A Sea of Debt

In this innovative legal history of economic life in the Western Indian Ocean, Bishara examines the transformations of Islamic law and Islamicate commercial practices during the emergence of modern capitalism in the region. In this time of expanding commercial activity, a mélange of Arab, Indian, Swahili, and Baloch merchants, planters, jurists, judges, soldiers, and seamen forged the frontiers of a shared world. The interlinked worlds of trade and politics that these actors created, the shared commercial grammars and institutions that they developed, and the spatial and socio-economic mobilities they engaged in endured until at least the middle of the twentieth century. This major study examines the Indian Ocean from Oman to India and East Africa over an extended period of time, drawing together the histories of commerce, law, and empire in a sophisticated, original, and richly textured history of capitalism in the Islamic world.

FAHAD AHMAD BISHARA is an Assistant Professor of History at the University of Virginia. He received his Ph.D. in History from Duke University in 2012, and holds an M.A. in Arab Gulf Studies from the University of Exeter. His research, in the fields of legal history and the history of capitalism, has been supported by the Social Science Research Council and the American Council of Learned Societies. He was also previously a Prize Fellow in Economics, History, and Politics at the Center for History and Economics at Harvard University.

Published in association with the Muhammad Alagil Chair in Arabia Asia Studies, Asia Research Institute, National University of Singapore.

ASIAN CONNECTIONS

Series editors
Sunil Amrith, *Harvard University*
Tim Harper, *University of Cambridge*
Engseng Ho, *Duke University*

Asian Connections is a major series of ambitious works that look beyond the traditional templates of area, regional or national studies to consider the trans-regional phenomena which have connected and influenced various parts of Asia through time. The series will focus on empirically grounded work exploring circulations, connections, convergences, and comparisons within and beyond Asia. Themes of particular interest include transport and communication, mercantile networks and trade, migration, religious connections, urban history, environmental history, oceanic history, the spread of language and ideas, and political alliances. The series aims to build new ways of understanding fundamental concepts, such as modernity, pluralism or capitalism, from the experience of Asian societies. It is hoped that this conceptual framework will facilitate connections across fields of knowledge and bridge historical perspectives with contemporary concerns.

A Sea of Debt

Law and Economic Life in the Western Indian Ocean, 1780–1950

Fahad Ahmad Bishara
University of Virginia

CAMBRIDGE
UNIVERSITY PRESS

CAMBRIDGE
UNIVERSITY PRESS

University Printing House, Cambridge CB2 8BS, United Kingdom

One Liberty Plaza, 20th Floor, New York, NY 10006, USA

477 Williamstown Road, Port Melbourne, VIC 3207, Australia

4843/24, 2nd Floor, Ansari Road, Daryaganj, Delhi – 110002, India

79 Anson Road, #06-04/06, Singapore 079906

Cambridge University Press is part of the University of Cambridge.

It furthers the University's mission by disseminating knowledge in the pursuit of education, learning, and research at the highest international levels of excellence.

www.cambridge.org
Information on this title: www.cambridge.org/9781107155657
DOI: 10.1017/9781316659083

First published 2017

A catalogue record for this publication is available from the British Library.

ISBN 978-1-107-15565-7 Hardback
ISBN 978-1-316-60937-8 Paperback

Contents

Figures and Tables

Figures

Tables

Acknowledgments

When I first began to conceive of this project as a graduate student at Duke University, I benefited from learning under the shade of two great masters of the craft: Ed Balleisen, to whom I owe my appreciation for all things legal and economic; and Engseng Ho, who showed me how to navigate the stormy waters of Indian Ocean history, but also taught me how to read and how to imagine. If I have done anything well in this book, it is because of the two of them.

I also benefited from the guidance of a number of other teachers, both at Duke and beyond. Bruce Hall asked the right questions at the right time; Timur Kuran guided me through the thickets of economic history while including me in his own work; Janet Ewald took a chance on me when I still had not yet found my sea legs; and the late Jonathan Ocko read and encouraged my work with his usual cheer and sense of humor. Sebouh Aslanian read the manuscript, gave me his usual sharp insight, and continues to support me in ways that I can only call humbling. Barbara Welke pushed me to refine my thinking from early on, but also showed me how to strike a balance between rigor and generosity. And Michael Gilsenan read, asked questions, wondered, exclaimed, and prodded; I am lucky to know him.

Over the course of the last decade or so, I got to know people who would forever change the way I think, read, and write. Daniel Bessner, Jatin Dua, Mitch Fraas, Paul Johstono, Ameem Lutfi, Robert Penner, Serkan Yolacan, and many others have left more of an imprint on this project – and on my life – than they could possibly know. Andrew Byers, Tamara Extian-Babiuk, Julia Gaffield, Doug Leonard, and Willeke Sandler all endured more of my work than anyone should ever have to, and their company made the writing process much more enjoyable than it would have otherwise been.

At Harvard University, the Prize Fellows' program at the Joint Center for History and Economics furnished me with a group of interlocutors, collaborators, and friends that helped me make the transition from being one kind of student to being another. My fellow fellows – especially Alexia Yates – kept me on my toes, helped me sharpen my thinking, and broadened my intellectual horizons. And though we were called the Prize Fellows, it is to Emma Rothschild that the real prize goes: Emma is the extraordinary architect behind it all; her vision, foresight, and generosity helped bring such a remarkable program into being. Crucial financial support for this project came from the JCHE, but also the Social Science Research Council, and the American Council of Learned Societies.

My colleagues at the College of William and Mary were perhaps the best that anyone could hope for. They shared in my enthusiasm as I worked through different readings and chapter drafts, kept up their sense of humor as I struggled through different course experiments, and took me out to celebrate or to hear me complain. And at the Omohundro Institute, Nadine Zimmerli helped me become a better writer; the book is leaner and sharper because of her editing.

Of course, I could not have completed this project without the help of a number of individuals from around the Indian Ocean. At the Zanzibar National Archives, Omar Sheha ensured that I received the kind of access I sought, but also integrated me into his family; our friendship is perhaps the best thing to have come out of this project. In Muttrah, Vimal and Dhruv Purecha opened up their family library to me, took me out to different meals, and met me in various parts of the world. I am grateful to them for their hospitality and to Calvin Allen for putting us in touch. In Manama, Ali Akbar Bushihri shared his family documents, put up with my questions, and regaled me with stories and cheesecake; I only regret that I wasn't able to use the Bahrain material here. And finally, I am grateful to the archive staff at the British Library, the Maharashtra State Archives, and the Zanzibar National Archives, who put up with my endless requests but also dragged their feet enough to make sure that I would sometimes leave them alone and find someplace to eat, think, and spend time with fellow researchers.

During my research travels, I met a number of people who quickly became my friends and interlocutors. Among others, Simon Layton and Johan Mathew made for excellent company while I was away from family and friends. Walks with Abdul Sheriff around Zanzibar allowed me the chance to become more intimate with my surroundings while learning at the hands of one of the masters of the craft of oceanic history. Ahmed Al-Dailami and Noora Lori immediately became some of my closest friends and most engaging conversation partners; I consider our meeting a blessing. And Thomas (Dodie) McDow – well, what can I say? There has been nothing better than getting to know him and his family, and researching and thinking alongside him in Zanzibar, Mumbai, Muscat, and the United States.

In Kuwait, my mother, my sisters, and my relatives all encouraged me to keep working and continued to put up with my interminable absence without knowing exactly what it was that I was doing and why. And my friends, most of whom I have known for at least twenty years, kept me anchored, even as I drifted from one city to another, degree after degree, and project after project. I cannot begin to imagine what life would be like without these people, even though they have gone through as many years without me around as they have with me there.

And of course, there has always been Rose, who has been there from the first proposal to the final draft. She has seen us through countless moves, made sure that our home was always in order, and that I always made time for my family, often taking time away from her own work to do it. Her love, her patience, her support, and her enthusiasm are what made this book possible; her unyielding dedication to our family is what keeps us all alive. Writing would have also been impossible without the constant help of my mother-in-law, Rosemary.

I dedicate this book to my son, Jossem, who made it just in time for the first draft to be completed, and to my father, Ahmad Bishara, who left us too soon to see this book in print. My father pushed me from early on to read, to learn, and to explore, and was the only family member who ever understood what I was trying to do; his departure has left me bereft of words. Thankfully, my son carries on his grandfather's boundless curiosity.

Prologue

Looking out across the ocean from his palace in 1800, the Sultan of Muscat, Sultan bin Ahmed Al-Busai'idi, had much to be proud of. Over the course of the past few decades, he and his family members had built an expansive maritime empire around the Western Indian Ocean. His father, Ahmed bin Sa'id, had brought most of coastal Oman under his rule, having won over many of the tribes who had plunged the countryside into civil war. Ahmed bin Sa'id and his sons had also expanded Busa'idi power regionally, working to exert some form of suzerainty over the vast littoral of the Western Indian Ocean. Having established themselves in Muscat, their sultanate gradually grew to include various town and port cities along the coast of South and Southeast Arabia; they leased the Persian port of Bandar 'Abbas and its environs from the ruler of Persia in 1780, they established themselves as the overlords of Gwadar, on the coast of Baluchistan, a few years later, and even tried to take the pearl-producing island of Bahrain further up the Gulf. After reaching a critical mass of revenue and manpower, they then set their sights on East Africa, imposing their domination over, though never really entirely possessing, port cities and islands from Mogadishu to Cape Delgado. By the time he took power in 1792, then, Sultan bin Ahmed had inherited a far-flung empire of port cities around the Western Indian Ocean.

But the Sultan's expansion into East Africa also forced him to confront the legacies of the dynasty whose mantle his family had inherited. His sultanate gradually chipped away at the holdings of his predecessors, the Ya'rubis, a dynasty that had led a successful offensive against the Portuguese in South Arabia and East Africa in the seventeenth century. The Ya'rubis had expelled the Portuguese from Muscat in 1650, and over the next fifty years had managed to wrest from them a series of forts along the East African coast, all the way down to Mozambique. To administer this sprawling network of forts and port cities, they had sent out different clans to govern on their behalf: the Busa'idis were their governors in Sohar, while other clans like the Mazru'is were their men in Mombasa.

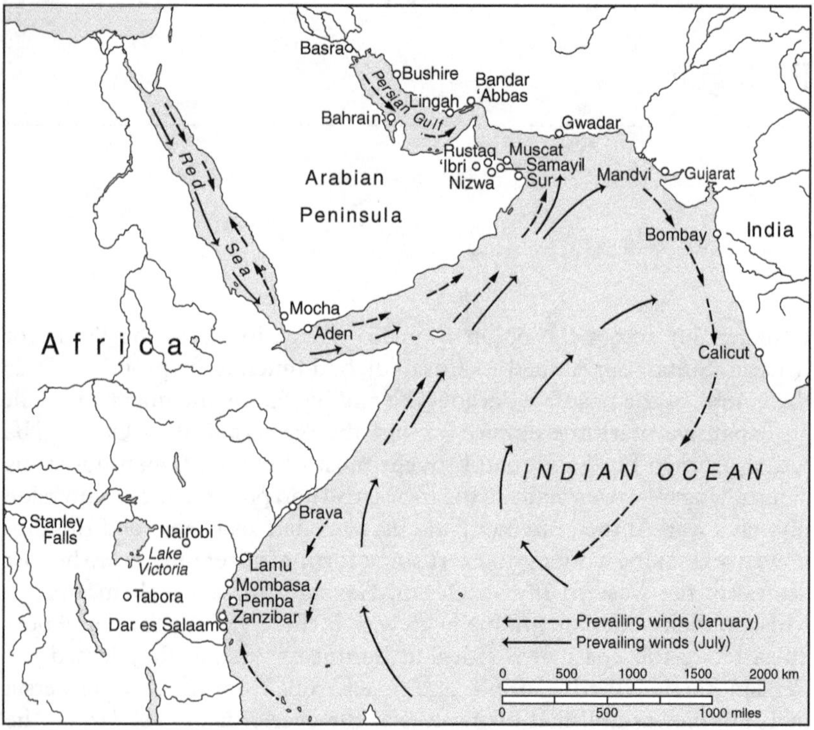

Figure 1 A map of the Western Indian Ocean

By the 1720s, rival factions within the Ya'rubi dynasty began to reveal the polity's seams; and after a protracted civil war, more challenges from within the family, and interference from Persia, the dynasty imploded.[1] Town by town and port by port, the Busa'idis picked up where their former overlords had left off.

The Busa'idi Sultan was thus heir to the spoils of early modern history, of the dismantling of the Portuguese Empire in the Western Indian Ocean and the emergence of a splintered political geography in the region, carved and re-carved again through battles, migrations, and usurpations. And the sultanate bore the imprint of its history of expansion in the region: it included Arab sultans born to Indian and African mothers, Gujarati customs masters, and Baluchi, Omani, and Hadhrami soldiers manning Portuguese cannons and forts, all littered around a sprawling inter-continental geography. By establishing themselves along the coasts

[1] John Wilkinson, *The Arabs and the Scramble for Africa* (Sheffield, UK: Equinox Publishing, 2015), 22–26.

of East Africa, South Arabia, and the Persian Gulf, the Busa'idi sultans hoped to direct regional trade through their ports and profit from the customs revenues that would follow.

But the Busa'idis hadn't done this alone. In building their trans-oceanic empire, they rode the tides alongside a range of different actors, all of whom played some role in shaping their expansion into the Western Indian Ocean. Their efforts, travels, and trajectories help us reflect on how we've mapped the Indian Ocean as a coherent space – how historians, but also historical actors, might have imagined connectivity in the region.

Arabia, Africa, and the Oceanic Turn in History

There was one moment in the history of Omani expansion into East Africa that early historians of the region all highlighted: the first face-to-face encounter between an expanding Busa'idi sultanate and the Mazru'i governor of Mombasa, a holdover from the previous Ya'rubi regime. Zanzibar's Chief Justice during the mid-twentieth century, Sir John Gray, recalled the moment in his first book, *The British in Mombasa, 1824–1826*. In Gray's telling of it, the young military commander Ahmed bin Sa'id Al-Busa'idi, arrived in Mombasa in January 1785, after a successful campaign to convince his recalcitrant uncle Saif to give Zanzibar back to Ahmed's father, who at the time was the ruler of Oman.[2] Emboldened by his success, Ahmed sailed to Mombasa and walked right into Fort Jesus; the gatekeeper who saw him and his men did nothing to stop them, as he "thought that they were trading Arabs, who had come down with the monsoon." Upon seeing Ahmed, the fort's governor "rose from his seat and showed him great respect"; when Ahmed asked him whom the fort belonged to, he replied "It is yours." Gray continues: "Then the Imam's son [Ahmed] said, 'Give me a writing to that effect.' So he gave him a document written with his own hand to the effect that he held the fort for the Imam's son." Ahmed then left the fort and sailed away to Muscat, 2,500 miles away.[3] Questioned later, he told his overlords that it was

[2] Ahmed was Sultan bin Ahmed's nephew; at the time, Sultan's brother Sa'id bin Ahmed was the ruler, though he would pass away shortly afterwards.

[3] John Gray, *The British in Mombasa, 1824–1826, Being the History of Captain Owen's Protectorate* (London: Macmillan & Co., 1957), 13; The account that Gray relies on is just one of many; important details, including names and dates, vary in other versions. See also Sa'id bin 'Ali Al-Mughairi, *Juhaynat al-Akhbār fī Tārīkh Zanjibār*, 4th ed. (Muscat: Ministry of Heritage and Culture, 2001), 210; C.H. Stigant, *The Land of Zinj: Being an Account of British East Africa, its Ancient History and Present Inhabitants* (London: Constable and Company Ltd, 1913), 24; M. Gullain, *Documents Sur L'Histoire, La Geographie, et Le Commerce L'Afrique Orientale* (Paris: Arthur Bertrand, 1856), 556–558.

clear that Ahmed would have been able to take the fort by force, and so he "gave him a piece of paper so as to avoid the evil of the hour."

Gray's narrative of the encounter at Fort Jesus, which drew on a handful of local chronicles, recalled a moment that historians would now consider to be emblematic of the oceanic turn in the histories of Arabia and Africa. The narrative brimmed with the very sorts of oceanic connections that historians have begun to highlight. The narrators mention Muscat and Mombasa, Arab traders, and aspiring Arab sultans and rogue governors in East Africa, all in one breath. Moreover, Gray's suggestion that the fort's gatekeeper had assumed that the Busa'idi walking into the port was one of the "trading Arabs who had come down with the monsoon" pointed to a common vector of the oceanic turn in historical writing: the role of the monsoon winds in shaping trans-regional connections. The monsoon winds formed a critical element of the Indian Ocean world, giving trade, migration, and agriculture their seasonal rhythm. From November to January, sailors could count on winds blowing from Arabia and India towards East Africa, and from China to Southeast Asia; from April to August, the winds would blow in the opposite direction, bringing with them the rains that farmers throughout the region had gambled their livelihoods on.[4]

The monsoons also constituted an integral component of how historians have written about the Indian Ocean as a zone of interaction. K.N. Chaudhuri began his pioneering work on the history of the Indian Ocean with a meditation on how the monsoon winds shaped patterns of circulation and food production along the Indian Ocean rim. Historians after Chaudhuri followed suit: it quickly became standard practice to begin books on Indian Ocean history with an homage to the natural forces of the monsoon as the most primordial expression of trans-regional connectivity.[5] And there is little reason to discount the role of the monsoon winds in regularizing contact between Arabia, Africa, and South and Southeast Asia. Indeed, the notion that the arrival of trading Arabs in Mombasa would have prompted no action by the gatekeeper suggests just how common movements between the Arabian Peninsula and East Africa were.

[4] Edward A. Alpers, *The Indian Ocean in World History* (New York: Oxford University Press, 2014), 7–8.

[5] K.N. Chaudhuri, *Trade and Civilization in the Indian Ocean: An Economic History from the Rise of Islam to 1750* (Cambridge, UK: Cambridge University Press, 1985), 21–29. See also M.N. Pearson, *The Indian Ocean* (London: Routledge, 2003), 13–26; Abdul Sheriff, *Dhow Cultures and the Indian Ocean: Cosmopolitanism, Commerce, and Islam* (New York: Columbia University Press, 2010), 15–25; and most recently, Sunil Amrith, *Crossing the Bay of Bengal: The Furies of Nature and the Fortunes of Migrants* (Cambridge, MA: Harvard University Press, 2014), 8–13.

But as the encounter also shows, other layers of historical forces reinforced the monsoon vectors of trans-oceanic history. As merchants in different port cities looked across the sea to find trading partners, others saw different opportunities. Well before the arrival of European empires in the Western Indian Ocean, regional sultanates and other potentates – the "empires of the monsoon," to borrow Richard Hall's evocative term – reached out across the ocean to realize their political ambitions. The Busa'idis and the Mazru'is are excellent examples of these impulses: both were products of the confluence of world historical forces and oceanic migrations that had given the Western Indian Ocean its distinct flavor, and both saw the ocean as an opportunity to exercise a form of local or regional suzerainty. Their meeting in Mombasa echoed a time of Indian Ocean economic and political expansion before Western colonization – a time in which local rulers vied with one another over the right to control key forts and port cities along the oceanic littoral, and access to commodities.[6]

For inhabitants of South Arabia, the coasts of East Africa constituted a key staging ground for their intertwined commercial and political aspirations.[7] Though prolonged contacts between the two regions go as far back as the tenth century, from at least the early modern period merchants and political aspirants from Southeast Arabia envisioned East Africa as a place where they could reinvent themselves as actors of consequence. Just as Hadhrami scholars established their trans-regional religious mission in India and Southeast Asia, political actors from Oman looked across the Arabian Sea, to East Africa. Ousted rulers and governors saw in the East African coast a place to assert independent political ambitions, backed by local tribes and access to the flows of commodities like gold, ivory, and slaves from the interior.[8] Those who were able to

[6] On the confluence of trade and political ambition in the Indian Ocean, see also Sebastian R. Prange, "A Trade of No Dishonor: Piracy, Commerce, and Community in the Western Indian Ocean, Twelfth to Sixteenth Century," *The American Historical Review*, Vol. 116, No. 5 (December 2011), 1269–1293; Roxani Margariti, "Mercantile Networks, Port Cities, and "Pirate" States: Conflict and Competition in the Indian Ocean World of Trade before the Sixteenth Century," *Journal of the Economic and Social History of the Orient*, Vol. 58 (2008), 543–577; Patricia Risso, *Merchants and Faith: Muslim Commerce and Culture in the Indian Ocean* (Boulder, CO: Westview Press, 1995).

[7] The best overview of this long, intertwined history can be found in Wilkinson, *The Arabs and the Scramble for Africa*, 14–40.

[8] The Pate Chronicle speaks to many of these themes. In it, the Al-Nabhani dynasty, which ruled the interior of Oman, was displaced by the expanding Ya'rubi dynasty and took refuge on Pate, in what is now the northern coast of Kenya, near Lamu. They intermarried with the local ruling dynasty and, over the course of two generations, established themselves as the rulers of Pate, where they developed plantations and established a trade with India and Arabia. Stigant, *The Land of Zinj*, 30–45; Al-Mughairi, *Juhaynat Al-Akhbār*, 169–172. The chronicle also recalls how the Mazru'is, who had been sent by the Ya'rubis to expel the Portuguese, established themselves as independent potentates and

mediate between the outward flows of East African goods and the inward streams of textiles and other products from South Asia, the region's principal bazaar, established themselves as political contenders. The monsoon-structured trade system thus underpinned regional political power.[9]

The South Arabian dynasties of the seventeenth and eighteenth centuries recognized the opportunities that lay before them. The Ya'rubi dynasty profited from a growing trade in ivory from the East African interior, but also generated revenue through maritime plunder and the imposition of protection costs on shipping in the Western Indian Ocean.[10] After the dynasty's collapse in the middle of the eighteenth century, the field was open for their former governors to either stand their ground and hold out for the possibility of establishing themselves as rulers of independent port cities, or to try to assert themselves as political suzerains over the tribes and clans that ran along the coasts of South Arabia and East Africa, profiting from the flows of commodities and people that characterized the region. The Mazru'is took the first route; the Al-Busa'idis chose the latter.

Thus, when the Busa'idis and Mazru'is met at Fort Jesus that day in 1785, at stake was not just a fort in coastal East Africa. At stake were the spoils of a regional commerce in ivory, slaves, and other commodities – a commerce that would underpin expansionist ambitions on both sides, and excite the intellectual agendas of historians centuries later. But lurking beneath this imperial expansion was another vector of oceanic history – the movements of merchants and other commercial actors.

Networks and Trade in World History

When the Kutchi merchant Sewji Topan Thakkur first arrived in Muscat from Gujarat in the 1780s, he could not have possibly imagined the world of trade and politics that he was about to step into. At the time, Muscat was only just beginning to come into being as a commercial entrepôt of serious consequence. The port city had benefited from a number of political transformations taking place in the Persian Gulf, and

even sought to extend their rule into Lamu. Stigant, *The Land of Zinj*, 55–73; Wilkinson, *The Arabs and the Scramble for Africa*, 31–32; Al-Mughairi, *Juhaynat Al-Akhbār*, 207–210.

9 M.N. Pearson, *Port Cities and Intruders: The Swahili Coast, India and Portugal in the Early Modern Era* (Baltimore, MD: Johns Hopkins University Press, 1998), 36–62.

10 Wilkinson, *The Arabs and the Scramble for Africa*, 24; Thabit Abdullah, *Merchants, Mamluks, and Murder: The Political Economy of Trade in Eighteenth-Century Basra* (New York: SUNY Press, 2000), 60; R.B. Serjeant, *Customary and Shariah Law in Arabian Society* (Hampshire: Varorium, 1991), 80–83.

its long-standing links with East Africa and India ensured that its bazaars were well stocked with the sorts of wares that inhabitants of the Gulf and Arabian Peninsula desired. Muscat had not yet become the regional commercial and political capital that it was going to be over the next seventy years or so, but it was on its way there; Sewji had arrived at the right time.

Kutchis like Sewji Topan constituted only one of what was a dizzying variety of merchant communities in the Indian Ocean: Arab, Persian, Armenian, Swahili, Gujarati, Chettiar, Chinese, Bugis, and more, all of whom engaged in a rich commerce with one another and with merchants from around the world. Their movements and activities undergirded the sultanates, empires, and petty chiefdoms that dotted the Indian Ocean rim. Mercantile activity formed the resource bases of these Indian Ocean polities: rulers derived revenues directly from commerce, established quarters for foreign merchants so as to attract trade, and spent money on patrols to protect merchant shipping. At other times, they profited from raiding merchant ships, flexing their military muscle along key trading routes, and using the proceeds to establish themselves as political contenders.[11]

The expanding Sultanate of Muscat and Zanzibar was no exception to this trend, housing (and profiting from the presence of) merchants from South Arabia, the Persian Gulf, East Africa, and India. Of these traders, Indian merchants – Kutchis like Sewji Topan, but also others – have attracted a great deal of scholarly attention, in part because of the visibility of their activities to imperial officials around the region, but largely because of their centrality to commerce.[12] They formed a core constituency in economic and political life in the Omani empire and the Indian

[11] Sanjay Subrahmanyam, "Of Imarat and Tijarat: Asian Merchants and State Power in the Western Indian Ocean, 1400 to 1750," *Comparative Studies in Society and History*, Vol. 37, No. 4 (1995), 750–780.

[12] Works devoted almost entirely to Indian merchants include: Uma Das Gupta (ed.) *The World of the Indian Ocean Merchant, 1500–1800: Collected Essays of Ashin Das Gupta* (New Delhi: Oxford University Press, 2001); Claude Markovits, *The Global World of Indian Merchants, 1750–1947: Traders of Sind from Bukhara to Panama* (New York: Cambridge University Press, 2000); Stephen Frederic Dale, *Indian Merchants and Eurasian Trade, 1600–1750* (New York: Cambridge University Press, 1994); Scott Levi, *The Indian Diaspora in Central Asia and its Trade, 1550–1900* (Leiden: E.J. Brill, 2002); Calvin Allen, "Sayyids, Shets and Sultans: Politics and Trade in Muscat Under the Al Bu Said, 1785–1914" (Ph.D. Dissertation, University of Washington, 1978); Pedro Machado, *Ocean of Trade: South Asian Merchants, Africa, and the Indian Ocean, c. 1750–1850* (New York: Cambridge University Press, 2014); Chhaya Goswami, *The Call of the Sea: Kachchhi Traders in Muscat and Zanzibar, c. 1800–1880* (New Delhi: Orient Blackswan, 2011); Charles Schaefer, "'Selling at a Wash:' Competition and the Indian Merchant Community in Aden Crown Colony," *Comparative Studies of South Asia, Africa and the Middle East*, Vol. 19, No. 2 (1999), 16–23; Ghulam Ahmed Nadri,

Ocean more broadly: they channeled commodities and credit around the region, but also bankrolled aspiring Sultans and petty rulers, financing their battles and providing them with the means to coopt potential rivals.[13]

Sewji Topan fit the mold well. Shortly after arriving in Muscat, he became a banker to Sultan bin Ahmed, the ruler of Muscat, financing many of his campaigns in East Africa.[14] To compensate Sewji for his financial support, the Sultan awarded him and his family the right to farm customs, first in Muscat and then in Zanzibar and East Africa – a right that Sewji's family held onto for more than sixty years. Moreover, Sewji's mercantile firm linked together resources and markets in South Arabia, East Africa, and India, channeling goods and credit around the Western Indian Ocean. The movement of commodities he and others stimulated constituted the life-blood of the Omani sultan's empire: it generated revenues, attracted merchants and settlers, and formed the basic outlines of commercial and imperial expansion.

To historians searching for a non-imperial lens through which they could write about the history of the Indian Ocean, merchants like Sewji Topan seemed to offer a clear possibility. Merchant communities cut across geographical boundaries, intersected with empires and other polities, and bridged regions that would otherwise have little to do with one another. For historians, Sewji Topan and others like him stood at the center of a historiography that first explored these worlds through the prism of cross-cultural trade and later developed into sophisticated accounts of trust and reputation within trade networks.[15] Here, the agents of history were the traders themselves: their quests for profit, their dogged efforts at

Eighteenth-Century Gujarat: The Dynamics of Its Political Economy (Leiden: Brill, 2009); Noor Mohammed Al-Qasimi, *Al-Wujūd Al-Hindī fī Al-Khalīj Al-'Arabī, 1820–1947 [The Indian Presence in the Gulf, 1820–1947]* (Sharjah, United Arab Emirates: Government Printers, 1996).

13 See also M. Reda Bhacker, *Trade and Empire in Muscat and Zanzibar: Roots of British Domination* (London: Routledge, 1994),12–14, 68–75, 117–128; John C. Wilkinson, *The Imamate Tradition of Oman* (New York: Cambridge University Press, 1987), 63–66; Goswami, *The Call of the Sea*, 79–238.

14 Bhacker, *Trade and Empire*, 72–74.

15 On trade networks and trust in world history, see also Philip Curtin, *Cross-Cultural Trade in World History* (New York: Cambridge University Press, 1984); Francesca Trivellato, *The Familiarity of Strangers: The Sephardic Diaspora, Livorno, and Cross-Cultural Trade in the Early Modern Period* (New Haven: Yale University Press, 2009), 1–2. Sebouh Aslanian, *From the Indian Ocean to the Mediterranean: the Global Trade Networks of Armenian Merchants from New Julfa* (Berkeley, CA: University of California Press, 2011). Machado, *Ocean of Trade*, 44–59; Trivellato, *The Familiarity of Strangers*; Jessica Goldberg, *Trade and Institutions in the Medieval Mediterranean: The Geniza Merchants and their Business World* (New York: Cambridge University Press, 2012).

overcoming obstacles on land and at sea to carve a niche for themselves, and their ability to navigate a world of regional politics, at times circumventing authorities and at other times drawing them into their agendas. In a sense, they brought back economic history of the Braudelian variety – histories in which state institutions developed to meet the imperatives of material life and capitalism, not the other way around.[16]

As revealing as they have been, discussions of networks and trust have been perhaps too narrowly focused. With only some exceptions, most studies of networks in economic history have told us little about how members of these networks interacted with actors outside the trust circle. The emphasis on trust within the network has also tended to obscure as much as they have revealed. As astute as these new Indian Ocean economic histories have been in their analysis of the internal legal dynamics of merchant networks, they have generally ignored the pivotal question of how these internal dynamics intersected with an external institutional world – courts, tribunals, and the state. By emphasizing merchants' proclivity for self-regulation, even in a formal institutional setting, these authors often paint a narrow picture of self-contained mercantile communities in a static institutional world, and risk flattening complex institutional experiences to highlight an internal equilibrium. After all, the world of Indian Ocean trade was not simply one of trust; it was one of law.

Law and Political Economy in the Indian Ocean

In the Indian Ocean, law was both everywhere and nowhere. It was hardly ever visible, but it left its mark on every actor, artifact, and action. It was present in that meeting between the Mazru'is and Busa'idis in Mombasa, where a deed infused with legal meaning exchanged hands between the parties. It was there throughout Sewji Topan's career and the journeys of thousands of others who crossed the Indian Ocean in search of profit, advancement, or a new life. It was there in the court of the Sultan and of his governors, in Muscat and in Zanzibar, where displays of power and authority intertwined with notions of justice in a public theater. And it was there whenever actors transacted with one another, whether they explicitly invoked it or implicitly understood it.

Law was a central part of how this Indian Ocean world took its shape. As a technology – a means of coordinating action – law furnished the institutions and instruments necessary to organize commerce and settlement between Oman, India, and East Africa, and to facilitate access to

[16] Fernand Braudel, *Civilization and Capitalism, Vol. 2: The Wheels of Commerce* (Berkeley, CA: University of California Press, 1992).

the capital necessary to fuel economic activity. As a discourse, jurisprudence furnished the intellectual underpinnings of this world, providing a philosophy to the nature and shape of the commercial obligations that ran through it, and the institutions that governed it. And as modality of rule – a medium for the expression of multiple and overlapping sovereignties – law was essential to the process by which a range of actors negotiated, established, and contested jurisdiction over communities and commerce.

Perhaps nobody could appreciate this more than the Omani jurist Nasser bin Abi Nabhan, born in 1778, just as the Busa'idi sultanate was beginning its expansion. An accomplished jurist in his own right, Nasser eventually accompanied the Sultan from Muscat to Zanzibar, where he penned a range of different tracts on theology, medicine, astronomy, and jurisprudence. He spent the rest of his life moving between South Arabia and East Africa on the decks of dhows, writing on law and religion and contemplating the changing economic and political world that he was born into. Nasser died in Zanzibar in 1847, but not before a number of other jurists and *qāḍis* joined him there, moving to East Africa from Oman and Hadhramaut.[17] As part of a trans-regional community of legal scholars, the jurist would have immediately understood how fundamentally constitutive law was to the world around him.

Nasser also belonged to a distinguished lineage of scholars, and formed part of a regional revival in theology and jurisprudence – a juridical *nahḍa* that had started in the late eighteenth century, just as the Busa'idni political project was beginning to take hold in East Africa. The *nahḍa's* fountainhead was Nasser's father, Ja'id bin Khamis Al-Kharusi, known to all of his peers and later jurists as "Abi Nabhan." Abi Nabhan was considered to be the greatest legal mind of his generation, but was also sympathetic to the demands of commerce; he is credited, among other things, with having disposed of the argument against coffee consumption in Oman.[18] Along with other contemporaries, Abi Nabhan spearheaded the renaissance in Ibadhi legal thought.

But though Abi Nabhan was largely responsible for the emergence of a renaissance in legal thinking, he was hardly the first jurist that wrote in service of a broader political and commercial transformation. Around

[17] Amal N. Ghazal, *Islamic Reform and Arab Nationalism: Expanding the Crescent from the Mediterranean to the Indian Ocean (1880s–1930s)* (New York: Routledge, 2010), 21; Wilkinson, *The Imamate Tradition*, 231, 355 n. 7. Anne Bang's *Sufis and Scholars of the Sea: Family Networks in East Africa, 1860–1920* (London: RoutledgeCurzon, 2003) highlights the movement of jurists and *qāḍis* from southern Yemen to East Africa.

[18] Wilkinson, *The Imamate Tradition of Oman*, 204.

the Western Indian Ocean, the administration of law and the expansion of political authority had been intertwined with one another for centuries; the spread of Islamic law in the Indian Ocean is thought to be through the vehicles of trade and empire, articulated through the networks of scholars that interlaced them.[19] When the Ya'rubis took over Portuguese holdings in South Arabia and East Africa in the second half of the seventeenth century, they did so in part with the encouragement and assistance of jurists like Khamis bin Sa'id Al-Shaqṣi, whose work laid out the entire corpus of Ibadhi law for the Ya'rubis to draw on, and who worked tirelessly to unite Omani tribes under their leadership.[20] Jurists like Nasser, his father Abi Nabhan, and others, going at least all the way back to Al-Shaqṣi and extending forward deep into the nineteenth and twentieth centuries, were as much a part of Omani expansion into East Africa as sultans, soldiers, and merchants were. They formed a juridical society that bridged Arabia and East Africa, articulating a legal framework for commerce and settlement between the two regions that would endure until well into the twentieth century.

The presence of jurists and *qāḍis* like Nasser bin Abi Nabhan who moved between South Arabia and East Africa highlights the legal constitution of the Indian Ocean world, revealing an oceanic space bound together as much by law as by nature, empire, or trade networks. Indeed, a jurist like Nasser bin Abi Nabhan would have seen law as a fundamental element of all of those dimensions of Indian Ocean history: politics and commerce were both fundamentally constituted by law, and even natural phenomena like the monsoons had their place in Islamic legal thought. All of the oceanic encounters that took place around him, then – from the mandarin to the mundane – would have been mediated by law, in all of its different forms and manifestations.

To Nasser bin Abi Nabhan, law – and especially Islamic law, the *shari'a* – encompassed a broad range of ritual and mundane matters, and was critical to how economic life might be imagined. Embedded in the legal thinking of jurists like him was a sort of economic thought – a political economy that involved reflections on nature, trade, wealth, taxation, and power, and how these all fit together. Around the Indian Ocean, jurists and *qāḍis*, but also scribes, market inspectors, and other legal officials, all articulated categories to describe a growing commercial

19 See also Risso, *Merchants and Faith*; Engseng Ho, *The Graves of Tarim: Genealogy and Mobility Across the Indian Ocean* (Berkeley, CA: University of California Press, 2006), 97–115; Chaudhuri, *Trade and Civilization*, 34–62; Sheriff, *Dhow Cultures of the Indian Ocean*, 239–261.

20 Wilkinson, *The Imamate Tradition of Oman*, 218–219.

world. Their voices and writings gave regional trade its shape, and the categories and ontologies they developed circulated around the region to lend it the coherence necessary for phenomena like trade and empire to take root, much like they did elsewhere in the Islamic world.[21]

When read through the intertwined forces of law and political economy, the Indian Ocean begins to look very different: the multiple and overlapping layers of sovereignty given expression through trade and empire come to the fore, and the trans-regional connective tissue that bound the shores of the ocean together suddenly begin to take shape.[22] Law in the Indian Ocean stretched "from the visible heights of formal political power to the unnoticed depths of everyday life" while helping to shape economic and political relations among empires, local actors, and diasporic communities.[23] It filled the crevices of commercial exchanges, defined the rights and obligations that actors could make claims to, and conjured into being the very objects – commodities, land, money, and time – that actors hinged their economic lives on.

Nasser bin Abi Nabhan would have seen all of this. For a jurist like him, law – especially the *shariʿa*, that complex of social, political, moral, and legal discourses given expression in a range of different texts – underpinned every aspect of political and economic life in the Indian Ocean. Where historians see trade networks populated by members of distinct ethnic or religious groups, he would have seen matrices of rights and obligations held together by contracts – intersections of nominate categories in Islamic jurisprudence and the conglomerations of commercial and juridical actors (himself included) and institutions that shaped them. Their circulation around the Indian Ocean was what gave the region its structure – not networks. To the jurist, the notion that abstract bonds of trust made the commercial world go round would have been misleading: if actors trusted one another at all, it was because they had a deep well of law to draw from – one which structured their exchanges with one another, shaped their expectations of one another, and furnished

[21] See also Ghislaine Lydon, *On Trans-Saharan Trails: Islamic Law, Trade Networks and Cross-Cultural Exchange in Nineteenth-Century Western Africa* (New York: Cambridge University Press, 2009); Timur Kuran, *The Long Divergence: How Islamic Law Held Back the Middle East* (Princeton, NJ: Princeton University Press, 2011); Gregory C. Kozlowski, *Muslim Endowments and Society in Colonial India* (New York: Cambridge University Press, 1985); Abraham L. Udovitch, *Partnership and Profit in Medieval Islam* (Princeton, NJ: Princeton University Press, 1970); Maxime Rodinson, *Islam and Capitalism* (London: Al-Saqi, 2007); Peter Gran, *Islamic Roots of Capitalism: Egypt, 1760–1840* (Austin, TX: University of Texas Press, 1979).

[22] Renisa Mawani and Iza Hussin, "The Travels of Law: Indian Ocean Itineraries," *Law and History Review*, Vol. 32, No. 4 (2014), 733–747.

[23] Engseng Ho, "Afterword: Mobile Law and Thick Transregionalism," *Law and History Review*, Vol. 32, No. 4 (2014), 884.

them with a set of institutions that they could fall back on when their trust gave way to suspicion. As long as there was exchange in the Indian Ocean, there was law.

But law wasn't only the handmaiden of commercial exchange: it was fundamentally constitutive of the wealth in the region. The natural and built landscapes and their relation to the worlds of commerce and empire were all infused with legal meaning. If the monsoon winds gave Indian Ocean trade its rhythm, they did less to define the rights to pearls, fish, and ambergris, to articulate the economic significance of trees or ivory, or to map out the multiple layers of value, rights, and duties that shaped the houses, shops, marketplaces, and walkways that made up the port cities that lined the ocean's shores. These forms of wealth, whether on land or at sea, formed the core of economic life in the region; they took up hundreds of pages in leather-bound volumes of Islamic jurisprudence, spilled over into even more loose sheets of questions and answers between merchants, *qāḍis*, and jurists in the form of *fatwas*, and generated tens of thousands of deeds, contracts, and receipts, all of which bore the imprint of law.[24] The Indian Ocean, then, was not only about connections across the sea; it was built on the circulation of wealth, and more fundamentally, on ideas of wealth, production, law, and exchange – of political economy in its most capacious form. And the Busaʿidi imperial project itself would have been given its shape through the circulation of these ideas and through the efforts of merchants, planters, *qāḍis*, scribes, and jurists like himself – economic and juridical actors that historians have until recently placed at the periphery of imperial history.[25]

At the same time, Nasser bin Abi Nabhan would have also known of a different world of law, political economy, and empire – one that was slowly beginning to take shape across the sea, in British Indian metropolitan centers like Bombay and Madras. He would have learned of British military victories in India against Muslim rulers like Tipu Sultan

[24] The anthropologist Brinkley Messick has highlighted the richness of these materials in 1960s Yemen. See also idem, "Property and the Private in a Sharia System," *Social Research*, Vol. 70, No. 3 (2003) 711–734; Textual Properties: Writing and Wealth in a Yemeni Sharia Case," *Anthropology Quarterly*, Vol. 68, No. 3 (1995), 157–170; *The Calligraphic State: Textual Domination in a Muslim Society* (Berkeley, CA: University of California Press, 1993).

[25] For examples in Atlantic history, see also Mary Sarah Bilder, *The Transatlantic Constitution: Colonial Legal Culture and the Empire* (Cambridge, MA: Harvard University Press, 2004); Daniel Hulsebosch, *Constituting Empire: New York and the Transformation of Constitutionalism in the Atlantic World, 1664–1830* (University of North Carolina Press, 2005); Lauren Benton, *Law and Colonial Cultures: Legal Regimes in World History, 1400–1900* (New York: Cambridge University Press, 2002); *A Search for Sovereignty: Law and Geography in European Empires, 1400–1900* (New York: Cambridge University Press, 2009).

in Mysore, but would have also heard news about the burgeoning system of courts, advocates, and legal codes that was slowly sinking its roots into Indian society. He would have been aware of the growing encounter between Muslim juridical society and these foreign institutions, and might have even seen some of the digests of Islamic law they produced. It would take some time before that world reached the shores of the Arabian Peninsula or East Africa, but a person as astute as Nasser would hardly have discounted the possibility that one day inhabitants of the region might have to contend with a British Indian legal system in their own home ports. When Nasser arrived in Zanzibar, all of this was still only a distant possibility. The British legal system in India was still taking shape, and there was much else to occupy the curious mind of a jurist in East Africa. But for other actors, the history of global empire in the Indian Ocean was beginning to sink its roots.

Oceans and Empires in World History

As he sailed out from Bombay in 1823 to survey the coasts of Arabia and Africa, Captain William Fitzwilliam Owen, a naval officer assigned to the Government of India, had a sense of the shifting waters he was entering into.[26] Owen's travels throughout the region brought him into contact with regional sovereigns and imperial outposts throughout Arabia and Africa. He met with the Busai'idi ruler of Muscat and Zanzibar and the Mazru'is of Mombasa, he traveled through Portuguese Mozambique, and had an extended audience with Radama I, the King of Madagascar. The oceanic space he moved through, it was clear, was shared by a number of local, regional, and global sovereigns and suzerains, but also offered Owen clear opportunities for intervention.

As part of his surveying assignment, Owen's ships docked off the coast of Mombasa, and the captain arranged a meeting with the island's governors, as he had done elsewhere. But this meeting was different: whereas his meetings with other rulers had yielded information about the geography, trade, and politics of the region, his meeting with the Mazru'is was more about their own aspirations. Decades after they had handed over rights to Fort Jesus to the Busa'idi Sultan, the Mazru'is were still in Mombasa, though in much straitened circumstances. Owen found himself feeling sorry for the ragged and impoverished-looking Mazru'i governors, "for these were the people who had successfully opposed the

[26] Heaton Bowstead Robinson, ed., *Narrative of Voyages to Explore the Shores of Africa, Arabia, and Madagascar; Performed in H.M. Ships "Leven" and "Barracouta," Under the Direction of Capt. W. F. W. Owen, R.N.*, 2 vols. (London: Richard Bentley, 1833).

Portuguese ... and, in later days, in fact up to the present moment, these Arabs had firmly resisted the whole force of the Imaum of Mukskat." The inhabitants of Mombasa had fought bravely against the Sultan, "but the power of their enemy had increased, whilst their own had long been on the decline, and they were now about to taste the bitter cup of slavery."[27]

Owen's arrival presented the Mazru'is with the opportunity to throw off the yoke of their Busa'idi overlords by placing themselves under British protection. They would have heard of the effectiveness of this strategy elsewhere around the Western Indian Ocean: they would have known of the Sultan of Muscat's appeals to British protection at different moments in Busa'idi rule, and would certainly have been familiar with the different British treaties with rulers of the small chiefdoms just up the coast from Muscat.[28] By appealing to British protection, they could stand up to their suzerains in Muscat and Zanzibar and reclaim for themselves the chiefdom that they had sought to establish decades before.

When the Mazru'is asked Owen if they could place their port under British protection, the captain considered it a clear opportunity to begin a new era in British imperialism. It was strategically situated, and offered an entry point for the expansion of British trade in the region: "Goods sent from England to that port could be conveyed by the Arab dows [sic] along the whole line of coast, where they would meet with a sure market," he wrote, adding that "as a possession of the English, it would be an excellent port for ships passing through the Mozambique Channel [in an age before the Suez Canal]... and the communication by this route to India [would be] more frequently attempted, while a lucrative trade might be entered into with Madagascar." He concluded that holding Mombasa as a military station "would be one of the most effectual steps towards the entire civilization of Eastern Africa" – one of the last frontiers of the British Empire.[29]

The driving force behind Owen's desire to place Mombasa under his protection, though, was his conviction that the move would form a critical step towards the suppression of the slave trade in the region. In writing out the protectorate agreement with the Mazru'is, he noted that "one of the principal articles on the part of the English... was the abolition of the slave-trade."[30] His dramatic letters to the Government of India, in which he pleaded with them to validate his treaties with the

[27] Robinson, *A Narrative of Voyages*, Vol. 1, 407–408.

[28] James Onley, "Britain and the Gulf Shaikhdoms, 1820–1971: The Politics of Protection," *Georgetown Center for International and Regional Studies, Occasional Paper No. 4* (2009), 506.

[29] Robinson, *A Narrative of Voyages*, Vol. 1, 413.

[30] Robinson, *A Narrative of Voyages*, Vol. 2, 148.

Mazru'is, bore out this conviction. After describing the slave trade out of East Africa in detail, he asked why his country had "refused the glorious duty of extending its protection to these poor creatures who sought it," adding that "the presence of a single Englishman in authority would prevent the continuation of any traffic in slaves" and that possession of the island would be far more effective in suppressing the slave trade than the practice of slave patrols might have been.[31]

A protectorate over Mombasa, Owen contended, would have also established a new British-headed property rights regime on the island. Of the inhabitants of Mombasa, he asserted that "The Koran is their law, and by it they pretend to govern their conduct," but argued that "right is ever made subservient to power, especially towards the Banyans, of whom there are many in the place." The island's Indian merchants, for whom he felt some responsibility, were "helpless and unprotected, [and] they are obliged to submit to be swindled out of their property with impunity by the higher classes of Arabs." He depicted a society with little regard for property rights in commercial transactions, for which the oath necessary to recover a debt "must be made in the presence of blood" – a ritual, he noted, that was "not required by the Koran, but it is here made a law in order to deprive the Banyans [*Banias*, a term used to describe Indian merchants around the region] of justice." Only with the establishment of the British protectorate on the island, he asserted, was the practice – "with many other abuses" – corrected, and "justice for a short period reigned at Mombas [sic]."[32]

Owen ultimately failed to have his protectorate confirmed, the Government of India deciding that it would be an affront to their latest ally in the region, the Busa'idi Sultan. But despite his failure, the naval officer was perhaps the perfect illustration of imperial history in the Indian Ocean. His anti-slavery bent, his push to establish a British-headed property rights regime in Mombasa, and his interventions in regional politics to further his agenda, were typical of the British in the Indian Ocean at the time – and did much to attract the attention of a whole generation of historians of the region.[33]

Owen's travels map the vectors of an empire in the making – impulses that historians have used to write oceanic history for several decades now.

[31] Gray, *The British in Mombasa*, 46.

[32] Robinson, *A Narrative of Voyages*, Vol. 2, 150–151.

[33] See also James Onley, "The Politics of Protection in the Gulf: The Arab Rulers and the British Resident in the Nineteenth Century," *New Arabian Studies*, Vol. 6 (2004), 30–92; Abdul Sheriff, *Slaves, Spices and Ivory in Zanzibar* (Oxford: James Currey, 1987) 201–244; Bhacker, *Trade and Empire*, 149–193; and most recently, Robert D. Harms, Bernard K. Freamon, and Michael Morony, eds. *Indian Ocean Slavery in the Age of Abolition* (New Haven, CT: Yale University Press, 2014).

The earliest histories of the region were effectively imperial histories, focusing on the role of gunpowder empires in diverting trade towards Europe, the ascendancy of European trade companies in the region, and their overwhelming subjugation of Indian Ocean communities.[34] Even the next wave of Indian Ocean histories, despite having been inspired by Braudel, could do little to rid themselves of the imperial framework. Work by historians like Chaudhuri try to take a different approach to the region's history, but ultimately fall back onto the very imperial frameworks they sought to avoid. Even as an older variant of land-based imperial history began to give way to oceanic history, historians of empire took to the ocean with gusto.[35]

But as historians have delved into empire's legal archives, they generated a narrative in which courts form the main locus of empire – a history in which Arab, Indian, African, and Southeast Asian litigants, lawyers, and judges played an important role in shaping imperial history. In this narrative of empire, the visions of imperial officials form only one weak strand: officials had to contend with the variegated legal landscapes that they had tried to map their empires onto. Historians have recently begun tracing the outlines of these legal histories, charting the development and articulation of imperial legal regimes throughout the region and the sophisticated claims by litigants to their rights as imperial subjects but also as members of religious communities. Imperial officials, then, had to share their juridical responsibilities with religious courts, mercantile tribunals, and other imperial jurisdictions, all of which came with their own notions of law, justice, personhood, and property rights.[36] Owen's comments about justice in Mombasa, however condescending they may have been, at least acknowledged the existence of another realm of law,

[34] See also Holden Furber, *Rival Empires of Trade in the Orient 1600–1800* (Minneapolis, MN: University of Minnesota Press, 1978); Richard Hall, *Empires of the Monsoon: A History of the Indian Ocean and its Invaders* (London: HarperCollins, 1998), and the countless histories of Portuguese, Dutch, and British trading companies and empires in South and Southeast Asia.

[35] David C. Armitage, "The Elephant and the Whale: Empires of Land and Sea," *Journal for Maritime Research*, Vol. 9, No. 1 (2007), 23–36. Sanjay Subrahmanyam criticized historians who skirted the tension between oceanic and national historiography by thinking of the region primarily within a European imperial frame: "to study the sea was hence to study the maritime empire, and to study the maritime empire was essentially to study the European presence in Asian waters"; Sanjay Subrahmanyam, "Introduction: The Indian Ocean Between Empire and Nation," in *Maritime India* (New Delhi: Oxford University Press, 2004), xii. Andre Wink repeats Subrahmanyam's suspicions, suggesting that although "the majority of studies in 'the new thalassology' are trans-oceanic in perspective," they were "albeit to some degree simply old wine in new bottles ('good old' colonial history repackaged as ocean-based 'world' history)"; Andre Wink, "Indian Ocean Studies and the "New Thalassology," *Journal of Global History*, Vol. 2 (March, 2007), 60.

[36] See also Elizabeth Kolsky, *Colonial Justice in British India: White Violence and the Rule of Law* (New York: Cambridge University Press, 2010); Mitra Sharafi, *Law and Identity*

even if he might not have seen the multitudes of actors and institutions that drew it together.

The issue, then, is not with imperial history as such, but with imperial history's tendency, on the whole, to obscure the indigenous ties across the Indian Ocean. The first wave of Indian Ocean histories, with some exceptions, left us with only a limited understanding of what the region looked like from the perspectives of those who inhabited it, rather than those who governed it. As Engseng Ho lamented, we know far less about the histories of "the Gujaratis, Bohras, Banias, Chettiars, Shirazis, and Omanis who settled across the ocean" than we do about the Europeans, whose dense archives have stimulated the imagination of historians and novelists alike.[37] The challenge, then, is to find the voices of the thousands of migrants who traversed these imperial realms and remade the boundaries between law, empire, and economic life.

in Colonial India: Parsi Legal Culture, 1772–1947 (New York: Cambridge University Press, 2014); Scott Alan Kugle "Framed, Blamed and Renamed: the Recasting of Islamic Jurisprudence in Colonial South Asia," *Modern Asian Studies*, Vol. 35, No. 2 (2001), 257–313; Julia Stephens, "The Phantom Wahhabi: Liberalism and the Muslim Fanatic in Mid-Victorian India," *Modern Asian Studies*, Vol. 47, No. 1 (2013), 22–52; Gagan Sood, "Sovereign Justice in Precolonial Maritime Asia: The Case of the Mayor's Court of Bombay, 1726–1798," *Itinerario*, Vol. 37, No. 2 (2013), 46–72; Arthur Mitchell Fraas, "'They Have Travailled into a Wrong Latitude': the Laws of England, Indian Settlements, and the British Imperial Constitution, 1726–1773" (Ph.D. Dissertation, Duke University, 2011); Bernard S. Cohn, *Colonialism and Its Forms of Knowledge: The British in India* (Princeton, NJ: Princeton University Press, 1996), 57–75; David C. Washbrook, "Law, State and Agrarian Society in Colonial India," *Modern Asian Studies* Vol. 15, No. 3 (1981), 649–721; Rohit De, "The Two Husbands of Vera Tiscenko: Apostasy, Conversion, and Divorce in Late Colonial India," *Law and History Review*, Vol. 28, No. 4 (2011), 1011–1014. Only a handful of very recent studies have traced the travels of this regime across the Indian Ocean, into the Middle East, East Africa, or Southeast Asia. One clear exception to this is the November 2014 special issue of *Law and History Review* entitled "Travels of Law: Indian Ocean Itineraries"; and Thomas Metcalf, *Imperial Connections: India in the Indian Ocean Arena, 1860–1920* (Berkeley, CA: University of California Press, 2008), 16–45; Nurfadzilah Yahaya, "Courting Jurisdictions: Colonial Administration of Islamic Law Pertaining to Arabs in the Straits Settlements and the Netherlands East Indies, 1860–1941" (Ph.D. dissertation, Princeton University, 2012). Fewer still have charted the movement of alternative systems of law that existed beneath the imperial winds; see also Iza Hussin "Circulations of Law: Cosmopolitan Elites, Global Repertoires, Local Vernaculars," *Law and History Review*, Vol. 32, No. 4 (2014) 773–795; and Bhavani Raman, *Document Raj: Writing and Scribes in Early Colonial South India* (Chicago: University of Chicago Press, 2012).

37 Engseng Ho, *The Graves of Tarim: Genealogy and Mobility Across the Indian Ocean* (Berkeley, CA: University of California Press, 2006), xxii.

Inscribing Oceanic History: A Legal History of Economic Life

Behind this shifting oceanic world of monsoons, empires, law, and political economy were people – merchants, planters, mariners, financiers, and other migrants who crossed the sea in search of fortune and new lives. And as they moved around the ocean, between India, Arabia, the Persian Gulf, Africa, and beyond, their actions shaped the world around them. They traded, planted, settled, and contracted, giving articulation to the interlinked worlds of Allah, Mammon, and empire that framed the history of the Indian Ocean.

The history of the Omani sultanate in the Western Indian Ocean attests to this. By the end of the eighteenth century, as the Omani ruler Sultan bin Ahmed Al-Busa'idi eyed his string of port cities across the Western Indian Ocean, a steadily expanding ivory trade and burgeoning plantation economy along the coast attracted growing numbers of migrants from India, South Arabia, and the Persian Gulf. In East Africa, they saw a chance to reinvent themselves as a propertied, slave-owning elite; and to get there, they drew on what little property, social connections, and money they had access to at home. Hopeful migrants hypothecated houses, shares of family estates, slaves, boats, and more in order to finance their journeys across the Indian Ocean. What began as a series of trans-oceanic connections facilitated by the monsoon winds had by the dawn of the nineteenth century evolved into a world fused together by capital, blood, and soil – and, more fundamentally, paper.

As different actors moved across the Indian Ocean, they took on debts to finance their new lives. The deeds they generated in contracting those debts – deeds they referred to simply as *waraqas*, literally "papers" – tell the story of their movements: of the familial property they hypothecated to Indian financiers to access the credit they needed to live, of the promises they made to deliver ivory, cloves, and other commodities in exchange for credit, and of the political, economic, and legal realms they navigated in order to make new lives. Through these *waraqas*, one sees what the Indian Ocean world might have looked like from their perspective: who they borrowed from, what they dealt in, and who they built houses next to as they made their homes across the water. And by looking *at* the *waraqas*, as well as through them, a richer picture of law and economic life in the Indian Ocean emerges.

By following the *waraqa* across the Indian Ocean, from East Africa to Oman, and from there maybe further up the Persian Gulf, or across the Arabian Sea to the Gulf of Kachhch, the bonds that formed a connective tissue across the Indian Ocean – bonds of nature, empire, trade networks, and even law and political economy – begin to take a more discernible shape. Through the *waraqa*, the ties that bound actors together in a changing economic and political world emerge as an alternative anchor for Indian Ocean history, bringing into focus the aspirations of different actors, the technologies they mobilized to realize them, and the shifting legal landscape that shaped the possibilities. The *waraqa* thus forms a narrative device that allows us to move between South Arabia, East Africa, and India, and from the realm of politics to the realm of trade – all through the multivalent idiom of obligation, which at once invoked all of the economic, moral, legal, and social dimensions of commerce.

The obligations that underpinned the *waraqa* gave it its moral and legal force. Obligation was the fundamental idiom of commercial society: it bound debtor to creditor, producer to retailer, and merchants to statesmen over the course of several generations. It coordinated action, working in a manner similar to trust, though far more textured in its ability to give expression to the realms of law, religion, and trade all at once. It structured economic life in the region, tethering itself to the natural rhythms of commerce and agriculture while stretching them to meet the demands of global capitalism. And it formed the basic building block of empire, shaping the actions and mutual expectations of sultans, governors, customs masters, and merchant-kings throughout the Indian Ocean.

The *waraqa's* journeys through Arabia, India, and East Africa allow us to bring to life an Indian Ocean world bound together by obligation. It emerges as a sinew of commercial and juridical society, binding together economic, juridical, and political actors across the imperial spectrum into a shared enterprise. It moved alongside other texts – books, treatises, and talismanic verses from the Qur'an and other scriptures – "graphic artifacts" that were essential to economic, political, and spiritual governance.[38] Through the *waraqa*, legal actors lent personhood to others, forging the ontological foundations of economic life. It brought the land to the sea, endowing property and rents with the ability to circulate around the Indian Ocean, and it gave articulation to the overlapping worlds of law, nature, commerce, and empire that surrounded them. The *waraqa* coordinated action within, and translated idioms and strategies between, the worlds it traveled through.[39] It allows historians to see how a regional arena came into being not just through the circulation of actors,

[38] Matthew Hull, "The File: Agency, Authority, and Autography in a Pakistan Bureaucracy," *Language and Communication*, Vol. 23, No. 3–4 (2003), 287–314.

[39] Miles Ogborn, "Writing Travels: Power, Knowledge and Ritual on the English East India Company's Early Voyages," *Transactions of the Institute of British Geographers*, Vol. 27, No. 2 (2002), 155–171.

but also of objects, and the categories, concepts, and standards that were embedded within them. Commercial society in the Indian Ocean was not the whole in which objects like the *waraqas* were embedded. Rather, commercial society traveled across the ocean through objects like the *waraqa*, calibrating connections throughout the region but also generating moments of disconnection and confusion, and offering opportunities to put forward competing interpretations about what those connections might look like.[40]

Law, then, was much more than the pronouncements of jurists like Nasser bin Abi Nabhan, however vocal and prolific he might have been in articulating its contours. Law emerged from the actions of merchants, planters, and moneylenders, from the inscriptions of scribes, from the assemblages of actors, instruments, and treatises that animated economic life in the Indian Ocean, and from the ideas, measures, experiments, and ontologies that pulsed through them all. In a sense, law was less an object than it was a language for commercial society – a means of giving the world of local and regional trade a particular shape, and an ever-evolving conversation about what the possibilities and limits of economic life might be.

But as a modality of trans-oceanic connectivity, the *waraqa* and the notions of law and obligation that ran through it were neither stable nor constant. As the world of Omani-East African commerce confronted a burgeoning British Indian empire, its participants had to cope with the growing presence of British judges, Parsi lawyers, and Indian court personnel, all of whom brought with them their own notions of law and economic order. The encounter between the two legal realms set into motion a long process in which merchants and plantation owners clashed over the legal and epistemological foundations of economic life, both in and outside of the courtroom.

Through the material plane of the *waraqa*, different actors made claims to what the role of law and obligations might be in a changing economic world: they marshaled intellectual resources from England, North Africa, Arabia, and India to harness the creative energies of merchants, planters, and scribes in an age of emerging modern capitalism, to shape commercial and political trajectories at a time of high imperialism, and to write new chapters in the economic and legal histories of the Indian Ocean. The *waraqa* might have moved through this world, but its movement was conditioned by a series of voices and actions.

[40] Here I am drawing on the eloquent thoughts of Bruno Latour, *Reassembling the Social: An Introduction to Actor-Network-Theory* (Oxford, UK: Oxford University Press, 2005), 241–242.

In the pages that follow, what I hope will emerge are the beginnings of an intertwined legal and economic history of the Indian Ocean: of an Indian Ocean commercial society and the practices and instruments its members mobilized to shape their commercial destinies; the discourses in law and political economy that those practices generated, both on the part of Muslim jurists and British officials; and the changing political, economic, and institutional landscape that opened up some possibilities while closing off others.

But this is also a legal history of *economic life* – which I take to mean "the history of human participation in the production, exchange, and consumption of goods."[41] By disaggregating the economy into its component activities and taking law as fundamentally constitutive of those activities, a clearer picture emerges of how law both emanated from and shaped the commercial arena. We can get a sense of how different legal voices contended with one another as they sought to clothe a range of economic practices and phenomena, from finance to consumption, in a legal garb.

The history I write in the pages that follow highlights these voices: Indian merchant-moneylenders and their debtors, whose contracts bound the interior of East Africa and South Arabia to markets in India and abroad; Muslim jurists, *qāḍis*, and scribes, whose actions and pronouncements shaped the boundaries between Islamic jurisprudence and a growing world of commerce; British consuls who had to contend with the different claims that merchants made to British jurisdiction over economic life; consular clerks, whose careful annotations and inscriptions silently directed the encounter between Muslim categories of contracting and an expanding Anglo-Indian legal empire; British judges and Indian lawyers, whose pronouncements on the border between law, empire, and economic life drew on far-flung legal systems and texts to make claims about Islamic law and what it might be capable of in an age of modern capitalism; and economic experts within the British Empire, who spoke out for stricter economic regulation as the global economy teetered on the verge of collapse.

The narrative unfolds in three broad movements: the first, starting from the Prologue and until the Interlude, explores the interlinked commercial and legal worlds that a trans-regional society of jurists, scribes, merchants, moneylenders, and planters created. The second, spanning Chapters 4 to 7, maps out the protracted legal encounter between this trans-regional commercial and juridical society and a growing

[41] William H. Sewell, Jr., "A Strange Career: the Historical Study of Economic Life," *History and Theory*, Theme Issue 49 (December 2010), 46.

Anglo-Indian legal empire. The narrative then resolves itself in Chapter 8 and the Epilogue, where the weight of the global economic depression of the 1930s and the regulatory impulses it brought with it gradually pulled this world apart and reconfigured it to meet the demands of the global economy in the mid-twentieth century. And at the center of it all lies the *waraqa*, which pulls us through the different eras and intertwined actors and histories – from the long chains of obligation that structured Indian Ocean economic life to the legal discourses, debates, maneuverings, and transformations it weathered.

1 A Geography of Obligation

By the time Sewji's son Jairam was born in 1792, the emergence of an intertwined world of commerce and empire was well underway. Jairam was born in Mundra, a port city in Kutch; his father Sewji Topan was already a known banker to the ruler of Muscat, Sultan bin Ahmed. Sewji had financed much of the state-building and expansion that had taken place over the previous couple of decades, and had secured for himself a range of different commercial privileges, including customs farming – the right to collect custom receipts in Muscat, and later, in his other dominions as well, in return for an up-front payment. When Jairam was just a young boy, the ruler had taken Sewji and another banker of his to Zanzibar, in part to gauge their interest in investing in East Africa's growing commerce. By the time Jairam came of age, his father was already well-entrenched in East African commerce and politics. When Sultan bin Ahmed died and his son Sa'id bin Sultan took over, Jairam built a relationship with him much like the one their fathers had with one another. And much like his father, Sa'id continued the practice of relying on Sewji's firm, which slowly passed to Jairam, to finance his intertwined undertakings in commerce and empire-making.

Together, Jairam Sewji and his father – and scores of other merchant-financiers like them – were at the vanguard of the commercial transformation of the Western Indian Ocean. Through their business partners in Bombay and Kutch and their agents stationed all along the East African coast, they bridged Western India together with South Arabia and East Africa, directing the movement of cloth, pearls, dates, ivory, and eventually cloves, around the Western Indian Ocean. Theirs was a commercial world that seemed to be constantly expanding, as consumers in East Africa, South Arabia, and the Persian Gulf demanded the goods that India and the world had to offer, while markets in South Asia, Europe, and America exhibited an insatiable appetite for the region's wares.

But the two merchants did more than just direct the movement of commodities and benefit from the profits it generated. They actively financed it, channeling credit from India to producers, traders, and rulers in South Arabia and East Africa. The credit they supplied to a growing commercial society, particularly in East Africa, bound together Arab, Persian, Swahili, and Indian producers and markets that were oceans apart, and bridged the commerce of the Western Indian Ocean with a burgeoning world economy. As demand for Indian Ocean commodities grew, capital supplied by Jairam and other merchants from northwestern India remade the regional landscape, binding it to their firms' portfolios and tethering it to markets in India, Europe, and America. As their credit and capital made its way through a network of brokers, producers, consumers, and rulers in South Arabia and East Africa, they forged a region-wide geography of obligation – a landscape in which creditors and debtors were yoked to one another in a common fate. Seen from their perspective, goods traveled within a geography constituted by shifting matrices of rights and obligations – one in which merchants could imagine the distance from Bombay to Zanzibar as a link in a network rather than an entire ocean.

Trade in the nineteenth-century Indian Ocean looked different from what it was before. By the mid-nineteenth century, markets had expanded to global dimensions, and merchant-financiers like Jairam secured goods to service those markets well in advance. Commodities traveled along pre-carved pathways, from the interior to Zanzibar, to Kutch or Bombay, and from there to Europe, along international commodity chains that would see an ivory tusk turned into a ball on a European pool table, or a pound of cloves distilled into a vial of oil. People knew where goods were going, and had sold them well before they even came into being. The market forces of supply and demand shaped the broader fortunes of these commodities, but within the region goods moved between actors who knew who they would be coming from, who they would be going to, and how much they would cost. Merchants like Sewji Topan and his son Jairam stood at the intersections of it all, brokering between an Indian Ocean world of production and consumption, and a growing world market.

Commodities, Consumption, and Credit

Jairam and his father's ability to do business in Muscat and Zanzibar was not only a product of their own entrepreneurial initiative and their connections to the ruling family; it hinged on the confluence of a range of different historical processes that would give them and a host of other Gujarati merchants access to capital and textiles at good rates, leaving them with plenty of room to profit. It also hinged on the allure of the goods they dealt in: their ability to signify distinction, and to meet the demands of an increasingly discerning regional population of consumers.

The trade in textiles and foodstuffs that merchants like Jairam were involved in was in large part financed through Indian credit networks – an indigenous banking network that ultimately linked back to financial centers like Surat. Even as Bombay eclipsed Gujarat as a regional political and manufacturing center by the mid-eighteenth century, Surat remained active in finance, providing merchants with extensive banking and credit facilities.[1] By drawing on contacts in Kutch and other parts of Gujarat, merchants like Jairam were able to procure textiles – a Gujarati specialty that was in high demand around the Western Indian Ocean – on credit. They also had access to other goods his customers in Muscat and Zanzibar would have demanded: rice, tea, sugar, and the occasional trinket.

Over the course of Sewji and Jairam's lifetimes, however, the contours of the regional commodity and credit markets they relied on would have changed dramatically. By the early nineteenth century, Gujarat's textile industry found itself competing with an influx of British-produced textiles, which manufacturers offered on credit at cheaper rates than the local piece goods. As British markets became oversaturated with capital, London bankers began to look to the colonies to invest their money, in the hopes of better returns than they might have at home. At the same time, deliberate policies by the British government aimed at protecting the British manufacturing industry gave it a competitive advantage over Indian textiles in colonial possessions, South Asia included.[2] These processes intersected in South Asian markets, where the confluence of London capital and Manchester textiles gave merchants like Jairam and his father the opportunity to purchase goods on cheap credit and re-export them to markets in Muscat and Zanzibar, where they could advance them at a higher interest rate.[3]

The arrival of cheaper British textiles into Indian Ocean markets did not completely displace the South Asian textile industry. When British textiles arrived in India, they had to be dyed and patterned according to the demands of consumers in the Persian Gulf, South Arabia, and East Africa, leaving ample room for a robust local textile processing industry.

[1] Machado, *Ocean of Trade*, 60–61.

[2] See also P.J. Cain and A.G. Hopkins, "Gentlemanly Capitalism and British Expansion Overseas I: The Old Colonial System," *The Economic History Review*, Vol. 39, No. 4 (1986), 501–525; idem, "Gentlemanly Capitalism and British Expansion Overseas II: New Imperialism, 1850–1945," *The Economic History Review*, Vol. 40, No. 1 (1987), 1–26.

[3] Ray, "Asian Capital in the Age of European Domination," 464, 480–481.

Moreover, consumers continued to demand Indian, rather than British textiles. In Zanzibar itself, lengths of cloth arriving from India (which may or may not have been British in origin), were sewn with gold thread and sold as *wizārs* (cloths wrapped around the waist, much like *lungis*) at a high profit.[4] Affordability was thus only one of the many dimensions of the textile market; consumers around the Indian Ocean sought distinction through different grades, colors, and varieties of fabric, and were willing to pay a premium for it.[5] Merchants like Jairam were aware of this and ensured that the textiles they dealt in catered to a broad range of consumers.

The infusion of surplus British capital into India also had another effect: it gave rise to Indian industrial manufacturing. As British financiers sought opportunities to profitably employ their capital in the colonies, they turned to infrastructural projects: railways, steamships, canals, and factories. As a regional metropolis, Bombay was a chief recipient of British investment: by the middle of the nineteenth century, it had firmly established itself as a regional manufacturing center and transport hub for goods moving between the interior of South Asia and its oceanic frontier.[6] The textile trade benefited directly from this transformation: Indian merchants in East Africa and Bombay who had business partners in Bombay were able to take advantage of the goods a growing industrial sector offered, further infusing cloth into the markets they served.

But not all textiles arrived from England, or even India. In 1819, Sewji Topan, Jairam's father, saw a new commercial opportunity in American vessels that began to call at East Africa, and invited them to do business in Zanzibar. The American merchants, the majority of whom came from Salem, brought with them a variety of goods to trade, but none were more popular than cotton cloth, which took the East African market by storm. By the 1840s, the *merekani* cloth, as it had come to be known, became the most popular in the region, desired by consumers from the coast all the way into the interior.[7] American traders also distinguished themselves in the terms of their trade, advancing cloth on four to six

[4] Jeremy Prestholdt, "On the Global Repercussions of East African Consumerism," *American Historical Review*, Vol. 109, No. 3 (2004), 764–770.

[5] See, for example, Richard Burton, *The Lake Regions of Central Africa: From Zanzibar to Lake Tanganyika*, Vol. 2 (London: Longman, Green, Longman, and Roberts, 1860), 531–533.

[6] See also B.R. Tomlinson, *The Economy of Modern India: From 1860 to the Twenty-First Century* (New York: Cambridge University Press, 2013), 92–97, 212–214.

[7] Prestholdt, "On the Global Repercussions," 767–773; William Ruschenberger, *Narrative of a Voyage Round the World During the Years 1835, 1836 and 1837, Including an Embassy to the Sultan of Muscat and the King of Siam*, Vol. 1 (London: Richard Bentley, 1838), 65–66.

months' credit so as to allow their customers to gather the commodities they wanted in return. Throughout the American merchants' time in East Africa, Jairam was their principal business partner, ensuring that all goods moving to and from Salem went through him and his business partner, the American Consul Richard Waters.[8]

Although access to textiles on credit played a big role in shaping the fortunes of the Indian merchant-financiers of the Western Indian Ocean, it could not account for all of it. Over time, as access to textiles became more widespread, they lost their ability to signify distinction, and consumers began to seek out other goods through which they could signal their status: muskets, clocks, music boxes, umbrellas, and luxury items that they could furnish their homes with.[9] These were not, after all, one-dimensional consumers; they saw in the world around them a range of goods that would enable them to engage in different forms of conspicuous consumption, and saw in their creditors the means to pursue them.

For merchants like Jairam, financing these desires proved to be an altogether different enterprise than supplying consumers with textiles. There was an established textile industry in Western India; the same could not be said for parasols, clocks, or music boxes. These required a different sort of credit than textiles: they required access to money, either to buy the goods and re-sell them on credit or to lend directly to their debtors. And over time, as the cash zone expanded deeper and deeper into the interior, where traders were no longer satisfied with giving up their ivory for measures of cloth and trinkets but instead wanted ready cash, access to money became even more important for trade.[10]

Fortunately, the same British capitalists who invested in the Bombay textiles industry also founded the region's first large banks – institutions with links to metropolitan European capital. They established banks in the Bengal and Bombay Presidencies in 1809 and 1840, setting up another bank in Madras just three years later.[11] By the second half of the nineteenth century, the Indian Ocean financial sector witnessed the arrival of a number of large financial institutions, including the Chartered

[8] Abdul Sheriff, *Slaves, Spices and Ivory in Zanzibar* (Oxford: James Currey, 1987), 96–97.

[9] Prestholdt, "On the Global Repercussions," 765; idem, *Domesticating the World: East African Consumerism and the Genealogies of Globalization* (Berkeley, CA: University of California Press, 2008), 88–116; Frederick Cooper, *Plantation Slavery on the East Coast of Africa* (New Haven, CT: Yale University Press, 1977), 75; Ruschenberger, *Narrative of a Voyage*, Vol. 1, 70–71; Robinson, *Narrative of Voyages*, Vol. 1, 385–386, 393.

[10] Jonathon Glassman, *Feasts and Riot: Revelry, Rebellion and Popular Consciousness on the Swahili Coast, 1856–1888.* (London: James Currey, 1995), 46.

[11] See also John Maynard Keynes, *Indian Currency and Finance* (London: Royal Economic Society, 1913), 140; S.G. Panandikar, "Banking," in V.B. Singh (ed.) *Economic History of India, 1857–1956* (Mumbai: Allied Publishers, 1975), 415–416.

Banks of India, Australia, and China; the National Bank of India; Lloyds Bank; and a number of other Dutch, French, and American institutions. As members of trans-regional mercantile firms with partners and assets in urban centers like Bombay, Jairam and others would have enjoyed access to credit from these banks, which they then re-extended to markets in the Persian Gulf, South Arabia, and East Africa – markets that the larger financial institutions would have found too risky because of the information gaps that persisted. These merchants' ability to exploit the informational arbitrage opportunities also allowed them to charge interest rates that reflected the information gap – depending on the customer, a "bazaar rate" that could match the bank rate, but often far exceeded it.[12] It was in that pocket – between the price they paid for money and the price they sold it for – that many merchants made their profits.

Whether dealing in textiles, trinkets, or cash, Indian merchants like Jairam made the flows of capital conform to seasonal trade needs around the Western Indian Ocean. They brought Indian capital to markets in Africa and Arabia, and linked up producers and consumers in Zanzibar, Mombasa, Lamu, Muscat, and Bahrain to carvers, jewelers, shippers, and retailers in Gujarat and Bombay. As markets around the world opened up to Indian Ocean commodities, and as Indian Ocean consumers themselves sought access to global wares, merchants like Jairam and his father skillfully rode the crest of a rising wave of commerce.

Arabia and Africa in Indian Financial Networks

For Sewji Topan, Muscat was a sensible place to set up a business. The port city was not far from Kutch: it was only just over 700 miles by sea to Muscat from the port city of Mundra, where Sewji Topan came from. Sewji would easily be able to communicate with his trading partners and producers at home, and would benefit from a steady movement of goods back and forth and a fast turnaround on the letters, credit instruments, and other documents necessary to facilitate trade. More importantly, Muscat offered a range of liberties to Gujarati traders, many of whom had been involved in the southern Red Sea's coffee trade for centuries. Many of the port's Gujarati merchants had come there from ports like Mocha and Aden, where increasingly oppressive policies pursued by the rulers of Southern Yemen against Gujarati traders forced them

12 Ray, "Asian Capital in the Age of European Domination," 480; Ray's "bazaar rate" or "intermediate rate" refers to the rate charged in internal money markets (i.e. between merchants), whereas the "rate charged by usurers" seems to refer to the amount charged for loans taken on by producers and consumers, rather than retailers and other merchants.

to leave for opportunities elsewhere in the Western Indian Ocean.[13] The first Busa'idi ruler of Muscat, Ahmed bin Sa'id Al-Busa'idi (who ruled from 1744 to 1783) was himself a coffee merchant, and immediately recognized an opportunity in the exodus of Gujarati merchants and financiers from Yemen. Through a mix of trading incentives and guarantees of religious liberty – policies that observers frequently praised him for – he managed to attract a significant number of traders to the port. By 1765, the Danish traveler Carsten Niebuhr could remark that "in no other Mahometan city are the Banians so numerous as in Maskat" – population of no fewer than 1,200, all of whom were "permitted to live agreeably to their own laws, to bring their wives hither, to set up idols in their chambers, and to burn their dead."[14] In Muscat, the Gujarati merchant community found a ruler who would afford them the same security they had previously enjoyed in other ports.

It was also a good time to be a trader in Muscat. The port city, which enjoyed the geographical advantage of being at the mouth of the Persian Gulf, had benefited greatly from political and economic shifts taking place around the Gulf and in the Arabian Peninsula. In Persia, the fall of the regime of Karim Khan Zand in the late eighteenth century took out one of the Muscat regime's main rivals in regional trade. Zand had pursued a conspicuously maritime-oriented policy, and his demise opened up the Gulf for the Sultan of Muscat to assert his hegemony. In around 1790, scarcely a decade after Zand's death, the Sultan leased a large area around Bandar 'Abbas, which the Busa'idi sultans held onto for more than sixty-five years. Customs receipts from the leased area provided nearly a quarter of the Sultan's income from his Gulf dominions, and the port opened up a large market for Muscat's merchants.[15]

Moreover, the political geography of the Gulf had undergone radical shifts by the end of the eighteenth century. A combined plague and Persian siege in Basra in the mid-1770s spurred on the emergence of smaller port towns around the region. Towns like Kuwait and Muhammarah, for example, quickly established themselves as alternatives to the unstable port of Basra, as merchants from Iraq moved their business operations there in response to the troubles they faced at home. Merchants were also attracted by the incentives offered by the rulers of the smaller ports, who assured prospective businessmen that they would take a hands-off

[13] Pedro Machado details how these policies pushed Gujarati Vaniya traders to pursue opportunities in Mozambique's growing ivory trade. Machado, *Ocean of Trade*, 20–24.

[14] Carsten Niebuhr, *Travels Through Arabia and Other Countries in the East*, Vol. 2 (London: T. Vernor, 1792), 116.

[15] Lewis Pelly, "Remarks on the Tribes, Trade, and Resources Around the Shore Line of the Gulf," *Transactions of the Bombay Royal Geographic Society*, Vol. 17 (1865), 57.

approach to mercantile affairs and would limit taxes. The development of these ports and the expansion of related families into ports like Bahrain, which was previously held by Karim Khan Zand's troops, helped reinvigorate trade between the northern Gulf, Muscat, and India.[16] The final feather in the Sultan's cap came with the fall of the Qawasim, a ruling tribe operating out of Sharjah, Ras Al-Khaima, and Lingah, just further up the Gulf from Muscat.[17] Qasimi ports were rocked by a series of British bombardments between 1797 and 1820; their ships were burned, their towns leveled, and their political and commercial ambitions decimated. Muscat's prominence was left virtually unchallenged up and down the Gulf.

By the beginning of the nineteenth century, then, Muscat was clearly poised for economic and political success, and everyone seemed to know it. During his visit to the port in 1823, British Captain William F. Owen noted that "the good faith of the Sultan, the security he derives from his connexion with the Government of Bombay, and the advantageous situation of the port (at the entrance of the Persian Gulf) has rendered it a sort of emporium for the Coasts of Africa, Madagascar, the Red Sea, the Persian Gulf, and India in general; and in being so, it has rather added to than diminished the trade of Cutch, Surat, Bombay, &c."[18] As the political geography of the Gulf was being remade during the late eighteenth century, more and more traders were drawn into the port's orbit. For Sewji's Arab and Persian customers from the Gulf who were looking for goods, Muscat was the safest bet in the region: from there, they could access the wares of India and the financial services that they would need to participate in a lucrative world of Indian Ocean trade. Those who wanted to bypass Muscat and trade with India directly had to pay a toll.[19]

For merchants like Sewji, Muscat offered an entry point into a large market for the goods he had on hand: foodstuffs such as rice, sugar, and tea, and sundries like tobacco, which had become staples in the region, but also textiles from Gujarat. Trade reports on the Gulf port cities all

16 Hala Fattah, *The Politics of Regional Trade in Iraq, Arabia, and the Gulf, 1745–1900* (Albany, NY: SUNY Press, 1997), 186–206.

17 The tribe has had a contentious history: some have claimed that they were engaged in piracy, while others have suggested that they were asserting their economic and political authority in ways that made the East India Company and its regional allies (who included the Sultan of Muscat) uncomfortable. For a good sense of the debate, see also J.B. Kelly, *Britain and the Persian Gulf, 1795–1880* (Oxford: Clarendon Press, 1968); *Sultan bin Mohammed Al-Qasimi, The Myth of Arab Piracy in the Gulf* (London: Routledge, 1988); Charles E. Davies, *The Blood-Red Arab Flag: An Investigation into Qasimi Piracy, 1797–1820* (Exeter, UK: University of Exeter Press, 1997).

18 Robinson, *Narrative of Voyages*, Vol. 1, 340.

19 James Onley, "The Politics of Protection in the Gulf," 36.

listed "piece-goods" – long measures of cloth that consumers would form into clothing and turbans – as the most popular import.[20] Buyers in the region also seemed to like guns: people traveling through the area in the early- to mid-nineteenth century noted the locals' fascination with firearms of different types and could not help but mention the number of people they saw carrying guns.[21]

In return for the textiles, foodstuffs, and guns they brought, merchants like Sewji accepted a range of different commodities: wool and woolen goods, which were mostly exported from the Persian ports; horses, which made their way from the interior of the Arabian peninsula to markets in India; and pearls, the Gulf's most notable export.[22] The pearls were fished from the pearl banks that surrounded Bahrain and lined the coasts of Eastern Arabia, but were carried to Muscat, the region's principal port city, before being shipped off to Bombay. An officer in the Indian Navy traveling through Oman in 1835 valued pearl exports from the Gulf at Rs 4 million a year, and noted that nearly two-thirds of the pearls were brought to Muscat and were then forwarded to Bombay on different ships – at least some of which would have belonged to Indian merchants like Sewji and Jairam.[23]

Sewji and others also engaged in a modest trade in dates from Muscat, the bulk of which went to India. Their preference was for dried dates, which Indians used in wedding ceremonies and other festivals, but they also dealt a few other varieties.[24] American ships calling at Muscat also constituted a market for Indian merchants; by the first few decades of the nineteenth century, Indian merchants could depend on a regular traffic of American ships coming to Muscat by way of Zanzibar, loading their ships with cargoes of dates to take back to New York, Salem, and other American ports (see Chapter 7). Over time, with the increasing

[20] Pelly, "Remarks on the Tribes," 35–112.

[21] Ruschenberger, *Narrative of a Voyage*, Vol. 1, 29–35, 122; Glassman, *Feasts and Riot*, 48–50.

[22] On the horse trade, see Fattah, *The Politics of Regional Trade*, 159–183.

[23] J.R. Wellsted, *Travels in Arabia*, Vol. 1 (London: John Murray, 1838), 24–25. I detail the system of loans and debts that structured the movement of pearls from Bahrain to India in "A Sea of Debt: Histories of Commerce and Obligation in the Indian Ocean, c. 1850–1940," 80–91, 103–110. At different times, the Sultan of Muscat attempted to take Bahrain by force so that he could profit more directly from its pearl trade, but was repelled by the combined forces of the Persians and the Arab tribes who ruled over the island. Allen, "Sayyids, Shets, and Sultans," 43–45. Over the course of the nineteenth century, one community of Sindhi merchants moved further up the Gulf to invest in the pearl trade more directly, bypassing Muscat altogether to send their pearls to Bombay. Allen, "Sayyids, Shets, and Sultans," 109.

[24] Allen, "Sayyids, Shets, and Sultans," 141.

migration of Omanis to East Africa, where the date palm could not grow, the market for dates grew substantially.[25]

As profitable as the trade in textiles, dates, and pearls in Oman and the Gulf may have been, more interesting commercial prospects in the early nineteenth century lay with the expanding Omani frontier in "Zanzibar" – a metonym for the islands and ports of East Africa stretching from Mogadishu to Mozambique. Commodities from East Africa had been making their way to Muscat in significant numbers since at least the seventeenth century, but by the first few decades of the nineteenth century things were beginning to look substantially more lucrative. Zanzibar had become a global commercial capital: merchants from India, Arabia, Europe, and the United States regularly visited the region to take advantage of its growing trade in ivory, gum copal, spices, and slaves, and to feed its insatiable market for textiles. International shipping routes, and flows of finance and commodities all converged on the small island.

Anyone looking to establish themselves in Indian Ocean trade, then, could do no better than to start with Zanzibar, where dozens of international merchants jockeyed for entry into the market. It was a seller's market: buyers came in from all over the globe to purchase Zanzibari wares, and merchants there found themselves confronted with an embarrassment of options to choose from. As one American merchant lamented in 1851, "there is entirely too much foreign trade for the place"; French Spanish, German, American, European, and Indian ships had all descended upon the island at the same time, and competition between them was fierce.[26] A couple of decades later, Richard Burton commented on how French merchants from Marseilles "found out that Zanzibar is overstocked with buyers" and that French firms were "eating up each other." Sure profits, Burton pointed out, "are commanded only by the Banyan system."[27]

And a "Banyan system" it was indeed. At least some of Zanzibar's emergence as a global commercial center was the result of the efforts of merchants like Jairam's father Sewji, who was in Zanzibar in 1819 when he heard of an American ship nearby and sailed to it to personally encourage the captain to trade in Zanzibar.[28] Along with other

[25] Allen, "Sayyids, Shets, and Sultans," 148.

[26] John F. Webb to Michael Shepard, Zanzibar (November 10, 1851), Ms Shepard Papers, Box 47, Peabody Essex Museum, transcribed in Norman R. Bennett and George E. Brooks, Jr., eds. *New England Merchants in Africa: A History Through Documents, 1802 to 1865* (Boston: Boston University Press, 1965), 488.

[27] Richard F. Burton, *Zanzibar: City, Island, and Coast*, Vol. 1, (London: Tinsley Brothers, 1872), 320.

[28] William Osgood, *Notes of Travel or Recollections of Majunga, Zanzibar, Muscat, Aden, Mocha, and Other Eastern Ports* (Salem: George Creamer, 1854), 54; Sheriff, *Slaves, Spices*, 146.

merchants in Muscat, Sewji may have also had a more direct hand in the expansion of Zanzibar's trade, encouraging the Sultan to conquer East Africa, and financing his military activities there.[29] Whether or not they were whispering into the Sultan's ears as he made his way across the Arabian Sea to East Africa, one thing is for certain: merchants like Jairam and his father Sewji Topan were instrumental in directing the vectors of commerce between Gujarat, Muscat, the Persian Gulf, and East Africa. Their ability to channel the flows of commodities and capital around the Western Indian Ocean, and between the global firms that competed for a foothold in Zanzibar's growing economy and the local entrepreneurs who supplied their wants, gave regional trade and economic life in the region its shape during the nineteenth century.

Binding the Elephant

By the time Jairam and his father Sewji made it to East Africa, there would have been a long history of Arabs, Africans, and Gujaratis trading in ivory out of the region. There are reports dating back to the medieval period of Arabs and Indians trading ivory and gold out of Kilwa and Sofala.[30] Under the Portuguese, traders from Mombasa to Mozambique bought and sold considerable amounts of the stuff, and the Ya'rubis, too, looked to East Africa as a source of ivory, which they carried to Muscat and sold to regional buyers there.[31] But it was through mercantile firms like Jairam and his father's that this trade reached new heights and that the ivory found its way to markets around the world.

Merchants were clearly aware that there existed a robust market for ivory in the Western Indian Ocean – particularly in Gujarat and in India more broadly, where ivory workers carved them into wedding bangles, knife handles, and other ornaments. In the middle of the eighteenth century, Indian traders from Diu and Daman had established themselves on the island of Mozambique, 700 miles south of Zanzibar, exchanging Gujarati textiles for increasing quantities of ivory, which they then carried across the ocean. Over time, these traders were displaced by Kutchis like Jairam, who managed to redirect the trade further north, towards

[29] Allen, "Sayyids, Shets, and Sultans," 110; Allen himself seems less than convinced of this possibility, citing the opinion of Abdul Sheriff that the Sultan encouraged Indian merchants to come to his East African dominions.

[30] Pearson, *Port Cities and Intruders*, 43–45; Randall L. Pouwels, *Horn and Crescent: Cultural Change and Traditional Islam on the East African Coast, 800–1900* (New York: Cambridge University Press, 1987), 24–31.

[31] See also Machado, *Ocean of Trade*; M.N. Pearson, *Port Cities and Intruders*, 84–93; Bathurst, "The Ya'rubi Dynasty of Oman," 173–179.

Zanzibar and ports along the Mrima coast like Bagamoyo, Pangani, and Saadani.[32] The geography of the ivory trade may have shifted slightly, but the principal markets remained the same through the beginning of the nineteenth century.

But by the middle of the nineteenth century, the market for ivory had expanded to include European and American consumers. In the aftermath of the industrial revolution, as the size of the upper-middle and upper classes swelled with the entry of the industrial *nouveau riche*, there emerged a demand for products like billiard balls, piano keys, combs, and cutlery with ivory handles – products that East Africa's soft ivory was perfect for.[33] This growing market made itself visible in swelling export figures: the value of ivory leaving East Africa for Bombay (where much of it would be re-exported) slowly climbed from Rs 227,000 in 1803 to more than half a million rupees in 1844 – and this did not even account for amounts that American merchants took directly out of Zanzibar, bypassing Bombay altogether.[34] For any enterprising merchant, then, there was a good deal of money to be made in the ivory trade.

As part of a trans-regional firm of Indian merchants and financiers who had followed the Sultan from Muscat to Zanzibar, Jairam was well-placed to take advantage of the boom in the ivory trade, and accounts made it clear that he wasted no time in capturing the opportunities it presented. Through his network of agents in Zanzibar and the coast – a growing firm that included Ladha Damji, who would ultimately succeed Jairam as customs master – the Kutchi merchant was able to tap into the increasingly lucrative ivory trade in the region, channeling goods and credit from his trading partners in Bombay and Kutch into the interior of East Africa, and sending back large shipments of ivory.

Through direct loans to caravan leaders or to merchants on the coast, Jairam, Ladha, and the scores of other ivory financiers like them bound the new hinterlands of East African ivory to markets in northwestern India and beyond, securing supplies of ivory for their business partners at home. A group of merchants described to a British official in 1875 how any Indian merchant on the coast who collected ivory coming in from the interior, if he had taken on loans from a Zanzibar merchant, had to forward the goods on to his creditor in satisfaction of the latter's right to them. As one merchant explicitly stated, "he who gives advances to constituents on the coast is entitled to a lien over all the goods of the

[32] I draw all of my information here from Machado, *Ocean of Trade*, 168–207.
[33] Pearson, *Port Cities and Intruders*, 160–161; Sheriff, *Slaves, Spices*, 87–91.
[34] Sheriff, *Slaves, Spices*, 249–252.

constituent sent by him for sale at Zanzibar, and is the only person to whom the goods can be consigned."[35] And at times, the pressures were clear: in 1874 one Indian merchant waited anxiously for a caravan he had financed to arrive from the interior. But he was not waiting alone: pressing him for the ivory were several creditors in Kutch, who wrote to the British Political Agent that they were keeping a close eye on his property there in case the ivory never arrived.[36]

A merchant like Jairam, or even any one of the lesser known Indian merchants in Zanzibar or on the coast, would not have gone into the interior himself. Like the Gujaratis who had done business in East Africa before him, he would have contracted with an ivory trader – an Arab or a Shirazi, who would take goods from the coast and traded them for ivory along the caravan routes and stations of the interior.[37] These "respectable men," Burton wrote, "by promising usurious interest to the *Banias*, can always borrow capital enough to muster a few loads, and then they combine to form one large caravan."[38] Through the trading goods and provisions they were able to advance to aspiring caravan leaders, merchants like Jairam cast their lines into the interior of East Africa – much like they did in the South Arabian date and pearl trade – hoping to reel in loads of ivory that would make them and their trading partners rich.

A successful ivory trader knew his customer's tastes in the interior – particularly their tastes in textiles and beads, both of which formed essential items of trade. While tastes fluctuated from season to season, cloth and beads, cowry shells – and, over time, guns – were almost universally accepted in the interior as payment for ivory or slaves.[39] A sharp caravan leader could get a *frasela* of ivory for 12 to 15 garments.[40] Caravan porters engaged in this, too: some took cloth and beads to trade on their own account during the caravan journey, while others converted them into more symbolic capital, for consumption. One traveler into the interior wrote that "when a young man [of the Wanyamwezi, a community

[35] *Jeta Anandji* v. *Lulu Haverchand* (1876) Zanzibar National Archives (hereafter, ZNA) HC 7/45.

[36] *Mahomed Laljee* v. *(1) Pragjee Jadiwjee (2) Cowejee Chapsee (3) Megjee Lila (4) Anundjee Moolchund (5) Mumla Morjee* (1875) ZNA HC 7/20.

[37] For an overview of the caravan routes and the role of financiers in shaping the caravan trade, see Jonathon Glassman, *Feasts and Riot*, 58–74; Stephen J. Rockel, *Carriers of Culture: Labor on the Road in Nineteenth-Century East Africa* (Portsmouth, NH: Heinemann, 2006), 8–23.

[38] Richard F. Burton, *The Lake Regions of Central Africa*, Vol. 2 (London: Longman, Green, Longman, and Roberts, 1860), 57.

[39] On shifting tastes in the interior, see Prestholdt, "On the Global Repercussions," 755–781.

[40] Heinrich Brode, *Tippoo Tib: The Story of His Career in Central Africa* (London: The India Office, 1907), 29.

of porters] possesses a few iron hoe-blades, some beads, or one or two "doti" of cotton-stuff, he is in a position to marry."[41]

Over the course of the nineteenth century, as the ivory trade underwent its boom, the young ivory and slave trader Hamed bin Mohammed Al-Marjebi emerged as the most famous of these traders. For Al-Marjebi, the journey into the East African interior was one that his father, and his fathers before him, had made several times in the past. East Africa might have been where they spent most of their days, but Muscat was their home. Al-Marjebi's great-grandfather Rajab bin Mohammed had first come to the Swahili Coast in the company of his friend, Mohammed bin Jum'a Al-Nabhani, whose father had gone off to the interior of East Africa and returned to Muscat a rich man. After arriving in East Africa at the end of the eighteenth century, Rajab married his friend's sister and fathered a boy, Jum'a. The young Jum'a went on to lead caravan expeditions as far into the interior as Lake Tanganyika. He later married the daughter of the Sultan of Tabora, and his son, Mohammed, proved to be as adept as his father at leading caravans. Mohammed also frequently moved back and forth between the East African coast and Muscat, where he married the daughter of a prosperous and well-respected Arab family, Binti Habib bin Bushir Al-Wardi – Al-Marjebi's mother.[42]

By the time the young Al-Marjebi sought to organize his first caravan into the interior, then, he would have been following on the heels of many who went in before him. Omanis from the Barwani family, most of whom hailed from the town of Ibra in the Sharqiya province of Oman, had been active in the ivory trade for some time, and had established trading colonies in interior towns like Tabora and others further upcountry, near Lake Nyasa.[43] Some of these individuals had developed reputations as traders and strongmen, and had even taken on local names: the Swahili Arab Mohammed bin Khalfan Al-Barwani came to be known as "Rumaliza," a name that he had purportedly taken from an interior town; another Arab, Jum'a bin Salim Al-Bakri, who came to be known as "Juma Merekani" for his dealings in American cotton cloth,

[41] Philippe Broyon-Mirambo, "Description of the Unyamwesi, the Territory of King Mirambo, and the Best Route Thither from the East Coast," *Proceedings of the Royal Geographic Society of London*, Vol. 22, No. 1 (1877–78), 34. As the work of Prestholdt and Machado has made clear, interior consumers were known to have discerning tastes; a merchant's success often depended on his ability to stay attuned to the vagaries of the market and to remit information to his financier. See Presthold, "On the Global Repercussions," 760–767; Machado, *Ocean of Trade*, 134–149.

[42] Brode, *Tippoo Tib*, 13–14.

[43] Wilkinson, *The Imamate Tradition of Oman*, 55.

had set up shop in Nyangwe, in the Congo.[44] Al-Marjebi's journeys, then, although exceptionally well documented, were among hundreds of others.

To finance his caravan journey upcountry, Al-Marjebi needed access to credit.[45] He needed money to pay his porters, but also provisions for the journey inland and goods that he could trade – textiles, glass beads, or whatever it was that consumers in the interior wanted. At first, he could only raise enough to finance small undertakings: his first trip into the interior was with his father, and it was not altogether clear that Al-Marjebi had borrowed anything for the journey. After he returned from his first trip, however, he had made his creditors a lot of money in small ivory tusks, which at the time were commanding more money than the larger variety. When he came to the coast to outfit another caravan in July of 1867, he combined his own credit with the burgeoning reputation of his half-brother Mohammed bin Masud Al-Wardi, who had been sailing back and forth between Zanzibar and Somalia.[46] His brother borrowed 5,000 Maria Theresa Dollars (hereafter, MTD) and promised to bring back 320 *fraselas* – nearly 11,200 lbs of ivory; Al-Marjebi borrowed six times the amount, from twenty different creditors.[47]

Over time, as he accumulated experience and a reputation, Al-Marjebi was able to ask his creditors for more. Upon his return to the coast from a long stay in the interior, he was accosted by the Sultan of Zanzibar, who directed him to Jairam's agent Ladha Damji. According to Al-Marjebi, Ladha was anxious to have him on board and offered him "goods to the value of 50,000 dollars" to trade in the interior. The caravan leader hesitated to take goods from Ladha, "because these fellows from Customs had

[44] Leda Farrant, *Tippu Tip and the East African Slave Trade* (London: Hamish Hamilton, 1975), 59; Wilkinson, *The Arabs and the Scramble for Africa*, 100–101.

[45] The historians Jonathon Glassman and Abdul Sheriff both emphasize how crucial credit was to the caravan trade of East Africa. Glassman's analysis in particular emphasizes that access to credit determined who could and could not participate in the increasingly lucrative ivory trade during the mid-nineteenth century. Sheriff, *Slaves, Spices*, 181; Glassman, *Feasts and Riot*, 57.

[46] Hamad bin Mohammed Al-Marjebi, *Maisha ya Hamed bin Muhamed El Murjebi, Yaani Tippu Tip, Kwa Maneno Yake Mwenyewe*, edited by W.H. Whitely (Nairobi: East African Literature Bureau, 1971), 13–15.

[47] Brode, *Tippoo Tib*, 25; ZNA AM 1/1, 72. Brode wrote that Al-Marjebi contributed nearly MTD 30,000 in credit from nearly twenty creditors; there is no record, however, of such a transaction. It is difficult to determine how much money MTD 5,000 was against a normal family's income, as there are no indicators as to what the cost of living in nineteenth-century East Africa might have been. Frederick Cooper, however, notes that in 1860 MTD 5,000 could buy a large estate. This must have been a considerable sum of money when considering that the total government revenue was only MTD 200,000, and that the annual subsidy that Zanzibar paid to Muscat following the Omani Empire's partition in 1856 came to MTD 40,000. See Cooper, *Plantation Slavery*, 59, 118, 249.

become very tyrannous, they acted like chiefs" but accepted Ladha's offer, reneging only when the Khoja Indian merchant Tharia Topan – who at one point worked for Ladha and Jairam's firm and would later become customs master as well – offered him access to unlimited credit.[48] Al-Marjebi was then able to pass off the amount Ladha offered him to his "brother," Jum'a bin Saif bin Jum'a.[49]

For Al-Marjebi and the hundreds of others who went into the interior like him, credit meant access to the goods he so desperately needed to trade for ivory, but also the opportunity to establish a name for himself, like Rumaliza, Juma Merekani, and others like them. By 1875, the Arabs of the town of Unyanyembe, more than two hundred miles from the coast, owed nearly MTD 270,000 to Jairam's firm alone; no doubt many of them had similar hopes.[50] But for Al-Marjebi it meant much more: with access to Tharia Topan's credit and Jairam's cashbox, which he accessed through the Jairam's agent Ladha Damji, he was able to build an empire in the interior, trading in ivory and slaves and forcing those who refused his goods to hand over their ivory at the risk of death. Indeed, it was through Jairam's cashbox and the cloth and beads – and, more importantly, the guns – it gave him access to, that he was able earn himself the sobriquet "Tippu Tip." His contemporaries suggested might have come from a twitch that caused him to blink like a local bird of the same name; Al-Marjebi, however, claimed that it derived from the sound of his guns firing off in the distance.[51]

By the middle of the nineteenth century, then, Indian capital had reconfigured the geography of the interior of East Africa. Through caravan leaders like Al-Marjebi and Rumaliza, it had remade it into a web of principalities and petty sultanates, bound to one another and to the coast through circulations of commodities, credit, and information that would ultimately make their way across the ocean, to Bombay and Kutch. The interior of the continent was now yoked to Zanzibar through a series of known routes through which ivory would move, traveling towards the sources of finance and marketing that brought them into being to begin with. What was once the daunting *nyika* (literally, the wilderness) had by the 1860s become *terra cognita* – an investment frontier that was constantly moving inland and searching for new sources of profit.

[48] See also Goswami, *The Call of the Sea*, 177; Jagdish Gundara, "Aspects of Indian Culture in Nineteenth Century Zanzibar," *South Asia: Journal of South Asian Studies*, Vol. 3, No. 1 (1980), 23; Mumtaz-Ali Tajddin Sadiq Ali, *101 Ismaili Heroes* (Karachi: Islamic Book Publisher, 2003): 416–421.

[49] Al-Marjebi, *Maisha ya Hamad*, 29–31; Jum'a was most likely his paternal cousin, not his brother.

[50] Wilkinson, *The Imamate Tradition of Oman*, 234.

[51] Brode, *Tippoo Tib*, 41.

Financiers like Jairam were the agents of capital, the conduits through which this all flowed; and traders cum petty sultans like Tippu Tip and Juma Merekani – actors whose names literally bore the imprint of modern capitalism in the region – were its handmaidens.

Al-Marjebi's story, however, is an unusual one. Most traders who went into the interior were not able to establish a trading empire; only a handful of others were able to assert themselves politically at all, though everyone knew of the political power that access to credit and commodities brought with it. Some traders took their creditors' money and never returned: Al-Marjebi's biographer wrote that many caravan leaders who went into the interior on borrowed money "preferred, instead of abiding by [their] obligations in Zanzibar, to lead a showy life in the interior with other people's money."[52] Others continued their work in the ivory trade, staying on in trading stations like Tabora and facilitating the movement of information and goods between the coast and interior. Most, however, moved away from the ivory trade altogether and opted for a more sedentary lifestyle.

Shackling the *Shamba*

Of the thousands of migrants who made their way from Oman to East Africa over the course of the first half of the nineteenth century, only a small percentage engaged in the ivory trade. The upcountry trade was risky: one had to brave the *nyika* and seek out opportunities that were uncertain. The caravan trade involved major risks: caravans often encountered dangers in the interior, and faced the very real prospect of death by disease or starvation. In a late-nineteenth century compendium of Swahili customs, the author, an African from Bagamoyo, began his discussion of men's work by asserting that "some people are unwilling to travel inland," in large part because of "the trouble in the bush" and the risks that accompanied it.[53] Even an experienced leader could find himself deserted by members of his own caravan. As Tippu Tip's biographer wrote, "it was no light matter, in view of the uncertain conditions, to stake much money on a caravan for the interior. How many of them never came back! Either the whole was wiped out by savages or the leader died, and all the property was made away with by his unskilful

[52] Brode, *Tippoo Tib*, 25–26. Burton, too, suspected that many of the Arabs in the interior who had been robbed of their merchandise chose to stay there rather than face their creditors on the coast. Burton, *The Lake Regions of Central Africa*, Vol. 2, 151–152, cited in Sheriff, *Slaves, Spices*, 186.

[53] Mtoro bin Mwinyi Bakari, *The Customs of the Swahili People*, trans. J.W.T. Allen (Berkeley, CA: University of California Press, 1981), 120.

[sic] or faithless followers."[54] Unless they were unable to make money any other way, then, there was little incentive for commercial actors in East Africa to join the caravans moving between the coast and interior.

Instead, those who had the resources chose to invest in agricultural plots, called *shambas*.[55] On the coast, planters grew a range of different food crops: manioc, sorghum, sesame, and different grains.[56] One French captain visiting Zanzibar in the 1840s wrote that many caravan traders, after three or four journeys, would acquire enough capital to invest in plantations in Zanzibar.[57] For most of these commercial actors, a *shamba* made for a good investment: the food crops they grew provisioned an expanding population of merchants and migrants from India, South Arabia, and other parts of East Africa, but also the growing number of settlements in the interior of East Africa.

Even for financiers like Jairam and Ladha, for whom ivory held the key to enormous profits, plantation finance was the safer investment. There existed a ready and steady market for agricultural products around East Africa that only grew as time went by. Moreover, some planters began devoting more of their land to export-oriented crops like millet and sesame which they exported to the Arabian Peninsula and to the nearby French islands of Bourbon and Île de France.[58] The more popular of their export crops, however, was the coconut, one variety of which they dried to make copra, which they then exported to India where it was pressed for oil or used in soap and candles. This was a profitable trade: between 1842 and 1857, the price of copra rose from just over MTD 2 to over MTD 12 for 1,000 pieces.[59]

Moreover, unlike the exchange of ivory for textiles or glass beads, there were fewer variables at play in the plantation business – fewer informational delays or misread signals that might jeopardize a trading enterprise. With only some exceptions, plantation finance was a local undertaking. Merchants like Jairam could directly observe conditions in the *shamba* and communicate with the planter, and in cases where they couldn't, they frequently dealt with intermediaries – shopkeepers who operated in the *shamba* area and kept accounts with the planter. These shopkeepers acted as factors for bigger

[54] Brode, *Tippoo Tib*, 25.
[55] On interior plantations, see Wilkinson, *The Imamate Tradition of Oman*, 59–60.
[56] The most comprehensive study we have of plantation agriculture in East Africa remains Cooper's *Plantation Slavery on the East Coast of Africa*, particularly 47–114.
[57] Captain Loarer, "L'Ile de Zanzibar," *Revue de l'Orient*, Vol. 9 (1851), 240–299, quoted in Sheriff, *Slaves, Spices*, 108.
[58] Cooper, *Plantation Slavery*, 80.
[59] Burton, *Zanzibar*, Vol. 1, 220–221.

merchants in town like Jairam, who would then forward the *shamba's* produce along marketing channels in East Africa, South Arabia, and India.

For most planters, agricultural life struck a good balance between productivity and leisure. Running a *shamba* required relatively little exertion on the part of the planter, whose slaves did the bulk of the work. The *shamba* was a place of production, but also a place of relaxation: families who lived in town and owned *shambas* would retreat to them on weekends, seeking respite from the closed quarters of urban life; during the clove harvest season, they might spend a few months there. Travelers would remark how planters lived "a life of indolent ease" on their estates, hosting visitors and leaving the seasonal work to their slaves.[60] In her memoirs, the Sultan's daughter Salma bint Sa'id recalled how she would host parties on the *shambas*, play with fireworks with her siblings there, and entertain guests.[61] As a member of the ruling family, hers was likely an exceptional case, but not altogether unique.

But it wasn't all about leisure – nor could it always be, for there were markets to serve. Over the course of the 1830s and 1840s, *shambas* that produced cloves quickly eclipsed all others in terms of profitability, shaking up the relationship between the planter and his *shamba*. Unlike the other crops that East Africa produced, Zanzibari cloves were almost exclusively export-oriented: one could not eat cloves, and even their use as a spice would have created only a limited market locally. Rather, cloves were meant to be exported to regional, and ultimately, global markets, where retailers would sell them as condiments, or, more commonly, where processors would distill them into clove oil, which they would then market as an antiseptic and as a key ingredient in a variety of medicines and confections. American and European pharmaceutical manuals from the middle of the nineteenth century make frequent references to the clove and its medicinal qualities.[62]

Cloves were not native to Zanzibar; like many of the island's settlers, they were transplants. Before 1820, cloves were mostly grown in Southeast Asia, in the Moluccas islands; from there, they made their

[60] Cooper, *Plantation Slavery*, 73–74.

[61] Emily Reute, *Memoirs of an Arabian Princess* (New York: D. Appleton & Co, 1888), 257–261.

[62] See, for example, Wooster Beach, *The American Practice of Medicine*, Vol. 3 (New York: Charles Scribner, 1852), 180; Ferdinand J.S. Gorgas, *Dental Medicine: A Manual of Dental Materia Medica and Therapeutics for Practitioners and Students* (Philadelphia: P. Blakiston, Son, & Co: 1884), 248. The clove also makes an appearance in 1853–1854 medical exams; see Joseph Hanaway and Richard Cruess, *McGill Medicine: The First Half-Century, 1829–1885*, Vol. 1 (Quebec: McGill-Queen's University Press, 1996), 134.

way to the Mascarenes, from which one Omani planter in Zanzibar imported them in order to experiment.[63] It took time for their popularity to take root: even two decades after the first clove trees were introduced to Zanzibar (and accounts of their introduction vary) most clove plantations belonged to the Sultan, who experimented with a range of export-oriented crops, and his entourage.[64] By 1840, clove plantations had begun to spread around Zanzibar, and by 1860, cloves rivaled ivory as East Africa's main export to India; their export soared from 315,000 lbs in 1839–1840 to nearly 5 million lbs just sixteen years later.[65]

The confluence of planting, laboring, and financing forces that bound *shambas* in East Africa to markets around the world made themselves most visible in the journey of the clove from *shamba* to ship hold. For the plantation owner, economic life involved mediating these forces as much as he possibly could, balancing nature's rhythms with the imperatives of labor management and his place in his financier's ledger book. And nature intervened in every step of the clove trade, mediating the demands of agrarian finance. Almost immediately, it placed brakes on the planter's ambitions. A clove tree did not bear fruit immediately after it sank its roots; it took at least seven years to begin producing cloves, and almost ten years before it fully matured.[66] Any aspiring planter, then, had to account for the natural lifetimes of his slow-bearing trees before he even bothered to approach a moneylender. For those coming to East Africa from Arabia, this would have been a familiar hurdle: date palms also took several years before they began to bear fruit and over a decade to reach full maturity.

Even when a planter's trees were able to start producing for the market, they would only bear cloves once a year: a tree would begin to bud in January or February, but picking took place between July and November, depending on whether it was a dry year or a wet one. In a dry season, picking would stop in October and November and recommence in January, giving rise to two distinct harvesting seasons (in the summer/fall and in the winter). Deciding when to pick was a balancing act: planters had to wait until just before the overlapping petals of the clove flower fell

[63] Ruschenberger, *Narrative of a Voyage*, Vol. 1, 72–74; Cooper, *Plantation Slavery*, 49–50. The planter, Saleh Al-'Abri, had his plantations confiscated by the Sultan.

[64] Cooper, *Plantation Slavery*, 47–51; Osgood, *Notes of Travels*, 24–25. In 1839, American merchants visiting Zanzibar noted that Captain Hassan bin Ibrahim, one of the Sultan's sea captains who had trained in India, owned a plantation containing nearly 12,000 clove trees. "The Journals of Richard P. Waters, 1836–1844," in Bennett, *New England Merchants in Africa*, 212.

[65] Sheriff, *Slaves, Spices*, 249–252; Cooper, *Plantation Slavery*, 52.

[66] Robert Nunez Lyne, *Zanzibar in Contemporary Times: A Short History of the Southern East in the Nineteenth Century* (London: Hurst and Blackett, Ltd, 1905) 247.

off and released the stamens, at which point the tube of the bud began to turn pink and then red. It was at that point that the clove had to be picked. If the planter waited too long, the clove quality would be sacrificed. At the same time, however, a planter had to balance quality with quantity: one writer observed that Arabs never began to pick "until there is a good show upon the trees, enough to make it worth their while to take an interest in the proceedings."[67]

Planters looking for loans to hold them over until the harvest thus had to time their debts to the natural cycles of clove production. Long-term loans lasted several years at a time, with the expectation that the debtor would deliver with every harvest.[68] Short-term loans, however, were more clearly tethered to the harvest season: planters made out contracts to deliver a certain number of *frasilas* of cloves to their financiers "at the end of the next new moon" (*fī inqiḍā' al-qirn al-dimiyāni al-muqbil*) or "at the confluence of the new moon and the [harvest] season" (*fī ḍarb al-qirn fil-mawṣim*).[69] At other times, they used more precise terminology: to deliver "in two months and ten days" or a similarly agreed-upon timeframe.[70] Finance, then, worked with the rhythm of clove planting and harvesting, not against it.

When it came time to deliver, the planter's slaves would set out into the *shamba* and pick the cloves off the tree. Whatever they collected was earmarked for the creditor – usually the factor. The cloves thus began their journey out of the *shamba*, through the ledger books, and back up the channels of capital that had conjured them into being. Upon receiving his cloves, the Indian factor working in the *shambas* then had to make sure they would reach his principal in town on time and in good shape. If he was in Unguja, the main island in Zanzibar, he would send them to town on a donkey or on the heads of porters. Factors working in Pemba, however, had to ship cloves to the island by one of the many leaky dhows that moved between the islands, and risked damaging their shipment through exposure or by contact with water, thereby lessening their value.[71] Any damages left their mark on the debt chains that held planter, factor, and clove merchant together.

But no matter where they came from, all clove shipments had to make it through the customs house. The customs house, Burton remarked during a visit, was "an Arab bourse, where millions of dollars annually change hands under the foulest of sheds, a long, low mat-roof supported

[67] Lyne, *Zanzibar in Contemporary Times*, 247–248.
[68] I discuss this in much greater detail in Chapter 3.
[69] ZNA AM 1/1, 38–39.
[70] ZNA AM 1/1, 36.
[71] Lyne, *Zanzibar in Contemporary Times*, 248–249.

by two dozen rough tree stems." In front of the customs house was the shore, lined with "shore-boats, big and small"; behind it lay "sacks and bales, baskets and packages, hillocks of hides, old ships tanks, piles of valuable woods, heaps of ivories, and a heterogeneous mass of waifs and strays."[72] There, among the piles of goods awaiting shipment, merchants from Bombay, Rotterdam, Marseilles, New York, London, Hamburg, and elsewhere would bid against one another for cloves; as customs master, Jairam or Ladha collected duties and handed out receipts to those who hoped to sell their produce in the marketplace. Their partners in Bombay and Kutch received some of the shipments, but most bags had already been earmarked for the international trading interests that had made their way to the island. The clove, after all, had become an international commodity whose price was worked out under that rude shed by the beach in Zanzibar and echoed all the way down to the *shamba* factor's ledger books.

The factor would have only seen some of the global dimensions of the trade. For him, what mattered the most were his own accounts, with Jairam – the amount he owed on the goods that lined his store's shelves, and any other outstanding debts he had with his principals. He made what Jairam told him he could sell his cloves for, minus the customs duties that he invariably had to pay; from those profits he would deduct his own commission and enter the remainder into the pages of his ledger book as a credit to his planter. The factor, then, acted as a conduit between the *shamba* and the flows of global finance that made their way into Zanzibar through the customs house. To secure supplies from his planter clientele, he would have to continually re-extend the credit that kept the planters going from one season to another, opening up his store for whatever they might need. In a good season, when prices were high and the clove crop good, the balance would be in his favor, and he might make a good commission as well. In a bad year, he would have felt a little more pressure from his creditor, but would have passed on most of his losses to his debtors.

From the perspective of the planter, too, the global dimensions of the clove trade – the clove's journey from the tree to the ship's cargo hold – were largely invisible. He would have known of Jairam and the general business that went on in the customs house, and would have had a sense of where his cloves ended up, but he would not have seen much further beyond the *shamba* shopkeeper's ledger book. As far as he was concerned, all that mattered was that the cloves had made it to town and that

[72] Burton, *Zanzibar*, Vol. 1, 93.

the money had been credited to his accounts with his factor; where they ultimately went to was Jairam's concern, not his.

And yet, whether or not he knew it, the circuits of finance and cloves that dictated the pace of economic life in East Africa had fundamentally redefined the place of the planter's *shamba* in the global economy. The journeys of a clove from the tree to the market, and of credit from the ledger books of Bombay firms to the *shamba* moneylender, carved the pathways that would bind the *shamba* to the international market – that made it a *plantation*, not just a farm. The practices of lending and borrowing against the rhythms of plantation agriculture may have mediated the forces of global capitalism, but they could not detach the *shamba* from them altogether. The leisure of *shamba* life, with all of its social gatherings and infused meanings may still have been a part of the planter's world as he understood it, but the broader flows of finance in which the *shamba* was caught up had effectively separated him from his trees. The land could have meaning, but the trees now had an assigned value – a metric against which a loan could be measured and a line in an account book entered. Thus, when the Sultan's son, Barghash bin Sa'id named his *shamba* "Marseilles," it was no big mystery why: the plantation's name literally bore the imprint of the global channels of finance and marketing that had conjured it into being.[73]

Slaves, Spices, and Ivory

Merchants like Jairam and Ladha were not only concerned with the vectors of commodities and credit around the Indian Ocean. As they sank their money into the land, they became more deeply invested in the structures of labor and production that underpinned economic life in the region – whether on the caravan trails leading to Tabora and the Congo, or in the *shambas* that they derived so many of their profits from. Through their finance, Jairam, Ladha, and the hundreds of other Indian merchants on the island either directly or indirectly invested in slaves.

The work of slaves permeated almost every dimension of economic life in the Western Indian Ocean.[74] Slaves accompanied ivory

[73] Lyne, *Zanzibar in Contemporary Times*, 55.

[74] The historiography of slavery in the Western Indian Ocean is both deep and long-standing, and I cannot hope to do the subject any justice here. For more comprehensive discussions of slavery, see Cooper, *Plantation Slavery*; Sheriff, *Slaves, Spices*, 35–76; Machado, *Ocean of Trade*, 208–267; Jonathon Glassman, Feasts and Riot; idem, "The Bondsman's New Clothes: The Contradictory Consciousness of Slave Rebellions on the Swahili Coast," *Journal of African History*, Vol. 32 (1991), 277–312; Matthew S. Hopper, *Slaves of One Master: Globalization and Slavery in Arabia in the Age of Empire* (New Haven, CT: Yale University Press, 2015); Elizabeth McMahon, *Slavery and*

on its journey from the interior of East Africa to the coast, and slave labor underpinned all forms of production in the region, from the date farms of Basra and Muscat and pearl banks of the Persian Gulf to the clove and coconut plantations of East Africa. They were a commodity, traded openly in the markets of East Africa and the Persian Gulf, and an item of conspicuous consumption for merchants, planters, and even other slaves. Their presence infused every transaction, every promise to deliver, and every line in the ledger book.

But slaves in the Indian Ocean also served a variety of social and political functions: they buttressed the followers that different clan heads and political aspirants amassed; they served as military leaders and governors for rulers around the region; and they served as concubines for the elite and commoners alike.[75] They engaged in a wide range of economic activities: slaves worked as commercial agents, sailors, pearl divers, sea captains, artisans, and even wage laborers.[76] A slave in the Indian Ocean, then, seemed to enjoy at least some opportunities for social and economic mobility.

Over time, however, one of the slave's roles – as an agent of productive labor – grew to surpass the rest. The expanding French sugar plantations in the Mascarenes created a large demand for slaves, first from Madagascar and then from the East African coast, which Arab and Swahili traders were keen to supply. The port of Kilwa, just south of Zanzibar, emerged as a major transit point for slaves captured in the interior; its control became the subject of fierce contestations between the French, the Omanis, and the local political actors through which the Sultan governed.[77] Moreover, the "northern" slave trade to Oman and the Persian Gulf, where slaves would work in date plantations and on pearling dhows, also continued unabated in the nineteenth century, picking up by the middle of the century.[78]

The rise of grain, coconut, and clove plantations in Zanzibar and the East African coast brought with it a marked transformation in the nature of slavery and a concomitant growth in demand for slaves to work on

Emancipation in Islamic East Africa: From Honor to Respectability (New York: Cambridge University Press, 2013); and several volumes edited by Gwyn Campbell.

75 Gwyn Campbell, "Introduction: Slavery and Other Forms of Unfree Labour in the Indian Ocean World," *Slavery and Abolition: A Journal of Slave and Post-Slave Societies*, Vol. 24, No. 2 (2003), vii–xxxii.

76 Jonathon Glassman, "The Bondsman's New Clothes," 288–298; Cooper, *Plantation Slavery*, 6; Thomas F. McDow, "Deeds of Freed Slaves: Manumission and Economic and Social Mobility in Pre-Abolition Zanzibar," in Harms et al, *Indian Ocean Slavery*, 160–179; Abdul Sheriff, "Social Mobility in Indian Ocean Slavery: The Strange Career of Sultan b. Aman" in idem, *Indian Ocean Slavery*, 143–159.

77 Sheriff, *Slaves, Spices*, 41–48; Cooper, *Plantation Slavery*, 42–43.

78 Sheriff, *Slaves, Spices*, 35–41; Hopper, *Slaves of One Master.*

plantations. What had once been a more flexible, less market-driven sector became more voracious in its appetite for slave labor. The expansion of plantations on the coasts and islands paved the way for an increased traffic in slaves from the interior, on many of the same caravans that brought ivory to the coast. Observers in the region noted the growth of the coastal slave population, particularly in the clove-growing areas of Zanzibar and Pemba, and the gradually diminishing proportion of Omani Arabs to slaves.[79]

For the most part, however, the nature of plantation work gave the relationship between masters and their slaves a particular hue.[80] On the clove plantation, labor was pegged to the rhythms of the crop itself: demand for labor was highest during the harvest season, where the planter would sometimes supplement his workforce with day laborers. During the rest of the year, the workload was comparatively light. Slaves would work from sunrise to noon, even when the work day was supposed to end at 4 pm, and would get Thursdays and Fridays off to tend to their own plots. Coconut plantation work was even more lax, with observers frequently noting that cultivation was irregular and collection haphazard. Only in the coastal town of Malindi, where land was abundant and planters grew a range of different crops, did slaves engage in regular, uninterrupted plantation work.[81]

The structures of plantation finance and produce marketing also placed clear limits on planters' incentives to produce at full capacity. When the planter handed off his produce to his creditor, he would have seen none of the profits or commissions from the sale of his cloves, though he did not necessarily need to. His debts to his factor may have grown or lessened according to the vagaries of a global market or the seasonal harvest, but they barely impinged on his access to the store or even his factor's cash box. When times were good, his factor opened up his stores even more than usual, but when times were bad he still had access to what he needed to preserve his status.[82] The threat of his creditor foreclosing on his *shamba* was always present, but it was a distant one: with few exceptions, merchants and factors were uninterested in owning plantations, preferring the bonds of debt and obligation to outright vertical integration.[83] Planters in South Arabia and East Africa were able to maintain a

[79] Cooper, *Plantation Slavery*, 56–57.

[80] In some areas – particularly sugar plantations on the coast – this gave rise to a more contentious relationship between planters and their slaves. Glassman, "The Bondsman's New Clothes," 298–310.

[81] Cooper, *Plantation Slavery*, 55, 63–64, 110–111, 157–160.

[82] Cooper, *Plantation Slavery*, 75–78.

[83] Historians have put forward a range of different explanations for Indian indifference to land ownership. See Cooper, *Plantation Slavery*, 142–143; Sheriff, *Slaves, Spices*, 65–67. The most likely explanation is that the profits derived from lending and marketing

more multidimensional relationship with their land: the plantation was never just their milch cow; it was infused with political, social, and cultural meaning, and constituted a source of status as much as it did profit.

The nature of plantation work in East Africa and the absence of the fear of commercial failure left its imprint on the relationship between planters and their slaves. With some exceptions, an individual slave's output was left unmeasured, and force rarely factored into plantation work.[84] In Oman, too, slaves were put to work on the date plantations on the coast and in the interior, but the nature of date plantation work, which was only seasonal and did not require intensive labor, meant that slaves were able to engage in other forms of labor and sociability there as well.[85]

Broadly speaking, then, slaves in East Africa and South Arabia exhibited a significant degree of economic autonomy, both on the *shamba* and off of it, participating in economic life alongside their masters. Planters granted their slaves a plot of land to work and allotted them two to four days a week to work on them, depending on the time of the year; others gave their slaves a share of the *shamba's* crop. In both cases, slaves enjoyed the ability to dispose of their crop on the market in whatever manner they wished.[86] Slaves that did not work on *shambas* hired themselves out as day laborers and enjoyed distinction as artisans, at times sharing their profits with their masters and at other times keeping them to themselves.[87] Others sought more direct participation in a regional economy of obligation, borrowing from moneylenders like Jairam and pledging what little they had against promises to return from the interior with ivory or to deliver a set amount of crops.[88] Like freeborn commercial aspirants, these slaves often sought textiles and other consumer goods that would endow them with the distinction and respectability they desired.[89] They sought out socio-economic mobility – a chance to purchase their freedom, to own property, and to enter as equals into a

outweighed those that would come from direct ownership while obviating the difficulties and expenses of *shamba* ownership.

84 In Malindi, however, plantation work did involve a degree of violence, and slave output was measured by the *ngwe*, a length of rope used to estimate the size of the plot to be cleared every day. Even then, however, there were limits to what a master could ask of his slave laborers. Cooper, *Plantation Slavery*, 170–173, 178.

85 Cooper, *Plantation Slavery*, 35–36; Hopper, *Slaves of One Master*, 126–133.

86 Cooper, *Plantation Slavery*, 162; Glassman, "The Bondsman's New Clothes," 290–291. Glassman argues, however, that this capacity diminished over time.

87 Glassman, "The Bondsman's New Clothes," 291–292.

88 McDow, "Deeds of Freed Slaves"; McDow describes the commercial trajectories of the manumitted, but there is ample evidence (which I discuss in Chapter 2) to suggest that slaves also participated in similar acts of lending and borrowing.

89 McMahon, *Slavery and Emancipation*, 114–156.

commercial arena in which access to credit and the ability to take on debt shaped entire commercial fortunes.

Despite their subservient status, then, slaves participated in a growing commercial economy as equals, seeking out ways to distinguish themselves as patrons and consumers; they aspired to host feasts, wear expensive clothes, own property, and even own slaves themselves. They sought participation in communal institutions, and saw engagement in market-driven work like the ivory trade or clove planting as a way to realize their aspirations.[90] And they sought the credit that would enable them to realize all of those aspirations: borrowing from Indian moneylenders in the region, they entered into the economic arena alongside their masters – socially subservient, yes, but economically equal, and of commercial consequence.

For financiers like Jairam and Ladha and their middlemen, then, engaging with slaves was unavoidable. Slaves frequently approached them for loans to participate in a growing commercial arena and to consume the goods that they stocked their shops with. When they lent money to a planter against promises to deliver cloves and coconuts, they understood that the *shamba's* productivity depended on a ready supply of slaves to plant, pick, dry, and deliver the produce. If Indian finance underpinned the expansion of the trade in ivory, cloves, coconuts, pearls, and dates, slaves and their labor filled the spaces in between the lines of the ledger book, stepping out from time to time to directly claim their place in the regional commercial economy.

Public Finance and the Customs House

No matter where a commodity began its journey – whether it was carried on the heads of porters from the Congo to the coast, on the backs of slaves from the *shamba* into town, or on dhows sailing down the Persian Gulf – it always ended up in the same place: the customs house. It was there, in those rude sheds, that the flows of a regional commerce ultimately converged, and that the imperatives of finance, global capitalism, and empire all intersected. As commodities funneled in from the interior of Oman and the port cities of the Gulf to Muscat, and from the deepest interiors of East Africa and the *shambas* on the coast to Zanzibar, the capillaries and main arteries of the Omani Empire in the Indian Ocean became clear. And it was there, at the customs house, where the bonds of debt that yoked producers to merchants began their climb into the realm

[90] This is the core of Glassman's argument, spread out over several chapters in *Feasts and Riot*.

of politics, binding customs masters and sultans together in a common enterprise.

To the first Sultan of Muscat and Zanzibar, Sultan bin Ahmed Al-Busa'idi, two merchants stood out from the hundreds that spread around the Western Indian Ocean during the late eighteenth and early nineteenth century: Sewji Topan, whom we have already met, and Mowji Rowji Bhimani, also a Kutchi. These were the bankers to his throne – the cashbox from which he liberally drew to finance his commercial and political expansion around the Western Indian Ocean. From early on, Sultan bin Ahmed turned to Sewji and Mowji when he needed a loan; he died owing Sewji MTD 12,000.[91] And as he was able to establish himself in East Africa Sultan bin Ahmed, and later, his son Sa'id, continued to rely on the two firms, the Sewjis and Bhimanis, for money. In return, they rewarded the two with the right to farm the customs houses throughout their growing dominions. Credit and debt ran from the top of Indian Ocean society to its bottom; from the commercial to the political and back again.

In the early part of the nineteenth century, it was not yet clear to either of the two firms which of the Sultan's dominions – his capital, Muscat, or the new frontiers of East Africa – would produce more wealth. At the time, Muscat had the upper hand, consistently generating two to four times more revenue than Zanzibar.[92] It was clear, however, that the Sultan saw potential in Zanzibar: in one of his visits there, he took members from both firms along with him, perhaps to gauge their interest in farming the customs receipts there. While the customs house in Muscat (and presumably the Bandar 'Abbas customs that were linked to it) had gone to the Bhimanis, the two firms competed with one another for the Zanzibar contract, which included with it all of the ports of coastal East Africa. By around 1818, however, Sewji had managed to gain control of the customs house in Zanzibar, and Mowji Rowji took over the Muscat customs house at some point over the next decade. The Zanzibar house, which by the mid-1830s proved to be the more lucrative of the two, stayed in the hands of the Sewji's firm for almost seven decades, passing from Sewji to his son Jairam, and from Jairam to his partner, Ladha Damji.[93]

[91] M. Reda Bhacker, *Trade and Empire*, 172; for a correction of Bhacker's account, see Goswami, *The Call of the Sea*, 192–193.

[92] Bhacker, *Trade and Empire*, 78; it is not clear whether Bhacker's figures for Muscat also include the Zanzibar revenues, but even when adjusted for that income Muscat remains ahead.

[93] Goswami, *The Call of the Sea*, 95–101.

Control of the customs house was not cheap: the winners had to supply the Sultan with all of his public revenues – a projected figure that they based on a combination of receipts from years past, estimates for the future, and the needs of the Sultan himself. In 1819, Sewji Topan paid MTD 84,000 for the right to farm the Zanzibar revenues; Jairam paid MTD 142,500 for the same right in 1847, and MTD 190,000 twelve years later.[94] It is not clear how much the Bhimanis paid for the Muscat customs farm, but it is likely that the amount included the Bandar ʻAbbas customs, which in 1864 cost "a Bunya" 95,000 Tomans.[95] The amounts the two firms pledged to farm the customs did not come in a single payment, but rather as a credit entry in the ledger books between the Sultan and his customs masters – an assurance that their cash boxes would be open to him should he need them.

For the rulers of Muscat and Zanzibar, the customs farm constituted the single most important source of public revenue. The sultans were independently wealthy; they owned many plantations and generated income from different sources around the Western Indian Ocean. Whatever they earned, however, was not enough to support the webs of governors, soldiers, sailors, and *qāḍis* that made up the imperial bureaucracy – to say nothing of the family members and competitors they had to pay off and the largesse they had to distribute to individuals and tribal leaders of consequence around the sultanate. For this, they had to rely on the cash boxes of their financiers cum customs masters, who were more than happy to convert the vectors of commerce that they controlled in South Arabia and East Africa into political resources for their royal debtors. It was in the customs house, then, that the spoils of commerce merged with the imperatives of empire.

As customs masters, Jairam and his firm mediated the flows of capital that ran through the polity's veins. As the Sultan expanded his authority along the East African coast, he disbursed payments to the many petty rulers in return for their fealty. In one 1839 document featured in the Omani historian Saʻid bin ʻAli Al-Mughairi's history of Oman and East Africa, one of the Sultan's agents announces a payment of MTD 150 to Mohammed bin Khamis Al-Mombasi, and another MTD 250 to the heads of the *Tisa Taifa*, nine ethnic groups scattered along the coast of what is today Kenya (and referred to in the document as the *aṣ-ḥāba tisʻat bulud*, or the heads of nine tribes) paid out by the Busaʻidi ruler

[94] "Administration Report for Zanzibar (1859)," Maharashtra State Archives (hereafter, MSA) Political Department (PD) 1859 Vol. 188, Comp. 1123; Sheriff, *Slaves, Spices*, 127.

[95] Pelly, "Remarks on the Tribes and Resources," 57.

Sa'id bin Sultan.[96] The payment, the document stated was not in cash; rather, it was to be deducted from the obligations they owed him – the customs duties (*'ushūr*) they were obligated to hand over.[97] In the same breath in which he mentioned the payments from Sa'id bin Sultan to the other rulers of the Swahili coast, the agent mentioned Jairam, warmly referred to as "*maḥabbunā Zayram*" or "our dear Jairam."

The reference to Jairam is perhaps unsurprising: Jairam (or rather, Jairam's firm) was the person responsible for the collection of customs along the Swahili coast, and his firm had by then already clearly situated itself at the nexus of commerce and empire in the region. At the same time, however, in its mention of Jairam the document brilliantly evokes the degree to which actors like Jairam and others like him (another letter, from 1826, refers to "*maḥabbunā Siwā*" – presumably Jairam's father Sewji Topan) were intimately bound up in this world of political and economic obligation.[98] *Banias* like Jairam mediated the payments that underpinned the political economy of the Swahili coast. As a banker to the Sultan, Jairam was the source of the Sultan's public finances and the person to whom public revenues, in the form of customs, had been farmed out. As a member of a class of Indian moneylenders and financiers, as a merchant and customs master, Jairam constituted the principal conduit through which the forces of emerging modern capitalism flowed into the Swahili coast's changing economic and political landscape. The casualness with which the agent mentions Jairam – that he had become "our dear Jairam" – betrays the degree to which he and others like him had become such a central, constitutive feature of this political economy.

The fact that the Mombasa clans and *Tisa Taifa* were to be "paid" with a release from their customs obligations further underscores the fungibility of obligations between the realms of commerce and politics in East Africa. Sa'id bin Sultan was able to deduct his payments to his debtors from money they paid into the customs because he himself was in a state of perpetual debt to the customs master, from whom he received a loan (taken out against the customs duties) every year. This was not a practice unique to the realm of customs; merchants from around East Africa regularly traded in debt (see Chapter 3). In the case of the transfers between the Sultan, the *Tisa Taifa*, and Jairam Sewji, the liquidity of obligations between actors whose work straddled the realms of commerce

96 The Mombasa Mazru'is also relied on Indian creditors for similar purposes; Gray, *The British in Mombasa*, 20.

97 Al-Mughairi, *Juhaynat Al-Akhbār*, 240–241.

98 ZNA AM 3/1, 47. Other *waraqas* also refer to *maḥabbunā* Zayram; see also ZNA AM 3/1, 22, 41.

and politics allowed for a form of negotiability between the two realms. Commercial obligations could be transmuted into political ones, and political obligations offset by commercial ones.

For Jairam, his father, and members of their firm, the customs house was the cornerstone of their business enterprise. On the one hand, the right to collect customs gave them the opportunity to earn money hand over fist, particularly in a growing commercial environment. The amount they paid the Sultan for the customs house was more than amply compensated by the amount they collected. In 1819, the total annual revenue for the East African dominions amounted to MTD 40,000, a figure which doubled by the early 1840s; and by the early 1860s, annual revenue was MTD 310,000, roughly 50 percent more than what the farmers paid for it.[99] A merchant who could accurately gauge the tempo of commercial activity thus stood to make a fair amount of money through customs receipts.

That said, there were years in which the customs receipts would not add up to what they paid for them – in which the Bhimanis and Sewjis willingly paid more than they knew they were going to be able to collect. The customs house, it was clear, was only partly about the money they could make from customs receipts: more than anything, it was about maintaining a hold on the information the customs masters were privy to. It was a listening post for the world of commerce: according to one observer in 1873, "the Custom's farmer's real security is in... the marvelous system of private intelligence, which is the keystone of native Indian commerce, and by which every great Indian trader seems to hear of everything which concerns him wherever it may happen."[100] Through the customs houses, Jairam and the other customs masters were kept informed of the supplies of the different commodities moving through the ports and whose hands they ended up in; they knew the prices their goods could fetch, the size of the market for any particular commodity going in or out, where the best commercial opportunities lay and what places to avoid. In short, they knew everything that a mercantile firm would want to know about their trading worlds, keeping their fingers on the commercial pulse.

[99] Sheriff, *Slaves, Spices*, 127. In early nineteenth-century Muscat, customs revenues fluctuated wildly; at times they reached MTD 180,000, and at other times they were only half that amount, not including the Bandar 'Abbas customs. Vincenzo Maurizi, *History of Seyd Said, Sultan of Muscat* (London: John Booth, 1819), 29; Bhacker, *Trade and Empire*, 78. It is not clear whether the "customs revenues" that Bhacker published refer to the amount that the customs master paid or the amount he realized; comparing his figures for Zanzibar with Sheriff's, however, suggests the former rather than the latter, though this could have resulted from different sources.

[100] Edward Hutchinson, *The Slave Trade of East Africa* (London: Sampson Low, 1874), 52.

Faced with the prospects of such valuable information and con customs masters made sure that they kept it all in house, inserting member of their firm at every node in the arena. In his listing of customs masters in East Africa, Burton wrote that "Ladha Damha [Damji, Jairam Sewji's agent] farms the customs at Zanzibar, at Pemba Island his nephew Pisu has the same charge; Mombasa is in the hands of Lakhmidas [Ladha's son], and some 40 of his co-religionists; Pangani is directed by Trikandas and contains 20 Bhattias, including those of Mbweni; even the pauper Sa'adani has its Bania; Ramji, an active and intelligent trader, presides at Bagamoyo, and the customs of Kilwa are collected by Kishindas." As he wrapped up his list, he added an important point: "I need hardly say that almost all of them are connected by blood as well as by trade."[101]

It is no wonder that Jairam, his father, and Ladha paid so dearly for the right to control the customs house, or that their former employee Tharia Topan would enter into a bidding war with them in an attempt to dislodge the firm from that small shed.[102] For the customs house was more than just a place to collect receipts; it formed one of the key nodes of commerce in the region – a hub through which commodities, credit, and commercial intelligence all traveled. Moreover, it lay precisely at the intersection between commerce and empire; whoever held the customs house ultimately held the imperial purse-strings as well. Through their control of the customs house, merchants like Jairam and Tharia did not simply derive benefits from commercial and political activity; they deeply embedded themselves in the political project, bridging land, sea, commerce, and empire.

Conclusion

The world of trade in the Indian Ocean during the nineteenth century was not the same one that merchants knew a hundred years before. Finance – the availability of capital, and of goods on credit – had remade the geography of the Indian Ocean, determining which ports would be in ascendance, and what the vectors of trade would look like. By the 1870s, chains of debt and credit had fastened together ports and hinterlands across the Indian Ocean in an unprecedented fashion. As they moved to capture new commercial opportunities, merchants and financiers – primarily Indians, but also Arabs, Africans, and Persians – linked together the markets of Arabia, Africa, and India in new ways, pushing beyond

[101] Burton, *Zanzibar*, Vol. 1, 328–329.
[102] Sheriff, *Slaves, Spices*, 107–109.

roping interior towns and villages into a burgeoning
ɔnal economy.

underpinned all of this, forging bonds of obligation ɔnal economy its shape. When any economic actor, the way down to a pearl diver, took on a loan, what not a debt in the strictest sense of the term – that is, a ɔn that had to be repaid. Rather, by taking on a loan, commercial relationship – or better yet, signaled their entry into a broader regional economy which at its very core was structured by horizontal and vertical ties of debt and obligation. For all of the stratification that it generated, indebtedness was a normal state of affairs in the Indian Ocean. Far from the stigma of improvidence to which it is attached today, indebtedness in the Indian Ocean meant inclusion – inclusion into a marketplace of commercial relationships, into the circuits through which goods and money traveled, and into the dense webs of economic, social, and political obligation that characterized life all around the Indian Ocean.

From the Zanzibar *shamba* to the London shopkeeper, and from the heads of the elephant to the wrists of the newlywed wife, commodities in the Indian Ocean followed the money. Before a caravan leader bartered for his tusk, and before a planter sank the roots of his clove tree, they knew where it was all going, how much they got for it, and how much more they would have to get. Cloves, coconuts, ivory, dates, and pearls had transformed into ink on a ledger book, into rows and columns on a customs master's accounts, and into loose sheets of paper acknowledging this debt or that loan. Capital, whether in the form of the Maria Theresa Dollar or the yard of cotton cloth, had remade the seascape, binding together chains of debtors, creditors, interior towns and port cities into an ocean-wide geography of obligation.

But this was not the work of "capital" in the abstract; rather, it emerged out of the deliberate actions of Gujarati moneylenders in South Arabia and East Africa – merchants like Jairam and Ladha, who sought to bind their debtors to them in order to secure supplies of the commodities they dealt in while shielding themselves from the risks of commerce. When Ladha loaned out money to an aspiring caravan leader or, through a *shamba*-based factor, to a clove planter, he passed the risk onto his debtor. The prices he was able to fetch for the goods would, after a commission, be entered into the books, and the debtor owed him whatever was left over. In a good year, Ladha's broad base of debtors might owe less, and in a bad year, or with a bad crop, they might owe more; but no matter what, there would always be a debt of one sort or another – one that shrank or grew from one year to another.

And though Jairam and Ladha's debtors could sleep knowing that their creditors were unlikely to call the debts and take their houses or *shambas*, they also knew that they could only hand their goods off to members of their firm. By taking on a loan from a member of Jairam's firm, they placed themselves in their ledger books, joining the dozens of suppliers whose goods moved in and out of the customs house every day. And from Jairam's customs house – from that rough-looking shed on the beach – commodities moved across the ocean to Bombay and Kutch, moving in the opposite direction of the flows of capital that had brought them to the customs house to begin with.

This, then, was the shape that economic life took in the Indian Ocean: rows of debts and credits between merchants, shopkeepers, caravan leaders, planters, and sultans petty and large, all of whom converged together in the ledger books of Jairam, Ladha, and the dozens of other financiers like them. The movement of a commodity from the *shamba* or the East African interior to the customs house and from there to Bombay, traced the outlines of a structure of mercantile activity made to reduce uncertainty: to centralize the movement of commodities, information, and capital, and to bind producers, brokers, merchants, and statesmen together into a singular structure of economic governance aimed at generating predictable flows of goods and mitigating the risks and uncertainties inherent in economic life.

But for these bonds of obligation to endure the hazards of commerce, they had to be based on a solid foundation of law. For if credit and debt, and the obligations that resulted from them, were integral parts of economic life, their durability – and, indeed, their very constitution – depended on a legal framework that could both define and sustain them. When a merchant like Sewji, Jairam, or Ladha gave out a loan, he did so with an eye towards the obligations it generated: economic, social, but also legal. How did Indian Ocean economic actors situate their economic relationships within the framework of the law? And how did juridical actors in the region make sense of this world of commerce, and give it articulation in their writings – that is, how did they conceive of a commercial society at work, and how did they imagine debt, wealth, law, and contracts as holding it all together? It was left to the region's merchants, planters, *qāḍis*, scribes, and jurists to work this out.

2 Life and Debt

In the fall of 1860, when the aspiring ivory trader Mohammed bin Gharib approached the Khoja moneylender Rehmetulla Haima for a loan of goods to trade into the East African interior, the Indian merchant knew better than to leave it unwritten. Mohammed was asking for a lot of money – nearly MTD 5,000, and was promising to return with over 1,300 lbs of ivory. Haima called a scribe, Muhyi al-Din bin Saleh, and had him record Mohammed's acknowledgment of his debt. The scribe wrote: "He acknowledges, Mohammed bin Gharib, that he owes Rehmetulla bin Haima al-Hindi a quarter *qirsh* [MTD], and twenty-one silver *qurush*, and nine-hundred silver *qurush*, and four-thousand silver *qurush*, and thirty-seven and a half *frasilas* of pure [*naqāwa*] ivory of Zanzibar weight, due twelve months from this date, the fourth of Rabi' al-Awwal, 1277."[1]

Haima was not the only person to record his transactions; the *waraqa* that the scribe (called a *kātib*) Muhyi al-Din produced was one of thousands that were generated around the Western Indian Ocean as commercial opportunities expanded and producers, merchants, and consumers bound themselves to one another in long chains of obligation. Their acknowledgments of debt to one another, such as the one Mohammed made in the presence of Haima and Muhyi al-Din, formed the legal basis of these bonds; they forged the concrete linkages in the chains of obligation that structured the movement of capital and goods in the Western Indian Ocean.

The acknowledgment of debt, called the *iqrār*, emerged from the moment the debt was contracted – from the critical juncture at which the abstract realm of law and the lived reality of commerce came face to face. For no matter what their length or provenance, and no matter who or what they involved, all debt-related *waraqas*, began with a simple three-letter word: *a-q-r* – *aqarra*, "[he] acknowledged." Of the scores of words that populated the physical space of the *waraqa*, none were more

[1] ZNA AM 3/1, 87.

important than that acknowledgment, for it was that acknowledgment of debt alone – that *iqrār* – that generated the obligation on the part of the debtor, and which gave the document the bulk of its legal force.

As the fundamental idiom of commercial society, the *iqrār* was intimately bound up in notions of personhood, which itself grounded in the field of contract.[2] In this world, obligation grew out of contract on the one hand and blood on the other, and formed the bedrock of economic life at a time of emerging modern capitalism. Through the vehicle of the *iqrār* and its material expression, the *waraqa*, merchants, moneylenders, planters, caravan leaders, and other actors on the East African coast forged a commercial society – one in which producers, merchants, debtors, laborers, and financiers all relied on one another for the fulfillment of their wants and needs.[3] And by bringing together notions of law, personhood, and obligation, all of which were bound up in the idiom of *iqrār*, to accommodate the growing commercial society of Oman and East Africa, actors developed an ontological basis for cross-cultural trade – one that accommodated prolonged credit relations between members of different ethnic communities under one legal carapace.[4] Put differently, in this emerging multi-ethnic and multi-confessional commercial society, virtually everyone had a recognized legal personhood.

As different commercial actors and their *kātibs* forged relationships based on *iqrār* through their *waraqas*, they stimulated discourses among jurists surrounding obligation and economic life – an actor's rights and duties, their ability to lend and borrow, and how these bound together different actors into a commercial society. Taken together, these scribal practices and juristic discourses wove a rich tapestry of debt and economic life in which multiple and overlapping notions of personhood and *iqrār* informed one another in an expanding commercial arena. Over the course of the early to mid-nineteenth century, as the arena of emerging

[2] For reflections on this phenomenon in twentieth-century Morocco, see Lawrence Rosen, *Bargaining for Reality: The Construction of Social Relations in a Muslim Community* (Chicago: University of Chicago Press, 1984), 60–164.

[3] I adapt this notion of commercial society from Adam Smith, *An Inquiry into the Nature and Causes of the Wealth of Nations* (Indianapolis, IN: Liberty Fund, 1982), articulated most forcefully on page 37. The idea of commercial society, however, has involved many more writers than Smith. See also Biancamaria Fontana, *Rethinking the Politics of Commercial Society: The Edinburgh Review, 1802–1832* (New York: Cambridge University Press, 1985).

[4] For a succinct and useful definition of cross-cultural trade, see Trivellato, *The Familiarity of Strangers*, 1–2. It is important to note that the *waraqas* here overwhelmingly involved "prolonged credit relations" between commercial actors who "belonged to distinct, often legally-separated communities." Although many *waraqas* included transactions between Arab merchants, or even between Muslim Indian merchants, none involved exchanges between *Banias*, whose transactions utilized a separate set of Gujarati instruments.

modern capitalism in Oman and East Africa grew to include Indians, Africans, slaves, freedmen, and firms, the region's commercial and juridical actors mobilized the *waraqa* to subtly clothe themselves in the garb of the law – or at least what they understood to be the law.

Debt and Commercial Society

Concerns surrounding credit, debt, and obligation in commerce featured regularly among questions posed to the Omani jurist Sa'id bin Khalfan Al-Khalili. That people turned to Al-Khalili for advice isn't at all surprising: of his contemporaries, he was among the most respected, and certainly the most prolific in his output. He was born in 1811, as the commercial boom on the East African coast began to take off, and the rest of his life would draw him ever closer within the orbit of commodities, contracts, and capital that increasingly characterized the nineteenth century. He commenced his studies at the age of sixteen and he spent the next few decades of his life moving between Muscat and the interior of Oman, studying with a range of different scholars.

Al-Khalili was also part of the juridical renaissance (*nahḍa*) that had unfolded across the Western Indian Ocean during the late eighteenth and early nineteenth century. The study groups he moved in and out of included jurists and *qāḍīs* who frequently moved between Oman and the expanding settlements in East Africa: Nasser ibn Abi Nabhan Al-Kharusi, who spent his life as a scholar shuttling back and forth between Oman and East Africa was one of his principal instructors, as was Sultan bin Mohammed Al-Baṭṭāshi, who served as a *qāḍi* during the reign of Sa'id bin Sultan and who frequently made the voyage to and from Zanzibar.[5] Although he never left Oman, Al-Khalili was an important member of a trans-oceanic Muslim juridical society of *qāḍis*, jurists, and scribes who circulated around the Sultan's dominions and beyond.

The jurist also kept correspondence with *qāḍis* in Zanzibar and Malindi, and was not unaware of the economic transformations taking place across the Western Indian Ocean.[6] He had directly witnessed or heard of many of the economic changes taking place in Oman and East Africa during the first half of the nineteenth century, and often fielded questions from merchants, planters, *kātibs*, *qāḍis*, and everyday consumers on the religious, moral, and legal anxieties that this emerging world of modern capitalism prompted. As a jurist whose credentials were

[5] Sa'id bin Khalfan Al-Khalili, *Ajwibat Al-Muḥaqqiq Al-Khalili*, Vol. 1 (Muscat: Maktabat Al-Jīl Al-Wā'id, 2013), 29–42.
[6] Al-Khalili, *Ajwibat Al-Muḥaqqiq Al-Khalili*, Vol. 1, 34–43.

beyond reproach, many looked to him as a moral compass of sorts; their questions, and his responses, were later collected in a volume of *fatwas*, many of which offer a dynamic window into the workings of Muslim jurisprudence in a changing world of commerce. When read alongside the *waraqas* that *kātibs* produced, Al-Khalili's *fatwas* help illuminate the intersections of obligation and legal personhood that Indian Ocean society was built on.

As practices of credit and debt grew to involve a wide variety of people around the Western Indian Ocean, many came to Al-Khalili with different concerns about their obligations and the moral burden they might bear. And when it came to questions of debt, the jurist, who showed a degree of conservatism on a range of different subjects, seemed to have no compunctions whatsoever. Those who felt compelled to borrow, he wrote, should feel no moral burden: "debt is *ḥalāl* according to the test of the book of Allah the Almighty," he declared, and there were enough verses in Quran to confirm it.[7] Even debts for consumption, rather than production, were valid. In one of his longer commentaries on debt in Omani society, Al-Khalili distinguished between two classes of debtors and their forms of conspicuous consumption: those who were wealthy enough to fulfill their obligations to their creditors, and those who were not. A debtor of the first category, he argued, could take on as much debt as he wanted to "with no comment or embarrassment." Being in a situation of power and artfulness (*iḥtiyāl*), "no harm follows his transactions (*lā ḍarar yalḥaq fi mu'āmalātih*), for he takes and provides (*bal ya'khudh wa yaqḍī*), and deals and gives (*wa yataṣarraf wa-ya'ṭī*), and he is bound by his obligations and moves quickly to fulfill them (*wa-sā'an fil-khilāṣ*)."

Furthermore, he asserted, the second class – "the weak – not in health, but in ability to fulfill their obligations to their creditors" – also had the right to borrow, for even the poor had to entertain guests and sometimes live slightly beyond their means. Although members of that class needed to economize (*yaqtaṣid*) when it came to such expenditures, there was no reason to cut them off completely from the world of consumption.[8] Consumer debt had come to constitute an indispensable part of sociability in Oman, despite what misgivings people might have had about it or about the moneylenders they had to deal with.

Al-Khalili expressed his commentary on credit and consumption within the framework of legal personhood – of the rights and obligations that the different classes had. Credit and debt, he made clear, were not without their legal implications. For all of his assertions that people had a

[7] Al-Khalili, *Ajwibat Al-Muḥaqqiq Al-Khalili*, Vol. 4, 247.
[8] Al-Khalili, *Ajwibat Al-Muḥaqqiq Al-Khalili*, Vol. 4, 261–265.

right to borrow for purposes beyond mere subsistence, the jurist affirmed that the right to borrow also placed a burden on the borrower, namely an obligation to his lender. His opinions emphasized time and again that no matter what the circumstances of the loan, a debtor was required to make good on his financial obligations, whether his creditor was local, foreign, Muslim, or otherwise.

In asserting a bond of obligation between lender and borrower, Al-Khalili was not simply engaging in a stale exercise of moralizing; he was commenting on a commercial society that was gradually taking shape along the coasts of Oman, throughout the Persian Gulf, and across the Arabian Sea, in Zanzibar and East Africa. Having seen dhows, mariners, planters, and moneylenders come and go between the two corners of the Western Indian Ocean, the significance of the ties that bound together creditors and debtors would not have been lost on him. He would have seen how throughout the Western Indian Ocean, lenders and borrowers were engaging in transactions with one another, signing *waraqas* here, and promising loads of ivory, cloves, or pearls there. The obligations that debt generated formed an organizing principle of commercial society – a magnetic core around which a range of different actors clustered to bring order and certainty to the world around them.

Through the acknowledgment of debt – the *iqrār* – debtors acknowledged that their obligation was binding upon them – that they were aware of what sort of relationship they entered into. As Islamic legal scholar Joseph Schacht explained more succinctly roughly a century after Al-Khalili, the *iqrār* was "in practice the most conclusive and uncontrovertible [sic] means of creating an obligation on the part of the person who makes it."[9] Al-Khalili put it this way: he asserted that when a person acknowledges something in writing, "it is *thābit* upon him" – the word *thābit* drawing on the multiple meanings "established," "fixed," and "enduring" all at once – and that "he will guarantee the meaning of the *iqrār*" whether he wrote it himself or not.[10]

If acknowledgments of debt formed such a constitutive component of this world of trade, it is because debt meant inclusion within a burgeoning commercial arena. As producers, merchants, and consumers looked to one another to help fulfill their wants in a world of plenty, taking on debt allowed them to participate in the reciprocal exchange of commodities, capital, and services that constituted the very basis of commercial society. Far from the stigma with which it is now associated, taking on debt meant signaling one's capacity to incur obligations – to be part of

[9] Joseph Schacht, *Introduction to Islamic Law* (Oxford: Clarendon Press, 1964), 151.
[10] Al-Khalili, *Ajwibat Al-Muḥaqqiq Al-Khalili*, Vol. 5, 373.

something bigger than a once-off transaction. It is thus not surprising that caravan porters in coastal East Africa eschewed wage labor in favor of debt; debt confirmed their self-image as aspiring entrepreneurs in the mercantile economy of the towns and as independent actors in mutually beneficial relationships with their creditors.[11]

The Most Enduring Obligation

Debt did more than bind people together in the reciprocal ties of obligation that constituted Indian Ocean commercial society; it also lent those obligations a sense of durability. Of all of the liabilities that characterized commercial associations in the Islamic legal episteme, debt was the most enduring and the least disputed. Debt created a bond of obligation between the lender and the borrower that the latter was liable to meet no matter what the circumstances. Partnerships may have been ephemeral, lasting only as long as the natural lifetimes of the partners, but debt was not.[12] Indeed, the very word that Muslim jurists used to describe debt, *dayn*, was synonymous with an outstanding obligation, and the temporal endurance of the bonds of obligation that debt created outstripped all others in Islamic commercial jurisprudence; an obligation generated by debt persisted until the debt was repaid.

Not even death offered the debtor any reprieve. The sixteenth century Shafi'i jurist Ibn Hajar Al-Haytami, who wrote a commentary on a *fiqh* manual that Indian Ocean jurists frequently referred to, wrote that even a man who was on his deathbed and contracted a debt would be liable for it; in the event of his death his heirs would have to pay it out of their inheritance.[13] Three centuries later, the issue seemed to have only grown in importance: the widely-read nineteenth-century Ibadhi jurist Mohammed ibn Yusuf Aṭfiyish devoted much of his discussion on obligations to the passing of a debt from a deceased man to his heirs.[14] To Aṭfiyish, even the bonds of family were not enough to override the obligation generated by debt: he wrote that a person who loaned his father money had, after his father's death, rights to his father's estate as both a creditor *and* an heir, cautioning him to approach his rights with a view to justice (*'adl*) rather than compassion (*'aṭf*).[15]

11 Glassman, *Feasts and Riot*, 60.
12 Kuran, *The Long Divergence*, 63–77.
13 Ibn Hajar Al-Haytami, *Tuḥfat al-Muḥtāj bi-Sharḥ al-Minhāj* (Beirut: Dār al-Kutub al-'Ilmiyya, 1971) Vol. 2, 346–347. His stance drew on similar positions taken by medieval Muslim jurists.
14 Mohammed bin Yusuf Aṭfiyish, *Sharḥ Kitāb al-Nīl wal-Shifā' al-'Alīl*, 3rd ed. (Jeddah: Al-Irshad Press, 1985) Vol. 13, 584–595. I explore Aṭfiyish's life more closely in Chapter 7.
15 Aṭfiyish, *Sharḥ Kitāb al-Nīl*, Vol. 13, 390.

All of these ideas resonated deeply with Al-Khalili, who frequently drew on works in Ibadhi and Shafi'i jurisprudence in his writings. As credit and debt became more integral to economic life during the nineteenth century, he made sure that debtors were aware of the long-term implications of their obligations. Whenever the question was posed, Al-Khalili asserted that the rights of creditors took priority over the rights of heirs.[16] Even when a debtor died and left behind a mother, sisters, and a pregnant wife with barely enough money to support themselves, he was unable to evade his responsibilities to his creditors. The rights of creditors, Al-Khalili argued, took priority over needy family members.[17] In response to one question, the jurist argued that even a "foreign" creditor – perhaps a veiled reference to an Indian – had rights to the debtor's estate that were just as strong as the heirs.[18]

In one illustrative instance a questioner, most likely a *qāḍi*, asked Al-Khalili for advice on a case he was grappling with: a man had passed away, leaving two wives, a son, and a sizeable debt to a number of different creditors. After having paid off some of the debt, his son also passed away, leaving behind two young boys aged thirteen and four, and an increasingly impatient mob of creditors anxious to be paid what they were due. The questioner also casually mentioned that the man had property somewhere on the Batinah Coast, a date-growing region of Oman located a few hundred miles away from Al-Khalili's interior residence. In his reply, Al-Khalili showed little compassion for the two orphans or the widowed wives. Whatever outstanding debts had been confirmed but not fulfilled, he asserted, were to come out of the deceased's wealth. "If the deceased has no executors, then you are to appoint an agent [*wakīl*] for him to fulfill what he owed from the debt, for the sake of justice [*bi-wajh al-ḥaqq*]," he contended, adding that "the heirs are to have nothing aside from what remains after the debt." As far as the obligation to repay the debt was concerned, he declared that both the mature and the orphan were equal.[19]

Inheriting a debt, however, was not the same as inheriting an obligation to perform a service – an obligation that grew out of debt. Although Al-Khalili had little to say about inheriting those sorts of bonds of obligation, commercial actors in the Western Indian Ocean frequently called on their deceased debtors' kin to make good on the family's outstanding obligations. In just one example of hundreds, the children of the deceased Sa'id bin Ahmed Al-Mufadhali acknowledged their father's

[16] Al-Khalili, *Ajwibat Al-Muḥaqqiq Al-Khalili*, Vol. 4, 248–259.
[17] Al-Khalili, *Ajwibat Al-Muḥaqqiq Al-Khalili*, Vol. 4, 251.
[18] Al-Khalili, *Ajwibat Al-Muḥaqqiq Al-Khalili*, Vol. 4, 258.
[19] Al-Khalili, *Ajwibat Al-Muḥaqqiq Al-Khalili*, Vol. 4, 250.

MTD 1,900 debt to the Indian moneylender Janmohamed Rawji, pledging to repay it within eight months.[20] And in many of the *iqrārs* between debtors and their creditors, members of the debtor's family members wrote themselves in as guarantors for the debt.[21] Indeed, in some parts of the Indian Ocean, the notion that a debtor's family were guarantors for his debts – that they would either repay the loan or continue to perform his obligations – had become enshrined in commercial custom. In the Persian Gulf pearl dive, for example, a deceased debtor's male family members were expected to stand in for him, diving for the captain in place of their deceased brother or father.[22]

At times, the parties made the inter-generational nature of their obligations explicit. On the same *waraqas* in which they acknowledged their debts to their moneylenders, for example, those who pledged their property stated that the property transfer was "for him and for his heirs after him" (although they sometimes used the plural), immediately pointing to the shared boundary between contract and bloodline. The bond between debtor and creditor, the parties asserted, was one that their children would inherit. Thus, even a debtor whose creditor had passed away owed the creditor's heirs: in 1879, nearly twelve years after the financier Jairam Sewji passed away, several of his debtors penned *waraqas* acknowledging their ongoing obligations to "*awlād Zayram bin Sīwjī Al-Banyāni*," the children of Jairam Sewji the *Bania*.[23] Through these declarations, Indian Ocean economic actors – or at least their scribes – drew on the spirit of declarations by jurists like Al-Khalili on the durable nature of debt and obligation; they, too, recognized that debtors and creditors could come and go as God wished them to, but that the debt always remained.

In confirming that members of a debtor's family acted as guarantors for his obligation after his passing, Al-Khalili (and Muslim jurists as a whole) and members of an Indian Ocean commercial society established debt as the ultimate obligation – indeed, as the most enduring obligation of them all. And by effectively grounding commercial contracts in the field of inheritance, jurists did more than just suggest that a person's inheritance might be garnished by a past debt; they created a system wherein actors could reasonably make claims on one another across generations. They subjugated the transient to the abiding, collapsing the precarious boundaries that actors hoped to erect between time, contract,

[20] ZNA AM 3/1, 319.
[21] This was a common practice in Muslim commercial society, and jurists often devoted chapters to discussing the nature of this sort of guarantee, which they designated *kafāla*, or surety.
[22] Bishara "A Sea of Debt," 80–91.
[23] ZNA AM 3/2, 98–100.

and blood. For in law's community, obligation and genealogy were not two distinct phenomena: they were concepts that were intimately bound up in one another.

Inscribing Personhood

Undergirding a creditor's ability to make claims on a debtor's heirs was an ontological schema that linked an actor's ability to buy, sell, borrow, lend, or inherit – their rights and their obligations in a world of commerce – to their kin. Fundamentally at play were ideas about an actor's legal personhood – their capacity to bear rights and obligations within a world of contracting that demanded it. For jurists, legal personhood and the capacity to incur obligations were inseparable elements of any contract. Indeed, one's legal personhood was the very seat of the obligation; without it, there was nothing in which to anchor the obligation. According to one medieval Muslim jurist, "the source of the capacity [to incur obligations] exists only once a legal personality [called *dhimma*] exists that is suitable to serve as a seat of obligations. This seat is the legal personality… [and] therefore, the obligation is attached to it and to nothing else." In articulating this link between personhood and obligation, the jurist marked out the starting point for the legal construction of credit.[24] By explicitly articulating their genealogies, then, Arab commercial actors signaled their ability to lend and borrow in a commercial society increasingly characterized by those very acts.

But jurists and other juridical actors made it clear that if some actors were born with a wide capacity, or a full legal personhood, others were not. In his observations on the world of contracting around him, Al-Khalili and Indian Ocean *kātibs* made distinctions between slaves, freedmen, Arab Muslims, Hindu Indians, and others when it came to entering into a relationship of obligation – of making an *iqrār*. The *waraqas* actors left behind bear witness to these distinctions, but also testify to the creative maneuverings that creditors, debtors, and *kātibs* engaged in to blur the boundary between legible and illegible legal persons and bridge multiple understandings of personhood, from the realm of jurisprudence outward.

[24] Baber Johansen, "The Legal Personality (*Dhimma*) in Islamic Law: How to Separate Personal Obligations from Goods and Secure Credit for the Insolvent." Paper presented at the workshop "Before and Beyond Europe: Economic Change in Historical Perspective," hosted by the Economic Growth Center, Yale University, February 25–26, 2011, 5–6. Elsewhere, Johansen explains that "since the seat of the obligation is the person itself, the meaning of dhimma as the seat of the obligation merges with the idea of the legal person." Baber Johansen, *Contingency in a Sacred Law: Legal and Ethical Norms in the Muslim Fiqh* (Lieden: E. J. Brill, 1999), 192.

Much of this work fell to the *kātib*. As an intermediary literate in the law, the *kātib* was crucial to the smooth functioning of commerce in the Indian Ocean, and was a vital actor in a dynamic juridical arena. The *kātib's* role was ambiguous: he was more than a scribe, but perhaps less than a notary. Like notaries in early modern Europe or Latin America, *kātibs* were expected to have a familiarity with nominate contracts and the formulas necessary to give them legal effect.[25] The process of creating a legally valid *iqrār* and written instrument hinged upon the *kātib's* ability to mediate between the transaction and the law, or the actual commercial landscape and imagined realm of commercial contracting in Islamic jurisprudence. He actively translated between the two, forging the links necessary to give an oral agreement the force of writing – and a written document the force of law – by infusing it with pivotal legal elements.

Unfortunately, the records that Indian Ocean merchants left behind limit what we can say about *kātibs*. Although one question posed to Al-Khalili suggested that some *kātibs* might have been chosen members of their community, and there were at least some instances in which notable *qāḍis* also acted as *kātibs*, these are rare glimpses.[26] Even the most detailed *waraqas* only very briefly identify their authors through the formulaic conclusion "and this was written by… by his own hand" (*wa katabahu… bi-yadih*). Available records greatly circumscribe what the historian can say about these important actors. They were frustratingly "absent writers."[27]

As absent as they were, *kātibs* were present throughout every step of the *waraqa* drafting process. Immediately after writing down the *iqrār*, the *kātib* identified the parties to a contract. This was not as straightforward a step as it seems: considering the range of different actors on the Indian Ocean commercial stage, the process of translating a cosmopolitan commercial society into an Islamicate social and legal lexicon required a degree of imagination on the part of the *kātib*. Not only did he have to find a way to identify the parties, but he had to render them in such a manner that, under Islamic law, they would clearly be considered

[25] On Latin American notaries, see Kathryn Burns, *Into the Archive: Writing and Power in Colonial Peru* (Durham, NC: Duke University Press, 2010); on notaries in early-modern Europe, see also Laurie Nussdorfer, *Brokers of Public Trust: Notaries in Early Modern Rome* (Baltimore, MD: Johns Hopkins University Press, 2009).

[26] Al-Khalili, *Ajwibat Al-Muḥaqqiq Al-Khalīlī*, Vol. 5, 374. A number of *waraqas* were written up by *qāḍis* who doubled as *kātibs*; see, for example, the *waraqas* in ZNA AM 1/5, the majority of which were penned by the *qāḍis* Burhan bin 'Abdul-'Aziz Al-Amawi and Taher bin Abibaker Al-Amawi, both of whom I discuss in greater detail in Chapters 7 and 8.

[27] Messick, *The Calligraphic State*, 226–230.

capable of contracting and of bearing durable rights and liabilities. In other words, he had to construct them as legible legal persons. Doing so meant far more than taking a pen to paper: it was to give articulation to an ontology of debt and credit – to establish who could lend and who could borrow in a world in which those actions formed fundamental building blocks of commercial society. And in a commercial arena like the Indian Ocean, where the range of different economic actors would have chafed against ontological boundaries in Islamic jurisprudence, the act of inscribing this sort of personhood brought with it unique challenges, but also unique opportunities.

That Omani Arabs in East Africa would bear a genealogy seems all but obvious to those who look at the *waraqas*. Indeed, every single one of the Arab actors on the document signaled their *nasab*, or genealogy, going back at least two, but often three, generations. Thus, actors identified themselves as Thani bin Salim bin Hammad Al-Ruwahi, or Hilal bin Majid bin Sa'id Al-Ma'miry. By signaling their genealogy at least two generations back, Arab commercial actors grounded themselves in a social landscape of known entities.[28] They drew on their membership in the clan to immediately signal to others the network of kinsmen that could identify them and their property and guarantee their obligations.

Their actions were not new. In signaling their genealogies, actors hearkened back to practices rooted in an early Islamic contractual culture. Ahmad bin Mohammed Al-Tahawi, the author of a ninth century notarial handbook, explained that identifying parties by their *nasab* formed a crucial part of writing a *waraqa*. While his early medieval Egyptian milieu might be far removed from the nineteenth-century Indian Ocean, his reasoning for identifying parties by their *nasab* can help explain what one sees in Indian Ocean *waraqas*. For Al-Tahawi, the central issue was *ta'rīf*, or identification. He writes that "we genealogized (*nasabnā*) each of them, the seller and buyer, to his father and to his grandfather and to his tribe, and so we said "fulān[29] son of fulān son of fulān al-fulāni" so that he [fulān] is identified (*yu'raf*) as present, absent, or dead." If the person had no genealogy, then some other identifier, such as his occupation, was acceptable. Al-Tahawi instructs the *kātib* that if the name of a contracting party "is genealogized (*nusiba*) to his profession, and it is said "fulān the caliph" or "fulān the qāḍi" or "fulān the emir" it is an [accepted] identification." Identification via *nasab*, real or constructed,

[28] According to John Wilkinson, through *nasab*, Arabs in East Africa "could locate themselves in the historical, geographical, and social structure of their home country, where a strong sense of regional identity finds expression in its own form of Islam and its notions of the Imamate state." Wilkinson, *The Arabs and the Scramble for Africa*, 5.

[29] The Arabic word *fulān* is simply a placeholder, equivalent to the English "so-and-so."

explained Al-Tahawi, sufficiently distinguished the party to the contract from someone else who might share his name or his tribe.[30]

But at the same time *nasab* was not simply a way of signaling one's Arab status in a clan-based creole society; it was a way of expressing one's legal personhood – and one not entirely limited to Arabs, either. By blurring the boundaries between genealogy and Arab tribal society, one risks flattening the texture of what genealogy accomplished beyond identification. *Nasab* did not have a fixed function; rather, its importance and what it signified varied across time and space. Most broadly, however, it symbolized both power and rights, and was "adjusted to demonstrate and symbolize, in an easily comprehensible way, social relationships that [were] already there."[31] In an Indian Ocean commercial society, genealogy – both real and fictive – formed the basis of legal personhood for a range of different actors, ethnicities, and entities.

The usage of genealogy to construct personhood through the *waraqa* was most striking when it came to Sanskritic Indian names. Not only did *kātibs* phonetically write out Sanskritic names in Arabic letters, they also appended a fictional tribal *nasab*, or genealogy. At first glance, the maneuver appears as a simple product of the act of translation: because the merchants had the deed drawn up in Arabic, then it was only natural that the names of the contracting parties, whatever their nationalities might have been, would appear in Arabized form. But there was another layer to this process – an act of rendering, of translating non-Arabic and often non-Muslim people into a distinctly Arabian social imaginary. And it is here that the attempt to make an Indian Ocean commercial society legible to an Islamic legal episteme comes across more forcefully than anywhere else.

Because Indian merchants stood at the center of the webs of finance in Oman and East Africa, furnishing them with the legal personhood necessary to forge bonds of obligation was critical to parsing out the rights and duties that a range of different actors would bear. *Kātibs* responded to the challenge directly: they gave them a genealogy.[32] Thus, to use a prominent example, the name of Zanzibar customs master Jairam Sewji was transcribed as "Zayrām bin Sīwah Al-Banyān," although an earlier *waraqa*, from 1842, referred to him as "Zayram bin Sīwa bin Tōban Al-Banyānī."[33]

[30] Al-Tahāwi, *Kitāb al-Shurūṭ al-Kabīr* in Jeanette Wakin, ed. *The Function of Documents in Islamic Law: The Chapter of Sales in Al-Tahawi's Kitab al-Shurūṭ al-Kabīr* (Albany, NY: SUNY Albany, 1972), Arabic section, 7–8.

[31] Zoltán Szombathy, "Genealogy in Medieval Muslim Societies," *Studia Islamica*, No. 95 (2002), 35.

[32] On Indian merchants in finance, see Chapter 1.

[33] ZNA AM 3/1, 4, 10.

The honorific suffix "ji" disappeared from Jairam's father's name, so that the son became "Zayram bin Sīwa" or "Jairam, son of Sewa." In another *waraqa*, Jairam's partner Ladha Damji appeared as "Lādah bin Dāmah Al-Banyāni."[34] The genealogy sometimes extended by another generation: Ladha Damji's son Lakmidas, for example, appeared as "Lakmīdās bin Lādah bin Dāmah Al-Banyāni."[35]

By adding the *nasab* "Al-Banyāni," the *kātib* mapped Ladha and Jairam onto an inscribed social world made up of tribes and clans in which *Banias* became an identifiable social group like the Al-Harthis of Oman or the Al-Barwanis in Zanzibar. The choice of the *nasab* "Al-Banyāni" further distinguished *Banias* from the larger body of other Indian shopkeepers and commercial actors, like the Khojas, many of whom were given the *nasab* "Al-Hindi" – the Indian.[36] There were many reasons to distinguish *Banias* from others: *Banias* were Hindu, whereas Khojas and others were Shi'a Muslims.[37]

In the realm of the law, however, the rendering of Sanskritic and other non-Arabic names into Islamic legal instruments did more than simply distinguish one group from another.[38] At a more fundamental level, it inserted a range of different actors into an Islamicate landscape, endowing the parties with the socio-legal capacity necessary to transact in debt and property. Through the medium of the *waraqa*, the actors underwent a process of what Al-Tahawi would have understood as *ta'rīf*, which tagged them as known parties capable of bearing the rights and liabilities that the contract placed upon them. *Ta'rīf* was thus more than identification: it was a process of transformation from illegibility to legibility – from a non-person to a known entity. Thus, for non-Arabs and non-Muslims living in a world in which the semiotics of Arabian Islam

34 ZNA AM 1/1, 146.

35 ZNA AA 12/19, Deed 100 of 1877 (pages in this volume were not numbered).

36 See also ZNA AM 1/1, 33–35, 37–40, 45–49.

37 The distinction between the two also appears in Swahili, wherein Banians are designated as Banyani while other Indians are known as Mhindi. Bakari, *The Customs of the Swahili People*, 207, 303.

38 My understanding of the *Banias'* Arabized genealogies expands on and slightly differs from the interpretations advanced by Mohammed Reda Bhacker. Bhacker, *Trade and Empire*, 139. Bhacker identifies *nasab* with its natural social expression, tribe. He notes that a number of different groups, including immigrants from Baluchistan "adopted their own *nisba* [i.e. *nasab*] of al-Bulushi to distinguish them from other groups in the tribal mélange of Oman." Bhacker, *Trade and Empire*, 19. This interpretation accords with a similar phenomenon that Richard Bulliet observes among early Persian converts to Islam, where the adoption of Arabized genealogies often signaled one's conversion to Islam. Within those milieus, a genealogy shored up one's socio-legal position. Richard Bulliet, *Conversion to Islam in the Early Period: an Essay in Quantitative History* (Cambridge, MA: Harvard University Press, 1979), 18–19.

infused both commerce and society, the artifice of genealogy furnished them with the legal personhood necessary to incur obligations, economic, and otherwise.

Moreover, to give otherwise unidentifiable economics actor a genealogy that would help others identify them, their male ancestors, and their social group rendered them capable of entering into long-term relationships of commercial obligation. If the obligations that debt created in the Indian Ocean bound different actors together into relationships that passed from father to son or brother to brother, then by giving actors a genealogy – however constructed it may have been – the *kātib* not only endowed them with legal personhood but also made it possible for others to hold their kin accountable for obligations they incurred.

For Indian merchants, these multi-generational obligations manifested themselves most clearly in the mercantile firm, which stood at the center of economic life in the region. As members of a single firm, merchants advanced loans over the course of many years, spanning several generations of producers and middlemen, creditors and debtors. But the problem was that Islamic law did not formally recognize the existence of corporations or companies as legal persons.[39] Only natural persons – human beings, not abstract entities – enjoyed legal personhood, and only they could bear the rights and duties associated with contracting. The *kātib's* response to this legal challenge was to personify the legal non-person – to collapse the multi-generational firm into a single corporeal body. Hindu family firms, which consisted of the pooled and undivided assets of a conglomeration of relatives, thus took on the persona of the founder.

This appears most clearly in documents relating to Jairam's firm: on the space of the *waraqa*, Jairam, the customs master, appears as "*al-sirkār*," a term that on the face of it referred to the government but seemed to have been used to denote the customs house. In other *waraqas*, members of Jairam's firm are described as "*wakīl al-sirkār*," or "the government's agent."[40] Through a simple flick of the wrist, the *kātib* both suggested that the customs house embodied the Omani government on the island – a move which speaks volumes of his understanding of the intersections between commerce and empire – and rendered it into a legal person capable of appointing an agent, which, strictly speaking, it wasn't.

[39] Timur Kuran convincingly argues that Muslim jurists did not conceive of a company as being a legal entity separate from the people who comprised it. Timur Kuran, "The Absence of the Corporation in Islamic Law: Origins and Persistence," *American Journal of Comparative Law*, Vol. 53 (2005), 785–834.

[40] See also ZNA AM 1/1, 12.

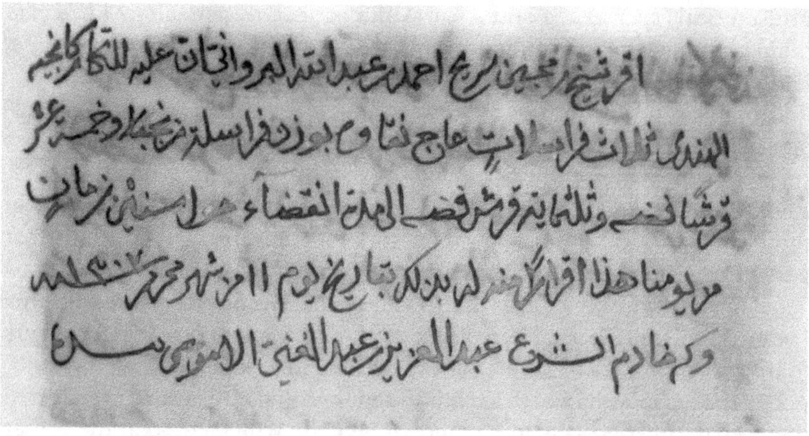

Figure 2 An *iqrār* of debt between a freed slave and an Indian moneylender

The process of anchoring Jairam's firm in the body of Jairam himself unfolded over some time. *Waraqas* that recorded transactions during Jairam's lifetime simply referred to him as "Zayram bin Sīwa" or "Zayram bin Sīwa bin Tōban"; there was no mention of the *sirkār*, except in reference to his *wakīls*. But when Ladha Damji, Jairam's agent, loaned out money, he was represented as "Lādah Dāmjī, wakīl Zayram" ("Jairam's agent") or *wakīl al-sirkār*.[41] Thus, the person of Jairam was, over the course of several years, transmuted into the *sirkār* – an enduring legal personality that those who took up the post of customs master would don well after his departure from Zanzibar in 1853 and death in 1866. In *waraqas* recorded after Jairam's passing, Ladha became *al-sirkār*; his son Lakmidas, as his agent, was referred to as *wakīl al sirkār* until he himself became the customs master.[42] Even as the post of *al-sirkār* moved from one person to another, the reference point on the *waraqa* remained constant. There was only one *sirkār*, who could have any number of *wakīls* – Lakmidas Ladha, Wala Bhanji, Kurji Ramdas, Kanji Chatterbhaji, and many others appear as *wakīls* of the *sirkār*, and many had their own *wakīls* as well.[43]

In inscribing the Indian firm as a natural legal person, *kātibs* actively engaged in a process of constructing a personhood for the parties to the

41 ZNA AM 3/1, 15, 214.

42 See, for example, ZNA AA 12/19, Deed 133 of 1877, in which Lakmidas is referred to as "*rijāl al-sirkār*," literally the *sirkar's* man. See also Goswami, *Call of the Sea*, 225–226.

43 In several *waraqas*, Hirachand Hansraj is referred to as the *wakīl* of Lakmidas Ladha. See ZNA AM 3/2, and ZNA AM 3/1, 315.

contract, giving them the legal capacity necessary to act within an Islamic legal framework. As entities that channeled commodities and credit around the Western Indian Ocean, Indian firms required the capacity to enter into relationships of ongoing obligation. By personifying the firm, the *kātib* not only lent it that capacity, he allowed the firm to continue to make claims on its debtors beyond the natural lifetimes of its members. Thus, when an agent of the customs master's firm lent out money as "*wakīl al-sirkār*," members of that firm could make claims based on that loan for many years after the lender's passing.

The *waraqas* attest to this practice. Well after Jairam passed away and the title of *sirkār* passed on to Ladha and others, the firm retained his name, and in several instances continued to contract as extensions of his person. His firm continued to operate under his name, dealing in significant amounts of money and property. Lakmidas Ladha, for example, was sometimes referred to as "*wakīl ahl bayt Zayram*," or the agent of the people of Jairam's house – an evocative way of describing Jairam's firm.[44] Slightly more bizarre was the continued appearance of Jairam as a lender on *waraqas* well after he passed away: debtors had *waraqas* drawn up acknowledging debts to "Zayram bin Siwjī Al-Banyānī" or "Zayram bin Siwā Al-Banyānī" in the mid to late 1870s, almost a decade after Jairam's death.[45] Others pledged property against loans from Jairam for periods of five or ten years, and did so well after he died, resulting in hypothecated properties and enormous debts to Jairam that would not mature for twenty years after he passed away.[46] Later on, in the 1880s – almost three decades after his passing – "Jairam Sewji" was able to appear on court case dust jackets as a litigant. In a sense, the boundary between the person of Jairam and his firm all but completely collapsed, and one became the other. Jairam, the *sirkār*, his agents, and their capital – all were bound together under his name, even as the title of *sirkār* shifted from one person to another.

The act of constructing a natural person out of a firm, it should be noted, was not unique to *kātibs* in the Indian Ocean, or even to Muslim legal culture. By anchoring the firm in the person of the *sirkār*, the *kātib's* actions reflected, to some extent, the practice within South Indian firms of conflating the "house name" – "formed by stringing together the initial letters of the names of three or four generations of lineal male ancestors, the last name belonging to the senior living male member" – and the firm's name. Colonial courts in South India recognized these names

[44] ZNA AM 3/1, 122.
[45] See, for example, ZNA AA 12/19, deed 171 of 1877.
[46] See, for example, ZNA AA 12/19 deed 151, 159, 161, and 191 of 1877.

as designations of business corporations.[47] Even in the Western common law tradition, in which only natural persons – beings with will – could sue or be sued, the advent of the corporation depended on a legal fiction surrounding its personhood. In order to give the corporation the ability to contract and to engage with the legal system, legal representatives characterized them as a "unit" comprising a group of natural persons and embodying their legal rights and duties. Lawyers and judges thus had to transmute the corporation into a legal "person" – a category which itself broadened as a result of the fiction – in order for it to sue and be sued, or for it to contract.[48]

The *waraqas* conjured legal personhood through a similar process. These documents may have omitted the reasoning process by which a firm became a legal person, but the result was the same. By flattening out the variegated organizational landscape, *kātibs* allowed for a range of contracting parties to come together as equal, legal "natural" persons. By rendering firms as natural persons and by constructing genealogies for non-Arabs and non-Muslims, they twisted the facts of the transaction to fit the rules of contracting. The *waraqas* mediated between the diversity of organizational forms and persons and the demands of the law. In the process of writing, the *kātibs* crafted a narrative of natural persons possessing the full legal capacity necessary to contract with one another. By inscribing genealogies onto the *waraqas*, and by having the genealogy stand in for the firm, *kātibs* placed the actors on an equal contractual playing field, allowing them to lend to and borrow from one another over the course of generations.

But not all actors enjoyed the precious gift of genealogy. Muslim jurists in the Indian Ocean and elsewhere in the Islamic world had long recognized that there existed categories of natural persons that did not – or indeed *could* not – enjoy full legal personhood. This was a subservient class – individuals whose right to lend, borrow, consume, and finance were broadly understood to be subordinate to others, and whose social and economic aspirations existed in tension with their legal standing, or at least with how others might have understood that standing.

A number of *waraqas*, for example, identified actors as belonging to different Swahili groups. The African Kombo Mwalimu from the island of Tumbatu, for example, appeared in *waraqas* as "Kombo bin Mu'allim Al-Tumbatu"; similarly, the Swahili Idi Mwalimu became "'Eid bin Mu'allim Al-Sawāḥili."[49] Like Indians, these actors received

47 David West Rudner, *Caste and Capitalism in Colonial India: The Nattukottai Chettiars* (Berkeley, CA: University of California Press, 1994), 109–110.

48 See also Lon Fuller, *Legal Fictions* (Stanford, CA: Stanford University Press, 1967), 12–13.

49 ZNA AM 1/1: 38; ZNA AM 1/3, 56.

Arab-looking *nasabs*. However, it is unlikely that *kātibs* would have understood Swahili economic actors as occupying a space equal to Arabs in terms of authority, privilege, and access to credit and consumer goods. Although there is little reason to think that Muslim jurists like Al-Khalili would have seen them as being at all deficient in their personhood, the distinct names – "Al-Sawāḥili," or "Al-Tumbatu" – suggests that *kātibs* might have understood them differently.[50] Moreover, the term Swahili might have been used as a euphemism by which slaves and others of low status could identify with inhabitants of the coastal towns, in which case their identification as such on *waraqas* would have had implications for how others might have understood their capacity to engage in credit relationships.[51]

Other subordinate forms of personhood were less ambiguous. The most obvious example is the slave, who captured jurists' imagination as the archetype of servility. For jurists, slaves' *dhimma* – their capacity to incur obligations, the very seat of their personhood – was constrained by their very ontological limitations. Because of their peculiar nature as both people and property, jurists considered slaves to have an inherently weaker *dhimma* than the freeborn. They could incur obligations, but only *in rem*, against their property or their person *as a commodity*.[52] Unlike the freeborn, their social standing – their blood – could not in itself serve as a guarantee for the obligations they incurred, and their personhood was considered insufficient for engaging in commerce on their own account, although many slaves did, with the express permission of their masters.[53]

Al-Khalili's stance on slaves and their rights was perhaps more ambivalent. Although he never took on the question of a slave's personhood in relation to debt and credit – perhaps in part because of the limited commercial opportunities available to slaves in Oman – his thoughts on whether a slave was able to make an *iqrār* were inconsistent. In one opinion, he argued that if a slave whose status was unclear acknowledged his enslavement (*aqarra bil-mulkih*), and if he was mature (*bāligh*), sound of mind (*ʿāqil*), and not under coercion (*ghayr majbūr*) – all of which

[50] In his autobiography, Tippu Tip identified only the Arabs by their *nasab*, while referring to the Swahili as *waungwana*, a term associated with Swahili civilization, and more recently translated as "gentlemen," though it was often used to describe freed slaves or free Swahili Muslims. Wilkinson, *The Arabs and the Scramble for Africa*, 5; Stephen J. Rockel, "Slavery and Freedom in Nineteenth Century East Africa: The Case of Waungwana Caravan Porters," *African Studies*, Vol. 68, No. 1 (2009), 87–109.

[51] Glassman, *Feasts and Riot*, 25.

[52] Johansen, *Contingency in a Sacred Law*, 193.

[53] Udovitch, *Partnership and Profit in Medieval Islam*, 150–151; see also the primary documents presented in John Hunwick and Eve Troutt Powell, *The African Diaspora in the Mediterranean Lands of Islam* (Princeton: Marcus Wiener, 2002), 26–27. I am grateful to Bruce S. Hall for these references.

were basic requirements for contractual legitimacy even for freedmen – then his *iqrār* was binding, or *thābit*, upon him, just like it would be for anyone else.[54] However, when slaves claimed to have been manumitted, their claim to manumission on its own did not suffice as proof (*da'wat al-'abīd lil-'atq laysa bi-ḥujja*), and they were considered to be enslaved until their manumission was clear.[55] The nature of the slave's *iqrār*, then, determined whether or not he had the legal capacity to make it.

The *waraqas* that *kātibs* generated in East African commercial society, however, suggested that slaves did often engage in debt acknowledgments – if not on their own, then by associating themselves with their masters. Of the slaves looking to take on loans and establish themselves as members of commercial society, a number were able to establish independent ties with creditors: slaves looking to trade in small amounts of ivory (around 150 lbs) could secure loans from financiers in town before setting out on a caravan.[56] Other slaves would have more direct access to credit through their masters, who in some cases were Indian moneylenders. One letter written by Gopal Mowji (of the influential Bhimani firm, which had farmed the customs in Muscat and Zanzibar at different times) to his slave in 1859, illustrates the close ties that a master and slave might share. In the letter, written in Arabic, Gopal refers to his slave Muftah as "the dearest, the most honorable, and the most respectable" (*al-muḥābb al-akram al-aḥsham*).[57]

By attaching himself to his master, a slave was able to transcend whatever ontological limitations might have kept him from participating in an increasingly lucrative world of commerce. And indeed, it seemed that slaves frequently borrowed with their masters' permission: "a slave," noted a group of Swahili commentators in the 1890s, "cannot incur a debt without his master's authority." The master, however, was not liable for the slave's dealings: "if the slave takes the money and goes inland or dies or runs away and does not return to the coast, [the creditor's] money has fallen into the sea. He cannot go to the master to claim it." By giving his slave the benefits of his personhood, the master endowed him with the ability to take on loans to finance agriculture, commercial ventures, and consumption, securing for himself a share of the profits and potentially of the slave's accumulated property, while

[54] Al-Khalili, *Ajwibat Al-Muḥaqqiq Al-Khalili*, Vol. 5, 373–374, 430.

[55] Al-Khalili, *Ajwibat Al-Muḥaqqiq Al-Khalili*, Vol. 5, 416–417; he gives a similar opinion on pages 430–431. Al-Khalili's ambivalence is difficult to explain. It could be that the evidentiary standards for claiming freedom were higher than those necessary for acknowledging servitude, but it could also be that in rules of evidence more generally, a claim required a higher standard of proof than an acknowledgment.

[56] See, for example, ZNA AM 3/1, 111–112.

[57] ZNA AM 3/1, 14.

shielding himself from the liabilities associated with the debt.[58] Over time, a slave's accumulated property could serve as security against the loan, and at times slaves could find other guarantors for their loans – but even then, *kātibs* made sure to inscribe the master's genealogy onto the slave's *iqrār*.[59]

Even after their manumission, former slaves did not have access to the fruits of genealogical belonging. This exposes yet another limit to legal reasoning – a gap between how jurists regulated legal personhood and how members of an Indian Ocean commercial society understood it. On the one hand, manumitted slaves were technically free, which theoretically meant that they enjoyed full *dhimma* in the eyes of Islamic law. The quality of being property, Muslim jurists argued, could be removed, allowing the slave to become a proprietor as he used to be.[60] On the other hand, the manumitted slave had no clear place in a society marked by genealogy: although manumission granted him the legal capacity to acquire rights and duties, it could not endow him with the genealogy necessary to participate in a fully reciprocal exchange of obligations.[61]

When a manumitted slave took on a loan, the *kātib* continued to express his personhood in reference to his former master: X, the freed slave (*'atīq* or *sarīḥ*)[62] of Y, son of Z. For example, the freed slave 'Abdul-Salam, who in 1867 entered into an agreement to deliver cloves to the Khoja Indian shopkeeper Mohammed Kurji in exchange for goods to get him through the harvest season, was identified as "'Abdul Salam, *'atīq* Hilal bin 'Abdullah Maddi."[63] And a year before, when another manumitted slave named Sangour outfitted an ivory expedition into the interior, pawning his property to two Indian moneylenders against the provisions he took, he identified himself as "the freed slave (*sarīḥ*) of Talib bin 'Abdullah Al-Hamdi Al-Ma'wali."[64] Thus, even freed slaves remained attached to the legal person of – and in a sense contracted *as extensions of* – their former masters. Whether this was an active attempt on the part of the slave "to be recognized through their owner's respected social status," an attempt by masters to retain some authority over their formal slaves, or simply a function of the *kātib's* rendering economic actors into legal persons on

58 Bakari, *The Customs of the Swahili People*, 176; Cooper, *Plantation Slavery*, 236; Elke Stockreiter, *Islamic Law, Gender, and Social Change in Post-Abolition Zanzibar* (New York: Cambridge University Press, 2015), 163–164.

59 See, for example, ZNA AM 3/1, 72.

60 Johansen, *Contingency in a Sacred Law*, 193–194.

61 Stockreiter, *Islamic Law, Gender, and Social Change*, 213–214.

62 The two terms both denote a manumitted status, though further research would be necessary to understand the differences between the two.

63 ZNA AM 1/1, 39.

64 ZNA AM 1/1, 8.

paper is unclear.[65] What seems apparent, however, is that in a society characterized by structures of belonging that generated the understood markers of personhood, those who did not enjoy those markers were subsumed by those who did.

Other nominally free actors were in a similar position. In a number of *waraqas*, *kātibs* sought to distinguish between a party who was a slave, for whom they used the unambiguous term *ʿabd*, and those whom they designated as *khādim*, a term which literally meant "servant." There is some ambiguity surrounding the term: while it broadly denoted some form of servile status, it was sometimes mentioned in the same breath as slavery, and at other times was used to describe a household servant – and in some cases, it was used to describe a freed slave that continued to entertain some form of association with his master.[66] Despite this confusion, his diminished personhood was clear: the *khādim*, like the *ʿabd*, was not given a genealogy of his own, but was attached to that of his master – sometimes a single person, but at other times, an entire clan. When one *khādim* named Zayed entered into a promise to deliver 350 lbs of ivory to the Indian Mohammed Kurji, the *kātib* wrote his name down as "Zayed, *khādim* of the *sayyid* Salman b. Hamad."[67] At other times, *khādims* were represented as having a slightly longer genealogy: one Jumʿa bin Saʿid bin Matar, the "*khādim* of the Rumāḥ," a clan, borrowed MTD 1,225 from Lakmidas Ladha in late 1878, pledging three *shambas* that he owned in Pemba.[68] Another, Saif bin Masʿud bin Saif, a *khādim* of the Al-Maskiry clan, took on a three-year loan of MTD 1,300, pledging two shambas in Pemba.[69] The *khādim* was thus just as mobile as the slave – or perhaps even more mobile, given the number of *shambas* and the size of the loans

[65] Stockreiter, *Islamic Law, Gender, and Social Change*, 211–216. Cooper argues that after abolition slaveowners continued to see themselves as the guardians of their former slaves, particularly with regard to the slave's right to marry. Cooper, *From Slaves to Squatters*, 189–190.

[66] Wilkinson, *The Imamate Tradition of Oman*, 96. In one of his opinions on slave manumission, Al-Khalili refers to the *khuddām* (plural of *khādim*) of the Batinah coast, though it is unclear whether he understood them to be separate from slaves (for which he uses the terms *ʿabīd* or *mamālīk*). Al-Khalili, *Ajwibat Al-Muḥaqqiq Al-Khalili*, Vol. 5, 431. It is possible that the term *khādim* was the more current term for slave in East Africa: in a number of *waraqas* from the 1850s and early 1870s that were registered at the British Consulate in 1877, the word *khādim* was translated as "slave"; ZNA AM 3/1, 19, 21, 23, 26, 27. At other times, however, *khādim* was translated as "servant" or "follower"; ZNA AM 3/1, 113, 124. It is also possible that the legal implications of being a *khādim* or slave were the same, and that the social understandings of those categories might have differed. On manumitted slaves using the term *khādim*, see Sheriff "Social Mobility in Indian Ocean Slavery," 149 – a practice Sheriff ascribes to habit.

[67] ZNA AM 1/1, 244.

[68] ZNA AM 3/1, 123.

[69] ZNA AM 3/1, 124.

Jumʿa was able to take. Still, when taking on those loans, his property was not enough; to signal the capacity necessary to borrow, he had to attach himself to the person of the master.

Genealogy, then, was far more than a marker of tribe or group: it was a marker of belonging, and the basis of personhood in Omani East Africa and the Western Indian Ocean more broadly. By furnishing actors with genealogies – or in the case of slaves or the manumitted, by anchoring those actors in other genealogies – *kātibs* and jurists rendered them as legal persons capable of incurring obligations. Genealogy thus formed the foundation of the ability of an actor (human or non-human) to enter into an enduring contractual relationship based on *iqrār*, which itself constituted the basis for commercial society in the region.

Conclusion

Even from his residence in the interior of Oman, Al-Khalili would have recognized many dimensions of the changing commercial society across the Indian Ocean as being familiar in fundamental ways. He would have recognized that this was a commercial world in which people sought access to commodities through credit – and alternatively, credit through commodities – and would have understood that access to credit necessitated an *iqrār*, an acknowledgment of obligation, which itself required that the two contracting parties were legible legal persons. And he would have been keenly aware of the social fact that genealogy formed the basis of one's ability to make an *iqrār*, and that these notions of genealogy and personhood, as well as their deficiency in certain actors, allowed some individuals to make claims to the obligations of others.

Through their *fatwas*, and in a carefully coordinated movement with *kātibs*, jurists like Al-Khalili developed a legal framework that would accommodate a range of different ethnic and religious groups, as well as different types of organizations and actors, together into one arena. By mobilizing the twin forces of *iqrār* and genealogy, they constructed an arena of cross-cultural trade populated by Hindus, Muslims, slaves, freedmen, and firms – all of whom enjoyed clear legal standing and were able to engage in prolonged, multi-generational relations of credit, debt, and obligation in an expanding commercial society. As lending and borrowing came to form increasingly critical components of the Indian Ocean's commercial fabric, jurists like Al-Khalili and *kātibs* articulated the ontological underpinning of a growing world of credit and commerce.

But an astute observer like Al-Khalili would have immediately known that though the *waraqas* and *iqrārs* infused commercial society across the Western Indian Ocean, they could not capture the entirety of the emerging Omani East African political economy. Instead, a more material dimension of East African economic life intervened in the debt relations that merchants, moneylenders, planters, and others formed with one another: property. Economic actors in East Africa, then, did not simply lend and borrow according to genealogy and status: they transacted in property. Indeed, the bulk of *iqrārs* between commercial actors in Omani East Africa involved some form of property or another – most often, urban or agricultural real estate, or a pledge of dates, cloves or ivory. Jurists like Al-Khalili thus had to contend with legal subjects that continually enmeshed themselves deeper and deeper into sets of property relations with other legal subjects. And having determined how subjects related to one another in this expanding commercial society, Al-Khalili and others could then turn their attention to how property fit into the dense webs of obligation that held Indian Ocean commercial society together – or, more broadly, how notions of property more broadly came to be constituted *within* these webs of obligation.

3 Paper Routes

Sometime during the middle of the nineteenth century, a correspondent from the interior of Oman wrote to Al-Khalili with an observation. "The Mazruʿis have wealth on the Swahili coast [*al-Sawāḥil*] and wealth in Oman." This in itself was no surprise: the Mazruʿi family included branches in both East Africa and South Arabia, and frequently appointed agents to manage their property abroad.[1] But lately, the correspondent suggested, things had been changing. Members of the Mombasa Mazruʿis were now coming to Oman armed with *wakalas* (powers of attorney) from unknown *kātibs*, authorizing them to sell off their familial properties in their ancestral homeland. "He [the Mazruʿi] sold what God likes from these properties and took the value… and the yield was separated from the property owners." The people's acquiescence to the state of affairs was of particular surprise to the questioner. Days, months, and years went by, he noted, and the property owners [*arbāb al-amwāl*] did not seem the least bit interested in changing the system, "and the people, as you well know, come and go via this sea, from Oman to the Swahili coast, with full confidence that they know [*bi-ḥukm al-iṭma'inana annahum 'alamū*]."[2]

In his suggestion that the Mazruʿis transacted in "in full confidence that they know," Al-Khalili's correspondent pointed to a critical dimension of a burgeoning Indian Ocean arena of debt, obligation, and capitalism: the ability of actors to move back and forth between the ocean's far-flung shores and transact in property and the rents it generated. More broadly, he pointed to a new development in regional contracting – one which allowed actors to separate a plantation's harvest, its yield, from the plantation itself, and move it from one port city to another, all while remaining confident in their ability to transact within a legible transoceanic grammar of contracting. As the frontiers of commerce and law

[1] Wilkinson discusses how the Al-Shaqṣī clan acted as agents for Mazruʿi property in Oman. Wilkinson, *The Arabs and the Scramble for Africa*, 33.
[2] Al-Khalili, *Ajwibat Al-Muḥaqqiq Al-Khalīlī*, Vol. 4, 290.

expanded, and as the Indian Ocean commercial arena found itself further integrated into a world market, this confidence formed the basis of a regional property regime. Indeed, if Indian Ocean actors were confident about anything, it was their ability to mobilize written instruments to transact in property within a common framework, whether in South Arabia or East Africa.

And transact in property they did. The *waraqas* that economic actors around the Indian Ocean generated and the questions they posed to Al-Khalili all highlight the fact that the dense webs of credit, debt, and obligation that structured economic and political life in the region were founded largely on a robust market for property. In their attempts to capture emerging commercial opportunities, a wide range of economic actors in South Arabia and East Africa mobilized whatever property they could get their hands on to pawn against the loans they needed to toss their hats into a commercial arena that seemed to only get more lucrative as the years went by. Planters, merchants, women, minors, and a range of different actors all drew on property in one form or another in accessing loans from their creditors. Even slaves and the recently manumitted tried to capitalize on their properties – usually small huts or plots of clove trees, but sometimes also slaves that they themselves owned.[3] For growing numbers of commercial aspirants, property held the key to socio-economic mobility.

But property was not always simply security, or even a means to mobility. For many Indian financiers, the property they received against the loans often held the very commercial object they hoped to attain, be it dates, cloves, or copra. Indian firms loaning out money against agricultural property, then, were less interested in the loan's repayment than they were in securing access to the plantation's crop, which they would then forward to their trading partners in India – hence Al-Khalili's correspondent's observation that "the yield was separated from the property owners." Omani planters could stay on their plantations and could consume the global commodities that Indian merchants and others gave them access to, but the plantation's crop was no longer theirs to sell.

For all of this to take place, actors had to rethink property and contract, and what both were capable of at a time of commercial expansion. As the commercial boom swept Oman and East Africa over the course of the nineteenth century, economic and juridical actors on both coasts began a

[3] Thomas F. McDow, "Arabs and Africans: Commerce and Kinship from Oman to the East African Interior" (Ph.D. Dissertation, Yale University, 2008), 152–164; ZNA AM 1/3, 36.

slow and subtle process of reformulating Muslim commercial contracts, stretching them to meet the exigencies of modern capitalism by allowing actors access to the capital and rents that formed the life-blood of commerce and politics. Slowly but surely, the demands of economic life pushed against the boundaries of legal categories: merchants and planters looked to *kātibs*, *qāḍis*, and jurists as partners in an enterprise of legal innovation that would come to define economic life in Oman and East Africa. As merchants and planters experimented, their *kātibs* gave their contractual experiments an Islamic legal lexicon on which to draw. When presented with questions surrounding the legal technicalities of these sorts of maneuverings, jurists like Al-Khalili responded by carefully placing them within a known universe of commercial contracting, grounding them in a matrix of rights and obligations that lent them the validity they needed to function in a changing world.

The *waraqa* served as a common platform for this dialogue – a medium through which merchants, planters, scribes, and jurists could all coordinate with one another, and an object they could focus their creative energies on. As jurists and scribes spoke through and around the *waraqa* to give shape to the abstract discussions of rights, obligations, and the agricultural ontologies that underpinned it, merchants and planters mobilized it to extract and circulate rents. And as different actors carried their *waraqas* with them from South Arabia to East Africa, the elaborate discussions of law, nature, standards, and forms that went into the crafting of contracts circulated from date farm to clove plantation. Through the *waraqa*, a common Indian Ocean grammar of economic life – one of mutually legible forms, instruments, and ontologies in an age of emerging modern capitalism – began to take shape.

Where the Land Met the Sea

As the commercial boom swept across the Western Indian Ocean, commercial aspirants and consumers around Oman and East Africa began to look to their property as a means of generating value. Men, women, and the free and unfree alike all turned to their property and began exploring ways of converting it into access to credit or goods. The *waraqa* was their answer: if the region was experiencing a commercial bonanza, the *waraqa* was their entry ticket into it – and *waraqas* make it abundantly clear that people in Oman and East Africa began to see their land primarily as a means of accessing credit. The bulk began with an *iqrār* of debt – an acknowledgment that the contract grew out of an existing obligation – followed by some sort of transaction in property, either a *shamba* or an urban dwelling. Debtors would acknowledge that they owed their creditors a certain sum of money, and then immediately declare a sale or pledge of property through the growing menu of contractual options available to them.

Not all sales of property in Oman and East Africa were a means of accessing credit: some were *bona fide* sales of property, with the clear intention of transferring title. These transactions, called *bay' qaṭ'* (*qaṭ'* sales, whose name suggested the act of "cutting off" the seller from his property) were sales in the more commonly understood sense of the term: a transfer of property, either for cash up front or as payment for a past debt. In some cases, there existed a customary understanding that the seller would retain the option of buying back the property, but this was rarely written out on the *waraqa*.[4]

The bulk of the property transactions that one sees in *waraqas*, however, were not straightforward property sales. Most commercial aspirants preferred more temporary forms of property hypothecation: the *khiyār* sale, discussed in much greater detail below, and the *rahn* – a pledge of land as security against a loan. Through the *rahn*, the debtor gave his creditor preferred access to the pledged property in case of default – or, as the *waraqa* itself states, a *rahn* "in which the [other] creditors do not share until after [this creditor] is given his claims, [through] an *iqrār* which [the debtor] has secured for him through that [*rahn*]."[5] The *rahn*, a pledge of property, allowed prospective debtors to put up their property against a loan, though only for a limited period of time. The repayment of the loan nullified the pledge, voiding any claims the creditor might have to the property.

The *waraqas* that Arab, Indian, and African commercial actors generated leave thousands of snapshots of moments in which a dazzling variety of people mobilized their property, using sales and *rahns* as a means of capitalizing on the transformations taking place around them. A series of *waraqas* narrate the story of 'Imran bin Saleh, a man from the town of Nizwa in Oman who had arrived in Zanzibar and taken up work as a broker (*dallāl*), and who approached Ladha Damji seven times for loans over the course of five years. Each time, 'Imran found some way to pawn via *rahn* his house in the Baghani neighborhood of Zanzibar for anywhere between MTD 200 and MTD 1,800, until he finally sold it to Ladha for MTD 3,000.[6]

[4] On the customary understandings that framed the *qaṭ'* sale, see McMahon, *Slavery and Emancipation*, 102–104. In cases in which the repurchase clause was written down on the *waraqa*, parties referred to the contract as a *khiyār* sale, which I will discuss in much more detail later.

[5] The precise wording on the *waraqa* is "*rahnan maqbūḍan lā yushārik fīh al-ghuramā' illā ba'd yusallim hāthā bi-haqqih, iqrāran ammanahū lah bi-dhālik.*"

[6] ZNA AM 3/1, 29–33.

Figure 3 A *khiyār* sale *waraqa*

Other *waraqas* show the two slave brothers, Jumʿa and ʿAmur bin Suweidan borrowing money from Ladha at around the same time, first selling him a house they owned for MTD 175 and then pledging a small plot in a *shamba* for MTD 19.[7] Another slave fared much better: he was able to pledge by *rahn* a farm and house in Zanzibar to a *Bania* merchant for a two-year loan of just over MTD 7,000.[8] One woman borrowed MTD 100 in 1858, putting up a *shamba* in Zanzibar as collateral.[9] The *waraqas* even show the

[7] ZNA AM 3/1, 44.

[8] ZNA AM 3/1, 319. Since *waraqas* tell us little about the size or productivity of the property being transacted, it becomes difficult to make sense of the amount debtors might receive when pledging them.

[9] ZNA AA 12/19, Deed 591 of 1876.

Sultan's brother, Khalifa bin Sa'id (who would later become Sultan himself) putting up his *shamba* against a loan of MTD 7,000.[10]

When they needed more than just a small, short-term loan, people turned to multiple properties at once. One debtor put up twelve of his *shambas* for a year in return for a loan of MTD 1,800 from a Khoja merchant, while another put up nine different properties in return for a ten-year loan of MTD 6,000 from Ladha.[11] A Swahili woman that had inherited several properties from her father put up two *shambas* in Mombasa for five months to the *Bania* agent of the firm of Wala Kanji for the smaller sum of MTD 145. When the due date elapsed, she pawned another property in Mombasa, this time a house, for another three months for MTD 50.[12] Unlike the other two, her loans were likely for consumption, being too small to constitute commercial capital.

Having lived in Oman throughout the expansions that characterized the nineteenth century, Al-Khalili was well aware of the contractual practices that his countrymen had grown accustomed to, both in South Arabia and in their new homes across the Arabian Sea. Omanis from all walks of life – merchants, farmers, *qāḍis*, and governors – frequently came to him for legal advice on how to conduct or regulate a range of commercial transactions. Of these, the majority revolved around questions of land, value, and rent – and, perhaps most importantly, the extensive menu of contractual forms and legal instruments they used to facilitate their circulation within a burgeoning economic arena.[13] The dialogue between Al-Khalili and his correspondents immediately suggests that economic and legal actors alike viewed the date, clove, and coconut plantations that they owned as the nexus of a range of different contracts – a locus of a brisk trade in rights to land, produce, water, labor, profits, and more.

When Omanis, whether in Oman or in East Africa, asked questions about their plantations, they asked about their rights: what they were, what they might be worth, and how they might transfer them to their kin or their creditors (and sometimes both). They traded in their rights to the land itself and the trees that grew upon it, asking their *qāḍis* and jurists when one might incorporate the other. They asked about bequeathing property

[10] ZNA AA 12/19, Deed 166 of 1877.

[11] ZNA AM 3/1, 201; ZNA AA 12/19, Deed 131 of 1877.

[12] ZNA AM 3/1, 105–106.

[13] When the questions came in are unclear; Al-Khalili's *fatwas*, like many others, are mediated through several layers of editing and abridgment that usually involved stripping away (*tajrīd*) of specificities of people and place, the omission of words and phrases not of legal relevance, and the omission of documents attached to or embedded in a primary *fatwa*. See David S. Powers, *Law, Society and Culture in the Maghreb, 1300–1500* (New York: Cambridge University Press, 2002), 7. It is more than likely, however, that the questions came in during the last two or three decades of the jurist's life.

to their heirs, and whether it was preferable to do so through wills, gifts while they were alive, or sales, and what the legal implications of each might be during their lifetimes and thereafter. They asked about renting out stalls in the marketplace to sell their produce, leasing out plantation land to foreigners, and the various intermediaries they would have to deal with. And they spent a great deal of time thinking about their rights to the irrigation canals (*aflāj*) that ran through their properties, posing question after question on how to contract out those rights, what the liabilities might be for damage done to the *aflāj* or adjoining properties, and how to apportion them. If Al-Khalili's *fatwas* are any indication at all, Omani planters spent a lot of time thinking about their property and the rights and value that grew out of it, particularly when it came to lending and borrowing.

But the rights that planters in Oman and East Africa had to their land were not always clear-cut. When economic actors looked to their land to drum up capital, they had to contend with the rights that others had to it as well. The plots of land they described in their *waraqas* were not fixed in space; not a single *waraqa* described a plot of land as being any number of *dhirā*'s long or wide, or even as containing any set number of trees.[14] Rather, they described their plots of land in relational terms: to the plantation of X son of Y to the north, Y son of Z to the east, and so on. Their very understanding of the terrestrial space that they had begun converting into different rights, then, was intimately bound up in the people they lived among. This was as much a social landscape as it was a terrestrial one: by including others in their visions of the land, planters and their *kātibs* signaled that this was a realm of transacting in which different parties would have a stake in what the land looked like, what rights creditors might have to the land, and to what degree they would be able to exercise those rights. In essence, they sought to link written legal documentation to systems of local, and oral, socio-legal knowledge.[15] As the plantation economies of Oman and East Africa spread along the coasts and interiors, where one planter's property ended and another's began was not something that could be looked up in a cadastral survey – indeed, no such survey existed. Rather, it was information stored in the archive of the

[14] The *dhirā*' was a unit of length that measured a cubit – usually about eighteen inches. Allen, *Customs of the Swahili People*, 232.

[15] Al-Tahawi, the author of a ninth-century notary manual, saw this strategy as a particularly useful means to resolve disputes over a property's precise boundaries. He noted that "when they have this sort of disagreement (*lamma ikhtalafū hādha al-ikhtilāf*) we looked to the people's talk (*kalām al-nās*) who know between them what this is, and we found them saying 'the house of so-and-so comes after the house of so-and-so'." Al-Tahawi, *Kitāb Al-Shurūt*, 12. The fact that merchants and planters in Oman and Zanzibar used similar terminology roughly a millennium later suggested that this was a landscape that was intimately familiar to those who lived in the area.

social – in what the communities knew of their surroundings – and was the subject of ongoing negotiation.

One ever-present claimant to a planter or merchant's property, whether in Oman or in East Africa, was his family. As a family estate passed from a planter's hand, Muslim inheritance laws intervened and, using a complex formula, established rights for a range of different heirs – siblings, wives, sons, daughters, and in some cases, even freed slaves.[16] And although Islamic inheritance rules did not directly stipulate how a testator was supposed to divide up his or her estate – whether into discrete parcels, monetary amounts, or any other way – an inheritance usually consisted of shares in an undivided property. Thus, heirs were less likely to end up with a smaller plot in a larger agricultural estate or a room in a house in their hometown than they were an assigned share of its value, ranging anywhere from a clean half to absurd fractions like 3/79.

For individuals eager to ride the rising wave of commercial optimism, absence of full title to a property was no deterrent. In fact, if anything, the splintering of estates enabled a broader range of actors to enter the commercial arena than before. Those who did not possess full titles simply hypothecated their shares in their family estates; in productive estates like plantations, this effectively amounted to signing over a proportion of the net profits every year. Questions posed to Al-Khalili suggest that in the middle of the nineteenth century Omanis were more than happy to assign dividends from their family estate to different creditors, and the jurist was eager to lend them guidance on a wide range of connected questions, including conditions of sale and the relative rights of coparceners.[17] Although Al-Khalili drew the line when it came to people borrowing against inheritance that they had not yet received, one questioner made it clear that this practice was already underway.[18]

In East Africa, too, commercial aspirants seemed to have caught wind of the possibilities that their shares in family estates might enable. When, in the spring of 1851, Sayyid Abu Bakr al-Shatiri sought a loan of MTD 870 from an Indian merchant, he hypothecated his share in a house he owned jointly with his brother. Three years later, he did the same with another share in a house – most likely the same property – to the same creditor, this time for MTD 914.[19] As commerce expanded along the coasts of Arabia and East Africa, the market for real estate of all kinds

[16] For a good overview of Muslim inheritance laws, see also N.J. Coulson, *Succession in the Muslim Family* (New York: Cambridge University Press, 1971).

[17] Al-Khalili, *Ajwibat Al-Muḥaqqiq Al-Khalili*, Vol. 4, 85–91.

[18] Al-Khalili, *Ajwibat Al-Muḥaqqiq Al-Khalili*, Vol. 4, 245. For an example of borrowing against a future inheritance, see also ZNA HC 2/1265.

[19] ZNA AM 3/1, 218–219.

similarly heated up, prompting entry by a range of different actors. One *waraqa* describes a three-year loan of MTD 1,750 taken on by Taleb bin Julait, a slave (*khādim*), from a Khoja merchant. As security, Taleb hypothecated four plots of agricultural land around Zanzibar as well as a one-third share in a plot in the coastal city of Malindi, just over 200 miles north of Zanzibar; how he came to own these is difficult to ascertain.[20]

At other times, family members chose to pool their resources to access even larger loans. In one *waraqa*, for example, all nine children of Sultan bin 'Abdullah Al-Barwani agreed to sell their family home in Zanzibar to Pirbhai Jivanji for MTD 8,000.[21] In another, the two brothers Ahmed and Mohammed bin Saif Al-Maskiry, sought to pledge by *rahn* three family *shambas* in Pemba, and approached the *Bania* Kanji Chatterbhaji, who loaned them a total of MTD 2,300 – MTD 1,150 each for a year; a third brother, Nasser, borrowed half that amount, MTD 575, repayable in six months.[22]

In looking to family estates as potential sources of capital, members of this commercial society actively commodified the landscape around them. What had once been imagined as an estate to be shared by members of a single lineage was parted out and liquidated. Capital and blood began to mix as individuals tugged at the loose fibers in the ropes that bound them and their kin to the land. In their place, they plugged in foreign creditors and capital, filling family title deeds with the names of individuals that bore no relationship to one another. The work that their ancestors had done to etch their family name into the land was now being washed away into the sea.

And indeed, across the sea it often went. For those willing to take their piece of property out of the bloodline, distance posed no obstacle. Commercial aspirants in East Africa regularly looked to family properties across the Arabian Sea, in Muscat and other towns in Oman. When the Zanzibari Arab merchant Sa'id bin 'Umar Al-Kharusi approached the Indian Wala Bhanji to borrow the princely sum of MTD 5,200 for one year, he hypothecated his date plantation in his ancestral homeland of Wadi Bani Kharus in Oman, just outside Muscat.[23] Another Zanzibari Arab merchant, Salim bin 'Ali Al-Sughri, borrowed MTD 3,300 from the customs master Lakmidas Ladha; as collateral, he offered his properties in Al-Sharqiyya, the Eastern province of Oman.[24]

20 ZNA AM 3/1, 113.
21 ZNA AA 12/19, Deed 149 of 1877.
22 ZNA AM 3/1, 132–133.
23 ZNA AM 3/1, 80.
24 ZNA AM 3/1, 77.

When Al-Khalili's correspondent asked him about the Mombasa Mazru'is trading in their family property in Oman, he was pointing to a similar phenomenon. The Mazru'is were drawing up *waraqas* in East Africa to trade in different rights to their familial properties in South Arabia, most likely to finance commercial or agricultural enterprises on the East African coast. The extent to which they were engaging in these sorts of transactions seemed to have caused some anxiety among Al-Khalili's correspondents, who were most likely either owners of adjoining properties or *qāḍis* having to assess the *waraqas* and deal with the claims arising from the property transactions. However, the property owners themselves – that is, the Oman-based Mazru'is – seemed to have no qualms about trading away their land rights to people across the sea. Al-Khalili's cool response further suggested that those sorts of long-distance transactions were not really much of a cause for concern: in cases like this, he noted, people were able to expand the regime of *iṭma'ināna* (*al-tawassu' bi-aḥkām al-iṭma'ināna*) – a term I explore in more detail below – to the extent that they did not violate ownership or possession (*al-istirāba*).[25]

But the question posed to Al-Khalili regarding the Mombasa Mazru'is wasn't only about whether someone could draw up *waraqas* in Zanzibar to trade in land in Muscat. The questioner suggested something specific – that "the yield had been separated from their property owners." The Mazru'is, it seemed, were not trading away their rights to land in general, but to the land's yield. When reading more of the dialogue between Al-Khalili and his correspondents in Oman, it becomes clear that what was taking place was something new: a form of contracting that counterparties took to calling the *khiyār* sale (*bay' al-khiyār*), that merchants, planters, and commercial aspirants in South Arabia and East Africa increasingly began to utilize in order to drum up the capital necessary to enter into the regional commercial bonanza.

Imagining the *Khiyār* Sale

Of all of the instruments utilized in nineteenth-century Oman and East Africa for trading different rights, the *khiyār* sale quickly grew to become the most popular, quickly outstripping the *rahn* as the preferred mode of mobilizing property to generate capital. Broadly speaking, the *khiyār* functioned as a form of pawnship: a planter or commercial aspirant would "sell" their property to a lender for an agreed-upon price (i.e. the

[25] Al-Khalili, *Ajwibat Al-Muḥaqqiq Al-Khalili*, Vol. 4, 290.

loan amount) that they would have to repay within a specified timeframe in order to reclaim the property and render the initial "sale" void. Like the *rahn*, the *khiyār* sale allowed a commercial aspirant to utilize property in order to access short- or long-term credit. However, unlike the *rahn*, in the *khiyār* sale a debtor was allowed to retain possession of the property, transferring only the rent to his creditor. Under a *rahn*, it was unclear whether the creditor (or pledgee) was allowed to derive any rent at all: although many Muslim jurists argued against the pledgee (*murtahin*) deriving benefits from the pledged property, Al-Khalili himself seemed ambivalent, granting him usufructuary rights as long as it was not a pre-condition of the loan.[26] Whatever the case may be, by the mid-nineteenth century, the *khiyār* sale had emerged as the preferred vehicle among the Arabs of Oman and East Africa to raise capital for commercial ventures or money for consumption.[27]

The *khiyār* sale was also a hot topic of discussion among commercial and juridical actors. Questions and concerns surrounding the contract took up much of Al-Khalili's time; of his recorded *fatwas*, no less than forty-six involved the new contract – so many that Al-Khalili's students, who compiled his *fatwas*, decided to devote a whole chapter to it.[28] The questions merchants and planters posed and the answers Al-Khalili gave them, which he recorded in the format of a dialogue, are remarkable in their illustration of the moral and legal anxieties – but also accommodations – that the new contract produced. What emerges most clearly is that throughout the *khiyār* experimentation process, Al-Khalili acted as a moral compass: while he was more than willing to facilitate the changing forms of contracting that modern capitalism demanded, he made sure to ground them in a universe of rights, obligations and ontologies that he saw as both familiar and equitable – and, more fundamentally, natural.

The *khiyār* sale was by no means a new invention. Muslim jurists originally conceived of it as a regular sale contract with the option (*khiyār*) for either party to rescind the contract within a specified period of time,

[26] Al-Khalili, *Ajwibat Al-Muḥaqqiq Al-Khalīlī*, Vol. 4, 277–278. At least some *rahn* transactions recorded in *waraqas* included explicit mentions of slaves or trees, suggesting that the creditor did have a right to derive benefit from the pledged property during the *rahn* period. See, for example, ZNA AA 12/19, Deeds 160 and 172 of 1877.

[27] Archival records from both regions include hundreds of *khiyār* sale *waraqas* dating from at least as far back as the late 1840s, though there were likely earlier ones that have not survived.

[28] This does not include questions directly or indirectly involving *khiyār* sales that fell under other chapter headings.

usually no more than three days.[29] By at least the seventeenth century, some Omani jurists began showing a little flexibility towards the time period allowed. Oman's leading jurist during the mid-seventeenth century, Khamis bin Sa'id Al-Shaqṣi, argued that different objects should be allowed different *khiyār* periods: although sales in animals should be subject to the standard three-day rule, those who buy clothes should only be allowed one or two days, while those who buy a room or house should be given at least a month.[30]

By the time Al-Khalili sat down to pen his opinions in the mid-nineteenth century, however, economic and juridical actors understood the *khiyār* differently. As the forces of emerging modern capitalism in the region pushed people to reimagine their relationship to their property, the *khiyār* became an option for a seller (or, more accurately, a debtor) to *redeem* the property within a specified timeframe – usually whatever length of time the operation itself necessitated. In the interim, the buyer (i.e. the lender) retained the right to the produce, harvesting and selling it until the redemption date. The option had become bundled into the transaction itself, creating the *khiyār* sale.

In some cases – particularly when it came to urban real estate, and perhaps also in *shambas* whose value was less than that of the loan – the seller (i.e. the debtor) would also agree to rent the property back from the lender in the interim. The parties would add a clause to the contract stipulating *qu'd* – literally the act of seating oneself, which allowed the debtor to retain rights to the property in exchange for an annual or monthly rent.[31] When the parties chose to go that route, the seller-cum-renter was responsible for rent payments in addition to the repayment of the principal. In both standalone *khiyār* sales and those coupled with *qu'd* clauses, however, the basic idea remained the same: an exchange of capital (i.e. a loan) for rents (i.e. harvest or monetary payments) for a finite period of time, after which the debtor could redeem the property or transfer it to his creditor.

Merchants and planters quickly adapted the *khiyār* sale to the rhythms of economic life in South Arabia and East Africa. *Khiyār* sales of clove plantations in Zanzibar, for example, would not exceed six months

[29] Ibn Rushd, *The Distinguished Jurist's Primer: A Translation of Bidāyat al-Mujtahid wa Nihāyat al-Muqtaṣid*, Vol. 2 (Reading, UK: Garnet Publishing, 1995), 250–255.

[30] Khamis bin Sa'id Al-Shaqṣi Al-Rusṭāqi, *Manhaj Al-Talibin wa Balāgh Al-Rāghibin*, Vol. 7 (Muscat, Oman: Maktabat Masqaṭ 2006), 301.

[31] Al-Khalili only discussed *qu'd* in relation to irrigation canals, though his understanding of the term as a form of rental or lease seems to have been the same as parties using it in other settings. Al-Khalili, *Ajwibat Al-Muḥaqqiq Al-Khalīlī*, Vol. 4, 440–481. I take this up in greater detail in Chapter 8.

(the time between two harvests) whereas sales of land as security against ivory-related loans could involve a period of one or two years, depending on the length of the expedition, or at least the settlement of accounts. Moreover, commercial actors frequently re-extended *khiyār* contracts if both the buyer and seller deemed it exigent. The demands of emerging modern capitalism expanded the contractual time that undergirded the *khiyār* option towards horizons more appropriate to prevailing commercial and agricultural cycles, thereby reformulating the purpose of the *khiyār* altogether. And in his answers to questions surrounding the expansion and contraction of the *khiyār*'s timeframe, Al-Khalili seemed sympathetic to the needs of his audience, allowing them the leeway necessary to perform whatever temporal sleight-of-hand they required. "The [*khiyār*] timeframe expansion and its contraction is all permissible," he wrote, though he added that "the shorter the timeframe the better."[32]

Al-Khalili voiced few objections to general practices surrounding *khiyār* sales around the Indian Ocean by the mid-nineteenth century, even when his questioners claimed that they amounted to interest-bearing transactions. One correspondent (most likely a *qāḍi*) noted that "the *khiyār* sale has spread these days, and has appeared in all regions," expressing concern that "it has become a path to usury (*sullaman ilā akl al-ribā*), and the general public (*al-ʿāmma*) have taken to it without a proper contract or permissible direction (*bilā ʿaqd ṣaḥīḥ wa lā wajh mubīḥ*)."[33] Al-Khalili disagreed: the *khiyār* in and of itself, he wrote, was unimpeachable; the famous Omani jurist Abi Nabhan Jaʿid ibn Khamis "whose dignity was known to all" made use of the *khiyār* to make short-term purchases if it helped the seller.[34] The usage of the *khiyār* as a vehicle for loans, then, was perfectly acceptable for those who needed them.

Faced with a series of questions surrounding the *khiyār* buyer's right to the plantation's harvest – which some suggested could amount to interest on the loan – Al-Khalili reframed the question as one of agricultural ontology. He declared that if a buyer purchased a property through the vehicle of the *khiyār* with the intention of owning the property, rather than simply to access its yield (*ghilla*) then he was permitted to harvest the yield during the *khiyār* period. In so doing, Khalili drew an ontological distinction between the land and its yield; the latter could not form a separate object of sale, but the former could, as a sale of land necessarily included a sale of its produce.[35]

[32] Al-Khalili, *Ajwibat Al-Muḥaqqiq Al-Khalīlī*, Vol. 4, 139.
[33] Al-Khalili, *Ajwibat Al-Muḥaqqiq Al-Khalili*, Vol. 4, 136.
[34] Al-Khalili, *Ajwibat Al-Muḥaqqiq Al-Khalīlī*, Vol. 4, 136–137.
[35] Al-Khalili, *Ajwibat Al-Muḥaqqiq Al-Khalīlī*, Vol. 4, 127–128, 132–133, 137–138, 141, 144–145, 150–151.

His creative reformulation of the issues of land, sale, and contract owed a great deal to the work of an earlier thinker – the seventeenth-century jurist Al-Shaqṣi, whose reflections on the question of value in an agrarian economy, articulated during the reign of the Ya'rubi dynasty two centuries earlier, formed the ontological basis for Al-Khalili's jurisprudential gymnastics.[36] In his discussion of the legal dimensions of the sale of palms, seedlings, and trees, Al-Shaqṣi began with the outright declaration that "whoever bought from another a palm whose fruit has matured (*qad balaghat thamratuhā*)... then that is permissible (*fa lā ba'sa bi-dhālik*) if he intended to buy the palm itself along with its fruit (*aṣl al-nakhl bi-thamratihā*)."[37] Al-Shaqṣi was able to clear the way for this sort of transaction by drawing an ontological distinction between the tree and its produce as objects of a sale contract. In a sale of a date-palm with a seedling (*sarm*), he argued, the seedling had to be treated as though it were fruit: if it had matured it belonged to the seller, but if it was too young to be uprooted then it belonged to the buyer.[38] For Al-Shaqṣi, it was as much a question of use-value as of nature itself: just as one could not sell a palm without the ground on which it stood, one could not sell unripe produce separately from the tree it depended on to survive. The palm formed part of its essence (*dhāt*), just as the ground formed part of the palm's essence; only when something could naturally exist on its own could it form a separate sale object.[39]

It took a significant degree of creative thinking to arrive at these conclusions. Rather than seeing the world around them as one populated by discrete parcels of property that were bought and sold on the market, Al-Khalili and Al-Shaqsi used the image of the flowering tree as a metaphor for the entire plantation. Trees and fruit naturally passed through several stages of growth and flowering; their ability to exist and to produce value all derived from the stage of growth they had attained. In the early stages of growth and flowering, fruit, tree, and ground were all one; as a tree passed through its natural cycles, the different components could be separated from one another as different objects of a sale contract. The plantation, then, was not singular; it was made up of many distinct layers, each of which could be bought, sold, or pledged. Thus, by combining Al-Shaqṣi's ontological schema of agricultural life with the temporal

[36] Al-Khalili was likely drawing on more than just Al-Shaqṣi's work; indirect discussions of ripening date palms and value can be found in texts as early as Ibn Sallam's *Kitāb Al-Amwāl*; see Abu 'Ubayd Ibn al-Qasim Ibn Sallam, *The Book of Revenue: Kitāb Al-Amwāl* (Garnet, NY: Ithaca Press, 2006).

[37] Al-Rustāqi, *Manhaj Al-Ṭālibīn*, Vol. 7, 151, 154.

[38] Al-Rustāqi, *Manhaj Al-Ṭālibīn*, Vol. 7, 152.

[39] Al-Rustāqi, *Manhaj Al-Ṭālibīn*, Vol. 7, 152–154.

demands of nineteenth-century agrarian capitalism, Al-Khalili was able to ground the novel practice of *khiyār* sales in a discursive universe of natural time and being, bringing together a series of "facts" about nature to enable the robust extraction and circulation of rents around the burgeoning world of Indian Ocean commerce.

Khiyār sales, however, were not once-off transactions between a lender and borrower. Restricting the *khiyār* to a singular exchange between the two would have missed the point altogether: financiers engaged in *khiyār* sales to secure supplies of goods – to bind planters into an ongoing relationship of mutual obligation. If the record includes isolated *khiyār* sale transactions between merchants and their borrowers, these were the exception rather than the rule. The mutual bonds that the *khiyār* sale created – the obligation to keep the produce flowing and the account ledgers open – were to pass from generation to generation, in the spirit of the *iqrār* with which a *khiyār* sale *waraqa* began. The parties to the *khiyār* asserted as much on the *waraqa* when they proclaimed that the contract was "for them and for their heirs after them" (*lahumā wa li-warthahumā min ba'dahumā*) for whatever timeframe they might have agreed to.[40] As part of the enduring bond of debt and obligation, the property relationship between the debtor and creditor was to continue until they or their heirs decided to end it.

Al-Khalili had no issues with multi-generational *khiyār* sales. He maintained that *khiyār*-based relationships between creditors and debtors that spanned multiple generations, lasting for as long as fifty years (a timeframe unimaginable in the *khiyār's* original conception), were completely valid.[41] His writings made it clear that because it was a contract arising from a debt, the *khiyār* sale created a bond between lender and borrower that transcended life itself, unless the counterparties clearly stated otherwise. A *khiyār* sale in which the debt had matured and was still unpaid could transfer the title to the land to the creditor, but one that was still active could be extended indefinitely.[42] But if the heirs to a *khiyār* arrangement chose not to extend it and had not made good on their commitment to repay the amount owed, then the *khiyār* creditor, as a buyer, was considered a preferred creditor to the estate; other creditors would be paid only after he was paid in full.[43] The boundary between the

[40] Although not all of the *khiyār* sales *waraqas* include this statement, the majority do. The longest single *khiyār* sale I have seen in a *waraqa* was for ten years, though this does not take into account possible extensions, which were likely. See also ZNA AM 3/1, 345.

[41] Al-Khalili, *Ajwibat Al-Muḥaqqiq Al-Khalīlī*, Vol. 4, 131–132, 149, 167–168.

[42] Al-Khalili, *Ajwibat Al-Muḥaqqiq Al-Khalīlī*, Vol. 4, 167–168. For a clear example of a matured *khiyār* sale and a transfer of land, see ZNA AM 3/2, 13.

[43] Al-Khalili, *Ajwibat Al-Muḥaqqiq Al-Khalīlī*, Vol. 4, 260.

khiyār as a *loan* and the *khiyār* as a *sale*, it seemed, depended mostly on the debtor's abilities to meet their obligations; in either case, the creditor enjoyed the full protection of the law.

And all creditors were equal, regardless of their background. The fact that the overwhelming majority of the creditors operating in the plantations of Oman and East Africa were Indians did not seem to concern Al-Khalili in the slightest bit. When asked about "the rights of a foreigner" (*ajnabī*) vis-à-vis the rights of an heir to property that had been put up as collateral against a loan, Al-Khalili's response was short and to the point: "he [the debtor] is to give his son the same rights as other creditors."[44] As creditors to the estate, the claims of foreigners – Indian, Arab, Muslim, or otherwise – were just as strong as those of family members. The commodification of family property had thus not only become a *de facto* phenomenon of nineteenth-century agrarian capitalism; it had also become recognized *de jure*.

The protections that Al-Khalili's writings afforded to creditors were just as important as the natural universe in which he grounded the transactions taking place around him. In a time of boom – a time in which there were profits to be had – a dearth of financial capital could mean missed opportunities. At the same time, however, a completely unregulated sphere of agricultural finance could result in the distortion of the basic rights and duties of parties to a contract – a distortion that a jurist with his credentials would simply not countenance. Rather than let his world spin out of control, Al-Khalili chose to regulate – mostly in favor of the creditor, though keeping in mind the basic rights of the debtors that surrounded him. If the *khiyār* sale had already become *fait accompli* in Omani Indian Ocean commerce, the intellectual work done by Al-Khalili and other jurists gave it the philosophical, ontological, and legal underpinnings necessary for it to enjoy widespread recognition as a legitimate contract.[45]

[44] Al-Khalili, *Ajwibat Al-Muḥaqqiq Al-Khalīlī*, Vol. 4, 258.

[45] Other jurists in Yemen also thought about contracts similar to the khiyār sale. See Linda Boxberger, "Avoiding Ribā: Credit and Custodianship in Nineteenth and Early-Twentieth Century Hadramawt," *Islamic Law and Society*, Vol. 5, No. 2 (1998), 196–213. As with Al-Khalili, their actions are comparable to those undertaken by thinkers in the nineteenth-century United States or jurists in eighteenth-century France, who were willing to reinterpret pre-existing legal categories in light of new social and commercial developments to facilitate the growth of commercial society. Tony Freyer, "Negotiable Instruments and the Federal Courts in Antebellum American Business," *Business History Review*, Vol. 50, No. 4 (1976), 435–455; Amalia D. Kessler, *A Revolution in Commerce: The Parisian Merchant Court and the Rise of Commercial Society in Eighteenth-Century France* (New Haven, CT: Yale University Press, 2011), 188–237.

Assembling the *Khiyār*

But we should not associate the *khiyār* sale too closely with Al-Khalili and his *fatwas*. The jurist's voice may dominate the *khiyār* discourse, with its elaborate temporal and agricultural ontologies and notions of property rights, but he certainly didn't conjure up the *khiyār*, nor did he lay the groundwork for its spread around the region. That work fell to the merchants, planters, and *kātibs*, who together with Al-Khalili managed to transmute the *khiyār* from a set of utterances in different plantations around South Arabia and East Africa to a collective decision – a contractual form that economic actors everywhere could mobilize, but also continually reshape. The remaking of Islamic legal categories to meet the needs of emerging modern capitalism in the Indian Ocean thus called for the combined energies of a broad range of economic and juridical actors, all of whom coalesced around the *khiyār* sale and its material expression, the *waraqa*, and contributed to shaping its form and content. Their work in creating the *khiyār* sale, and their mobilization of the graphic artifact of the *waraqa* itself, helped forge the philosophical, commercial, and bureaucratic world the *waraqa* inhabited – helped author the unfolding text of the *khiyār* sale in the world of Indian Ocean capitalism.

The *waraqa* itself attributes authorship to only one of these actors: the *kātib*, from whose perspective the contract was narrated and whose name appears at its bottom. Like his efforts in inscribing legal personhood onto the contracting parties through the *waraqa*, the *kātib's* work was central to fashioning the *khiyār* sale as a legally valid contract. This was no small task: Al-Khalili could not emphasize enough the weight that correct legal syntax and formulation (*lafẓ*) had in assessing the validity of a document. He and countless other jurists spent a great deal of time thinking about grammar, syntax, and intended meaning in law – particularly when it came to deriving legal rulings from the sayings of the Prophet Muhammad.[46] An incorrect *lafẓ*, Al-Khalili declared – drawing on what he had heard from his teacher Nasser ibn Abi Nabhan – could render a perfectly acceptable *waraqa* invalid even if off by just a letter.[47] Alternatively, proper *lafẓ* in a *waraqa* could eclipse other considerations: even in the absence of witnesses to the contract, correct *lafẓ* could endow the *waraqa* with legal validity.[48] Thus, in creating a legally valid document, access to a knowledgeable *kātib* was vital.

[46] Bernard G. Weiss, *The Spirit of Islamic Law* (Athens, GA: University of Georgia Press, 1998), 58–59.

[47] Al-Khalili, *Ajwibat Al-Muḥaqqiq Al-Khalīlī*, Vol. 4, 152.

[48] Al-Khalili, *Ajwibat Al-Muḥaqqiq Al-Khalīlī*, Vol. 5, 375. Al-Khalili's opinion here suggests a counterpoint to recent arguments on the relative weight of written and oral evidence in

The fact that *kātibs* played such an integral role in commercial and legal dealings yet left no trace of themselves aside from the names they left on the *waraqas* is telling, pointing to their very banality and ubiquity – that they constituted an unremarkable feature of commercial society in the Western Indian Ocean, almost completely blending into a larger commercio-juridical mass. The *kātib* may have penned the *waraqa* and may have done much of the work in mediating between the commercial world and the legal word, but, like Al-Khalili, he could not claim sole authorship – neither of the *waraqa* itself nor of the *khiyār* sale contract. To transmute something like the *khiyār* sale (and, by extension, its written articulation, the *waraqa*) from a set of utterances and isolated practices to a collective decision required more than one actor. It required coordinated action – a carefully constructed exchange between merchant, *kātib*, and jurist (and the overlapping roles therein), and a complex interplay between *waraqa* and *fatwa*.

The two genres, *waraqa* and *fatwa*, are hardly mutually exclusive: *fatwas*, especially those surrounding the *khiyār* sale, often included mentions of *kātibs* and *waraqas*. Al-Khalili, in a particularly revealing *fatwa*, acknowledged the sometimes problematic role that the *kātib* played in the process. Replying to a query as to whether the *kātib* was punishable for drafting a *waraqa* that assigned a creditor a plantation's yield rather than the plantation itself (the latter forming a necessary component of the sale's validity) Al-Khalili contended that although the *kātib* shouldered no liability for something a financier (*rabb al-māl*) asked him to do, the financier should not ask that of him.[49] A later jurist would ask Oman's *kātibs* to join him in breaking their pens in the face of requests to engage in this sort of chicanery, if they had any respect for the integrity of their religion at all (see Chapter 7).[50] Broadly speaking, jurists suspected that the alliance between commercial actors and *kātibs* could potentially conceal illicit gains.

The jurists' concern regarding the possible collusion between commercial actors and *kātibs* in their documentary maneuverings was not misplaced. For most people, whether in the plantation, in town, or on the caravan trail, the jurist was too distant of a legal actor to really shape their experience of the law. He might have been the most authoritative

Islamic law. See Lydon, *On Trans-Saharan Trails*, 280; see also idem, "A Paper Economy of Faith Without Faith in Paper: A Reflection on Islamic Institutional History," *Journal of Economic Behavior and Organization*, Vol. 71 (2009), 647–659.

49 Al-Khalili, *Ajwibat Al-Muḥaqqiq Al-Khalīlī*, Vol. 4, 131.

50 'Abdullah bin Humayyid Al-Salimi, *Jawābāt Al-Imām Al-Sālimi [Imam Al-Sālimi's Responses]*, 2nd ed. (Muscat, Oman: Ministry of Awqaf and Religious Affairs, 1999), Vol. 4, 302–303.

voice, but he was usually not physically present. Indeed, the vast majority of questions posed to jurists were in writing, from distant questioners who seemed to have already coordinated some of their actions with their *kātibs* – or, in some other cases, third parties who were commenting on some form of association between planter and *kātib*.

Read one way, the *fatwas* might suggest that by the time word of the merchants' and *kātibs'* experiments reached the jurist they were already *fait accompli*. None of the questioners were asking the jurists for *permission* to engage in the *khiyār*; they simply wanted clarification as to what their rights and liabilities were for transactions *that had already taken place*. Some questioners went so far as to ask the jurists to furnish them with competing opinions, signaling that they were less interested in an authoritative stance than they were in finding a legal carapace to their contractual maneuverings. And indeed, the art of crafting a *fatwa* question would have been an instrumental part of the process. Because the jurist could only answer what he was asked – there was no room for him to ask for factual clarification – his field of response was largely determined by the formulation of the question.[51] Through a cleverly crafted question, a merchant was able to elicit from the jurist a favorable response to his actions – a moral and legal justification for his contractual experimentation.

But jurists were not passive pawns in a broader commercial agenda, manipulated by the linguistic and documentary maneuverings of a merchant-planter community. Rather, jurists like Al-Khalili and others were active participants in the crafting of the *khiyār* sale contract. In responding to the carefully crafted questions posed by their correspondents, jurists furnished a supple legal framework within which commercial actors could place their transactions, allowing them to ground their contractual experimentations in a known universe of forms, standards, rights, and liabilities. The *khiyār* form continually circulated between the jurist, the *kātib*, and the planter, precipitating a multiparty interaction through which authorship and agency over the new contract was distributed over a broad network of actors, each of whom left their imprint on the *khiyār's* form and helped establish its place within a burgeoning plantation economy.[52]

[51] Muhammad Khalid Masud, Brinkley Messick and David S. Powers, eds. *Islamic Legal Interpretation: Jurists and their Fatwas* (Cambridge, MA: Harvard University Press, 1996), 22.

[52] For this idea, I draw on the brilliant work of Matthew Hull, whose reflections on files and bureaucracy in modern Pakistan inspires many of my thoughts here. Matthew Hull, *Government of Paper: The Materiality of Bureaucracy in Urban Pakistan* (Berkeley, CA: University of California Press, 2012), 138.

Waraqas, Grammar, and the Construction of an Indian Ocean Arena

The ability of jurists, *kātibs*, merchants, and planters to shape the *khiyār* sale and to give it expression through the *waraqa* was only one part of the puzzle. What commercial actors did with their *waraqas*, and how their actions gave shape to a burgeoning Indian Ocean economy of obligation at a time of emerging modern capitalism – that was what ultimately gave it commercial meaning. In a world in which people transacted in land, dates, cloves, ivory, slaves, and countless other commodities and rights in commercial centers separated by mountains, valleys, jungles, and an entire ocean, the *waraqa* formed the common denominator and supplied a unified grammar. The *waraqa* provided a space in which actors between the two coasts could employ the same measures for date and clove trees, mobilize identical contractual forms to facilitate the extraction and circulation of rent and value, and contract within a common ontology of agricultural life, be it in Muscat or Mombasa.

As brief as it was, the question posed to Al-Khalili recounted at the beginning of this chapter spoke volumes on the world that the *waraqa* and its multiple authors created. In describing the Mazru'i sales of land in Oman through different *waraqas* as taking place "with full confidence that they know (*bi-ḥukm al-iṭma'ināna annahum 'alamū*)," the questioner pointed to the framework necessary for a regional property market to emerge – one based on *iṭma'ināna*, or confidence. Even though the *kātibs* who penned the *waraqas* in question were unknown locally (*majhūlūn*), the correspondent noted that the transactions went on without incident or comment. Al-Khalili's short reply only confirmed the validity of the Mazru'i's transactions: in cases like this, he noted, people were able to expand the regime of *iṭma'ināna* (*al-tawassu' bi-aḥkām al-iṭma'ināna*), to the extent that it did not conflict with doubt (*tu'āriḍ fīh al-istirāba*)."[53]

But what might *iṭma'ināna* have meant in a world in which people transacted in property, harvest, and credit, from the interior of Oman to the East African coast and beyond? Here, *iṭma'ināna* might be best understood as a confidence that the forms, standards, and grammars of commercial contracting would be legible wherever one traveled within this world. And this is certainly what one encounters when looking beyond *fatwas* and into the *waraqas*, the material artifacts of commercial life itself. As *waraqas* circulated between the coasts and hinterlands of Oman and East Africa, so too did the standards, measures, and forms they contained – grammars of economic life that formed the sinews of a

[53] Al-Khalili, *Ajwibat Al-Muḥaqqiq Al-Khalili*, Vol. 4, 290.

shared commercial arena and the language of a burgeoning commercial society. Indeed, it is difficult to overstate the importance of the standards and measures that the *waraqa* transported with it in allowing the plantation economies of Oman and East Africa to become comparable units. Through the material plane of the *waraqa*, commercial and juridical actors between the two coasts mobilized the same quasi-standards to describe date and clove plantations. In a sense, they achieved the incredible feat of transposing one site onto another without deformation or dislocation, articulating a regional grammar that allowed for trans-oceanic commensurability.[54]

Among the main standards that the *waraqa* circulated between Oman and East Africa was the *frasila*, a regional measure of weight that equaled roughly 35 lbs, used to describe a wide variety of goods, from dates and cloves to ivory and frankincense.[55] Other measures, such as the *qora*, also appear in *waraqas* from time to time, but these seem to be far less widespread than the *frasila*, which one encountered throughout the coasts and hinterlands of South Arabia and East Africa. The stability of forms that the *frasila* provided around the coasts formed a critical dimension of the shared lexicon of commerce in the region. The fact that one does not encounter the *frasila* in non-Omani plantation societies – say, in Basra or Hasa – is equally significant, as it points to the outer limits of the commercial regime.

Just as important as the measures that allowed for commensurability between the plantations (and produce therein) in Southeast Arabia and East Africa were the similar agricultural ontologies that allowed for the extraction and circulation of rents between the two regions. The distinctions that Al-Khalili, Al-Shaqṣi, and others drew between the land, tree, and yield may have been articulated in an Omani milieu, but they were just as applicable to the East African context. The circulation of the *khiyār* form brought with it distinctions grounded in a more universalist natural law and adapted them to a local setting and subject matter. Depending on where one traded in the Western Indian Ocean, a *frasila* may have been used to measure a quantity of cloves, dates, or orchilla.

[54] Here, I am drawing liberally from the ideas and eloquent phrasings of Bruno Latour, *Reassembling the Social: An Introduction to Actor-Network-Theory* (Oxford, UK: Oxford University Press, 2005), 222–223.

[55] Depending on where one was, a *frasila* could range between 35 and 36 lbs. See also William Walter Augustine Fitzgerald, *Travels in the Coastlands of British East Africa and the Islands of Zanzibar and Pemba* (London: Chapman and Hall, 1898) 263–264, 524, 535; Bakari, *The Customs of the Swahili People*, 232. A mid-nineteenth century Somali report, however, identifies a *frasila* of frankincense as comprising only 20 lbs; see C. J. Cruttendren, "Notes on the Mijjertheyn Somalees," *Journal of the Asiatic Society of Bengal*, Volume 13, Part 1, No. 149 (1844), 332.

However, no matter where one stood, *when* an object formed a separate subject of a commercial contract remained constant.

The ontology of the flowering date palm thus easily transposed itself onto the flowering clove tree. And in Al-Khalili's imagining of it, the leap from date palm to clove tree would have been a short one. The two might have been grown in different parts of the world, produced different types of fruit, and looked and smelled differently, but they were ontologically similar; after all, they were both trees. The jurist suggested as much when he responded to a question posed to him about a mango tree. When asked if it was possible to sell the tree without that land on which it stood, Al-Khalili responded that the date palm needed its land to survive, and that rulings on the date palm could be extended by analogy to the mango tree.[56]

On the space of the *waraqa* itself, the complex juristic distinctions between land, tree, and fruit, and all of the rules surrounding when something formed an independent object of sale were compressed into the pithy statement that the plot was sold "with its boundaries, rights, and land, and whatever it might include from coconut and clove trees, and any other trees it might contain" (*bi-ḥudūdihā wa-ḥuqūqihā wa-arḍihā wa-mā fīhā min ashjār al-nawārjeel wal-qaranful wa ghayruhā min al-ashjār*).[57] This shorthand, appearing on *waraqas* throughout East Africa, captured the *khiyār* buyer's (i.e. the creditor's) contractual rights, signaling a legally valid purchase of land while suggesting an intention to collect its yield, indicated by an explicit mention of trees as part of the sale contract.

Through the compression of these rights and distinctions onto the space of the *waraqa*, merchants opened the door to the world of negotiability. A creditor in need of cash, or who had outstanding obligations of his own could, in lieu of cash or physical property, transfer his *waraqa* and the rights that it entailed, simply by signing over the document. The *waraqa* thus became an asset in itself – one that actors could circulate among themselves with little hassle. In this regard, they functioned in a manner similar to bills of exchange, with one important exception: unless the original debtor managed to find someone to stand as surety for him, his obligations remained fixed. As a *waraqa* moved from one creditor to another, so too did the original debtor's obligations;

[56] Al-Khalili, *Ajwibat Al-Muḥaqqiq Al-Khalili*, Vol. 5, 411–412. Al-Khalili was most likely responding to a *qāḍi*, as he furnished competing opinions on the permissibility of analogical reasoning when it came to trees – a debate that only *qāḍis* would have been interested in.

[57] At other times, the statement also included mention of mango (*embā'*) trees. ZNA AA 12/19, Deed 102 of 1877.

whatever payments he had initially agreed to make, or whatever rent he might have pledged, would be to his new creditor. *Waraqa* negotiability meant that real estate – a quintessentially immovable asset – and the rents that accompanied it were endowed with the fluidity necessary for them to travel through the dynamic and increasingly mobile credit networks that spanned the Indian Ocean.

As new markets emerged in East Africa and the Arabian Peninsula over the course of the nineteenth century, and as credit chains extended further into the interior from the coastline, the *waraqa's* negotiability allowed creditors to transfer outstanding debts and secure obligations between one another in a fluid manner, facilitating the extension of credit chains farther and deeper into new and distant markets. By the mid-1870s, creditors in East Africa frequently used *waraqas* to settle claims against one another. In 1874, for example, a Pangani-based Indian merchant transferred to his Zanzibar creditor *waraqas* worth a whopping MTD 13,000 – the value of nearly three large plantations, slaves, and all – to settle his accounts.[58] The next year, an Arab creditor transferred his two year old *waraqa* for a debt of 40 *frasilas* of ivory to his Khoja creditor as partial settlement of his accounts with him.[59] And when the time came in 1876 for one Arab to settle his accounts with his *Bania* financier, he transferred over his own outstanding claim of MTD 1,040 on a *khādim*.[60] Transfers like these often left their mark on the *waraqa* itself, through a witnessed addendum to the text – either at the bottom or on the back – in which the creditor agreed to transfer the claim to someone else.

Merchants even pledged *waraqas* to their creditors as collateral against their own loans. In 1856, a Khoja merchant signed over to Ladha Damji (acting as agent of Jairam Sewji) a *waraqa* through which he bought three storage rooms (*godowns*). The *waraqa* was collateral for his own debt to Damji of MTD 1,425.[61] Another Khoja merchant hypothecated his title deeds to four houses in Saadani, on the East African coast, to a Zanzibar merchant for MTD 190.[62] Even as late as the summer of 1896, when one Khoja merchant sought to borrow MTD 300 from another, he pledged (by *rahn*) seven *waraqas*, five of which were titles to *shambas* he

58 *Ramdas Jethani* v. *Dowarka Liladhur and Kanjee Liladhur* (1875) ZNA HC 7/5. In another 1880 claim against the Tanga-based debtor Noorbhai Ebrahimji, the Zanzibar merchant Esmailji Jivanji collected ten *waraqas* that Ebrahimji had in his possession – *waraqas* signed by Ebrahimji's debtors in the interior. *Esmailji Jeevunji* v. *Noorbhai Ebrahimji (Tanga)* (1880) ZNA HC 7/155.

59 ZNA AA 12/19, Deed 516 of 1875.

60 ZNA AA 12/19, Deed 127 of 1877.

61 ZNA AM 3/1, 16.

62 ZNA AA 12/19, Deed 94 of 1877.

had amassed over the course of his career; the other two were personal guarantees for MTD 96.5. He also pledged two mud huts, which he had presumably collected from his debtors.[63] The *waraqa* thus evolved into more than a transferable obligation; in its negotiability, it took on many of the characteristics associated with cash.

More generally, as it circulated between Oman and East Africa and changed hands between different actors, the *waraqa* reinforced the position of the actors responsible for its production. Its usage called forth the juridical assemblage that brought it into being, constantly re-inscribing the primacy of a juridical field comprised of merchants, planters, *kātibs*, and jurists to the smooth functioning of commerce. Even those who were not able to read the *waraqas* would have entertained conceptions about them: the material qualities of the *waraqa* that were to count as signs, what sorts of agents were involved in them, how they were (and ought to be) produced and used, and how they fit into a universe of commercial and legal instruments.[64] Thus, if jurists and *kātibs* helped assemble the *waraqa*, its production and circulation among different economic actors in an Indian Ocean arena enacted that very bureaucracy, day in and day out.

All told, then, it should come as no surprise that a man from Mombasa, carrying *waraqas* penned by *kātibs* in East Africa, would be able to transact in the Omani interior "with full confidence." Doing business in Oman, he would have encountered a world that was immediately legible to him: common measures for the goods he was transacting in, a common understanding of what land rights he was trading in, and a familiar group of actors drawing up the paperwork in a form that he would have instantly recognized as bearing all of the necessary marks of legitimacy. His ability to instantly comprehend the legal grammars of economic life around him, coupled with the ability of those around him to instantly place his transactions within a known universe of contracting, formed critical dimensions of the confidence he would have felt in doing business and the fundamental elements of the stability of the world around him.

Conclusion

At a time in which everyday economic actors began to think of their world in terms of credit, debt, production, consumption, and generating value, people began to rethink the instruments through which they engaged in

[63] ZNA AM 1/4, 38.
[64] Hull, *Government of Paper*, 14.

those activities. Faced with an agricultural frontier that seemed to continually unfold, and distant markets whose presence manifested itself in shopkeepers and moneylenders, they began to ask themselves and their legal guides how they might use the wealth they had available to them – their property – to tap into this seemingly endless supply of cloth, beads, and watches – goods they could immediately convert into status. Their genealogies might have given them the legal capacity to lend and borrow, but their property gave them the means to access the worldly goods and credit they needed to attain social, political, and commercial mobility. And as the forces of emerging modern capitalism pushed against the expanding agrarian landscapes of South Arabia and East Africa, land, tree, and yield separated themselves out from one another, each attaching itself to contracts whose scope expanded and shrunk to meet the cycles of wind, water, and agriculture that shaped Indian Ocean commerce.

As the frontiers of commerce and agriculture moved further inland, it fell to groups of merchants, planters, *kātibs*, *qāḍis*, and jurists to extend the reach of their legal systems to new towns, plantations, and caravan routes. As these commercial and juridical actors moved into towns like Tabora, Nyangwe, and Ujiji, the Sultan and his soldiers remained in Zanzibar, moving only as far westward as Mombasa or Bagamoyo. Merchants, *kātibs*, *qāḍis* – these were the people clothing new commercial actors, transactions, and activities in the garb of the law, stretching out and reshaping legal categories to make their commercial expansion both profitable and secure. They were, in many respects, doing the expansionist work of "empire" as they and others before them would have understood it – an extension of a commercial and legal regime that allowed them access to capital, commodities, property, and ultimately status.

And as long as the markets were strong and pockets were flush, nobody seemed to think twice about the transformations in property rights that they had set in motion or the contractual sleights-of-hand that they had become so committed to. This was, after all, a time of plenty, in which the focus was on reaping as much of the commercial windfall as possible – not a time to be distracted by legal technicalities. Their questions to jurists like Al-Khalili indicated some concern about rights and obligations, but they did not stop them from continually experimenting and pushing the boundaries of what may or may not have been permissible. People didn't give much thought to what might happen at a time of failure; they asked questions on how to enable contracts – how to make things happen – not how to divide up rights after things had fallen apart.

But that was when things were going well. If things were to go poorly, people were less likely to be as enthusiastic and brazen with their contracts. And that is what happened at the end of the 1860s and the years that followed, when economic downturns in East Africa coincided with political crises, setting in motion a series of juridical changes that would have enormous implications for what economic life in the Western Indian Ocean would look like over the next seventy-five years or so. The 1870s would bear witness to a rising tide of British imperialism in the Western Indian Ocean – one that would sweep away Al-Khalili and his partners, ushering in a new regime of writers, commentators, and bureaucrats. And it all began with the Indian merchant and the *waraqas* he held in his hands.

Interlude

During the cool spring of 1860, as the jurist Sa'id bin Khalfan Al-Khalili penned his responses to questions from around Oman on contracts and economic life, he was also laying the groundwork for big changes. The ruler of Muscat and Zanzibar, Sa'id bin Sultan, had died just four years earlier while shuttling back and forth between his capitals, and Al-Khalili hoped to seize the opportunity to establish his own political vision: an Imamate that would stretch across Southeast Arabia, and perhaps reaching out into East Africa as well. It was a vision grounded in Ibadhi ideology and law, in which the elected Imam formed a central part of the political landscape – a vision that past jurists had tried to realize, before the Busa'idis were able to carve out their own vision of political suzerainty in the region.[1] But now, times were different: the winds of change had been blowing in the world of commerce; now could be the time to redirect them into the world of politics as well.

From his residence in the Omani interior, Al-Khalili saw an opportunity to take down the Busai'idi rulers, who in his view were unable to extend their writ beyond Muscat or Zanzibar, and who relied out of weakness on the British to prop up their regime.[2] The jurist never tired of labeling the Al-Busa'idis *jabābira*, "unconstitutional rulers" – a term often reserved for non-Imamate rulers, but used particularly liberally to describe rulers operating under foreign influence. For Al-Khalili, the Al-Busa'idis were *jabābira par excellence*: not only were they not Imams, but they also relied on foreign powers to put down legitimate claimants to the Imamate.[3] His plotting against prospective rulers from Sa'id's line (or at least those who were unwilling to submit to his guidance) characterized

[1] Wilkinson, *The Imamate Tradition of Oman*, 177–226.

[2] The Busa'idis were the Government of India's principal ally in its fight against piracy and the slave trade in the Western Indian Ocean, and Busa'idi rulers often relied on British diplomatic support for their military campaigns in the region. Kelly, *Britain and the Persian Gulf*; Wilkinson, *The Arabs and the Scramble for Africa*, 55–56.

[3] Wilkinson, *The Imamate Tradition of Oman*, 190–191.

the third quarter of the nineteenth century – and, not coincidentally, the last two decades of the jurist's life.

In Oman's interior, Al-Khalili found a sympathetic ally in ʿAzzan bin Qais Al-Busaʿidi, Saʿid's cousin, who was then the governor of Sohar, just over 120 miles northwards along the coast from Muscat. ʿAzzan's father – Saʿid's paternal uncle – had established himself as an independent potentate in coastal Oman during his brother's reign, and only pledged allegiance to Saʿid after a failed attempt at seizing the throne during the power scramble that ultimately resulted in Saʿid's ascendancy to the throne in 1806. He died two years later, leaving the governorship of Sohar to his son ʿAzzan. After Saʿid's death at sea in 1856, ʿAzzan slowly began building up a strong base of opponents to the new Sultan – a base that consisted mostly of tribal Ibadhis from the interior who saw in ʿAzzan a chance to fully re-establish the Imamate and do away with the Sultanate, the British, and undesirable foreign influences.

While Saʿid bin Sultan's death did nothing to dismember the deep ties of blood, capital, migration, and property that bound South Arabia to East Africa, Muscat suffered deeply from his death. Following Saʿid's death, Muscat was administratively severed from Zanzibar: under an arbitration award by the Government of India, the two realms were to be governed separately, Muscat by Saʿid's son Thuwaini and Zanzibar by his son Majid; to compensate for the loss of the Zanzibar revenues, Majid was to pay his brother MTD 40,000 every year.[4] In Muscat, the promise of revenues from the Zanzibar subsidy prompted jostling from within the Busaʿidi family; Thuwaini's son Salim ended up killing his father and taking control of the Sultanate, while in Zanzibar Majid's brother Barghash launched a failed coup and was sent to Bombay, where he would spend the next two years.[5] The rifts within the Busaʿidi family created an opening for Al-Khalili and ʿAzzan, who played on the family's weaknesses to challenge them.

Al-Khalili's relationship with ʿAzzan had not developed overnight. While in his thirties, Al-Khalili had moved to Rustaq to serve under ʿAzzan's uncle, whom he had nominated to head the Ibadhi government in the interior.[6] Later, when ʿAzzan emerged as a potential head of the Ibadhi Imamate, Al-Khalili married his daughter Shamsa to him, thereby

[4] Sheriff, *Slaves, Spices*, 208–17; Bhacker, *Trade and Empire*, 179–193. The Government of India's involvement in mediating the succession crisis following Saʿid's death was in large part due to their desire to ensure that they had a stable ally in their anti-slavery and anti-piracy campaigns.

[5] Wilkinson, *The Imamate Tradition of Oman*, 236; Sheriff, *Slaves, Spices*, 217–221.

[6] Al-Khalili, *Ajwibat Al-Muḥaqqiq Al-Khalili*, Vol. 1, 29; Robert G. Landen, *Oman Since 1856: Disruptive Modernization in a Traditional Arab Society* (Princeton, NJ: Princeton University Press, 1967), 295.

securing the ties between them.[7] In 'Azzan, Al-Khalili found a potential challenger to Sa'id's line on the coast from within the Al-Busa'idi family – one who already had support on the Batinah coast. From 'Azzan's perspective, Al-Khalili's religious pedigree would help shore up his political credentials in the interior, where he would have otherwise enjoyed little or no support.

The two were further backed by Saleh bin 'Ali of the Al-Harthi tribe, one of Al-Khalili's students.[8] Saleh had recently tried to back Barghash's coup in Zanzibar; after the plot had been uncovered, he left Zanzibar for Somalia, and from there returned to Al-Sharqiyya in Oman.[9] With Saleh and 'Azzan on board, Al-Khalili had formed the coalition he needed to dislodge the Sultan. Together, they succeeded. In September 1868, their combined forces delivered an attack on Muscat from two directions, and by the end of October, 'Azzan's forces had taken over Muscat and Muttrah, proclaiming the establishment of the Ibadhi Imamate on the coast.[10]

The establishment of the Ibadhi Imamate in Muscat was Al-Khalili's moment in the sun: he had supported 'Azzan bin Qais from the beginning, and was widely acknowledged to be his adviser and ecclesiastical guide.[11] Shortly after establishing his rule on the coast, 'Azzan appointed Al-Khalili as his governor and chief *qāḍī* in Muscat, giving the jurist a temporal jurisdiction that bolstered his religious and legal authority. Others saw him as exercising more authority than 'Azzan himself, shaping the new regime's domestic policies, heading its legal administration, and establishing its overall tone.[12]

The reaction in the British Indian press to the establishment of the Imamate in Muscat was one of horror. The *Times of India* reported in August 1869 that "it should be premised that the real ruler of Muscat at present is Azim's [sic] lieutenant Kuleylee [sic]," adding that Al-Khalili "appears to be a bigoted and vindictive secretary, possessing just sufficient skill and forethought to turn his lawless proceedings to his own and his chief's immediate purposes." The article went on to paint Khalili as Muscat's "grand inquisitor," suggesting that Muscat was "under a reign of terror, and subjected to the merciless caprices of a knot of

7 Al-Khalili, *Ajwibat Al-Muḥaqqiq Al-Khalili*, Vol. 1, 30.
8 Landen, *Oman Since 1856*, 291.
9 Wilkinson, *The Imamate Tradition of Oman*, 230.
10 Landen, *Oman Since 1856*, 293; Wilkinson, *The Imamate Tradition of Oman*, 252.
11 Goswami, *The Call of the Sea*, 104. Saleh bin 'Ali, by contrast, receded to the background of the political machinery after the establishment of the 'Azzan and Al-Khalili government, though he did re-emerge as a commercial and political presence in the early twentieth century. Landen, *Oman Since 1856*, 298; see also Chapter 7.
12 Landen, *Oman Since 1856*, 296.

narrow-minded zealots." The combined rule of 'Azzan and Khalili, the article's author suggested, was likely to bring ruin to the prosperous port city of Muscat.[13] In another article on the two, the author referred to Al-Khalili as 'Azzan's "fanatical lieutenant" who entertained designs on the nearby port of Bandar 'Abbas; in yet another, he was the "puritane [sic] but reckless" leader of 'Azzan's "fanatical adherents."[14]

The British press's reaction to Al-Khalili's coup – particularly their usage of the language of fanaticism and zealotry – partly stemmed from their fears of Islamic extremism in British India. During the same months in which the *Times of India* published views on 'Azzan and Al-Khalili's rule over Muscat, authorities in British India arrested two businessmen on suspicion of financing "Wahhabis" – a term used to designate various Islamic reform movements – fighting the British in the northwestern frontier of India. The case attracted a significant amount of attention in the press, which was awash in an anti-Muslim paranoia surrounding religious fanaticism, imagined as part of a much wider plot to bring down the British Empire.[15] The Government of India's perceptions of Al-Khalili and 'Azzan's aims, then, were shaped by its own domestic fears.

Officials observing the situation from India also had other reasons to be concerned. One of Al-Khalili's first priorities in Muscat was to reform the customs administration, which had previously been under the control of the Bhimanis.[16] While he may have been willing to help furnish Indian firms like theirs with the legal personhood and property rights necessary to secure their finance in agriculture and commerce, their deep involvement with Muscat's customs administration was a source of discomfort for Al-Khalili, who understood how deeply intertwined the customs house and the Omani Empire were. The jurist-cum-governor sought to dislodge the Bhattias by encouraging one Arab candidate to bid for the customs administration and later, realizing the candidate's "ignorance of port practices and his general inefficiency," inducing a Khoja Indian merchant to bid for the concession – perhaps under the notion that it was preferable to have a Muslim Indian at the customs house than a Hindu one.[17] When the merchant was unable to produce the MTD 95,000 that had been bid, Al-Khalili resorted to threatening

[13] *Times of India* (August 5, 1869), 2.

[14] *Times of India* (September 25, 1869), 2; *Times of India* (October 30, 1869), 2.

[15] There is no better analysis of this case than Julia Stephens's "The Phantom Wahhabi: Liberalism and the Muslim Fanatic in Mid-Victorian England," *Modern Asian Studies*, Vol. 47, No. 1 (2013): 22–52.

[16] See Chapter 1.

[17] In Zanzibar, Sultan Barghash, who entertained close relationships with conservative Ibadhis, similarly chose to farm the customs administration out to a Khoja, Tharia Topan.

him with a MTD 5,000 fee and imprisonment.[18] The plan ultimately proved unsuccessful: 'Azzan himself later had to ask the Bhimanis to re-take the customs house.[19] Despite Al-Khalili's familiarity with commercial practices, his understanding of fiscal governance seemed weak at best.

For the Indian merchant community of Muscat, the threats to the customs house proved a disaster to business; the institution formed a key node in the flows of commodities and information that gave their commercial world its shape and regularity.[20] Moreover, despite Al-Khalili's general commitment to property rights, merchants found it increasingly difficult to advance any claims based on past debts. Even before they lost the customs, Indian merchants complained of their inability to collect from 'Azzan's government money owed to them by past sultans. In one petition to the British consul, they claimed more than MTD 47,000 in outstanding loans. 'Azzan's government denied any responsibility for his predecessors' debts, and so the merchants turned to the British Consul – who, it turned out, was equally unwilling to help them. He argued that "the petitioners should be informed that their advances to the late Sultan of Muscat have been made at their own risk," adding that the debt would cause an undue hardship on 'Azzan's government.[21]

Al-Khalili and 'Azzan's takeover of the government at Muscat and his repudiation of past debts formed just one source of the Indian merchants' woes. More generally, commercial life was becoming more and more difficult for Indian merchants living in Muscat. In September 1869, shortly after the effort on the customs house, 'Azzan issued a proclamation forbidding Muscat subjects from traveling or sending their goods by vessels that sailed under the British flag unless they received special permission. Only after protests by the Indian merchant community and a strongly worded disapproval by the British Consul did he rescind the proclamation.[22] Other regulations, including a ban on tobacco use (and, by extension, a ban on collecting debts owed on tobacco) and restrictions on the Hindu community's ability to practice its religion, caused further uproar, prompting some Indian merchants to leave for other ports in the region. As a result, the *Bania* population of Muscat dropped from nearly 2,000 to around 250.[23]

[18] Landen, *Oman Since 1856*, 310; Goswami, *The Call of the Sea*, 99–100.
[19] Goswami, *The Call of the Sea*, 100.
[20] I address this in much more detail in Chapter 1.
[21] MSA Political Department Vol. 87, Comp. 172 (1869).
[22] Goswami, *The Call of the Sea*, 105.
[23] Goswami, *The Call of the Sea*, 106–107; Allen, "Sayyids, Shets, and Sultans," 112.

As time went on, Indian merchants' cries for help grew louder. The cash-strapped 'Azzan and Al-Khalili government, it seemed, was less interested in enforcing debts than it was in raising money: merchants alleged that far from upholding their property rights, the governing authorities in Muscat took to extorting money from them and threatening them with imprisonment if they did not comply.[24] Indian merchants frequently complained of the authorities' lack of commitment to "the enforcement of the Muhammadan law of creditor and debtor."[25]

The Indians were not alone in their unhappiness with the 'Azzan and Al-Khalili government. Although the Hinawi alliance of tribes supported 'Azzan's rule, the Ghafiri alliance and other southern tribes were less content.[26] The Ghafiris perceived 'Azzan to have enmity towards them, and to have implemented policies that alienated them from the regime in Muscat.[27] While some Ghafiris did submit to the 'Azzan regime, many did not; 'Azzan reacted by directing his first pacification expeditions against Ghafiri tribes just outside of the port city. The humiliation they experienced at the hands of the 'Azzan and Al-Khalili government generated a resentment that the regime at Muscat had to contend with for years to come.[28]

The Government of India was also hesitant to endorse the 'Azzan government, and stopped its payment of the Zanzibar subsidy, which it had handled since the erstwhile Sultan Salim's accession.[29] Officials contended that 'Azzan and Al-Khalili, who had no prior treaty standing with the Government of India nor any right to inherit from Sa'id, had no right to the Zanzibar subsidy. Starved of revenues from trade and from the subsidy, 'Azzan and Al-Khalili often found themselves with an empty treasury, with little or no money to finance governmental operations.[30]

24 MSA Political Department 1870, Vol. 93, Comp. 816.

25 J.G. Lorimer, *Gazetteer of the Persian Gulf, Oman and Central Arabia*, Vol. 1 (Historical) (Slough, UK: Archive Editions, 1905/1987), 488.

26 Goswami, *The Call of the Sea*, 109–110.

27 Wilkinson, *The Imamate Tradition of Oman*, 238.

28 Landen, *Oman Since 1856*, 300, 306–307.

29 C.U. Aitchison, ed., *A Collection of Treaties, Engagements, and Sunnuds Relating to India and Neighboring Countries*, Vol. 7 (Calcutta: Foreign Office Press, 1876), 194. When Salim killed his father Thuwaini and took the throne at Muscat, Sultan Majid in Zanzibar had withheld the subsidy, arguing that Salim had no right to inherit from his father because of his parricide. The British government disagreed, arguing that whatever the circumstances of his accession might have been, Salim was *de facto* ruler of Muscat and retained his right to his inheritance. It is unclear why the British government handled the Zanzibar subsidy, though it is possible that the political fallout that might have resulted from Majid's refusal to pay prompted them to take control of the purse-strings.

30 Landen, *Oman Since 1856*, 312–313.

Emboldened by the general discontent felt in Muscat, Turki bin Sa'id, another son of Sultan Sa'id's who had just spent the past three years in voluntary exile in Bombay, launched a military campaign to recapture the capital from 'Azzan. His advances on Muscat were funded by his brother Majid in Zanzibar, who encouraged Turki to bring the port city back under their branch of the Busa'idi family – in part to keep more conservative Ibadhi groups from attacking or instigating revolution in Zanzibar.[31] As he advanced toward Muscat, Turki made liberal use of Majid's purse, drawing almost MTD 80,000 in total to bribe Omani tribes in nearby ports.[32] The money was paid out to Turki in Bombay and Muscat by agents of the firm of Jairam Sewji, the customs master in Zanzibar, who billed Majid for the expenses.[33] Money from the commercial boom that had unfolded in Zanzibar thus made its way into war chests in South Arabia and the Persian Gulf.

Turki's well-funded campaign proved successful. After taking towns near the vicinity of Muscat, warriors from tribes that Turki bribed or convinced to join him marched up the coast and entered Muscat from Muttrah. In January 1871, 'Azzan was killed while defending Muttrah. Having heard of 'Azzan's death, Turki, who was fighting in the southeast of Muscat, "rushed to the capital city escorted by 500 camelmen to claim his prize."

Al-Khalili's fate was far less noble. Having supported two coups against the Sultan of Muscat, and posing an even more considerable challenge than the weak-willed 'Azzan, Al-Khalili constituted a prime target for Turki bin Sa'id. The jurist, desperate to preserve his rule over the port, went so far as to ask the British to guarantee the rule of another candidate, 'Azzan's brother Ibrahim, in return for a yearly tribute of one-quarter of Muscat's revenue. He received no such commitment.[34] Meanwhile, Turki was hot on his heels, and after cornering the jurist in one of Muscat's forts, it was clear that he intended to have him killed. The British Consul A.C. Way intervened, arguing instead that Al-Khalili should surrender peacefully and be guaranteed safe passage and protection. Turki agreed, but then quickly seized Al-Khalili.

What happened next was the subject of speculation. Reports in the Indian press suggested that Turki imprisoned Al-Khalili in a dungeon, where he either died of diarrhea or was "sabred" to death.[35] Others gave

[31] Landen, *Oman Since 1856*, 316.
[32] Landen, *Oman Since 1856*, 317–318.
[33] "Bill drawn by the Sultan of Zanzibar upon the firm of Jairam Sewjee to a considerable amount in favor of His Highness Syed Turkee" MSA PD 1870 Vol. 144, Comp. 1198.
[34] Landen, *Oman Since 1856*, 319.
[35] *Times of India* (March 16, 1871), 2.

a more graphic version of the events: upon Al-Khalili's exit, Turki seized him and had him and his son buried alive, announcing to the British Political Agent that they had died of diarrhea and fright.[36] Which is the truer version is unclear. What *is* known, however, is that A.C. Way, who had witnessed Al-Khalili's brutal death, shot himself just a few months after the incident.[37] The jurist who had guided Oman's merchants and planters through the biggest period of growth and experimentation they had ever seen was now dead.

The Age of British Extraterritoriality

When the British Political Resident Lewis Pelly took up his position in 1863, he knew how messy things could be in the Gulf. Pelly had moved between a series of different political posts between India, the Persian Gulf, and East Africa since the early 1840s and had overseen more than a few military campaigns, having served in the military in India and taken part in an expedition to place Bahrain under British protection in 1861.[38] The shifts that would take place in Muscat between 1868 and 1871 would not have been too unfamiliar. However, little could have prepared Pelly for the commercial shocks that would have followed and the demands they would have placed on him as a British officer.

With Al-Khalili and 'Azzan gone, Muscat returned to the sons of Sa'id. Turki, however, had walked into a political and financial mess. Even after he agreed to compensate Indian traders for their losses during 'Azzan's reign and the subsequent war, the Sultan's ability to exact any fines from his governors and the tribes involved was hamstrung "in consequence of the extreme weakness about this time of [his] government."[39] The war with 'Azzan had depleted Turki's coffers, and his inability to service his family's debts to Indian merchants or compensate them for their losses left him unable to farm out the customs house to raise public revenues as others had done in the past. Indeed, so desperate for money was Turki that the British Agent at Muscat reported that the port's merchants were contributing to a MTD 5,000 purse so that he could meet his administrative expenses.[40]

[36] Muhammad bin 'Abdullah bin Ḥumayd Al-Salimi, *Nahḍat Al-A'yān bi Ḥurriyat 'Umān* (Cairo, n.d.), 332, quoted in Wilkinson, *The Imamate Tradition of Oman*, 237.

[37] *Times of India* (May 11, 1871), 2. Wilkinson suggests that Way's suicide was related to the "nastiness" of Al-Khalili's death; Wilkinson, *The Imamate Tradition of Oman*, 237.

[38] "Pelly, Lewis," *Dictionary of National Biography, 1885–1900*, Vol. 44 (London: Smith, Elder & Co, 1895).

[39] Lorimer, *Gazetteer of the Persian Gulf, Oman and Central Arabia, Vol. 1 (Historical)*, 513–516.

[40] Goswami, *The Call of the Sea*, 110–111.

The cash-strapped Sultan of Muscat and the region's exhausted merchants also had to contend with occasional disturbances from 'Azzan's younger brother Ibrahim and Saleh bin 'Ali Al-Harthi, who had supported 'Azzan's government early on. Barely a year after Turki's return, Indian merchants in Sohar and Seeb began complaining that Ibrahim was extorting money from them, the Sohar merchants claiming losses of over MTD 2,200 and those of Seeb more than MTD 6,000.[41] And in 1874, Saleh bin 'Ali and his Al-Harthi tribesmen marched on the market town of Muttrah and occupied it, plundering Indian shops and causing losses of nearly MTD 5,000. Powerless to do anything to fight the Al-Harthis, Turki came to a compromise with Saleh and Ibrahim. In return for their agreement to accept his rule, Turki confirmed all of the property that 'Azzan had confiscated and given to Ibrahim, Saleh, and the Al-Harthi and Beni Ruwayh tribes, and agreed to restore all of the property that Al-Khalili had amassed to his heirs.[42] His actions, however, did little to shore up his precarious authority.

Commercially, matters were no better. Even before Al-Khalili and 'Azzan had taken Muscat, the Indian mercantile community was suffering from a commercial downturn in western India. The outbreak of the American Civil War in 1861, which cut off cotton supplies to English textile mills, had given a boost to Indian cotton production; between 1861 and 1865 metropolitan centers in western India (especially Bombay) witnessed an explosive growth in the number of cotton mills, accompanied by a rising speculation in land reclamation projects in the city. However, after the war ended and American cotton came back online, the Indian cotton boom turned into a bust, resulting in an endless string of business failures.[43] Indian merchants in Muscat and Zanzibar with ties to Bombay – merchants who dealt in the very piece goods that these mills produced – would have undoubtedly seen the failures of their business partners reverberate into their ledger books. Al-Khalili and 'Azzan's coup could not have been more poorly timed.

By the time the Indian mercantile community had recovered from the cotton market crash in the early 1870s, Muscat was back under the control of Sa'id's sons. However, the port's role as an entrepôt for goods moving between the Persian Gulf and Indian Ocean was facing serious challenges. The advent of the steamship, which called at the port but also made stops in Bandar 'Abbas, Bushire, and Basra, rendered it

[41] Goswami, *The Call of the Sea*, 111–112.

[42] Political Agent, Muscat, to Gulf Resident (February 6, 1874) MSA Political Department, Vol. 154, Comp. 530 (1874).

[43] Dwijendra Tripathi, *The Oxford History of Indian Business* (New Delhi: Oxford University Press, 2004), 100–110.

unnecessary for those looking for global consumer goods to purchase them from Muscat as they had in the past. Meanwhile, constant political intrigues from challengers in the interior injected geopolitical uncertainties into the commercial environment, threatening to drag the port city back into a security abyss.[44] Although merchants who stayed behind eventually benefited from a later boom in the date trade, commercial prospects during the late 1860s and early 1870s looked bleak at best, to say nothing of the dampened mood that years of political upheaval had created. In 1876, the Muscat customs yielded only MTD 110,000, less than half of what it had been during Sa'id's more prosperous reign.[45]

Economic conditions in East Africa worsened even more dramatically than in Muscat. In the decade following the booming 1860s, the clove and ivory trade went through a painful downturn. In Zanzibar, a global depression in agricultural prices after 1873 was delayed by another disaster: in 1872, a hurricane swept across the island and decimated its clove plantations, prompting a shift to clove and coconut production on the nearby island of Pemba.[46] The hurricane and subsequent drop in clove supply generated a brief spike in prices: in the immediate aftermath, the average price per *frasela* was around MTD 9; however, because of declining global demand clove prices cratered, with the price stabilizing at just over MTD 3 in the 1880s.[47] Although the downward trend in clove prices was most likely due to overproduction in Zanzibar and Pemba, a drop in global demand would have only further undermined prices.

The trade in ivory – a luxury good that would have been of marginal use in a depressed economy – faced a similar collapse in global demand. In Mombasa, the total volume of exports dropped from between 87,000 and 105,000 lbs in 1849, to less than half that in 1872, and all the way down to 25,000 lbs just a year later.[48] By 1874, attacks on Arab traders at Unyamwezi in the interior had entirely disrupted the caravan

[44] Landen, *Oman Since 1856*, 113–127.
[45] Landen, *Oman Since 1856*, 350.
[46] Sheriff, *Slaves, Spices*, 54, 234. Pemba cloves generally commanded less money on the market, too, since many of them arrived in Zanzibar wet from conditions of their transport.
[47] Cooper, *Plantation Slavery*, 131. Within the broader world economy, the year 1873 marked the beginning of a long period of depressed commerce that many historians have dubbed the Long Depression. During the third quarter of the nineteenth century, cut-throat competition and reduced profits, punctuated by the failure of key financial institutions in Europe and the United States, knocked back the sense of commercial optimism that had marked most of the century and gave way to trepidation. Giovanni Arrighi, *The Long Twentieth Century: Money, Power and the Origin of Our Times*, 2nd ed. (London: Verso, 2010), 176; Eric Wolf, *Europe and the People Without History* (Berkeley, CA: University of California Press, 1984), 311–313.
[48] Sheriff, *Slaves, Spices*, 171.

traffic: pleas from the Arabs of the interior to the Sultan in Zanzibar to send them "guns and ammunition and munitions, that [they] may be able to stand before the enemy" amounted to nothing. Strapped for cash because of the shocks to Zanzibar's plantation economy, the Sultan could not afford to assist them and declared "his fixed determination to leave the Arab colonists to fight their own battles."[49] The downward trade in ivory exports continued, compounded by a series of high taxes on goods coming in from the interior; exports reached a low of 17,500 lbs in 1887.[50]

The governments in Muscat and Zanzibar were unequipped to deal with the fallout and plummeting trade receipts that resulted from these crises. The sultans were able to personally intervene in high-profile cases or personal appeals from financiers close to them: Sultan Barghash was in some instances able to mediate between Lakmidas Ladha and his higher-profile debtors, and in other instances confirmed the transfer of pledged properties from defaulting debtors to their creditors in places under his jurisdiction.[51] Generally, however, they were unable to do much to help the hundreds of smaller lenders who did not have as close an association with the government. Faced with falling prices, outstanding debts that were looking more like defaults with every day that went by, and governments that were unable or unwilling to enforce their contracts, Indian merchants began to seek out a new overlord: the British consul.

By the time Pelly had reached the Persian Gulf, he had served in different judicial positions in Baroda, Sind, and Karachi for nearly ten years. Because of his experience in courts and consulates around the Western Indian Ocean, he would have known all too well that merchants who could successfully claim British protection would enjoy clear advantages in navigating the economic and political upheavals of the time. He was a part of the decision to dispatch warships to assist Indian merchants during the successive hostilities that marked the 1860s and 1870s in Oman, loading them and their goods onto the vessels and transporting

49 "Correspondence with British Representatives and Agents Abroad, and Reports from Naval Officers, Relating to the Slave Trade," *Accounts and Papers of the House of Commons, Vol. 70* (London: Harrison and Sons, 1876) 30–31.

50 Goswami, *Call of the Sea*, 144; Sheriff, *Slaves, Spices*, 171.

51 See ZNA AA 12/19, Deed 129 of 1877, which is a registered letter from Salim bin Sa'id Al-Harthi to Sultan Barghash regarding an arrangement he had come to with Lakmidas pertaining to an agreement to deliver 50,000 coconuts. The fact that it was addressed to Barghash, coupled with its registration at the British Consulate (presumably by Lakmidas or his clerk) suggests that Barghash may have had a role in mediating between the parties. In another registered letter, Barghash ordered the *liwali* of Pemba to hand over the *shamba* of a Matar bin Zayed to a *Bania* named Kisu; see ZNA AM 3/1, 183. See also Glassman, *Feasts and Riot*, 73–74, in which he points to the privileged access to state enforcement mechanisms that high-profile moneylenders enjoyed.

them to safer ports.[52] And he would have also known that merchants who suffered losses during the various raids and counter-raids often lodged their claims with the British Consul, who normally pressed the prevailing authority in Oman to compensate them for their pecuniary losses.[53]

He wasn't the first to deal with those sorts of claims. The summer before Pelly arrived in the Gulf, his predecessor Captain Felix Jones, described a recurring difficulty that officials in Muscat confronted while performing their consular duties. Members of Muscat's Indian trading communities had recently approached the British Consul there and, claiming to be British subjects, asked him to extend his protection to them and their property – the real property they owned, but also the outstanding debts that planters, middlemen, and merchants around the country owed them. The difficulty in extending protection to the merchants, however, was that the Indians "possess houses, temples, mosques, and lands in common, in some parts, and indeed so engrafted are all their business transactions with those of the aborigines of the soil, that to define or disentangle them, when controversy arises, is out of the question by a single British Authority."[54]

Pelly and others worried that indiscriminate declarations of jurisdiction over Indian merchants would open the floodgates to endless petitions, unnecessarily burdening the chronically under-staffed British Agencies in the region. When Pelly asked his assistant to comment on the possible extension of British jurisdiction in the Persian Gulf during the disturbances in Oman, the assistant expressed this anxiety in very explicit terms. He prefaced his long response by letting Pelly know that "on the Arab Coast much [of the Agency's] work is created by the very numerous petitions filed by Banyans [sic] for the recovery of sums they have lent out," and then launched into his tirade, which is worth quoting at length:

> "This is the 'modus operandi':- so soon as a Banyan has sucked his man dry, and still can show a balance in the books against him, he writes a petition to the Assistant Resident at Bassidore [Basidu, a British naval base off the coast of Persia], claiming so much against so and so, usually with a large margin in his favor, to allow of the claim being taxed without much damage to himself. This done, the petitioner feels he has nothing to do but wait, say two months, before he sends in another to say he awaits a reply to Petition No 1. No 1, when received, is as usual duly filed in the Assistant's office to be attended to in due

52 Lorimer, *Gazetteer of the Persian Gulf, Oman and Central Arabia, Vol. 1 (Historical)*, 477–478.

53 Lorimer, *Gazetteer of the Persian Gulf, Oman and Central Arabia, Vol. 1 (Historical)*, 501–516.

54 Political Resident, Persian Gulf, to Political Agent, Muscat (Bushire, March 23, 1860) MSA PD Vol 35, Comp. 181.

rotation. But meanwhile, disturbances – it matters not at what point of the Gulf – have required the Assistant's presence for some weeks. When he returns to his post, No. 2 petition has come in, on which, if the Assistant has worked up to this number on the file, he usually writes to the Petitioner to attend with his evidence &c. at some named port, and the case is regularly gone into. But, in very many cases, it is at this point that the Assistant's difficulties begin. The Banyan, having already twice petitioned, takes no further thought of his case, and fails to attend when called, saying to himself: "I have written twice to the Asst; next time I shall write to the Resident: the (Sirkar) Government's duty is to see I get my rights."

This scenario, he emphasized, was often the least frustrating. "There is another class of petition that may be classed as the 'frivolous and vexatious' where, after careful enquiry and expenditure of temper and patience the Petitioner is found to be absolutely without an atom of proof to adduce in support of his claim."[55] The assistant's views on legal strategies employed by Indians in the ports of the Western Indian Ocean at least in part reflected British experiences with the legal administration of India, where the stereotype of the litigious Indian had by the mid-nineteenth century become firmly entrenched in officials' imaginary.[56]

Those wanting to restrict the scope of British jurisdiction in the Indian Ocean were also concerned about relations with the region's rulers. In the earliest instructions that Pelly's predecessor sent to the Agent at Muscat regarding the protection of property owned by British subjects, he added an important caveat. "You must first satisfy yourself," he cautioned, "that parties seeking protection are really what they represent themselves to be, and that they are not seeking to impose on you for the purpose of defrauding the local authorities at Muscat."[57] He further pursued this theme in a dispatch to the Agent's successor, telling him that he "cannot indeed be too cautious in the exercise of protection, as we are not authorized to abrogate the rights of a Sovereign Prince over subjects who are *bona fide* his by law," adding that that "the more you can narrow the circle of British protection, the less likely you will be to come into vexatious collision."[58]

Officials in Bombay felt that any extra-territorial jurisdiction in the Indian Ocean had to be built upon an unassailable legal foundation – one that accorded with the treaties they had signed with local rulers

55 Assistant Resident, Persian Gulf, to Political Resident, Persian Gulf (October 20, 1870) MSA PD 1871 Vol. 91, Comp. 1481.

56 On this issue, see also Fraas, "They Have Travailled into a Wrong Latitude," 182–290; Bernard S. Cohn, "Some Notes on Law and Change in North India," *Economic Development and Cultural Change*, Vol. 8, No. 1 (Oct., 1959), 79–93.

57 Political Resident, Persian Gulf, to Native Agent, Muscat (June 22, 1856) MSA PD 1856 Vol. 93, Comp. 155.

58 Political Resident, Persian Gulf, to Political Agent, Muscat (March 23, 1860) MSA PD 1861 Vol. 33, Comp. 181.

and that reflected established principles of the law of nations. However, articulating a set of legal principles by which British officials could confidently claim jurisdiction over Indian merchants in the Persian Gulf, South Arabia, and East Africa was no easy task. The variegated character of the Indian communities in the Western Indian Ocean, the activities they engaged in, and the degree to which they were enmeshed in dense, cross-cutting webs of obligation and property posed unique problems for the Law Officers of Bombay – officers like Sir Michael Roberts Westropp, the Acting Advocate General of the Government of Bombay, who could only rely on established principles of jurisprudence and experiences of British officials in other parts of the Empire. Westropp had taken up his post in 1861, after spending more than fifteen years practicing law in Dublin.[59] His attempts to tailor the jurisprudence he had become so familiar with to the facts in places he had never seen required some legal gymnastics: namely, the construction of a legal fiction of Indian domicile predicated on a presumed permanent residence in India itself.

As a guiding principle, domicile was perhaps a little too vague to be of immediate use to British officials on the ground in Muscat and Zanzibar; it lacked the specificity they needed to make decisions on very particular sets of claims. In an attempt to pin down a useable definition, Westropp drew on a long list of jurists and philosophers of the law of nations – including Emerich de Vattel, Joseph Story, Eugene Pottier, Hugo Grotius, and Samuel von Puffendorf – and placed them in conversation with one another. After weighing different definitions against one another, Westropp decided that domicile was best defined as the place in which a person's "habitation is fixed, without any intention of removing therefrom," clarifying that "two things must come to constitute domicil [sic]: first, residence, and secondly, the intention of making it the home of the party."

To more directly address the situation of the Indians of Muscat, Westropp discussed at length the question of changing one's domicile, and the concomitant status change that it would imply. At the core of his discussion rested the notion of allegiance – specifically, whether emigration from one's country at a time of danger meant that one had effectively cast off allegiance to that sovereign. Although the jurists Westropp relied upon failed to give him a clear answer, he drew on a number of comparable cases from Great Britain to argue that when one country was conquered by another, a person was released from any allegiance to his former ruler; however, "if he be unwilling to become the subject of

[59] Hugh Montgomery-Massingberd, *Burke's Irish Family Records* (London, UK: Burkes Peerage Ltd, 1976), 1199.

the conqueror, and if he be willing totally to abandon his native country and to settle elsewhere, he is at liberty so to do, and to enter afresh into the social compact in the country to which he emigrates." A temporary absence did not suffice to constitute the act of abandonment necessary to have removed oneself from one jurisdiction to another.

For Westropp and others, the question of abandonment stood out as a key determinant of the jurisdictional status of Indians in Muscat – and, by extension, those in Zanzibar. The Indians at Muscat were thought to have come from Sind – a notion that was most likely only true for some of them, but which had important implications. Because the British had only annexed Sind to their Indian dominions in 1843, Indians who had migrated to Muscat following the conquest would have, following Westropp's logic, signified an unwillingness to be British subjects and so were subjects of the Sultan. Investigating when an Indian petitioner had actually left India for Muscat and whether they intended to do so permanently, however, would have been an administrative nightmare. Instead of dealing with these complications, Westropp sidestepped them altogether by stating unequivocally that if claimants "had not by their words or acts clearly signified at or about the time of the subjugation of Sind an intention then to abandon their Native Country finally in consequence of its subjugation… they ought to be regarded as British Subjects." He finished off his lengthy opinion on the subject by adding, almost as an afterthought – but one that carried tremendous consequences – that "the immediate families of such men (wives, children, and grandchildren) should also… be so regarded [as British subjects]."[60]

Put simply, Westropp's opinion, which served as the basis for British policy on extraterritorial jurisdiction for the next two decades, was that any Indian who wanted to claim British protection only had to assure the Consul that they, their husband, their father, or their grandfather had never intended to leave Sind or any other part of British India and permanently settle in Muscat, or establish domicile there, and that they maintained a residence in British India. Effectively, the policy aimed to take Indian merchants living in ports where British officials had only limited jurisdiction and anchor them in parts of India where British jurisdiction was uncontested, thereby establishing unassailable grounds for its exercise in places like South Arabia and East Africa.

The idea that "domicile" could act as a guiding principle in parsing out claims to British subjecthood, however, quickly ran into obstacles, since it rested on flawed assumptions regarding the nature of the Indian

[60] Opinion of M.R. Westropp, Acting Advocate General (Forwarded on October 17, 1861), MSA PD 1861 Vol. 33, Comp. 181.

mercantile presence in the Indian Ocean. Theoretically, British consular agents could distinguish between permanently settled Indians in Muscat and mercantile sojourners. But whether a merchant kept a residence in British India did not really furnish a clear indicator of one's political status or identity. Mercantile families in the Indian Ocean were rarely, if ever, isolated units. In fact, individual merchants typically belonged to a much broader familial firm with relatives and assets spread over a wide geographic area. The most influential Indian mercantile families in Muscat and Zanzibar would have been more likely to have family and property in India – or, to be more precise, access to a network of people and property from which they could draw the resources necessary to finance economic activity. Any one branch of an Indian firm would thus have held titles to properties in a range of different places around the Western Indian Ocean – not least of all in India itself.

It did not take long for the Indian mercantile communities of Muscat and Zanzibar to identify the gaps in the emerging British policy on jurisdiction and take advantage of them. Almost immediately after Westropp issued his opinion, the Political Resident wrote to the Government of Bombay that in Muscat "the domiciled [Indians], when in difficulties, having a general knowledge only of international law, deem themselves to have the same privileges in respect to protection as the undomiciled of their race. They have heard of the government Resolution in favor of Hydrabadees and Sindians [sic] in general and at their convenience interpret it as they please, unmindful of the allegiance they owe to the ruler of the place of their domiciliation; unmindful in short of everything save their own individual interests."[61]

As the situation in Oman and East Africa worsened over the next decade, officials in Muscat and other ports in the Indian Ocean had to contend with countless claims to British protection, many of which were put forward by applicants who claimed that they met any combination of the different criteria for British subjecthood. In one claim put forward in 1871, towards the end of 'Azzan's reign in Muscat, six Khoja Indians successfully claimed that their fathers or their grandfathers were born in and owned property in British India or a British-protected state. Moreover, although all of them owned homes in Muscat, they claimed that they frequently moved between India and the Gulf. The Agent, however, expressed some doubts, as "their residence from its character and length of time has been such as constitutes domicile," but suspected

[61] Political Resident, Persian Gulf, to the Acting Secretary to the Government of Bombay (September 16, 1861) MSA PD 1861 Vol. 33, Comp. 181.

himself of applying incorrectly.[62] And in his letter to the Agent, Lewis Pelly, who had brought up the issue of jurisdiction years earlier, could only fall back on general instructions and the injunction to dispense a general kind of justice: "every case of claim for national protection," he relented, "would require to be decided on its merits, after enquiry."[63]

British policy on how to define a British subject and how to correctly apply the principle of domicile never achieved much clarity. There was no legal bright line separating British Indians from Indians owing allegiance to the Sultan. In the 1870s Indian Ocean, even after a series of petitions and decisions, the principle remained ambiguous. And as time went on, claims to British protection only multiplied, growing to include Arabs and Persians as well as Indians. That members of all of these communities could claim some sort of residence in India, either personally or by proxy through their fathers or grandfathers, created a jurisdictional nightmare for British officials, who had increasingly viewed themselves as having little choice but to admit their claims as meeting the ill-defined requirements for protection.[64] Deep into the late nineteenth century, then, the jurisdictional arena in the Western Indian Ocean remained wide open.

By the time the scope British jurisdiction had unfurled to include savvy Indians and other self-proclaimed subjects of the Raj in the Persian Gulf, South Arabia, and East Africa, Westropp had moved on from the position of Acting Advocate General and had become one of the Chief Justices at the High Court of Bombay. From his new position, Westropp still had to contend with issues of British jurisdiction around the Western Indian Ocean, but from an altogether new perspective. As a member of the High Court's bench during the 1870s and early 1880s, Westropp heard appeals from British consular courts around the region; an expanding jurisdiction, then, would have directly affected the volume and scope of cases that came to his attention.

On the ground, however, discussions of British jurisdiction and British Indian personhood had to cope with ongoing petitions from merchants around the Western Indian Ocean, who gradually accumulated a much clearer understanding of British jurisdictional policy than the officials themselves did. Indeed, throughout this period, traders continued to play on the ambiguity surrounding British jurisdiction in the region, tugging at the corners until they were able to enrobe themselves in the protection

[62] Acting Political Agent, Muscat, to Political Resident, Persian Gulf (January 16, 1871) MSA PD 1861 Vol. 33, Comp. 181.

[63] Political Resident, Persian Gulf, to Acting Political Agent, Muscat (January 28, 1871) MSA PD 1861 Vol. 33, Comp. 181.

[64] Bishara, "A Sea of Debt," 214–276.

of the Raj. For some, inclusion within the pale of British India's growing extraterritorial empire had by the late 1870s become *fait accompli.* In East Africa, the Sultan gradually ceded jurisdiction over those who were subjects of different British-protected Native Princes in India to British officials by 1870; in Muscat, this happened six years later.[65] Thus, by the end of the 1870s a sound legal basis for British extra-territorial jurisdiction in the Western Indian Ocean had worked itself out in practice, if not in theory.

Those who were able to convince British consuls that their claims to protection were valid acted quickly. An Indian merchant could walk into a British Consulate in Muscat, Zanzibar, or anywhere else, and register whatever *waraqas* he might have in the hopes of establishing his claims and, most likely, call on the Consul to enforce them sometime down the road. And over the course of the 1870s, Indian merchants registered their *waraqas* at the British consulate in droves, drawing British officials into their disputes with their Arab debtors and with one another. In doing so, they slowly paved the way for British India's legal expansion into South Arabia and East Africa. By 1881, the Political Agent in Zanzibar could remark to his superiors in India that "there can be no doubt the real source of our paramount influence here is the hold we have kept over immigrants from India in whose hands the trade of the mainland rests, and to whom half the property in this island is hypothecated."[66]

[65] Sheriff, *Slaves, Spices*, 202–208; Aitchison, *Treaties*, 109. For other communities, such as Arabs and Persians, the question remained open, and the strategies looked familiar. Petitioners from Persia continued to approach British officials for commercial protection, alternatively claiming domicile, naturalization or birth in British India. MSA PD 1884 Vol. 161, Comp. 1205.

[66] Political Agent, Zanzibar to the Secretary to the Government of India, Foreign Department (March 6, 1881) MSA PD 1881, Vol. 217, Comp. 61.

4 Translating Transactions

On the morning of November 27, 1877, the Khoja Indian merchant Rehmetullah Haima walked into the British Consulate, with five *waraqas* in hand. The *waraqas* recorded transactions between him and five different debtors, all during the months of September and October of 1860, over sixteen years earlier. There was good reason for Haima to choose to register his *waraqas* – there was a lot of money involved. Individually, the *waraqas* acknowledged debts of anywhere between MTD 570 and MTD 4,900, promising deliveries of ivory of between 7 *frasilas* (or about 250 lbs) and 37.5 *frasilas* (nearly 1,350 lbs). In total, over the span of just one month, Haima had lent out over MTD 12,200 – the price of nearly three large plantations – to caravan leaders who had promised to bring back just over 3,000 lbs of ivory![1]

As he entered the building, Haima would have encountered the consular clerk, Mancherji Pestonji Talati, a Parsi who had only recently arrived on the island to take up work in the consulate. By the time Talati had made it to Zanzibar, Parsis like him were already well-entrenched in the legal bureaucracy in India, where they worked as lawyers, judges, clerks, and other legal personnel. A number made their way to British colonies around the Indian Ocean – particularly to Rangoon, where British courts had been in operation since the 1850s.[2] Zanzibar, however, was different. There, the British Consulate worked within a juridical landscape that consisted of a range of different authorities, all of whom had established bureaucratic cultures and paper technologies. Talati's acceptance and registration of Haima's *waraqas* constituted one of the many points of contact between the consulate and the legal world around it – a world that becomes visible through the *waraqa*.

As the heady optimism that characterized the first two-thirds of the nineteenth century turned into frustration or outright despair during the late 1860s and 1870s, and as hundreds of Indian merchants in Muscat

[1] ZNA AM 3/1, 87–89.
[2] Sharafi, *Law and Identity in Colonial South Asia.*

and Zanzibar rushed to the consulate to register themselves as subjects of the Raj, a slow sea change began taking place in the legal administration of commerce in the region. Recognizing the protections that British Indian law might afford them, Indian merchants took their *waraqas* to the consulates and began registering them in droves, bringing in several at a time. Their actions unwittingly set into motion a long process of imperial legal expansion into South Asia and East Africa, spurring on a prolonged encounter between the expanding British Indian imperial legal regime and the Islamicate contractual cultures of the Western Indian Ocean.

Situated at the center of the enormous commercial and legal transformations that were sweeping the Indian Ocean, the consular registry into which actors like Talati copied *waraqas* emerged as a bureaucratic, legal, and economic genre of its own – a veritable grab bag of different contracts and declarations that reflected the diversity of people, organizations, and practices that animated the commercial economy of the Western Indian Ocean. In it, one sees contracts written in English, in Arabic, and in Gujarati; declarations, *iqrārs*, *khiyār* sales, Indian mortgages, British sales contracts, hire contracts, and more sitting side by side. In its repetitiveness, the registry comes across as an ordinary – even unremarkable – site of colonial legal administration.

At the same time, however, the registry emerges a site of legal encounters – of the interpretations and translations that came to characterize the early British legal administration in Muscat and East Africa, and the competing economic and legal epistemologies that underpinned each.[3] As merchants had their *waraqas* copied into the consular registry, consular clerks carefully – or casually? – annotated them, giving them a defined status in an Anglo-Indian system of legal and commercial instruments. The annotation seemed simple enough: the clerk noted the parties' names, the amount transacted, and the type of transaction the *waraqa* involved. The act of annotation, however, signaled far more than its brevity suggested; through it, the clerks initiated a long process whereby members of an Anglo-Indian legal bureaucracy grappled with the maneuverings, ontologies, and discourses that underpinned commerce in the region – and, more broadly, the actors and personnel that gave it shape.

At the foundation of the process of annotation lay a fundamental problem: how to take a set of categories from one legal culture and translate

[3] A caveat is in order here: because there do not exist any consular registries from Muscat, the discussion here must necessarily be restricted to Zanzibar.

them so as to become legible to an altogether different one.[4] Here, every act of decoding became one of encoding at the same time. As Talati recorded hundreds of *waraqas* into the registry, he had to search for terminology that would help him accurately reflect who the parties to the contract were, and what sort of transaction they might have understood themselves as entering into. The process of transcribing *waraqas* into consular registries required him to engage in a series of subtle translations and annotations, ultimately transforming it from a piece of paper into a registered legal document that could be called upon in court. And as he copied it into the registry, the tensions between the transcribed text of the *waraqa* itself and the markings that rendered it comprehensible to an Anglo-Indian legal bureaucracy emerged forcefully.

The process by which clerks, but also judges – and later, lawyers – grappled with the *waraqas* and the terminologies, epistemologies, texts, and actors they drew on to make sense of them reveal the anxieties, uncertainties, and uneasy translations that characterized the early Anglo-Indian imperial legal enterprise in East Africa. Faced with a body of subjects whose daily transactions enmeshed them in a series of legal disputes, British officials in East Africa were forced to rely on the assistance of other juridical actors in the region. In determining the substance of the law and the procedures by which it ought to be applied, they turned to Indian merchants, Muslim *qadis*, *kātibs*, governors, and Indian lawyers, all of whom helped shape the legal contours of British India's newest frontier, while also drawing on their own legal lexicon to make sense of the world around them.

Hedging Bets, Crafting Narratives

Rehmetulla Haima may have been exceptional in the number of *waraqas* that he registered in a single day and the amounts that he had loaned out through them, but he was hardly alone in hoping to get his sixteen-year-old transactions recognized by the consulate. Over the course of the late 1860s and 1870s, merchants registered thousands of *waraqas*, precipitating a long process through which litigants, clerks, judges, and others shaped the document's meaning. Their movement between the pieces of paper that the *kātib* produced and the pages of the consular registry suggested a sharp legal consciousness on their part, and a keen sense of what strategies might best suit their objectives.

[4] For a useful perspective on this phenomenon in Southeast Asia, see Michael Gilsenan, "Translating Colonial Fortunes: Dilemmas of Inheritance in Muslim and English Laws across a Nineteenth-Century Diaspora," *Comparative Studies of South Asia, Africa, and the Middle East*, Vol. 31, No. 2 (2011): 355–371.

Like Haima, on any given day an Indian merchant might walk into the consulate and register any number of *waraqas*, all from different dates. In September of 1867, for example, the merchant Khalfan Lalji simultaneously registered seven different *waraqas* covering a twelve-year span beginning in 1855.[5] Six years later, Ramdas Jeta registered six different *waraqas*: the oldest was a decade old and the most recent only two weeks old.[6] In just one morning in November 1877, Lakmidas Ladha, the customs master's agent, registered eighteen different *waraqas*, each between one and three years old. And in one particularly interesting example, the moneylender Megji Anandji registered an entire ledger book in 1897, containing no fewer than 600 *waraqas* issued over the previous two years.[7]

Sometimes, members of the same firm registered *waraqas* that did not belong to them personally, but belonged to members of their firm. On September 27, 1877, for example, the clerk to Jairam Sewji's firm – now run by Lakmidas Ladha – registered eleven different *waraqas*. The *waraqas*, spanning the twenty-year period between July 1857 and February 1877, were made out to different members of the firm: Jairam Sewji (who had passed away ten years earlier), Ladha Dhamji (who had died five years earlier), Wala Bhanji, and Lakmidas Ladha.[8] The clerk did the same less than a month later, registering twenty *waraqas* from between 1842 and 1875, made out to seven different members of the firm – the *sirkār*, as the *waraqas* identified it.[9] Scores of other merchants employed similar tactics, some with *waraqas* almost twenty-five years old.

The consular registries themselves immediately attest to the importance of registering a *waraqa* for a court case. As *waraqas* made it into the consular registry, the clerk assigned them a number – "No. 209 of 1877" or "No. 310 of 1879," for example – making them reference-ready in the context of a dispute in court. And there was good reason to register them: notices in 1865 from both the British Consul and the Sultan made it clear that anyone entering into a pledge (*rahn*) or *khiyār* sale contract (referred to as a sale "where the property sold is not actually taken possession of by the purchaser") would have to register their *waraqas* at the Consulate if they wanted to base any legal claims on them; four days later, the Consul established the first official deed registry.[10] The preamble to an 1881 Order in Council confirmed the registered *waraqa's*

[5] ZNA AM 1/1, 36–39.
[6] ZNA AM 1/1, 189–92.
[7] ZNA AM 1/5.
[8] ZNA AM 3/1, 1–7. Later entries refer to the clerk as "Abdulkadir Bohra" or "Abdulkadir, the writer of Jairam Sewji."
[9] ZNA AM 3/1, 9–19.
[10] Notifications in Arabic and English (July 10, 1865) ZNA AM 2/13, 1–2. I am grateful to Hollian Wint for bringing these to my attention. See also ZNA AA 3/22, 1–2.

status in litigation, announcing that British Consular offices would not consider any instrument relating to property as evidence of the transaction being disputed unless one of the parties had registered it at the Consulate.[11] Paper or writing on its own was not enough to make claims about a commercial relationship; only registered writing met the evidentiary requirements of the British court.

The strategies they employed in registering their *waraqas* testified to the merchants' legal savvy. Recognizing the advantages that registering their transactions with the British consulate could yield, they moved quickly to shape the written record – perhaps with an eye down the road to whatever legal proceedings might grow out of it. It is difficult to tell whether they learned this strategy from partners in India, where British courts had long been established, or from their own past court experiences. What their actions suggest, however, is that they quickly perceived the difference between a registered *waraqa* and an unregistered one. In the *shambas* or out in the ivory corridors that linked Zanzibar to the Congo, a registered *waraqa* may not have meant any more than any other. However, in a courtroom, it meant the difference between a successful claim and an unsuccessful one. And as the commercial setbacks of the early 1870s sent waves throughout the mercantile communities of East Africa and South Arabia, a courtroom victory or loss could mean the difference between surviving a short-term shock or drowning under a swelling tidal wave of bankruptcies.

But the act of registering a *waraqa* meant more than supporting a successful claim in a courtroom. In registering multiple transactions, separated by decades or by a single instant, merchants were actively intervening in and shaping a written record that they would have immediately recognized as being "official." Compared to the loose *waraqas* they carried around in their pockets or stored away in their offices – *waraqas* that constituted snapshots of one dimension of an agreement at a particular moment in time – registration gave them the opportunity to craft an official narrative of an ongoing commercial relationship, documenting the property rights they secured at every step.[12]

To take just one example: on one day in mid-December 1878, the Khoja moneylender Pirbhai Jivanji registered three different *waraqas* from the same debtor at the consulate: an *iqrār* for MTD 5,750 for one year beginning mid-March 1878, a *khiyār* sale of a *shamba* in Pemba

[11] "Rules respecting the Registration of Non-Testamentary Instruments under The Zanzibar Order in Council, 1881 [Approved by the Secretary of State for Foreign Affairs, November 28, 1893]." I am thankful to Mitch Fraas for bringing this document to my attention.

[12] For more on this sort of strategy, see Trivellato, *Familiarity of Strangers*, 160–161.

for three years for MTD 10,000 in late May of the same year, and a rental (*qu'd*) agreement by the debtor for MTD 1,500 a year for the same *shamba* on the same day as the *khiyār* sale (see Chapter 6). By registering his *waraqas*, Jivanji was doing more than hedging bets against a future default, which he would have seen many of in the mercantile community around him.[13] The three *waraqas* were effectively all part of the same agreement: the debtor, 'Abdullah bin Jaber Al-Rajebi, had borrowed a total of MTD 15,750 and agreed to pay back MTD 4,500 in interest over the life of the loan – a rate of 9.5 percent interest per annum – in addition to whatever yield he had assigned in the interim. However, in his simultaneous registration of the three agreements as separate transactions, Jivanji disaggregated the exchange, raising the possibility that he might make individual claims based on single transactions rather than as part of the more multi-dimensional relationship that others would have likely understood it to be.

Interruptions in that narrative also left their imprint. When the resolution of a dispute nullified a *waraqa* and its contents, the dissolved bond between lender and borrower sometimes left its mark on its copy in the registry. In one case, a *rahn* of a property by Saif bin Salim Al-Harthi to Purshottam Chatterbhaji was struck out, the clerk explaining that "this is cancelled, the deed never having been satisfied, and has accordingly been destroyed."[14] In another instance, a line was drawn through a rental agreement between Mohammed Al-Barwani and the British merchant Archibald Smith, with a note that the agreement had been cancelled due to another, more recent deed.[15] At times, the consulate's copyist stopped transcribing a *waraqa* halfway through because the debt had been paid: in one instance, the clerk noted that a half-copied *waraqa* "was a deed for acknowledging a debt of $40, and as the said debt was paid during the writing of the above and the Sultan's signature was wanting, the deed was not signed [by the Consul, after registration]."[16] Cancellations like these attested to the evidentiary weight of a *waraqa*, or at least the perception that it might have implications for future disputes.

Waraqa registration, then, wasn't only about registering deeds at a consulate. In the act of registration lay an unarticulated legal consciousness – a cognizance of what the downstream implications of registration might be, and of how to craft a particular narrative out of a set of utterances. If the *waraqa* was a space for experimentation with different contractual

[13] ZNA AM 3/1, 340–341.
[14] ZNA AA 12/19, Deed 542 of 1876.
[15] ZNA AA 12/19, Deed 517 of 1875, referencing Deed 527 of 1875.
[16] ZNA AA 12/19, Deed 141 of 1877. The note itself uses "$" rather than MTD, which I use throughout this book.

forms, and the *fatwa* a medium through which those experiments were given confirmation, then the registry was an alternative medium – one in which *waraqas* could be arranged or disaggregated into different sorts of transactions. By registering their *waraqas*, merchants were crafting a secondary narrative out of *waraqas* – one that projected and confirmed their own version of events at a time when commercial optimism had soured into fear, and open hands had turned into closed fists.

But the merchants were not the only ones intervening in the record. In the process of registering their *waraqas*, they were engaging in a silent dialogue with another actor – one who was just as actively intervening in the court's archive: the consular clerk. As he received the *waraqas* and transcribed them into the registry, the clerk shaped meanings, encounters, and ultimately outcomes. And by shaping the archival foundation on which the consular court was built, the clerk, along with merchants who registered their *waraqas*, established the registry as one of earliest sites of legal encounter in East Africa, and perhaps in South Arabia as well.

Clerical Consciousness

For Talati and other clerks, the different approaches to registering *waraqas* at the Consulate and the different sorts of contracts they had to contend with meant a significant amount of work. And yet, we know too little about them. In many ways, clerks were like *kātibs* – simultaneously everywhere and nowhere, rarely leaving their name on the written record while spilling their ink on nearly every document in the archive. They were faceless bureaucrats, overshadowed by judges and consuls but crucial to the functioning of the nascent British Indian legal administration in the Western Indian Ocean. In fact, were it not for two of them leaving their names at the bottom of a handful of registered deeds out of thousands, we would hardly even suspect they ever existed.

But their names are there, recorded so casually that one might easily overlook them: "Mancherji Pestonji," on contracts registered in his presence in Zanzibar in August and September of 1878, and "Bamanji Dhunjibhoy," on another contract in November of that year.[17] There was also a third, a Hormusji Nouroji, and there was some indication that the three might have been related. Decades later, the outgoing Political Agent and Consul General at Zanzibar remembered them fondly: "There are three names that I can never forget," he declared to the official gazette

[17] ZNA AM 3/1, 280, 285–286, 320–321. One historian has suggested the first clerk to arrive was "Mancherji P. Talati," who arrived in 1875–1878; John R. Hinnells, *The Zoroastrian Diaspora: Religion and Migration* (Oxford, UK: Oxford University Press, 2005), 267.

upon his departure in October 1908. "Bomanji Dhunjibhoy Talati, Mancherji Pestonji Talati and Hormusji Nouroji Talati – for how much the name of Talati stands in Zanzibar – men who have held in turn the post of Head Clerk at His Majesty's Agency and Consulate General, as loyal and faithful public servants as could be found anywhere."[18] It is difficult to tell what the extent of the Talatis' relationship to one another might have been – whether they were cousins or brothers, or simply members of the same occupational group.[19]

The work that the Talatis did might be considered almost mechanical and banal were it not so revealing about the nature of the British encounter with East Africa's contractual culture. Upon receiving a *waraqa* to be registered, the Talatis (or perhaps someone else) copied it into the registry, assigned it a number, and then briefly annotated it with the parties' names, the debt amount, and a one or two word description of the nature of the contract. And they did this over and over again, to the point where it seems so routine as to not even be worth noticing. And yet it is through their annotations that we come to know them the best.

When they entered *waraqas* into the registry, the Talatis described them using terms that they were most familiar with – terms that they might have learned from having worked as court clerks in India or other legal work that they might have done. In the process of annotating them – of coding them in a legal language other than that which they had been written in – they hoped to render the *waraqas* legible to an Anglo-Indian system of law. What they ended up doing, however, was unwittingly generating the first epistemological encounter between the two systems of contracting that characterized the two distinct Indian Ocean empires – the Islamicate Omani and the Anglo-Indian. The clerks actively translated between the two, setting into motion a long process whereby one lexicon of personhood and property rights slowly sought to come to terms with another.

The Talatis thought of law in comparative terms. When it came to describing the contracts around them, they scrambled to find appropriate terminology. Faced with the most basic of the transactions – the *iqrār*, the basic acknowledgment of obligation, in which one party acknowledged that he owed another a sum of money or a delivery of goods – the clerks grasped for terms that could approximate the transaction. Depending on who was annotating the *waraqa*, the *iqrār* became a "deed of debt," an "owing deed,"

18 Reported in *The Gazette for Zanzibar & East Africa* (October 28, 1908), quoted in Hinnells, *The Zoroastrian Diaspora*: 272.

19 The title "Talati" referred to the position of village accountant in Northwest India. Vinayak Chaturvedi, *Peasant Pasts: History and Memory in Western India* (Berkeley, CA: University of California Press, 2007), 40.

or a "bond." Their efforts to find an accurate term to describe the *iqrār* suggest that they were at least somewhat familiar with the complexities of debt and obligation in the region – and perhaps they ought to have been, when considering that they had arrived in Zanzibar from India, where similar debt relations were commonplace, and that they kept company with the island's Indian community and would have been familiar with their ways of doing business. The terminology they used was hardly legal – "deeds of debt" and "owing deeds" were not, strictly speaking, established categories for instruments in British India – but they did reflect the Talatis' attempts to translate *iqrārs* into terms legible to the court.

If the range of terms they deployed in describing the *iqrār* at least attempted to approximate its multi-dimensional nature, when it came to transactions involving property, which formed the bulk of registered *waraqas*, the Talatis picked decidedly less robust terms, choosing instead to code them as legal contracts. The *rahn*, for example – a pledge of land against a debt – invariably came to be annotated as a "mortgage." Thus, to take just one example of many, when one Indian merchant came to the consulate in October 1878 to register a month-old *waraqa* issued to him by another who pledged his house as a *rahn* against a debt of MTD 224 due in a year, one of the Talatis (it is unclear who) annotated the *waraqa* as a "Deed of Mortgage of a House at Tanga for $224 for 12 months."[20] Though barely noticeable, the slippage was telling: a *rahn* was not a mortgage, and in fact, no equivalent to the mortgage existed in the lexicon of Islamic commercial contracting – a point that different litigants would raise in British courts later on (see Chapter 6).

The most curious of all, however, was the category of "time sale," which they used to describe the *khiyār* sale, which by the 1870s had become significantly widespread in South Arabia and East Africa. Not only was the *khiyār* sale not a time sale, it is unclear what the term itself might have alluded to, or where it might have come from. The Talatis took pains to distinguish the *khiyār* sale from a *qaṭʿ* sale, which they described using the more straightforward term "sale" or "complete sale," but one does not get a sense of how a "time sale" might have been understood in a British legal episteme. Nowhere in the record does anyone describe the "time sale," and there are no references to time sales in works on English or British Indian law.[21] And in at least one moment a clerk recorded a *khiyār* sale using the label "Mortgage (Time Sale)," pointing to the

[20] ZNA AM 3/1, 302.

[21] In one 1834 report on the sale of corn (wheat), the authors assert that "Time-sale is a term applied to purchasing a quantity of grain deliverable at a certain period; at the expiration of a month; then if not delivered, whatever the difference of price is in the

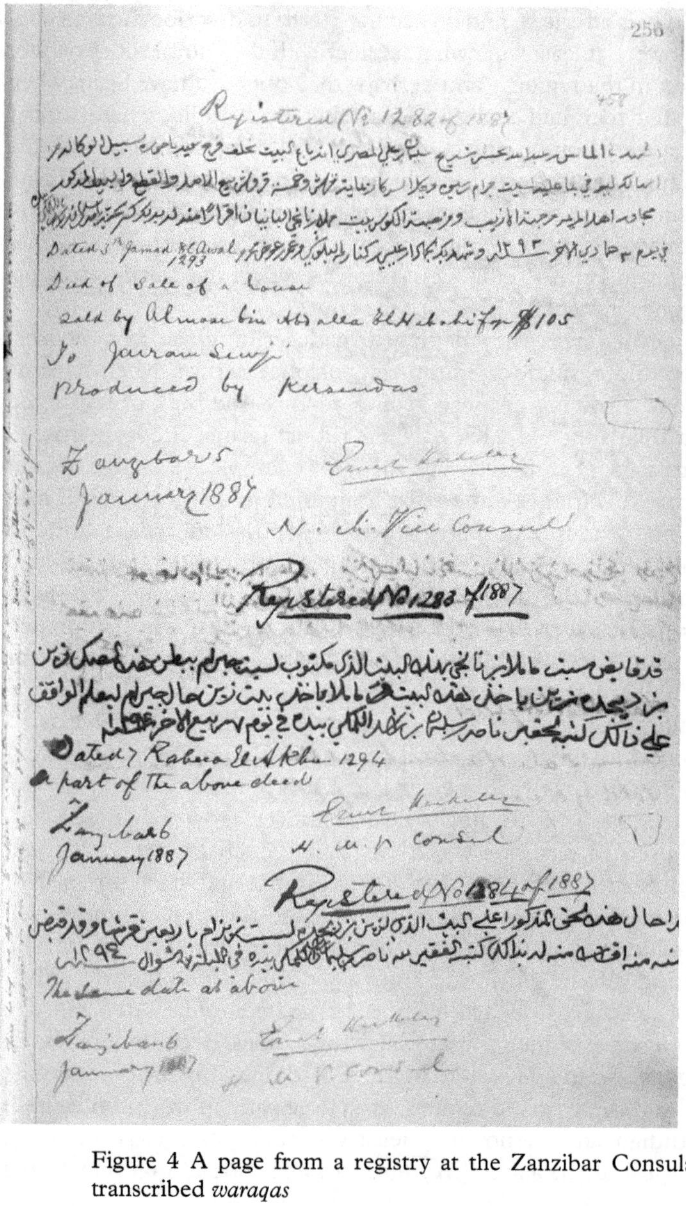
Registered No 1282 of 1887

Dated 3rd Jamad El Awal 1293

Deed of Sale of a house

sold by Almaas bin Abdalla El Habshi for $105

To Jairam Sewji

Produced by Kersandas

Zanzibar 5 January 1887

H. M. Vice Consul

Registered No 1283 of 1887

Dated 7 Rabeea El Akhar 1294

A part of the above deed

Zanzibar 6 January 1887

H. M. V. Consul

Registered No 1284 of 1887

The same date as above

Zanzibar 6 January 1887

Figure 4 A page from a registry at the Zanzibar Consulate showing transcribed *waraqas*

precarious boundaries between different forms of contracting that he was trying to erect.[22]

The lack of clarity surrounding the "time sale" might have been related to the Talatis' inability to fully comprehend practices associated with the *khiyār* sale. On the inside cover of one of the registers, someone – either one of the clerks or the British Consul – wrote a brief description of what he understood to be the *khiyār* sale: "AB has sold the house to CD for $1000 for the period of one year bai khiyar [sic] to him and his heirs; CD then executes another deed, renting the same house to AB for $100 per year."[23] The note more accurately described a combination contract of a *khiyār* sale and *qu'd* (rental) agreement, which was only one of a handful forms the *khiyār* could potentially take, the more common being an assignment of yield, which required no additional agreement. Moreover, the fact that the writer used the term "bai khiyar" – that they chose to *transliterate* the term rather than *translate* it – suggested the challenges the staff at the Consulate faced in making sense of the documents before them.

Just as they struggled to translate the variety of contracts they saw before them, the Talatis also had to grapple with the types of *people* that were entering into contracts, sometimes with important implications. In the dozens of *waraqas* involving parties of a current or former servile status, the clerks transposed a vocabulary borrowed mostly from their British employers. Thus, when a *waraqa* identified its protagonist as a *khādim* – a term that could denote a broad range of different forms of servility – the clerks annotated it as "slave," a particular sort of legal person with a particular status in Anglo-Indian law.[24] At other times, they translated it into "follower," a term which better approximated the *khādim's* status, but signaled that the clerk struggled to translate the category.[25] Similarly, the two terms *'atiq* and *sarih* were translated into the decidedly less textured term "freedman," which itself had legal implications for how the actor's personhood might have been understood – an understanding that not always mapped itself very neatly onto the commercial and legal realities of life in Zanzibar.[26]

market, of course it must be made good." *Report from the Select Committee on the Sale of Corn: With the Minutes of Evidence, Appendix, and Index* (House of Commons, July 25, 1834), 80.

22 ZNA AA 12/19, Deed 154 of 1877.

23 ZNA AM 1/1, 1.

24 See, for example, ZNA AM 3/1, 8.

25 ZNA AM 3/1, 142.

26 See, for example, ZNA AM 3/1, 16. For a fuller treatment of the law and practice of slavery in English colonies, see Alan Watson, *Slave Law in the Americas* (University of Georgia Press, 1989), 63–82.

Clerks like the Talatis did not necessarily fundamentally misunderstand the world of contracting that was taking place around them; rather, they struggled to translate the changing world of contracting that they confronted into terms that they might have understood to be more legible in a British court of law: a "slave," a "freedman," a "bond," a "debt deed," a "mortgage," or even a "time sale." Like their counterparts in Islamicate legal cultures, the *kātibs*, clerks sought to clothe people and practices around him in the garb of what they understood to be established categories of commercial contracting. They sought to extend an Anglo-Indian legal lexicon to the changing forms of contracting that were taking place around them, rendering them legible and comprehensible within an Anglo-Indian legal episteme.

But none of this should suggest that they did all of the work on their own. Indeed, the Talatis seemed to know the people around them fairly well. The shorthand they often used to describe those that came in to register *waraqas*, or parties to the *waraqa*, suggests a familiarity with those around them and their occupations. When a merchant registered a *waraqa* involving the daughter of Hamad bin Sa'id, they recorded her as "the daughter of Hamad, the old vazeer [sic]."[27] At another time, a party identified by the *kātib* as 'Ali bin Saleh Al-Shīʿī (the Shi'ite) was identified by the Talatis as "Ali bin Saleh El-Bahrani, the Interpreter," suggesting that they knew him in a more professional capacity.[28] And when they copied *waraqas* involving members of Jairam's firm into the register, they frequently identified the person presenting the *waraqa* as "Abdulkadir" or "Abdoolkadir Bohra, the writer of Jairam Sewji," or simply "Abdulkadir, their writer," all of which indicated that they had so many interactions with the man – and, indeed, he seemed to be a frequent visitor to the consulate – that they hardly needed to describe him in any detail.[29]

The fact that the Talatis were familiar with those who lived and worked in the small island is unsurprising, but is nonetheless revealing about the personal nature of the nascent British legal bureaucracy in East Africa. Though the official markings on a registered *waraqa* – its neat copy, and the number it was assigned – suggested distance and formality, the moments in which the clerks identified the people around them by using familiar language breaches that image, replacing it with a more intimate picture – one of a consulate embedded in a small society of merchants, shopkeepers, *kātibs*, and government officials. In part, it attests to the

27 ZNA AM 3/1, 14.

28 ZNA AM 3/2, 61. Ali bin Saleh was most likely the British consulate's Arabic interpreter; see "Misc. Papers: Arabic and English Translations by Ali bin Saleh," ZNA AA 5/3.

29 See, for example, ZNA AM 3/2, 66, 70, 77.

degree to which legal administration on the island was dependent on other actors, all of whom could be called on for pronouncements of law, statements on the meaning of documents, and clarification of different transactions.

There was nothing inherently problematic about the ways in which the Talatis chose to represent the actors and transactions they saw in the *waraqas*. Whether one called the practice of pawning land against a loan with a temporary assignment of harvest a *bayʿ khiyār* or a time sale or even a mortgage wasn't itself the problem. Both were simply labels – signs that existed in equal distance from their referents. The problem lay in the context – in the ability of the contracting parties and others to call attention to what they might have perceived to be the mismatch between the sign (i.e. the contractual category) and its referent (i.e. the practice), or to make claims that the contract signaled something else altogether.

And herein lay the difference between the clerk at the consulate and the *kātib*. Whereas the *kātib* would have seen the *waraqa* as an accounting device – a snapshot of a broader relationship, and an instrument that enabled a variety of commercial relationships to come into being – the clerk would have seen it differently. Through the act of recording it into the register, assigning it a number, listing the parties to the transaction, and annotating the *waraqa's* details, the clerk hoped to create a document that could constitute evidence in litigation. The act of translation, then – the movement from the space of the *waraqa* to that of the register, and the accompanying translations of names, practices, and transposition of dates – altered the instrument's very purpose, and opened it up to a range of new readings.

But recording a *waraqa*, or even annotating it, was a very different exercise than interpreting it. If the act of recording and translating was largely left to the clerk, the act of interpreting the *waraqa* in the courtroom was decidedly different. There, a range of different commercial and juridical actors were called upon to pronounce how a *waraqa* or the practices surrounding it might be understood, and they all played equally important roles in determining its place within a legal bureaucracy that was still taking shape.

A Sea of *Qāḍis*, c. 1870–1890

When the Legal Vice-Consul Erskine Foster arrived in Zanzibar in 1879, he might have found the administration of law there surprising. Foster, an Oxford graduate who had studied at Inner Temple when he was only twenty-one, had been called to the Bar just five years earlier; Zanzibar was his first post within the Indian Civil Service.[30] And when he first walked into the consular courtroom on the island, he would have witnessed a sight that might have shaken his belief in the order that the British Empire brought to these different territories. There, he would have seen largely informal, ad-hoc proceedings involving a rather motley group of individuals: a Consul-cum-judge, the parties to the dispute, and perhaps a group of merchants or a *qāḍi*. But rather than reflecting any sort of chaos or disorder, the scene would have suggested the very malleability of law and legal procedure during a time when British jurisdiction in the region was still in its formative years. Judges, many of whom were only civil servants, were unclear as to what they had jurisdiction over and what the substance of the law they were to administer might be. In these early years, the British court formed but one element of a broader juridical fabric on the island – a field that included a variety of overlapping mercantile, Islamic, and governmental forums and legal authorities, all of whom commercial actors appealed to at different junctures, and all of whom made claims to the right to determine law.[31]

The earliest surviving consular court cases from Zanzibar, from roughly 1866 to 1869, illustrate just how informal court proceedings were. The first register of court cases, in which each case was given a separate entry – often brief, like a *qāḍi's diwān* – paints a picture of a court that facilitated the resolution of disputes more than it adjudicated in favor of one party or another. The Consul's judicial work frequently involved facilitating assessors' work in their division of a bankrupt merchant's belongings or giving weight to the rulings of other tribunals, like the *panchayat*.[32] When the Consul did hand down rulings, he rarely did so on the basis of his understanding of law – just on his reading of evidence presented by the different parties. In a handful of instances, he ruled on the basis of custom, which he drew from "the testimony of several respectable merchants."[33] However, more often than not, he based his decision on oral evidence supplied by the parties and witnesses, supplemented by written records – bills, contracts, and ledger books.

[30] Joseph Foster, *Men-At-The-Bar: A Biographical Hand-list of the Members of the Various Inns of Court, Including Her Majesty's Judges, Etc.*, 2nd ed. (London: Hazell, Watson, and Viney, 1885), 164.

[31] While I have no evidence from Muscat, work that I have done on Bahrain in the 1920s and 1930s illustrates that it was administered in the same way, suggesting that Muscat may have been similar. See Bishara, "A Sea of Debt," 348–361, 378–386.

[32] See, for example, ZNA E/25, entry for 17 May, 1866. Bankruptcy proceedings are present throughout the volume.

[33] ZNA E/25: entry for August 21, 1867. The consul also ruled on the basis of what he understood to be commercial custom in the entry for November 20, 1863.

Foster would have been the only one among his peers who knew anything about law. From early on, British consuls in Zanzibar found themselves bewildered by the flexibility that merchants, rulers, and *qāḍis* showed towards commercial practices on the island – particularly those that confounded their understanding of the mutual rights and liabilities that shaped property transfers. When the Acting Consul William Francis Prideaux wrote to London in 1874 to inform them of a property dispute between the head of the Central African Mission and Zanzibari authorities, he bemoaned the legal difficulties he faced. Although the mission's head asserted that his rights were enshrined in local custom and stated that he had polled local *qāḍis* on the matter, Prideaux did not feel that these sufficed to prove his claim. "I can scarcely assure Your Lordship," he wrote, "that in a place like Zanzibar the opinion of one Kazi [sic] can always be counterbalanced by that of another."[34]

When it came to matters of commercial custom, consuls often proved more than willing to cede authority to leading merchants. In one 1875 dispute between two Indian merchants over their father's estate, the Consul transferred the case to the Zanzibari *panchayat*, a tribunal run by the town's leading merchants, for adjudication.[35] In another case that same year, the Consul referred a debt disagreement between Indian merchants to a group of Indian assessors and confirmed their judgment.[36] Only Foster, a trained judicial officer, was able to weigh in on the question of commercial custom: in at least two of his surviving judgments, Foster contended that unless a custom was long-standing and universally practiced among merchants it could not enjoy the force of law.[37] Even then, however, he was drawing on broad legal principles – the sort he would have found in his textbooks – rather than English or Anglo-Indian law in particular.

If what constituted commercial custom seemed clear enough, consuls and judges found themselves on much shakier ground when trying to determine questions of Islamic law. Shortly after beginning his work in the court in Zanzibar in the mid-1870s, the British Consul John Kirk pointed to his lack of familiarity with Islamic law, stating that "a knowledge of the principles of Mussulman law are constantly demanded in the Consular Court and still more in obtaining justice for British subjects before the Arab judges or the Sultan." Kirk tried to partially overcome

[34] William Francis Prideaux to the Secretary of State for Foreign Affairs, London (August 24, 1874), ZNA AA 2/14.

[35] *Khamis Soomar* v. *Hirji Soomar* (1875) ZNA HC 7/1.

[36] *Rhemtulla Hermani & Valji, Ebji Sivji's agent* (1875) ZNA HC 7/5.

[37] See also *Premji Khimji* v. *Tyabji Mamooji* (1878) 1 ZLR 7; *Purshottam Kesowji* v. *Cooverji Chapsi* (1880) 1 ZLR 18.

his handicap by reading the French translation of Khalil ibn Ishaq Al-Jundi's *Mukhtaṣar*, a Maliki legal manual.[38] Unfortunately for Kirk, Al-Jundi's manual would have offered only very little relevant guidance, as Zanzibar's Sunni Muslims were adherents of either the Ibadhi or Shafi'i schools of jurisprudence.

Only in a handful of any of these early cases, however, was there any discussion of the substantive law that applied to Zanzibar and East Africa. Indeed, until the 1890s, it was unclear even to the judges whether they were to decide commercial disputes according to Islamic law, English legal concepts, declared commercial custom, or general notions of equity. The judge, it seemed, decided in favor of whoever could produce the most convincing argument for the existence of an established rule: the litigant, a *qāḍi*, or even a prominent merchant. Despite the court's common-law heritage – which, one would have imagined, meant that it operated according to the principle of *stare decisis* – in practice, judgments during the 1870s and 1880s were largely ad-hoc and highly contingent in nature, muddling their way through both substantive and procedural legal issues. Only Foster, a trained lawyer, could take on the issues with any confidence.

But then tragedy struck: in 1881, scarcely two years after arriving on the island, Foster died, having fallen victim to "the coast fever."[39] With his death, officials in Zanzibar found themselves in a desperate situation, as few others knew enough about law to run a court. In their letters to officials in India, they pleaded for help – if not for a replacement judicial officer, then for money to purchase a small library of books Foster had left behind, before his widow left the island with them. The library consisted of fifty-four treatises on a range of different substantive and procedural matters (including Almaric Rumsey's *Chart of Mohammedan Inheritance*, published in India ten years earlier) and "a lot of old and miscellaneous law books," all worth Rs 390. The books, they wrote, were "much needed for the use of the Judge, who has cases frequently before him of legal difficulty and involving large interests."[40]

There was good reason to ask for the books. Over time, the Consulate's case load grew to a size that it was no longer tenable for a consul to do all the work of determining legal matters on his own. Col. Samuel Miles, who had moved to a temporary position as Political Agent in Zanzibar in 1881 from Muscat, where he had spent the past seven years overseeing the establishment of jurisdiction over the port's Indian community, was

[38] Political Agent, Zanzibar, to the Officiating Secretary to the Government of India, Calcutta (March 13, 1876), MSA Political Department, 1880, Vol. 23, Comp. 87.
[39] Leopold Hoffer, ed., *The Chess-Monthly*, Vol. 2 (September, 1880–August, 1881), 265.
[40] MSA Political Department 1881 Vol. 217, Comp. 61.

in a strong position to comment on changes taking place in East Africa. "The continued progress of the commerce of Zanzibar," he commented, "has been naturally followed by a corresponding increase of the Indian population who hold the trade of this part of the East African Coast in their hands." To Miles, this development carried with it legal implications. "British interests assume more importance daily in consequence," he noted, "and more responsibility and work are thrown on this Consulate."[41]

Miles's commentary highlighted a long regional transformation. In Zanzibar, enough merchants had begun to use the British court by the 1880s that it had become, *de facto*, the principal dispute resolution forum on the island. There alone, the population of Indians under the jurisdiction of the British consulate by 1883 numbered around 6,000 – double that of twelve years before. Miles chronicled the growing number of civil cases that the Consular Court had to deal with over the past three years: 446 in 1880, 443 in 1881, and a staggering 571 in 1882, many of which took days or weeks to resolve. These statistics marked a major shift: in 1871, the total number of cases, both civil and criminal, involving British subjects had numbered a mere 279 – only 67 of which were heard at the Consular Court.[42]

As the number of cases heard at the Consular Court grew, so too did the need for a better understanding of how to run a court. To enjoy jurisdiction was one thing; to effectively exercise it was an entirely different matter – one that most British officials lacked preparation to consider. Books, Miles made it clear, were not going to be enough. He emphasized the court's need for people capable of staffing the growing bureaucracy, including a Gujarati interpreter, a clerk, and a qualified accountant. None of these positions was as important to the court, however, as someone with a sharp understanding of the law itself. "The importance of an English barrister to preside over the court," Miles reflected, "has for a long time been recognized."[43] Foster's death had left a gaping void in British India's nascent legal bureaucracy on the East African coast, and a time where they needed him more than ever.

Thankfully, they did not have to wait very long. When Foster passed away in 1881, he was immediately succeeded by Walter B. Cracknall, a trained barrister who had been appointed to his post five years after completing the Bar at Middle Temple.[44] But even as Cracknall sat down

[41] Miles, Acting Political Agent, Zanzibar, to the Secretary to the Government of India (March 3, 1883), MSA PD 1883 Vol. 225, Comp. 157.
[42] MSA PD 1883 Vol. 225, Comp. 157; MSA PD 1871 Vol. 142, Comp. 179.
[43] Miles, Acting Political Agent, Zanzibar, to the Secretary to the Government of India (March 3, 1883), MSA PD 1883 Vol. 225, Comp. 157.
[44] Lyne, *Zanzibar in Contemporary Times*, 195.

to begin his work, it was clear that he could not do it all on his own. Faced with a demand for a legal framework for an increasingly complex world of economic activity, the judge grasped at whatever resources were around him in constructing his judgments: books, general ideas about the law, notions of equity, and most importantly, other juridical actors. Even with the advantage of legal training, Cracknall would have immediately recognized that he was simply one judge among many – a single actor in a juridical field that included *muftis*, *qāḍis*, Sultans, and tribunals of leading merchants. That he might have imagined himself in that capacity is evident from an 1885 Arabic letter to a Zanzibari official, in which he referred to himself as "the English State's *qāḍi*" (*qāḍi al-dawlah al-ingilīziyya*).[45] His pluralistic juridical imaginary was particularly evident when it came to the *waraqa*, for which there were a wide range of different interpretations and confusions arising from an equally broad range of actors. One case illustrated these uncertainties, and the attendant problems of translating personhood and practice, strikingly well.

The Case of Musabbah's *Waraqa*

In February 1887, Cracknall walked into his courtroom to find before him an unusual cast of characters. The Sultan, Barghash bin Sa'id, had sent his *qāḍi* to the Consular Court to litigate a case against Jairam Sewji's firm over an empty plot of land to which they both had competing claims. Sewji's firm based its claim to the lot on a twenty-one year old *khiyār* sale *waraqa* that recorded a transaction between Sewji's agent at the time, Kurji Ramdas, and a freed slave (*sarīḥ*) named Musabbah who had taken on a loan to outfit a caravan for the interior of East Africa.

When Musabbah had taken on the loan in 1866, it had been a good year for the ivory trade. That year, Zanzibar had exported ivory worth nearly Rs 848,000 to Bombay – a figure lower than what it had been five years earlier, but nonetheless a good amount. More importantly for Musabbah and Ramdas, the per *frasila* price for ivory was climbing every year, from MTD 44 just five years earlier to just over MTD 54 that year.[46] For Musabbah, as for many others like him, his *waraqa* constituted an entry ticket into a regional commercial bonanza – one that allowed actors the chance to reinvent themselves during a time of commercial boom, and to mobilize what little property they had towards that end. And for financiers like Kurji Ramdas, the *waraqa* could mean a number of things: the chance to secure a supply of commodities like ivory, but also, in a time of

[45] *Suleman b. Musa* v. *Musa Abdool Rasool* (1885) ZNA HC 7/230.
[46] Sheriff, *Slaves, Spices*, 252, 255.

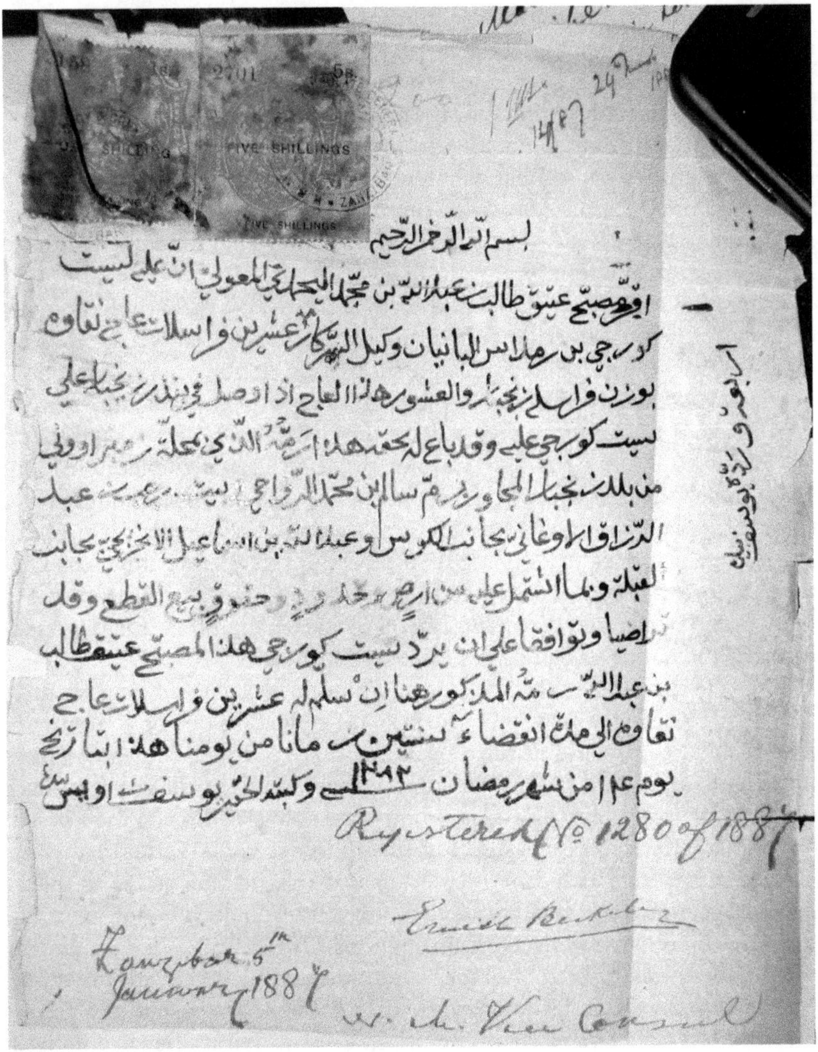

FIVE SHILLINGS

بسم الله الرحمن الرحيم

Registered No. 1280 of 1887

Zanzibar 5th January 1887

Vice Consul

Figure 5 Musabbah's *waraqa*

economic downturn – as came to pass in 1887 – an opportunity to make legal claims to the land that underpinned it.

The problem was that Musabbah never returned from his journey into the interior. Perhaps he died in the interior as many others did, his dreams of fame and fortune dying along with him. Or perhaps he simply chose to abscond with Kurji's money, deciding instead that he would make a name for himself in the interior, where he would no longer be someone marked by the stain of his enslaved past, but a commercial actor of means and importance. He would not have been the first to do so. There were scores of runaway debtors and other merchants in the interior: Richard Burton noted as much, and illustrated how the strategy could sometimes pay off handsomely. He relayed the story of a Baluchi who absconded from his creditors on the coast and wandered all the way to Uganda, where the favor of the sovereign there landed him wealth in ivory and even a harem.[47]

Whatever might have happened to Musabbah, by 1887 the commercial environment seemed uncertain: that year, ivory receipts had reached an all-time low; exports had plummeted to around 500 *frasilas*, a fraction of what they had been before. Faced with the prospect of default, Sewji's firm decided to claim the plot of land that Musabbah had sold to them via *khiyār* so many years ago – a plot that had grown tremendously in value since they first accepted it in 1866. One of the members of the customs master's firm – most likely the firm's writer, Abdulkadir – registered the *waraqa* at the consulate less than three months before the case. The *waraqa* bore the marks of registration: scrawled across its bottom were the words "Registered No. 1280 of 1887," a clear sign that it had passed through the hands of one of the Talatis.[48]

That the customs master's firm could make a claim based on a twenty-one year old *waraqa* is worth pausing and reflecting on for a moment. The firm's head wouldn't have been the first to do so; scores of other merchants registered older *waraqas*. However, by the time the firm had come to make its claim, Ramdas, whom Musabbah had made the *waraqa* out to, had already passed away. But that didn't seem to matter to anyone in that courtroom: everyone seemed to understand that as far as questions of personhood were concerned, a creditor could die, but his right to claim the obligation lived on through his firm. Ramdas had made out the document as "*wakeel al sirkār*," and although he was dead, the *sirkār* was alive and well. Indeed, when the firm brought the case to the court, they did so under the name of the original *sirkār*, Jairam Sewji, who had at that point been dead for almost thirty years.

47 Burton also suspected that many of the Arabs in the interior who had been robbed of their merchandise chose to stay there rather than face their creditors on the coast. Burton, *The Lake Regions of Central Africa*, 152–153, 402–403. Tippu Tip's biographer wrote that many caravan leaders who went into the interior on borrowed money "preferred, instead of abiding by [their] obligations in Zanzibar, to lead a showy life in the interior with other people's money." Brode, *Tippoo Tib*, 25–26.

48 ZNA HC 7/265.

Representing the customs master's firm was the recently arrived Indian lawyer, Camruddin Amiruddin. We know little about Amiruddin's trajectory, but it was clear that he had some legal training. In different case that year, he represented the influential Indian merchant Tharia Topan in his dispute with the British shipping company Gray Mackenzie. At different times, he referenced the Indian Evidence Act, *Addison on Contracts*, and C.D. Field's *Law of Evidence in India and Pakistan* to support his argument that oral evidence was not admissible in court.[49] His arrival hinted at the beginning of a new era in East African legal history, but it would not be for another few years that more Indian lawyers would begin to arrive on the island, heralding the region's legal transformation (see Chapter 5). At the time Amiruddin found himself in the consular court arguing about the nature of Musabbah's *waraqa*, he had only just begun his career.

To Amiruddin, the *waraqa* established the firm's claim to the plot of land in unambiguous terms: Musabbah had sold the firm the lot, reserving the right to reclaim it if he returned with the ivory within two years. The land sale constituted security against Musabbah's promise to deliver ivory, and because Musabbah had never returned, the land was rightfully his client's. Moreover, the firm had taken the trouble of registering the *waraqa*, however old it might have been, and there was thus no question of its authenticity or its admissibility in the British consular court.

The *qāḍi* representing the Sultan, however, offered a different interpretation of what the *waraqa* meant. When it was written more than two decades earlier, he stated, "there were many *waraqas*, thousands such as this, and no doubt many exist up to this time." They were issued to "every Arab who traveled upcountry (*sāfara ilā fawq*) and received an advance before his journey, and the *waraqas* were written as guarantees (*'alā wāṣiṭat ḍāmin*) should they not return or if they died or became bankrupt and they were several times allowed to stand over without annulling for many journeys." In a sense, the *qāḍi* was arguing what everyone who had previously contracted in South Arabia and East Africa already knew: that the *khiyār* sale and other instruments like it were there to enable commercial activity – to facilitate the flows of credit to commercial aspirants, and to circulate value and rents around the Indian Ocean. If the customs master's firm enjoyed any title to the plot of land at all, it was only in theory; practically speaking, nobody was going to make a claim based on a *khiyār* sale *waraqa*.

[49] *Messrs Smith Mackenzie & Co., Agents of BISN Co* v. *Tharia Topan* (1887) ZNA HC 7/270.

But there was more to the *qāḍi's* claim. As he stood in front of the British consul, he argued that the Sultan also had his own sale deed – one which stated that he had bought the plot from *another* person, who had purchased it from Musabbah at around the time he had executed the deed with Sewji. Moreover, he argued, any *bona fide* sale of land had to be confirmed by either a *qāḍi* or the Sultan himself.[50] In making the argument, the *qāḍi* was making a claim about the nature of title in the *khiyār* sale – that because the *khiyār* sale was an instrument meant to generate credit, title did not automatically transfer from the debtor to the creditor, and that a formal transfer of possession of the land constituted an altogether different transaction.

But at the heart of the claim was the unspoken assumption that Musabbah, being a freed slave, did not enjoy the full legal capacity to buy and sell property anyway, at least not without the express consent of his former master, Talib bin ʻAbdullah Al-Maʻwali, or of the Sultan, both of whom would have retained some authority over him even after his manumission. By contrast, to the Indian lawyer Amiruddin, Musabbah was a "freedman" and thus enjoyed full legal rights to buy and sell, borrow and lend. It was here that the ontological and legal tensions – between the mortgage and the *khiyār* sale, the *sarīḥ* and the freedman – expressed themselves most forcefully. Indeed, the inability of parties to fully comprehend one another could not have been made clearer: when the *qāḍi* submitted his written statement about the *waraqa* and the alleged transfer of ownership, he identified Sewji's position in the original transaction as "the holder of the obligation" (*ṣāḥib al-ḥaqq*). In the translation provided to the judge, the term had been rendered as "mortgagee."

For Judge Cracknall, who in the six years since he had arrived on the island had moved up the ranks to become the Judicial Assistant, the core of the matter was the question of possession: whether Sewji or his firm had ever demonstrated any form of possession over the land in question. It is unclear why he singled out the issue of possession, since neither the *qāḍi* nor Amiruddin the lawyer had raised it at all. The *qāḍi* contended that because neither the Sultan nor any *qāḍi* confirmed the sale, the *waraqa* simply amounted to an acknowledgment of debt rather than an actual transfer of title. By contrast, Amiruddin argued that the *waraqa* was an out-and-out sale. One likely explanation for Cracknall's position was that the law textbooks he and others came to rely upon might have highlighted possession as an essential element of a sale transaction.

[50] *His Highness the Sultan of Zanzibar* v. *Jairam Sivji* (1887), (ZNA) HC 7/265.

After hearing owners of neighboring plots give testimony on the empty lot's history, Cracknall ruled in favor of the Sultan – not on the strength of the Sultan's *waraqa* vis-à-vis Sewji's, but because of the circumstances following the *waraqa's* issue. He asserted that during the nearly twenty-one years that had passed between the time the *waraqa* was drawn up and the court case filed, Sewji's firm "could show no single act of ownership, while on the other side by [the Sultan] or his predecessors in title there seems to have been a continual act of possession for more than 20 and continuing for more than 12 years."[51] The firm's inability to demonstrate custodial possession of the land in over two decades rendered its claim to it unenforceable. Possession, it seemed, was truly nine-tenths of the law – even in Zanzibar.

As facile as it seems, Cracknall's argument about the necessity of possession reflected the multiple legal epistemologies that shaped how the court understood *waraqas* – and how it understood law more broadly – during the 1870s and 1880s. In a sense, Cracknall was drawing on multiple sources of legal thought: the *qāḍi's* claim that *khiyār* sales did not necessarily transfer title, Amiruddin's argument that the document related an out-and-out sale, and his own legal training, which would have suggested to him that possession was a necessary element of any sale contract. The indeterminate nature of his judgment, which neither addressed the *qāḍi's* claims about the nature of the *khiyār* sale nor Amiruddin's claims about what the document ostensibly stated, was less a product of his uncertainty about what law to apply than the robust exchange and creative interweaving of different ideas about law that characterized the British court until the 1890s. Rather than constituting a clear instrument, the *waraqa* formed the object of regulatory impulses from a range of different actors: *qāḍis*, jurists, clerks, lawyers, and judges.

Conclusion

When Cracknall highlighted possession as a necessary element of the *khiyār* sale, he may have thought that he was making a final pronouncement on the requirements of the contract, but he wasn't. Instead, his opinion foreshadowed what would become a decades-long battle in the courtroom over how to make sense of the *waraqa*. And as the economic, political, and juridical landscape in East Africa shifted, many fought over what the *khiyār* sale and *waraqa* could mean: whether possession of or title to the property in question ever changed hands, whether to

[51] *His Highness the Sultan of Zanzibar* v. *Jairam Sivji* (1887) ZNA HC 7/265.

interpret it as a sale deed or some other kind of instrument, and how to interpret the obligations that underpinned it. Cracknall's decision in Musabbah's case provided neither answers nor guidance; it was but one utterance – one pronouncement of how one might interpret the document – among many.

At issue in the dispute over Musabbah's *waraqa* was much more than a single plot of land on the island of Zanzibar. At the heart of the dispute was the fundamental problem of representation – of whether a written instrument could represent a commercial reality, of the different genres that made competing claims to understanding that reality, and of the different legal lexicons actors mobilized to render it legible within their own systems of law. As the *waraqa* moved from *kātib* to consular registry and then to the courtroom, it moved between systems that delineated the boundaries between law, writing, and economic life in starkly different terms. When the *qāḍi* argued that Musabbah's *waraqa* could not transfer title, and that a land sale by Musabbah would have to be confirmed by the Sultan, he was making claims about the nature of property and personhood – claims that rested on decades of *fiqh* and *fatwas* that wrestled with what these instruments could do in a commercializing economy. Meanwhile, Amiruddin based his claim on his own reading of the *waraqa* – one that coupled his understanding of sales with a reading of the annotated *waraqa* in the register. To both parties, the *waraqa* represented a commercial reality, but the problem was that they were unable to agree upon what that commercial reality looked like.

The issue hardly got any easier as the decades wore on. Over time, as East Africa began to emerge as a destination for imperial economic development and settlement, British companies, and other investors began to see it as a place where they could potentially make a good amount of money through speculation. At the heart of race to Africa was the Uganda Railroad, a massive infrastructure project that sought to link Mombasa to Lake Victoria, over 650 miles inland. And with the Uganda Railway, and the speculative frenzy it brought with it, came an expanded British Indian legal presence. The 1890s and 1900s witnessed the arrival of even more judges, lawyers, and legal personnel, and the formation of a full-fledged Anglo-Indian legal bureaucracy in the region. If Cracknall was the only British official with legal training in the 1880s, by the mid-1890s he found himself in good company.

Standing at the center of all of these legal and economic transformations was the *waraqa*, and all of the notions of land, law, and rights that came along with it. With a changing economic landscape, fluctuating clove and ivory prices, and a lingering sense of economic vulnerability among merchants and financiers, more actors took their *waraqas* to the courtroom and sought to make claims to land, rent, and debts. Their disputes prompted a heated discussion in the courtroom between judges, lawyers, and *qāḍis* on the place of the *waraqa* – and of Islamic law more broadly – in a developing regional and world economy.

5 Making Africa Indian

In the ten years after the dispute over Musabbah's *waraqa*, Judge Walter Cracknall had seen a lot change in East Africa. Over the course of a decade, the region had witnessed the emergence of new courts in Mombasa, Lamu, Zanzibar, and other cities, the arrival of lawyers, new judicial personnel, and a growing number of laws and acts from India. What had started as a motley group of commercial and legal actors hashing out claims in Cracknall's small courtroom in Zanzibar during the 1870s and 1880s had grown into a full-fledged legal bureaucracy that covered large swaths of the coast and interior. Gone were the days in which *qāḍis*, clerks, and merchants could each make equally authoritative claims to lawmaking in the face of a judge whose legal knowledge was shaky at best. By the last decade of the nineteenth century, the region witnessed the arrival of a steady stream of professional barristers and appointed judges, virtually all of whom held law degrees from London and had experience administering law elsewhere in the British Empire. And by 1897, Cracknall found himself in a position that did not even exist when he first started his work as a legal adviser nearly two decades before: he had become Zanzibar's first Chief Justice.

Cracknall's tenure in East Africa also witnessed important political changes – namely the establishment of a British protectorate in Zanzibar (in 1890) and the "East Africa Protectorate" (in 1895), which covered the bulk of what is today Kenya. The declaration of the protectorates heralded the dawn of a new era in the legal history of the region. Over the course of the next few decades, Anglo-Indian statute and case law arrived *en masse* onto the shores of East Africa, making their way across the Rift Valley and Lake Victoria and into Uganda. The only exception was Tanganyika, which was under a German colonial administration and was thus not subsumed into British India's legal empire until after Germany's defeat in World War I.

For Cracknall, however, it would have been clear that much of the legal and political change he saw in the region grew out of a single watershed event: the development of the Uganda Railway. The railway was the largest infrastructural project the region had ever seen, seeking to connect Mombasa to Lake Victoria, over 650 miles inland. Much like railroad projects in the United States, England, and India, the Uganda Railway brought with it a complete reconfiguration of East Africa's commercial and legal geography, but also the region's demographics. It necessitated a rethinking of British India's juridical presence in the region, raising big legal questions as growing numbers of lawyers, judges, shopkeepers, and railway speculators began to clash with moneylenders, plantation owners, and local legal authorities over the laws that governed property.

The railway project and the legal bureaucracy it helped give rise to highlighted the interpretive tensions that resided in the land at a time of imperial expansion. If the regional economy of obligation was underpinned by a robust market for property, the changing legal landscape in the Western Indian Ocean – one that offered creditors a chance to register their *waraqas* and make claims based on them – offered litigants a chance to tug at the corners of the regional legal fabric. As land became more firmly integrated into the world economy, merchants and speculators fought for the right to determine precisely how it might fit, and how the changing trajectories of empire might work to their advantage. Judges like Cracknall and other actors in the courtroom were thus forced to grapple with how to govern the parcels of property that surrounded them in view of the transformations that were taking place in the region. And throughout, they looked to India for guidance.

Empire's Advocates

During the mid-1880s, the Indian lawyer Camruddin Amiruddin could sleep well knowing that he was the only game in town: those who wanted to lodge anything beyond the most rudimentary of contractual claims in the British court had to go through him. And he knew that he could convince the judges of his client's claims, largely by looking to Indian law. In an 1886 case from Zanzibar, for example, he invoked articles from the Civil Procedure Code and court decisions from Calcutta to show that the plaintiff was barred from suing his client for rent. In his judgment, Cracknall wrote that the materials the lawyer cited established "undoubtedly a very strong authority in his favor on the point raised by him" and proceeded to decide the case in his favor.[1] Similarly, in an 1887 dispute, he represented the influential Indian merchant Tharia Topan in his dispute with the British shipping company Gray Mackenzie. To argue

[1] *Khimji Jairam Sivji* v. *Nasur Lilani* (1886) ZNA HC 7/240.

that oral evidence was not admissible in court, he referenced the Indian Evidence Act, *Addison on Contracts*, and C.D. Field's *The Law of Evidence in British India*. The judge, impressed by the textual support Amiruddin marshaled, dismissed the case against Topan.[2]

But Amiruddin wouldn't be alone for very long. As the British juridical presence in Zanzibar and the rest of East Africa grew, the region witnessed the arrival of a steady stream of lawyers. Servicing the needs of a growing body of litigants, and faced with judges that struggled with substantive legal issues and Anglo-Indian procedural law, lawyers were primarily responsible for the extension of a distinctly Anglo-Indian body of legislation and case law from India to Zanzibar – and later, from there to East Africa's ports and hinterland. Their arrival in Zanzibar signaled the beginning of a legal sea change – one that almost completely fastened the East African legal landscape to British India by the end of the century. By invoking Anglo-Indian case law and procedural codes in the courtroom, lawyers gradually established British courts as forums for the administration of the laws of British India, tethering them securely to a burgeoning legal system in the Subcontinent.

Who were these newly arrived legal professionals? The earliest court records in which they appear recount names such as Hormasji Lascari, and Framji Rabadina, and later Maneckji R. Boyce, and Framroze P. Doctor, most of which indicate the same Parsi Indian background as the clerks that first copied *waraqas* and other deeds into consular registries.[3] Even the clerks themselves joined in the fray: after subtly inscribing Anglo-Indian legal terminology onto *waraqas* during the 1870s and 1880s, the Talatis recognized that there were real opportunities in lawyering. At some point during the 1890s, they bought out an English law firm, establishing their own legal practice in Zanzibar.[4]

Despite the fact that most of the lawyers were of an Indian background, many received their legal training in London rather than India. For example, Hornius Lascari – a Parsi who newspaper reports referred to as "the head of the bar" at Zanzibar – completed his studies at Middle Temple in London in 1889, after earning a B.A. from Bombay University.[5] Lascari was the son of a Bombay merchant, Farduaji Laskari, and had apparently changed his first name to the more Latin-sounding

[2] *Messrs Smith Mackenzie & Co., Agents of BISN Co* v. *Tharia Topan* (1887) ZNA HC 7/270.

[3] This is in line with what Mitra Sharafi observes with regard to Bombay, where members of the Parsi flooded the legal community. See also Sharafi, *Law and Identity in Colonial India.*

[4] Mitra Sharafi, *Law and Identity in Colonial India*, 117 n. 201.

[5] *The Gazette for Zanzibar and East Africa*, Vol. 12, No. 624 (1904), 5; "Personal Intelligence," *Indian Magazine and Review*, Vol. 13, No. 264 (December, 1892), 661.

Hornius from the original, Hormasji.[6] Although a number of other Parsi barristers studied law at the London Inns, how many of them ended up practicing in Zanzibar is difficult to determine. In India, lawyers like Lascari had become a common part of the legal process from early on in the nineteenth century.[7] The timing of their arrival in East Africa was no coincidence: over the 1880s, the Indian law market had become oversaturated with barristers, solicitors, and *vakils*; those who hoped to make a living practicing law had to turn to imperial courts around the Indian Ocean.[8]

In contrast to British judges, many of whom would have had no experience in British India, these advocates intuitively imagined the courts of the Western Indian Ocean as extensions of those in the Subcontinent. In the Zanzibar courts, lawyers routinely cited Anglo-Indian case law, as though the court at Zanzibar was only down the street from a Bombay district court. Although they tacitly acknowledged that Anglo-Indian rulings did not establish any strict precedent outside of India, lawyers looked to them as establishing guiding legal principles – and in some cases deciding on the main questions. In court proceedings, lawyers made frequent references to opinions published in Indian law reports. To them, the ports of the Indian Ocean formed a shared arena of common law centered on India and fanning out into the Persian Gulf, South Arabia, and East Africa; Bombay, the highest court of appeal in this arena, was the metropole from which legal guidelines flowed.[9] In an 1889 case surrounding the administration of an Indian merchant's estate, to cite just one example of hundreds, the lawyer for the defendant cited law reports from Bombay and Madras in support of his argument that the merits of the case had already been decided and should not be brought up in the hearing.[10] In another case just two years later, when an Indian sued the two executors of the estate of his debtor for *waraqas* he held as security for money owed, lawyers for both parties relentlessly pursued their claims. Lawyers for

[6] H.A.C. Sturgess, ed. *Register of Admissions to the Honourable Society of the Middle Temple. From the Fifteenth Century to the Year 1944* (London: Butterworth & Co., 1949), Vol. 2, 674.

[7] See also Samuel Schmitthener, "A Sketch of the Development of the Legal Profession in India," *Law & Society Review*, Vol. 3, No. 2/3 (November, 1968–February, 1969), 337–382; Sharafi, *Law and Identity in Colonial India*.

[8] Charles R. DiSalvo, *M.K. Ghandi, Attorney at Law: The Man Before the Mahatma* (Berkeley, CA: University of California Press, 2013), 22–30.

[9] To this, one might add Southeast Asia – specifically, Malaya and Burma – as well. See also Sharafi, *Law and Identity in Colonial South Asia*; Metcalf, *Imperial Connections*, 16–45.

[10] *Fazal Issa, Administrator of the estate of Nasser Lilani, Deceased* v. *Mahomed Nasser* (1889) ZNA HC 7/300.

the executors argued that the suit was void according to the Indian Limitations Act, while the plaintiff's lawyer drew on a range of Anglo-Indian law reports to make the case for his client.[11]

Moreover, lawyers routinely cited relevant Indian acts and codes, sometimes to block claims by the other party to the dispute on procedural grounds, but often to establish substantive points of law. In theory, the various Orders in Council decreed in Zanzibar had already extended Anglo-Indian acts and procedures like the Indian Code of Civil Procedure and Indian Code of Criminal Procedure to different ports in the Indian Ocean. The actual execution of these codes and acts, however, was left to be fought out in the courtroom. In this theater, Indian lawyers – who, by virtue of their training, were already familiar with the substance of the statutes – helped determine what disputes deserved entry into the courtroom but also the specific form they had to take to be constituted as proper legal arguments.

Their ability to navigate legal procedure sometimes took on wide spatial dimensions. Lawyers who were particularly savvy could sometimes sidestep a consul's authority altogether by taking their clients' cases across the ocean to Bombay and appeal to a new overlord: the High Court of Judicature at Bombay. Because the Orders in Council designated the Bombay High Court as the ultimate court of appeals in the Western Indian Ocean, judges there had the authority to overturn the decisions of all political agents in the region. Litigants who were unhappy with a ruling handed out to them in a political agent's court simply had to file a motion to appeal; those with a good lawyer could push to have their cases decided at Bombay, circumventing the Consular Court altogether.[12]

Lawyers would gesture to the wide contours of the legal arena even when they weren't trying to lodge an appeal. In an 1891 case from the Zanzibar courts, the plaintiff's lawyer, citing the Civil Procedure Code, argued that because a linked question was being heard at the High Court in Bombay, the present suit could not be heard until that case was decided. After further citing a series of cases from the *Indian Law Reports*, he succeeded in persuading Cracknall to adjourn the hearing for another six months.[13] Legal proceedings across the ocean colored the particulars of cases in East Africa even before they were decided.

Far from always working hand in glove, lawyers and British imperial officials often found themselves at odds with one another, both in their interpretations of the law and their short- and long-term agendas. And

[11] *Luxmidas Ladha* v. *(1) Dayal Gopal and (2) Shivji Haji, Executors of Maula Naranji* (1891) ZNA HC 7/367.
[12] See, for example, *Allarakhia Wulli, Insolvent* (1889) ZNA HC 7/307.
[13] *Moloo Pira* v. *Jivraj Lalji* (1891) ZNA HC 7/350.

faced with such stiff opposition in the courts of India and East Africa, imperial authorities went to great lengths to prevent lawyers from practicing in other parts of the Western Indian Ocean. They frequently denied petitions by India-trained lawyers requesting that they be permitted to practice elsewhere in the region. In 1888, the British administration at Aden refused to allow an Armenian barrister to practice there, arguing that there existed "an inclination amongst the petty Arab traders to fraud, and litigation, and it is by no means desirable that their inclination to such litigation should be stimulated, as it undoubtedly would be, by the presence of pleaders."[14] Later Political Agents in Muscat further judged the arrival of pleaders in British courts there a "wholly undesirable contingency."[15]

Underpinning British officials' fears surrounding the lawyer presence and the potential for litigiousness in the region, however, lay a concern that a lawyer presence might unnecessarily complicate the administration of justice in the Indian Ocean ports, posing an unwanted challenge to the Political Agent or judge's authority. Reflecting on the relationship between the bench and the bar in East African courts, Gilchrist Alexander, a Tanganyika judge, wrote that "the reason the Governor of Tanganyika and many other Governors sought to exclude lawyers from the Courts was that they distrusted their influence on the tribunals [i.e. the bench]. Naturally if you have a weak bench you will find them unduly swayed by professional lawyers."[16]The aims of empire, Alexander's memoirs suggested, were not always served by the work of lawyers.

Officials' anxieties surrounding the presence of lawyers were largely unfounded. Though lawyers often did complicate legal proceedings and force judges to reckon with an intimidating body of Anglo-Indian case law and statute, they weren't able to dominate courtroom conversations about the law. During the 1890s, as British courts began appearing in East African port cities like Mombasa and Lamu, the region witnessed a steady influx of appointed judges, virtually all of whom had legal training, if not experience in the courtroom. Cracknall, who ten years earlier was the only legal officer in the region, spent his time shuttling back and forth between the courts of Zanzibar, Mombasa, and Lamu.[17] He was now one of many, with a strong cadre of trained judges and assistant judges

[14] Court of the Resident at Aden to Judicial Department (November 1888), MSA Judicial Department, 1888, Vol. 10 Comp. 1376.

[15] Memo by Political Agent, Muscat (July 30, 1900), IOR R/15/6/67.

[16] Gilchrist C. Alexander, *Tanganyika Memories: A Judge in the Red Kanzu* (London: Blackie and Sons, 1936), 19. Alexander's solution to the persistent lawyer presence called for "strengthen[ing] the bench, and not… exclud[ing] the lawyers" – a reflection on changes that had already taken place in East Africa in the three decades leading up to his appointment. idem, 16–17.

[17] *The Gazette for Zanzibar and East Africa*, No. 68 (17 May, 1893), 2.

wherever he went, and a growing body of court decision, notices, and appointments that were announced to the public through the medium of the *Gazette for Zanzibar and East Africa*, published in English and Gujarati.

The Uganda Railway and the Anglo-Indian Legal Bureaucracy

Over the course of his career in the 1890s and 1900s, Cracknall saw the British court's jurisdiction expand in significant ways. By the 1890s, officials witnessed the implementation of a more structured and entrenched legal bureaucracy on the East African coast – one that claimed an expansive jurisdiction. Before 1893, all cases involving non-British litigants had to include a *qāḍi* in one way or another. That year, however, British officials managed to leverage a concession from the Sultan to the effect that all cases involving even one British subject fell under consular jurisdiction, with no *qāḍi* presence necessary.[18] The court's reach further expanded to include other Europeans as well: through a series of treaties, capitulations, and other diplomatic exchanges with other European countries, the British court assumed jurisdiction over the rest of the Europeans living in Zanzibar and the East Africa Protectorate.[19]

British legal jurisdiction expanded spatially, too, in no small part due to the construction of the Uganda Railroad, an event that marked a transformation in the political, economic, and legal history of East Africa.[20] During the 1860s and 1870s, British officials in India saw what a railroad might help them realize in terms of expanded traded and imperial control; they wanted the same for their expanding dominions in East Africa.[21] With the development of a railway system in East Africa, officials sought to open up the interior to British investment in ways that were simply impossible with the caravan routes, while also ensuring the protection of the source of the Nile from Britain's enemies. The project would also give Britain the basis it needed to claim "effective occupation" of the East Africa Protectorate under the protocols set forward during

18 "The Administration of Justice in Zanzibar," *Gazette for Zanzibar and East Africa*, No 56 (February 22, 1893), 9.

19 Some of these are found in "Treaties between Zanzibar and Foreign Powers" ZNA AB 27/40.

20 The only available work on the Uganda Railway is M.F. Hill's two-volume study *The Permanent Way: The Story of the Kenya and Uganda Railway* (East Africa Literature Bureau, 1976).

21 On Indian railroads, see also Ian Kerr, *Building the Railways of the Raj, 1850–1900* (Oxford, UK: Oxford University Press, 1995); Ritika Prasad, *Tracks of Change: Railways and Everyday Life in Colonial India* (New York: Cambridge University Press, 2015).

the Berlin Conference.[22] The result, however, was the most monumental infrastructural project that the region had ever seen – one that served as a catalyst for British imperial legal expansion in East Africa.

The work of building the railway was first tasked to the Imperial British East Africa Company (IBEAC), a company whose shareholders included the international shipping mogul William Mackinnon, former consul John Kirk, and the Sultan of Zanzibar, Barghash bin Sa'id.[23] The Sultan had granted the IBEAC the right to engage in trade in his dominions in East Africa, part of which involved a commitment on the IBEAC's part to developing a railway line to Lake Victoria, facilitating the movement of people and goods from the coast to the heart of the continent.[24] But when the IBEAC began to show signs of financial troubles in the mid-1890s – troubles aggravated by the armed conflicts it had become embroiled in – the British Government took over the territory and the management of the railway's construction.[25] It soon began moving its personnel from the coast inland to oversee its expanding interior jurisdiction: Gerald Porter, who in 1890 was the British consul in Zanzibar and who oversaw the beginnings of the island's legal transformation, was appointed to the post of Imperial Commissioner in Uganda just three years later.[26] By July 1895, the Government proclaimed the territory the East Africa Protectorate, extending from the Indian Ocean coast inland to Uganda and the Great Rift Valley.

The process of building the Uganda Railway brought with it a tremendous change in the region's demographics. From 1890 onwards, indentured workers from India began arriving in Mombasa to provide the labor necessary for the railway's construction: workers from Sindh, Punjab, and other centers in South Asia were loaded onto dhows and steamships and made the passage across the Western Indian Ocean.[27] Along with them came scores of shopkeepers, merchants, and moneylenders, all of whom saw in the railway project a chance to build a business in East Africa, largely through supplying railway laborers. All told, the Indian population of Zanzibar and the East African protectorate rose

22 Andrew Fitzmaurice, *Sovereignty, Property, and Empire, 1500–1900* (Cambridge, UK: Cambridge University Press, 2014), 283–290.

23 *The Gazette for Zanzibar and East Africa*, No. 19 (July 5, 1893), 2.

24 "The British East Africa Company," *The Gazette for Zanzibar and East Africa*, No. 19 (June 29, 1892), 6–9.

25 The IBEAC's troubles generated many news and opinion columns in *The Gazette* between 1892 and 1894.

26 "Departure of Sir Gerald H. Porter, C.B., K.C.M.G., for Uganda," *The Gazette for Zanzibar and East Africa*, No. 49 (January 4, 1893), 5.

27 For first-hand accounts of the journeys of indentured laborers, see Cynthia Salvadori (ed.) *We Came in Dhows*, Vol. 1 (Nairobi: Paperchase Kenya Ltd, 1996).

from just over 6,300 in 1887 to a staggering 54,434 by 1921; Indians could be found all over East and East Central Africa.[28]

The railway proved to be a blessing to Indian merchants in East Africa. As early as 1892, one columnist for the *Gazette* acknowledged that "the entire trade of East Africa has long been in the hands of wealthy resident British Indian merchants" and suggested that the opening up of the interior was going to deepen their involvement. "With the support of the Indian authorities," he wrote, "it is anticipated that Africa may in the future become to the natives of India, what America and the British colonies have proved to the mother country and Europe."[29] The notion may have been slightly exaggerated, but was not altogether off the mark; for some merchants, the opening up of the interior was nothing short of a windfall to their business. The Khoja merchant Allidina Visram, for example, had his beginnings in the pre-railroad world – he started out as an employee of Sewa Haji Paroo, one of the caravan trade's most active financiers – but rose to commercial prominence after supplying railway laborers. By 1909, Visram had a network of shops and agents that extended as far inland as Uganda and the Congo, and along all of the railway's stops, and also operated steamers on Lake Victoria.[30] And he wasn't alone in capitalizing on the opportunity that the railway presented: hundreds of other merchants also followed the railway tracks into the interior, where they set up shop and ultimately settled.

Indians were not alone in trying to capture the opportunities that the railway presented. As the investment frontier began its inland expansion, scores of European firms came in to take the place of Mackinnon's IBEAC. Some were firms involved in the Zanzibari clove, coconut, and ivory trade that began to look to the interior as a possible destination for European capital as the railway brought cities like Mwanza, Entebbe, and Nairobi to the fore.[31] Others saw opportunities to profit from the railway itself, speculating on the land that they presumed it would pass through.

Perhaps unsurprisingly, the massive transformations in commerce, politics, and demographics that the railway brought with it also prompted

[28] Robert C. Gregory, *South Asians in East Africa: an Economic and Social History, 1890–1980* (Boulder, CO: Westview Press, 1993), 11–12.

[29] "Imperial British East Africa Co." *The Gazette for Zanzibar and East Africa*, No. 19 (June 8, 1892), 2–3.

[30] A concise summary of Visram's life can be found in Gaurav Desai, *Commerce with the Universe: Africa, India, and the Afrasian Imagination* (New York: Columbia University Press, 2013), 112–113.

[31] See also Laird R. Jones, "The District Town and Articulation of Colonial Rule: The Case of Mwanza, Tanzania, 1890–1945" (Ph.D. Dissertation, Michigan State University, 1992).

rapid juridical developments along the coast. The first step was the establishment in 1890 of a court at Mombasa whose decisions were, at least for the time being, subject to revision only by the High Court at Bombay.[32] A stream of professional judges followed: one of the first appointees was George B. Piggott, a Middle Temple graduate who arrived on the island as Assistant Judge in 1890, after spending time as a judicial officer in the Central Africa Protectorate and after having practiced in London.[33] He was followed in 1892 by Arthur Charles William Jenner, who had studied law at Lincoln's Inn in London.[34] That same year, Havilland Walter de Sausmarez, who had studied at Inner Temple eight years earlier and had legal experience in Lagos, took up the post of Assistant Judge in Zanzibar.[35] Over the next decade, the numbers of trained judges swelled as the British legal bureaucracy in East Africa expanded.

The establishment of the Mombasa court marked such an important move for the British legal administration of East Africa that one of the judges appointed to it declared that it would one day likely become a court of appeal for other courts planned for the Imperial British East Africa Company's territories.[36] Shortly after the establishment of the East Africa Protectorate, officials upgraded the court and renamed it the High Court of East Africa at Mombasa. It became the regional appellate court, the East Africa Court of Appeals, in 1909.[37] The juridical separation of East Africa from India was purely bureaucratic: Indian statutory and case law maintained their privileged place in the courtroom even after the administrative ties between East Africa's courts and India were severed. The move, however, cut off one of the strategies that litigants and their lawyers had previously turned to. Rather than appealing to authorities in a distant metropole, lawyers now had to take their cases to a regional appellate court staffed by judges who had previously served on the lower-level circuit. The symbolic power of shifting ultimate legal authority from Bombay, the regional imperial metropolis, to Mombasa,

[32] Like the Zanzibar court, the basic laws of the East Africa Protectorate also came from India; the same legislation applied. Anthony Allott, "The Development of the East African Legal Systems," in D.A. Low and A. Smith, eds. *History of East Africa*, Vol. 3 (Oxford: Clarendon Press, 1976), 361.

[33] *Who's Who 1903: An Annual Biographical Dictionary*, Part 2 (London: Adam and Charles Black, 1903), 1093.

[34] *The Gazette for Zanzibar and East Africa*, No. 16 (May 18, 1892), 5; *The Solicitor's Journal and Reporter*, Vol. 34 (November 23, 1889), 65.

[35] *The Gazette for Zanzibar and East Africa*, No. 48 (December 28, 1892), 6. The following year saw the arrival of Horshanji Lascari from India, Francis Henry Owen Wilson from London, and J. Collinson from the Cape Colony.

[36] *The Gazette for Zanzibar and East Africa*, No. 20 (June 15, 1892), 2.

[37] Allott, "The Development of the East African Legal Systems," 379.

the terminus of the Uganda Railway, would not have been lost on the lawyers or their merchant clientele.

At the same time, political developments were taking place in Zanzibar that had profound implications for the position of British courts there. In the decade after the British Government established a protectorate at Zanzibar, a series of decrees and acts reordered the island's court system and set in place a dual system of legal administration that made provisions for British and Islamic law. Within the system, British Indian law and Islamic law were to be administered in two different courts drawing on two different bureaucracies, with two different appellate structures – at least in theory.[38] In reality, the dual court system was perhaps more of a bureaucratic artifice than a substantive division of legal responsibility. By 1904, both courts operated out of the same building – the High Court building, designed in the Indo-Saracenic style by the architect J.H. Sinclair.[39] More importantly, at the top of either court system stood a panel of British imperial judges. Piggott, for example, sat as a "Her Britannic Majesty's" Judge for Zanzibar, but also "as Judge in Arab matters on the highest judicial tribunal of His Highness the Sultan of Zanzibar."[40] Even Arab *qāḍis* made frequent appearances in British courts – although they rarely decided on key matters.[41]

To anyone paying attention it would have been clear that by the end of the nineteenth century, an all-encompassing legal bureaucracy headed by British judges had more or less taken shape along the coast of East Africa, and was on the cusp of bursting into the region's interior along the tracks of the Uganda Railway. And as greater numbers of merchants and laborers began to make their way to East Africa to engage with the growing infrastructural project, either through their labor or their capital, questions of law became more pressing than ever before. The money that firms brought, the speculations they engaged in, and the land that the railway ran through were all grounded in fundamental questions of law and empire.

[38] For a good overview, see Stockreiter, *Islamic Law, Gender, and Social Change*, 35–45; J.H. Vaughn, *The Dual Jurisdiction in Zanzibar* (Zanzibar: Zanzibar Government Printers, 1935).

[39] 1 ZLR xi. On Indo-Saracenic architecture in the Indian Ocean as a form through which British India projected its imperial authority, see Metcalf, *Imperial Connections*, 56–67.

[40] *Who's Who 1903*, Part 2, 1093.

[41] Bang, *Sufis and Scholars of the Sea*, 153–172.

Governing Property: The *Charlesworth Pilling* Case

One early dispute in particular stood out in the breadth of the implications to the questions it raised surrounding the place of Islamic law in an East African world of emerging modern capitalism and high imperialism – questions that eventually made their way before the Privy Council, the highest juridical authority in the British Empire. Around 1895, Messrs. Charlesworth Pilling, a British firm that had been trading in East Africa for at least a few years, had purchased four *shambas* from different Arab and Swahili planters in Mombasa in the months before the Uganda Railway engineers began their work there. The purchase was speculative: the land was situated near the projected railway terminus, and firm hoped to reap profits by selling it to the British Government just as the project was beginning. The problem, however, was that the engineers began construction before the Government had undertaken a valuation of the land. When the time came, the Government Collector offered a total of just over Rs 40,000, a figure that the firm rejected as being too low.[42] Pilling's lawyers filed a suit against the British Government, in which they called into question the valuation process and disputed the land's acquisition by the government, the work the government claimed to have done on the land, and more. The core issue, however, was the land's value – and, more, specifically, the firm's ability to demand compensation for government buildings erected on their land as part of its valuation.

In arguing the case, Pilling's lawyers, the firm of Francis Wilson and Gerald Mead, raised the fundamental question of what law applied to the dispute. Drawing on William Edward Hall's *A Treatise on International Law*, published in 1880, the lawyers argued that the question fell under the umbrella of exterritoriality: that land acquired by their client, a British subject, must, by virtue of the principle of extra-territorial jurisdiction, be subjected to English law. Extra-territorial jurisdiction, they effectively argued, wasn't only over people – it was over the land they held as well. To them, the issue could not have been any more straightforward: this was a transaction between Englishmen and the British government, and fell under English law, which awarded compensation for buildings erected in matters like these.[43] The East African landscape, then, ought to appear as a patchwork of territorial jurisdictions – one that constantly shifted as land changed hands.

[42] *The Gazette for Zanzibar and East Africa*, Vol. 6, No. 289 (August 11, 1897), 2–3; see also R.W. Kostal, *Law and English Railway Capitalism, 1825–1875* (New York: Oxford University Press, 1998), 144–180.

[43] *The Gazette for Zanzibar and East Africa*, Vol. 6, No. 289 (August 11, 1897), 6.

The British government, however, contended that the issue fell under Islamic law – or, rather, "Mahomedan Law" – under which, they claimed, the plaintiffs had no right to compensation for any of the buildings. They called two *qāḍis* from Zanzibar as witnesses, and both affirmed "that in cases such as the present the landowner cannot claim possession of buildings placed upon his land by a trespasser but can only call upon the trespasser to remove the buildings and restore the land to its original state."[44] The ontological dependencies between fruit, trees, and the land (see Chapter 3) did not extend to the built environment; houses that had been built after the purchase were not an essential part of the landscape, and could thus be removed at either side's behest.

The stakes associated with the case were high. Even the judge presiding over the case – the judicial officer in Mombasa, Ralph Bertie Cator, who had arrived in Mombasa a year earlier – admitted that the legal questions it raised caused him "considerable anxiety," not only because of its effect on future railway work, but also for its implications for all future transactions.[45] A victory by Pilling would thrust the gates wide open for speculators to try and squeeze profits out of the railway project. More importantly, the ruling would have unequivocally established a new legal framework governing disputes surrounding property, and would have ushered in a new phase of British India's growing legal empire in East Africa.

Surprisingly, Cator was unwilling to apply English or Anglo-Indian law to the dispute at hand – at least not in 1897. Challenging the lawyers' interpretation of Hall's principles, the judge, who received a law degree from Lincoln's Inn just four years earlier,[46] argued that Hall's treatise gave only a limited endorsement of the principle of exterritoriality – that he "qualifies it by saying that 'the immunities have been granted partly out of convenience and partly out of courtesy.'" Cator declared that "the universal rule that questions relating to land must be governed by the *lex loci rei sitae* has reason on its side," adding that he did not think that "the privileges conferred by exterritoriality could ever be intended to infringe it." Exterritoriality was an exception – a privilege: the general rule in the politics of the protectorate was that the local law governed the land transactions. In East Africa, the judge noted, the British government was acting as an agent of the Sultan, "a Mahomedan prince, to whom unquestionably Mahomedan law would apply."

[44] *The Gazette for Zanzibar and East Africa*, Vol. 6, No. 289 (August 11, 1897), 6.

[45] *The Gazette for Zanzibar and East Africa*, Vol. 6, No. 289 (August 11, 1897), 5; *St. Peter's College, Radley, Register, 1847–1904* (Oxford, UK: Alden and Company, 1905), 106.

[46] "Appointments," *The Law Journal*, Vol. 40 (London: The Law Journal, 1905), 314.

For the time being, then, Islamic law, rather than English or Anglo-Indian law applied to the case – and it was up to the judge to administer it. "Besides my duties as a Consular Judge," Cator wrote, "I sit here as one of the Sultan's judges, and in that capacity I have to administer, with the help of native judges, the Sheria or Mahomedan Law, which is the local law here."[47] By framing his position in East Africa as one that straddled both juridical realms, Cator reserved for British judges like himself the right to weigh in on questions of Islamic law as well as British law. The nature of the dispute, rather than the forum, determined which law would apply. His long judgment was published in full, in a nine-page spread in the *Zanzibar Gazette*; there was no question of its importance to the region's commercial future.

Unhappy with Cator's decision, Pilling's lawyers appealed the ruling to Zanzibar, where Judge Cracknall – who had by now been deciding cases in Zanzibar and East Africa for nearly fifteen years – and an assistant judge heard the case again. To the two judges, the notion that Islamic law would govern land transactions flew in the face of decades of practice and treaties between the British Government and that of the Sultan of Zanzibar – specifically the Treaty of 1886, which stated that subjects of the British government enjoyed the rights of exterritoriality within the dominions of the Sultan. The principle of exterritoriality, they argued, declared "a separation of persons enjoying that right and their property from the country in which they are, that is to say that British subjects are justiceable by their own laws and their property subject to the law governing them in their own country." Cracknall contended that the court "has always acted on that principle, gifts *inter vivos* contracts, torts, wills, and intestacies being thus construed (as in India) of Christians, Mahomedans, Hindoos, Parsees, &c." and that there was never a restriction by "Mahomedan law," except in the case of testamentary power.[48]

The judges rested their argument on two pillars: first, that the Order in Council of 1884, which stated that "the common and statute law of England [is] in force," could not mean that Islamic law applied; and second, that the principle of *lex sitae* invoked by Cator fell under the scope of international law, "within the pale of which at the time of the Order in Council it is doubtful if Zanzibar had entered."[49] Because of the Sultanate's subordinate status in international politics, principles of international law had no place in the British courts in East Africa – not

[47] *The Gazette for Zanzibar and East Africa*, Vol. 6, No. 289 (August 11, 1897), 6.

[48] Judgment of High Court, Zanzibar (November 28, 1898) *Charlesworth Pilling & Co.* v. *Secretary of State for Foreign Affairs and Others* (1898) ZNA HC 5/3H, 43.

[49] *Charlesworth Pilling & Co.* v. *Secretary of State for Foreign Affairs and Others* (1898) ZNA HC 5/3H, 45.

even exterritoriality, which "involves confusion and differences… [which] could be removed by the practice of this Court, which regards easements as running with the land."[50] Moreover, they asserted, Cator's argument that the Secretary of State was the agent of "a Mahomedan prince" to whom Islamic law would apply had not been raised in court before, and could not be carried to its logical conclusion. The judges doubted, for example, whether "the agent would have obeyed his principal if he had ordered the railway to be stopped and the staff removed."[51]

Like Cator, Cracknall was concerned with developing a general property rights framework – one that would facilitate the railway project while establishing clear principles for determining compensation to affected property owners. By this point, British judges would have had decades of experience in India and England on how to deal with the land titles that railroads invariably ran into; the Zanzibar judges and Cator would all have been familiar with the need to address the matter.[52] However, where they differed was on their understanding of where those property rights emanated from: general principles of international law, or treaties between the British government and the Sultan. Put differently, they disagreed on whether to follow law in its abstract wisdom or in its particular manifestations. For now, the latter would prevail.

But for the British government, the Zanzibar court's ruling was unacceptable; not only would it disrupt railway work at a critical juncture, it would unnecessarily complicate the administration of law in East Africa, creating multiple, fluctuating jurisdictions for property disputes. To reflect the seriousness of the matter, they appealed the case to the Judicial Committee of the Privy Council – the highest court of appeal in the British Empire. There, Mombasa officials argued that the Orders in Council referred to did not impair the principle of *lex sitae*, and that no matter how one looked at the matter, Islamic law prevailed. If the court were to follow English law, then they would have to revert to local law to govern the matter; in English law, local law governed land transactions. Moreover, if the court were to hold that Zanzibar was a district of Bombay (which, administratively speaking, it was), then British Indian law would also cede the matter to Islamic law.[53]

[50] *Charlesworth Pilling & Co.* v. *Secretary of State for Foreign Affairs and Others* (1898) ZNA HC 5/3H, 44.

[51] *Charlesworth Pilling & Co.* v. *Secretary of State for Foreign Affairs and Others* (1898) ZNA HC 5/3H, 47.

[52] See also Kostal, *Law and English Railway Capitalism*; Peter Satyanand Samuels, "Dysmorphic Sovereignty: Colonial Railroads, Eminent Domain, and the Rule of Law in British India, 1824–1857" (Ph.D. Dissertation, Stanford University, 2014).

[53] *Privy Council Judgments on Appeal from India, Vol. 8, 1901–1905* (Phowinapore: Sreenath Banerjee, 1908), 3.

In their rebuttal, Pilling's lawyers argued that the notion that English and Indian law would ultimately revert jurisdiction to Islamic law meant that a treaty that provided for exterritorial rights "leaves all the incidents of landed tenure as intra-territorial, as they were before or without the treaty." The Government's definition of exterritoriality, they suggested, ultimately nullified itself, leaving no room for the administration of property through the laws of the empire. Their argument then took a different tack. Drawing on an English translation of the *Hedaya*, a Hanafi text used as a standard reference in British India,[54] they suggested that if Islamic law *were* to govern the matter, then the rule of usurpation (*ghaṣb*) declared that a landowner had a right to the land with the buildings that were on it at the time he paid for it – that the land and the buildings were inseparable as sale objects at the time of the transaction.[55] Searching the texts of Islamic jurisprudence, they found a useful resource in a manual produced for an Indian context – one that they hoped would support their client's claims to the buildings even if the judges decided against them on the question of exterritoriality.

The members of the Privy Council dealt with the questions swiftly. On the question of extraterritoriality, they first noted that textbooks defined the concept as "a fiction by which the house and land occupied by a foreign sovereign or his ambassador was treated in law as part of his dominions, and that it is a convenient word to denote any group of privileges belonging to that class." In the Zanzibar court, they argued, Cracknall and Collinson "pushed the metaphor very far, holding that the term works a complete separation of the British subject and his property from the country in which they are." The Council was not yet ready for this interpretation: while it conceded that the Sultan of Zanzibar had reserved an incomplete list of instances in which British subjects could appeal to their own laws, it was "going a long way beyond that, and beyond the reason for these immunities, to say that the moment a plot of land is purchased by an Englishman it is stamped with the same character… [that] would belong to it if it were actually transferred to England and surrounded by other English land."[56] As far as land disputes were concerned, exterritoriality in East Africa required the application of the "local law," which they took to mean Islamic law.

But how did one administer Islamic law? Neither the original *Pilling* case, the appeal, nor the Privy Council decision would resolve the matter.

[54] For a good account of the career of the Hedaya and other "Anglo-Mahomedan" legal texts, see also Kugle "Framed, Blamed, and Renamed"; Cohn, *Colonialism and its Forms of Knowledge*, 57–75.

[55] *Privy Council Judgments on Appeal from India, Vol.* 8, 4.

[56] *Privy Council Judgments on Appeal from India, Vol.* 8, 7.

Indeed, over the next few decades, lawyers and judges would find themselves in the courtrooms trying to understand what they meant by "the Sheria or Mahomedan Law," and exactly how to administer it. In the original *Pilling* judgment in Mombasa, Cator suggested one possible approach. He noted that "the Defendant called in two of the Sultan's Cadis [sic] or Judges from Zanzibar… [and] they gave their evidence well and referred to text books… and although I may not make use of my knowledge of the Mahomedan Law directly, I think there can be no harm in my saying that I in no way disagree with them."[57] By relying on *qāḍis* who would buttress their own opinions with textual references, one could effectively decide on questions of Islamic law.

In their review of Cator's judgment, members of the Privy Council approved of his decision to poll the *qāḍis* and supplement it with his own opinion, "which his experience as a Mahomedan judge qualified him to form." However, they went a step further, going where Cator was unwilling to go: in forming their opinion, they turned directly to the translated *Hedaya* for guidance on the questions of Islamic law before them, much as they would have for imperial possessions like India or Burma. In their reading of it, the textbook suggested that as landowners, the firm of Charlesworth Pilling had no right to compensation for the buildings on the land, only the right to ask that the buildings be removed.[58] After more than four years of petitions and appeals, Pilling had lost its case.

In its movement from Mombasa to Zanzibar, and from there to London, the *Pilling* case revealed the interpretive tensions that resided in the East African soil. It highlighted the many layers of law that shaped the meaning of property within this world, stretching out over multiple legal traditions. If land – or, more fundamentally, property – constituted the material foundation of economic life in the Western Indian Ocean it formed an unstable bedrock, throwing up question after question about law, empire, and capitalism in the region. The *Pilling* case was but the first of many.

And yet, despite all of the opposing opinions and impulses it highlighted and the bigger questions it posed, the *Pilling* decision had clearly ushered in a new era in the legal history of East Africa. The case settled several of the most important issues of imperial legal administration in the region, including what exterritoriality might mean in a region with a legal history as layered as East Africa, and what laws imperial judges were to administer in a changing commercial landscape. More importantly, the decision left no question as to who was in charge of the legal

[57] *The Gazette for Zanzibar and East Africa*, No. 289 (August 11, 1897), 6.
[58] *Privy Council Judgments on Appeal from India, Vol. 8*, 8.

administration, even in the heart of the Omani Empire in East Africa: whether it was a question of Islamic law, English law, or Indian law, and whether it was in Mombasa, Zanzibar, or London, it fell under the domain of British judges. Armed with law degrees from London, it was up to them to call on *qāḍis* or directly look to legal texts to settle fundamental questions of law and economic life in the region.

Conclusion

Little could attest to the establishment of new era of legal administration as much as one moment in 1904, scarcely one year after the first services on the Uganda Railway began. Judge George Bettesworth Piggott, one of the judges that oversaw the transformation of the legal bureaucracy in East Africa during the *Pilling* years, was leaving Zanzibar after five years on the Bench to take a position as Assistant Judge for the Dominions of the Sublime Ottoman Porte. There, he would serve with Cator, who had just been promoted to the head of one of the most sought-after legal posts in the empire.[59] In a ceremony that took place three days before his departure, the island's judges and lawyers – including a delegation of Indian lawyers headed by the celebrated Hornius Lascari – gathered to celebrate their accomplishments over the past decade or so. In his speech, Piggott declared that "this Court of Zanzibar [is] unique in position" and that there was "hardly any Court in the world which administered so varied laws and dealt with such varied questions as this Court of Zanzibar."

Expressing his gratitude to the judge for his service, Lascari noted how "members of the local Bar felt that in the Court and especially at the hands of His Honour Judge Piggott, they had been treated with great patience often at times when a Judge must be sorely tried by Counsels' offences in repetitions during the course of cross examination." He ended by asking that the departing judge "forget any such instances and recognize that such was all done for the benefit of the client." Piggott replied that he, too, "owed much to the patience of the Bar."[60] Indeed, there was much to be proud of. By the time Piggott left East Africa, a deeply-entrenched legal bureaucracy had taken shape all along the coast and interior, stretching the long arm of British imperial law into places that they weren't even sure existed forty or fifty years before. And the

[59] *The Law Journal,* Vol. 29 (June 19, 1904), 324.

[60] "Local News," *The Gazette for Zanzibar and East Africa,* Vol. 12, No. 628 (February 10, 1904), 4.

judges and lawyers that had gathered to celebrate that evening had done it all together – all for the sake of their clients and the empire.

For all of the hearty backslapping that took place that evening, the exchange that took place during the ceremony hinted at some of the tensions that characterized the development of British India's legal empire in East Africa. The partygoers had little to say about the anxieties over the contours and substance of British jurisdiction in the region that judges experienced, nor about the litigants, court clerks, and *qāḍis* who shaped the life of imperial law. Theirs was a narrative of legal development grounded firmly inside a courtroom that was removed entirely from the forces of commerce and empire that had shaped the history of the region – a courtroom that was devoid of any voice untrained in the art of law.

Nor did they say much about the confusion over which laws to administer and how to administer them. Despite their claims to Islamic law, Cator, Cracknall, and the members of the Privy Council had only the vaguest ideas of what those laws were – a combination of textbooks, Anglo-Mohammedan digests, and *qāḍis*' opinions, coupled with their own notions of what that law might be. In a sense, their approach to Islamic law hearkened back to the days in which they were grappling with the law more generally – a time when they looked to other legal actors for guidance while pleading with their superiors in Bombay to send law textbooks to help guide them.

By declaring their right to adjudicate on matters of Islamic law – by declaring themselves agents of the Sultan – judges like Cator unwittingly opened the door to a decades-long debate, played out over scores of courtroom decisions, over what Islamic law was and what it meant for *waraqas*, land, and economic life. Over time, they would develop a corpus of rulings on Islamic legal matters which they could look to in order to guide their decisions, but that, too, was a process involving *qāḍis*, lawyers, and litigants who sought to delineate the boundaries between Islamic law and economic life at a time of high imperialism. And to take utterances in the courtroom – to take the competing arguments about land, value, and contract that were nested in the *khiyār* sale – and craft a corpus of law out of them required deliberate action.

6 Muslim Mortgages

When James William Murison arrived in Zanzibar in the summer of 1905 to take up the post of Assistant Judge, the circulations of lawyers, texts, statutes, and codes that had ushered in a new phase in East Africa's legal history had already set in motion. Indeed, his arrival formed part of that history: Murison was a Cambridge graduate, and had been called to the Bar at Middle Temple just nine years before; Zanzibar was his first imperial post.[1] In the sixteen years or so before he arrived, judges like Ralph Cator, William Cracknall, and George Piggott, along with cadres of Indian and British lawyers, had worked out the basic contours and substance of British jurisdiction in the region; decisions like the one in the *Pilling* case directed their attention to their dual roles as imperial and Sultanic judges, and years of Sultanic decrees had ironed out some of the more pressing questions on the place of Indian law in East Africa.

But the job was not done. As in the past, Murison and others like him had to work out what that jurisdiction meant for commercial contracting in the region: how to define the *khiyār* sale and *waraqa* in a changing world of commerce, and how to balance their responsibilities toward Anglo-Indian law and Islamic law with the imperatives of economic life. The development of the Uganda Railway and the infusion of international capital into the East African landscape had done nothing to displace earlier forms of contracting. The *khiyār* sale, the *rahn*, and the *waraqas* they were inscribed onto were just as central to regional commerce in 1905 as they had been a half century earlier.

And yet, much had changed. The clove and ivory trades, both pillars of the East African economy during the nineteenth century, were by the 1890s experiencing enormous transformations. The changing political landscape of the East African interior redirected much of the ivory trade away from the hands of Zanzibari Arabs and the coffers of the Sultanate, while annual fluctuations in global clove markets left many of

[1] Douglas Brooke and Wheelton Sladen, eds. *Who's Who, 1907: An Annual Autobiographical Dictionary*, Vol. 58, Part 2 (London: Adam and Charles Black, 1907), 1229.

the region's planters saddled with debt and unsold stocks of cloves. The Uganda Railway project, which had promised to transform the region's commercial landscape, had done little to provide opportunities for the region's producers – the debtors that frequently found themselves being dragged to court by creditors and lawyers who hoped to foreclose on their plantations and homes.

Faced with an economic environment characterized by uncertainty and vulnerability, judges resolved to develop a property rights regime that would regulate the *khiyār* contract. Their experiences with agrarian debt and peasant dispossession in India, coupled with the precarious situation of landowners and debtors in East Africa, drove them to approach *khiyār* transactions in ways that emphasized stability over certainty, equity over incentives, and legibility in the eyes of the law over all else. They sought to build a property regime that would preserve the positions of individual landowners, whom they saw as constituting the foundation of political community; and law was a means of realizing this vision. The process was neither streamlined nor certain, and involved competing opinions, texts, and agendas from a range of different actors, all of whom made claims about the applicability of Islamic law or Anglo-Indian law to the matter. Nor was the process decisive in any way: although judges declared opinions that asserted finality, decisions were frequently reversed, amended, or disregarded altogether.

But for Murison, a messy series of decisions was not enough. To legally administer an empire, one needed guidance – a corpus of local decisions that judges and lawyers could look to for guidance when grappling with the disputes before them. To get there, he needed to craft a singular narrative out of a series of disconnected pronouncements and interpretations of law – a narrative that was unmistakably authoritative in its presentation and form. Drawing from the large archive of court cases that had been amassing in the consular court, Murison published the *Zanzibar Law Reports* in 1919, a narrative of law and empire – of legal positivism – in which court decisions, many of which he was involved in, gradually tethered the changing practices of a growing commercial society to the imperatives of imperial legal administration.

The *Zanzibar Law Reports* dealt with a range of different issues that litigants in the region grappled with: marriage and divorce, religious practice, and unsurprisingly, the *khiyār* sale, which formed a visible strand in the narrative braid that Murison and others had woven. The *khiyār* sale cases in the *Zanzibar Law Reports* highlight how the contract stood in as a metonym for Islamic law and economic life – the practices, concerns, and discourses that shaped what Islamic legal categories and commercial practices might be capable of in a global economy. They also reveal how actors turned to the law to mediate the pressures of a fluctuating market. At the same time, the narrative of the *khiyār* sale as presented in the *Law Reports* suggests that by the early twentieth century it fell to British judges to work out the boundaries between Islamic law in the books, British Indian statute, and the commercial practices they found themselves confronted with. If commercial actors had once determined how they were going to capture changing commercial opportunities, this role had now shifted decisively to the courtroom. In a post-*Pilling* world of contracting, the voices of commercial actors intervened in the narrative, but the voices of lawyers and judges dominated it.

Creating a Corpus: The *Zanzibar Law Reports*

Murison's *Zanzibar Law Reports* weren't the first time that legal decisions had been published. A summary of a bankruptcy case was published in the very first issue of the *Gazette for Zanzibar and East Africa* in 1892; subsequent issues publicized a range of different legal matters, including court proceedings, judicial opinions, insolvency declarations, declarations of *wakfs*, and more. And like the law reports that Murison would compile decades later, the *Gazette* aimed at a readership from among British officials, judges included. However, it became clear very early on that the *Gazette* aimed at a readership beyond British officialdom: entire articles and pages were reprinted in Gujarati, and reporters devoted as much space to international news, local cricket matches, and advertisements as they did to legal matters. The *Zanzibar Law Reports*, however, constituted an altogether different genre of writing: through them, Murison hoped to create a reference book for how to administer law in East Africa – to form a corpus of authoritative rulings and landmark cases to guide newly arrived judges in the region.

To do this, he had to be selective as to which cases to include. By the time he published the *Law Reports* in 1919, there were thousands that he could have chosen from: British courts had by then been in operation for more than fifty years, and judges had issued countless opinions on a range of different matters. The bulk of these, however, would be confined to the archives: even illustrative cases like that of Musabbah's *waraqa* (see Chapter 4) were doomed to be tied up in twine and filed away in a storage room, not to be opened until more than 100 years later. As illustrative as they might be to historians, those cases offered nothing by way of guidance to the judge – Cracknall's judgment offered little engagement with substantive legal issues – and could hardly be thought to highlight the legal work that Murison and his colleagues had engaged in over the years.

By contrast, the cases in the *Law Reports* were supposed to fit within a narrative of the triumph of Britain's imperial legal administration in East Africa – to supplement a similar narrative that had been established in other domains. Murison suggested as much in his introduction to the first volume, in which he framed the establishment of British courts in Zanzibar as the last episode in a history of Britain's involvement in the Sultanate, from the separation of Muscat and Zanzibar onward. After listing all of the different governments that surrendered their right to exterritorial jurisdiction to Britain, he named all of the decrees that had given Britain's legal bureaucracy in East Africa its shape.[2]

But the *Law Reports* were meant as more than a celebration of judicial accomplishments in East Africa. In compiling a selection of court decisions, Murison hoped to create a common law corpus that would guide judges who came after him. He took what were a series of utterances in the courtroom – opinions, arguments, and rebuttals – and crafted a narrative of legal positivism. Through the process of collecting cases, writing the headnotes, and selecting the keywords to index them with, he transformed a sprawling archive of thousands of court cases into a lean body of judicial decisions on key social, economic, and legal issues. Judges who came after him could now refer to a clear body of cases – a transcribed, catalogued, and indexed archive of Zanzibar's legal past, or at least the parts of it that mattered for its future.

To Murison, separating out Zanzibar's legal wheat from its chaff was all the more important when considering the variety of laws the court had to deal with. "The law of Zanzibar," he wrote, "even after the German, French, Austrian, American, Belgian, Italian, and Portuguese systems of law have been eliminated from it, still remains fairly polymorphous." It incorporated "the substance of the Common Law, the doctrines of equity, and the statutes of general application in England" by 1897. At the same time, he acknowledged that "many of the Zanzibar Decrees are based on the Indian Codes and Acts, with the result that a great part of the law of India is in force in Zanzibar." Also, with only some exceptions, "the substantive body of the Mahommedan law is also in force" – in all of its variations – as well as Hindu law. "And finally," he declared, "is to be added the multiplicity of customs prevailing among the various communities of Zanzibar."[3]

By publishing a small selection of cases, Murison hoped to guide judges on how to maneuver through the thickets of juridical life in a

[2] 1 ZLR vii-ix.
[3] 1 ZLR ix-x.

region characterized by multiple legal traditions – not the least vexing of which was Islamic law, which Murison affirmed "is the fundamental law of the Protectorate and in certain matters is administered in the British court, [and] plays a considerable part in the Zanzibar Law Courts." While he began his discussion of Islamic law by highlighting its "difficulty and obscurity," he also wanted to highlight the work that had been done in domesticating the legal tradition – work exemplified in the cases he highlighted. By the time he wrote his introduction, he felt confident in claiming that because of the combined efforts of British judges and East African *qāḍis* "much of the local Mahommedan law is fairly well settled, and in time it will no doubt be ascertained for practical purposes, wholly and with certainty."[4]

The *khiyār* sale formed one thread in this juridical tapestry. There were many possible cases to choose from, going back to before the case of Musabbah's *waraqa*; there were at least nine different cases between 1918 and 1922 that dealt with the question of rent alone. To choose a handful of cases that conveyed a narrative of the transformation of the contract from *khiyār* sale to Muslim mortgage required deliberate action – an awareness of which cases reflected that narrative and which did not. Instead, Murison chose to highlight two cases, both of which he presided over – cases that reflected the reconstruction of possession in the *khiyār* sale to reflect its new legal status as a mortgage, first based on Anglo-Indian precedent, and then on a blend of Islamic jurisprudence and Anglo-Indian law. What had started off as a series of bouts of confusion and conflict ultimately settled into a neat narrative of Islamic law and economic life – of the *waraqa's* place in a changing economic and political world, and of the role of judges in shaping that place. Moments like the case of Musabbah's *waraqa*, in which judges, *qāḍis*, lawyers, and other actors all made authoritative claims to interpretation were sidelined, or silenced altogether. In their place, Murison highlighted cases like the *Pilling* case and the two *khiyār* sale cases – ones that emphasized certainty over disagreement, precedent over context, and judicial authority over all else. In the *Zanzibar Law Reports*, law would not appear as an arena of conflict, but as a positive text: a frictionless flow of decisions from beginning to end, that could both guide and mislead judges and lawyers – and later, legal historians who let Murison's selections guide them through the archive as they reconstructed narratives of law and economic life in the Western Indian Ocean.[5]

[4] 1 ZLR x.

[5] On "law as text" versus "law as an arena of conflict," see also Hendrik Hartog, "Pigs and Positivism," *Wisconsin Law Review* (1985), 899–935.

Boom and Bust in East Africa, c. 1890–1925

For commercial actors in East Africa, the late nineteenth and early twentieth centuries were nothing to be excited about. Although the railway promised to transform the scale and scope of commerce in East Africa, merchants' prospects between 1875 and 1925 looked uncertain at best. Profits from the clove trade, which was Zanzibar's mainstay, fluctuated from year to year: the hurricane of 1874 had dealt a severe blow to the island's clove trade, and it took a while for the island's planters to recover. Many chose to shift their planting activities to Pemba, though a number did stay behind in Zanzibar and start their work over again. The problem was that clove trees did not produce right away: the English horticulturalist and agricultural reporter Robert Nunez Lyne, who spent much of his career in East Africa, noted that clove trees took seven or eight years to blossom, and ten years until they brought any real returns.[6]

The years between 1874 and 1882, then, were marked by low export figures, although financiers did receive high prices for them. When the newly planted trees did finally begin to mature, exports soared, as there were now producers in both Pemba and Zanzibar. The years 1883 to 1885, for example, saw the export of nearly 17 million lbs – more than the previous five years combined – and by the 1890s merchants were exporting anywhere between 12.5 million to 18 million lbs annually, a figure which seemed to only climb as the years went by.

However, even as exports increased, planters were unable to fight slowly declining prices.[7] In April 1892, the *Gazette* published a column bemoaning the long-standing depreciation of clove values on the world market. The author, most likely Lyne himself, suggested that in 1889, 6 to 7 ducats per lb. of cloves was considered a low price, but that the price had recently dropped to just over 3 ducats; he later noted that between 1894 and 1904, prices in London varied between 2½ ducats and 6 ducats per lb.[8] This, he suggested, was a result of overproduction – that the annual crop greatly exceeded the world's consumption (which he estimated at about 11.2 million lbs) and that London's warehouses were "burdened" with a stock of no less than 4.76 million lbs of

[6] Lyne, *Zanzibar in Contemporary Times*, 247.

[7] Here, I am relying on figures and analysis in Cooper, *From Slaves to Squatters*, 125–135. Cooper's analysis of the vicissitudes of the clove trade is by far the most compelling one to date.

[8] "Zanzibar and the Clove Trade," *The Gazette for Zanzibar and East Africa*, No. 12 (April 20, 1892), 2; Lyne, *Zanzibar in Contemporary Times*, 246.

unsold cloves.[9] In the summer of 1892 alone, unsold stocks of cloves in Zanzibar and Pemba amounted to over 5 million lbs.[10]

To planters, the unsold stocks of cloves were the product of a market that they could never fully come to terms with. The distance between their *shambas* and the markets they sold their goods in – markets as far away as Bombay, Marseilles, and London – left a lot of room for delay. Although clove prices between 1890 and 1925 were generally on the rise, the profits from season to season fluctuated wildly, varying by as much as 75 percent within a single year.[11] Planters who looked to the market for signals often found themselves chasing after the ghosts of markets past. The informational lag, and the time it took to adjust production to that information, invariably led to frustration: in a good season, everything suggested that planting more clove trees would bring in more profits, but if prices had dropped by the time the cloves reached the market, the planters, who had already sunk their money into trees, could only make up the difference by trying to sell more of their crop.[12] The unsold stocks of cloves, then, were sometimes the result of a glut in the market, but at other times a bet that things might turn around next year.

Planters also had to contend with a changing labor force. As the British presence in East Africa expanded, efforts to eradicate the slave trade gained traction; slavery was "de-legalized" by decree in 1897, and although planters were allowed to keep the slaves they already had, the closure of the slave trade and the open process of consular manumission ensured that the region's labor force would no longer be the same. Between 1897 and 1907 the British government freed nearly 11,000 slaves in Zanzibar and Pemba, and planters manumitted another 6,000 via non-governmental manumission processes.[13] Rather than leave, many manumitted slaves often stayed on the plantation, hiring themselves out as wage laborers. The rates planters paid to seasonal laborers cut into their already meager profit margins, which were already being eaten up by the high rates of interest they paid on their accounts and taxes they had to pay on their clove exports.[14] What had once been a pursuit of leisure and profit had now become a race to keep from drowning in red ink.

The state of the region's ivory trade was only slightly more promising. Although the total exports for ivory grew at a reasonably steady rate

[9] "Zanzibar and the Clove Trade," *The Gazette for Zanzibar and East Africa*, No. 12 (April 20, 1892), 2.
[10] See the August 1892 issues of *The Gazette for Zanzibar and East Africa*.
[11] Cooper, *From Slaves to Squatters*, 140 n. 48.
[12] Cooper, *From Slaves to Squatters*, 139–141.
[13] Harms, "Introduction" in idem (ed.) *Indian Ocean Slavery*, 11–12.
[14] Cooper, *From Slaves to Squatters*, 140.

between 1889 and 1913, the onset of World War I crippled ivory exports to Europe, and the post-war years saw little by way of revival. In the 1890s, Zanzibar exported an average of 530 tons of ivory to Europe – a figure which rose only slightly, to about 570 tons over the next ten tears. The years 1911 to 1914 were very good, averaging roughly over 600 tons a year, but the next five years were the worst ever reported, averaging only 320 tons per year; the following decade was only marginally better, with exports of roughly 390 tons per year until 1930.[15] All told, the regional ivory trade in the early twentieth century was a mere shadow of what it had been in its heyday.

The gradually shrinking ivory export figures and the fears that merchants had surrounding the future of the ivory trade owed a lot to the shifting political landscape of the East African interior. Bowing to international pressure, the Sultan of Zanzibar ceded the administration of the mainland to the German East African Company in 1888; soon afterwards, a rebellion broke out, spreading to many of the ivory-exporting towns on the coast and disrupting the ivory trade.[16] In 1890, Germany took control of the territory from the company, declared much of Tanganyika a German colony, and sought to redirect trade through Dar es Salaam.[17] With the establishment of the colony, the number of white settlers rose dramatically, as did the number of regulations relating to the export of ivory; as a result, the movement and marketing of ivory gradually shifted out of Arab and Indian hands.[18]

At the same time, another European power had come into the picture. The Belgian Government, which had been seeking its own colonies in Africa, had settled on the Congo as its principal foothold. After a series of armed battles in the Stanley Falls and around Lake Tanganyika, the Belgians defeated Arab traders (including Tippu Tip's son) and closed off the Congo to ivory caravans moving back and forth from the coast.[19] The ivory trading frontier, which had stretched from the coast all the way to the Congo, had by the end of the century come up against serious

[15] I am indebted to Jonas Kranzer for providing me with these figures. See Jonas Kranzer, "Warengeschichte des Elfenbeins im 19. und 20. Jh." (Unpublished Ph.D. Dissertation, University of Konstanz, Germany, 2010).

[16] For the best analysis of this rebellion, see Glassman, *Feasts and Riot*, especially 177–248.

[17] John Iliffe, *A Modern History of Tanganyika* (Cambridge, UK: Cambridge University Press, 1979), 88–122. Norman R. Bennett, *Arab Versus European: Diplomacy and War in Nineteenth-Century East Central Africa* (New York: Africana Publishing Company, 1986), 129–143, 211–216.

[18] Bernhard Gissibel, "German Colonialism and the Beginnings of International Wildlife Preservation in East Africa," *German Historical Institute Bulletin*, Supplement 3 (2006), 121–142.

[19] Bennett, *Arab Versus European*, 217–253; Wilkinson, *The Arabs and the Scramble for Africa*, 422–435.

barriers, and although it continued until well after the Belgian takeover of the Congo, it hardly held the same stature that it did in the past. Visitors to Zanzibar after 1900 rarely took the trouble to mention the island's commerce in ivory – a subject that had been a pillar of nineteenth-century travel narratives.

For moneylenders reading about the European victories in the interior of East Africa and of the subsequent ruptures in the caravan trade, the news would have added to their already-increased anxieties about their future business prospects. They received weekly reports on markets abroad – in India, in Europe, and elsewhere – and were sensitive to how prices for the commodities they dealt in fluctuated from week to week.[20] Moreover, they read about the financial health of their debtors: the *Zanzibar Gazette* included regular notices on insolvencies, bequests of properties, and results of court cases between merchants. When added to the news and rumors that spread through the marketplace and through merchants arriving from the interior, it would have heightened their sense of vulnerability – their paranoia surrounding the likelihood of a series of defaults leading to their own business failure.

To shield themselves from the fluctuations of the export economy, moneylenders turned to urban property. This made perfect sense in the bigger picture: urban property stood at the intersection of a number of different types of economic activities and their corresponding loans and debts. Plantation owners, ivory traders, shippers, and other actors all invested in urban real estate, and it formed the most conspicuous form of consumption for the well-to-do: the more successful an economic actor was, the larger the house.[21] Urban property – the house – thus stood in for the range of different loans, debts, and accounts that characterized economic life in East Africa.

But urban real estate also made sense as a financial investment. Because of the increased migration to towns as a result of the region's growing (albeit unevenly so) economy, urban property became increasingly lucrative. The rent that property owners could charge constituted a more stable source of income than agricultural profit, and urban property was more versatile, offering more potential than the plantations did even in their good years.[22] From the perspective of the moneylender,

[20] Lyne also started a short-lived newspaper called *The Shamba* in which he reported on the shifting market values of Zanzibar's agricultural exports. Philip Sadgrove, "The Press, Engine of a Mini-Renaissance, Zanzibar (1860–1920)" in Philip Sadgrove (ed.) *Printing and Publishing in the Middle East* (Oxford: Oxford University Press, 2008), 161–163.

[21] William Bissell, *Urban Design, Chaos, and Colonial Power in Zanzibar* (Bloomington, IN: Indiana University Press, 2011), 29–35.

[22] Cooper, *From Slaves to Squatters*, 206–213; see also Hollian Wint, "Credible Relations: Indian Finance and East African Society in the Indian Ocean, c. 1840–1930"

Indian or Arab, it was more fruitful to try to foreclose on a debtor's urban real estate than it did his hypothecated *shambas*.

The rising speculation in urban real estate, coupled with the uncertain situation of East Africa's economy from one year to another meant that questions of debt, land, and Islamic law – given expression in *waraqas* and *khiyār* sales – were going to take up a great deal of the court's attention. And indeed, they did: in the period between 1897 and 1930, the court heard scores of disputes surrounding *khiyār* sales of agricultural and urban property. And faced with a body of subjects for whom commercial failure was a growing concern, British officials saw to it that the courtroom was a place where they could stave off the threat of dispossession that sometimes accompanied the short-term fluctuations in the economy.

Emerging from the competing interpretations, opinions, and judgments that the court articulated between 1890 and 1930 is one trend: a clear tendency to maintain the terms of the *khiyār* well after the redemption period had expired and thus to allow the debt to accumulate. Through an admixture of Anglo-Indian law and Islamic law, judges effectively saw to it that the bulk of *khiyār* related disputes would result in an extension of the credit arrangement rather than the transfer of hypothecated property from debtor to creditor. Without a court decree, a creditor was unable to take over his debtor's property, effectively shielding the debtor from the possibility of foreclosure when a bad harvest, a glut in the market, or depressed demand left him at the mercy of his financiers and their lawyers.

In some respects, the principles that guided the judges in their approach to land disputes reflected a broadly Lockean philosophy. For Locke, private property formed the material foundation of civil society and of political community; the looming threat of dispossession of their East African protégés by their creditors – and British subjects, no less! – would have undermined that very foundation.[23] As a matter of principle as well as political expediency, then, judges had to keep property in the hands of Arab and Swahili landowners. And in taking a stance against foreclosure, British judges were also drawing on their long experience with the problem of peasant agrarian debt in the Subcontinent. Although British imperial expansion in India depended largely on the assistance of

(Ph.D. Dissertation, New York University, 2016), 148–203 for an analysis of the move to urban moneylending. Nelida Fuccaro's study of merchants in Bahrain sees similar trends. See Nelida Fuccaro, *Histories of City and State in the Persian Gulf: Manama since 1800* (New York: Cambridge University Press, 2009), 43–72.

[23] For an illuminating discussion of Locke, property, political community, and empire, see Andrew Sartori, *Liberalism in Empire: An Alternative History* (Berkeley, CA: University of California Press, 2015), esp. 13–50.

Bania financiers, the protections the British afforded them resulted in a system of agrarian finance characterized by heavy debt, expropriation, and dispossession.[24] The East African experience mirrored the Indian narrative: an explosion of credit in the nineteenth century in the context of the rapid expansion of commodity production for the world market, followed by the precariousness and uncertainty that came along with shifts in the market and the burden of debt that accompanied those shifts.[25] Having seen the fallout that could ensue from an unregulated credit market, particularly in agricultural regions, judges in East Africa approached financial transactions with an awareness of the past, but also an eye to the future. It was in the courtroom and in the *Law Reports* that they would pen the narrative of law and economic life that they had failed to write in India.

The *Khiyār* as Anglo-Indian Mortgage, 1897–1914: The *Mahfuz* Case

The first *khiyār*-related case Murison entered into the *Zanzibar Law Reports* was one that he presided over himself. In June 1903, an Arab by the name of Mahfuz bin Ahmed executed a *khiyār* sale in which he put up his house against a one-year Rs 1,700 debt to another Arab named Sa'id bin 'Awad. On the *waraqa*, he stated that he agreed to rent back the house for Rs 300 per year. Not much is known about either of the two parties; all the record states is that their arrangement continued uninterrupted until February 1905, when Sa'id came to court and filed a case against Mahfuz for Rs 150, unpaid rent for six months, and claimed a title to the house on the grounds that that redemption period had expired. When the judge looked into the consular register, he found that it was not the first time Mahfuz had put up his house via a *khiyār* sale. He had previously executed a similar deed in favor of two *Banias* for debts that he owed them, and had originally approached Sa'id for a loan to pay them off. Sa'id had effectively taken over as Mahfuz's new creditor.

To Murison, the central issue was how to interpret the *waraqa*: was he to consider it as a sale, in which case they would transfer title to the house to Sa'id, or a mortgage, in which case Mahfuz would only be liable for the unpaid rent and would retain possession of the house? The issue

24 Lakshmi Subramanian, *Indigenous Capital and Imperial Expansion: Bombay, Surat and the West Coast* (New York: Oxford University Press, 1998); I.J. Catanach, *Rural Credit in Western India: Rural Credit and the Cooperative Movement in the Bombay Presidency* (Berkeley, CA: University of California Press, 1970), 10–55.

25 Sugata Bose, *Peasant Labour and Colonial Capital: Rural Bengal since 1770* (Cambridge, UK: Cambridge University Press, 1993), 122–135.

wasn't simply one of semantics: if they understood the *khiyār* to be a sale, judges would have to uphold the creditor's right to the hypothecated property when the debt matured, unless the creditor chose not to pursue the claim. As a mortgage, the default would have been to keep the arrangement between the creditor and debtor alive, preventing a *de jure* dispossession of debtors who had not repaid their debts on time.

To a judge like Murison, the *Pilling* case (see Chapter 5) might have established that Islamic law governed all land-related transactions, but it offered far less guidance on how to deal with practices surrounding *waraqas* and land – transactions that formed the bedrock of economic life in the Western Indian Ocean. These did not just concern finance, either; contracts like the *khiyār* sale and the web of practices that emerged around it were fundamental to how Islamic legal precepts were given articulation in a commercial arena. How Murison regulated them in a courtroom, then, would have broad implications for how judges like him approached Islamic law in an age of emerging modern capitalism and high imperialism.

The issue was further complicated by the arrival in 1897, just after the first *Pilling* decision in Mombasa, of the Transfer of Property Act (hereafter, TPA) – a fifteen-year old piece of Indian legislation that sought to introduce a range of different categories of contracts for transactions relating to land. The TPA, organized into five chapters, sought to define the different types of sales and mortgages that came before Indian courts, and the rights and liabilities attaching to them. In its movement from India to East Africa, the TPA effectively displaced the categories that consular clerks had developed over two decades of their work in registering *waraqas*, translating them into categories that were better established in the Indian legal system (see Chapter 4). For judges looking to find useful parallels, the *khiyār* sale was most comparable to the "mortgage by conditional sale," which was a situation in which "the mortgagor ostensibly sells the mortgaged property on condition that on default of payment of the mortgage-money on a certain date the sale shall become absolute, or on condition that on such payment being made the sale shall become void, or on condition that on such payment being made the buyer shall transfer the property to the seller."[26]

On the face of it, the mortgage by conditional sale seemed almost exactly like the *khiyār* sale, the one clear distinction being that the *khiyār* sale, at least as economic actors understood it, did not necessarily imply a transfer of possession. Judges who ruled on *khiyār* transactions often

[26] Transfer of Property Act, 1882, Chapter 4, Section 58(c).

seemed comfortable with allowing *khiyār* sales to take place without any property changing hands. Indeed, for those concerned with keeping the wheels of commerce turning, it only made sense to turn a blind eye to what might have at first seemed like a charade of a contract. Only when litigants and their lawyers called the practice into question were the judges forced to articulate their views. The *Mahfuz* case was one such instance.

To determine what the status of the contract was in Islamic law, Murison polled three Zanzibari *qāḍis*, asking them whether the *khiyār* sale *waraqa* was "to be treated as an out and out sale or as a mortgage so that although the period of one year has gone past the mortgagor is still allowed to redeem [the house]." The first *qāḍi* to respond, a Shaikh Qasim bin Salim, wrote that because the *waraqa* clearly described a *khiyār* sale, and because the redemption period had expired, the sale had to stand. Whether the transaction constituted a mortgage was moot; the term would have been virtually unrecognizable to him. The other two *qādis*, both of whom regularly appeared in British courts – Shaikh Ahmed bin Sumait, who had actually written the *waraqa*, and Shaikh Tahir bin Abibaker Al-Amawi – agreed with Qasim's take on it. Strictly interpreted, the transaction could only result in the transfer of the house to the creditor.

Sa'id's lawyer, the Parsi barrister Framji Dorabji Rabadina, concurred with the *qāḍis*' assessment of the *waraqa*, but sought to buttress his case with evidence that he was more familiar with. Having graduated from St Xavier's College at Bombay University only seven years before, Rabadina was far more familiar with Anglo-Indian case law and legislation like the TPA than he was with questions of Islamic law.[27] In his reading of the *waraqa*, Islamic law was inconsequential; no matter how one looked at it, the *waraqa* was a sale. First, it didn't meet the requirements of a mortgage as laid out in the TPA, which required two witnesses: "the culture here is for the Cadi [sic] to write documents without witnesses," he stated; the TPA's formalities were never taken into consideration in the production of the document. Moreover, Rabadina argued, the court had misconstrued the transaction altogether. "There is a regular mortgage deed; this is not it," he declared. A mortgage deed stated that "so and so is indebted to so and so and has therefore mortgaged his *shamba.*" Citing three court decisions from Allahabad, Madras, and Bombay, he contended that the document could only be construed as a sale; the *qāḍis'* opinions only supplemented what was already a clear reading of the *waraqa* through Anglo-Indian law.[28]

[27] *University of Bombay: the Calendar for the Year 1906–1907, Volume 1* (Bombay: 1906), 217.
[28] *Said bin Avad* v. *Mahfuz bin Ahmed of Munguni* (1905) ZNA HC 7/775, 11–12.

The debtor Mahfuz's lawyer, the Parsi R.H. Boyce, read the *waraqa* differently. The *qāḍis*' opinions, he argued, held little weight; the transaction was governed wholly by the TPA, having taken place just before the TPA's introduction in 1897. And under the TPA, "the transaction must be a mortgage [by conditional sale] and not a sale."[29] Whether or not it looked like a regular mortgage deed made no difference; what mattered was that under the TPA, there was only one way to define the substance of the contract, no matter how it appeared on paper and no matter how the clerk might have annotated it.

Judge Murison agreed, asserting that while the *Pilling* case established that Islamic law governed all land-related disputes, "Indian Acts" dealing with questions of land that arrived in Zanzibar after *Pilling* "must over-rule *pro tanto* the Mahomedan Law." Even though he polled *qāḍis* on their reading of the *waraqa*, he wrote, "I cannot feel myself bound by their opinions in so far as they conflict with the law contained in the Transfer of Property Act."[30] Because the *khiyār* sale most closely approximated the mortgage by conditional sale as laid out in the TPA, there was only one way to categorize the contract. "It seems to me that in the absence of some explanation to the contrary, this document is just one of the kind that the section aimed at," he argued. "It is the common form of what is known as a Baikhiyar mortgage [sic]. It is never referred to in common parlance as a sale. It is always called a mortgage."

Murison's declaration that the *khiyār* was never referred to as a sale and was always called a mortgage brought into immediate relief the semantics of commercial practice. On the face of it, it was only partially true: nothing suggests that anyone but those working for the court called the *khiyār* a mortgage. The court records themselves are deceiving; while they make it seem as though witnesses only used the term "mortgage" or "mortgagee," one has to keep in mind their mediated nature. By the time it made its way into the documentary record, any utterance in the courtroom, no matter what the original language, had already been translated into English by the Court Reporter – a Parsi whose vocabulary, and perhaps basic familiarity with Anglo-Indian legal terminology, framed the recorded proceedings. This alone makes it difficult to ascertain whether the *qāḍis* in the case referred to the *khiyār* as a mortgage. When, for example, the *qāḍi* Qasim bin Salim wrote that "the mortgagor has no right of redemption after the expiration of the year

[29] *Said bin Avad* v. *Mahfuz bin Ahmed of Munguni* (1905) ZNA HC 7/775, 14–15.
[30] *Said bin Avad* v. *Mahfuz bin Ahmed of Munguni* (1905) ZNA HC 7/775, 19–20; 1 ZLR 191.

mentioned in the document" it is uncertain that he ever used the term "mortgager" – a term that had no equivalent in the lexicon of Islamic law. In a sense, the *Mahfuz* proceedings highlighted the process by which, subtly or otherwise, Islamicate categories became re-clothed in the garb of an Anglo-Indian contractual terminology through clerical translations and Anglo-Indian legislation. By insisting on calling it a mortgage rather than a sale – and, indeed, by asserting that *everyone* called it a mortgage and not a sale – Murison was commenting on a transformation that had slowly been taking place in British consular registries and in the courtroom over the course of many years.

And yet, to Murison and other judges like him, the semantics mattered. Through semantic maneuvers – through simple declarations on what to call something – the court redefined the contract in a way that benefited debtors in a time of uncertainty. As a mortgage rather than a sale, the expiration of the *khiyār* period did not necessitate a transfer of property from the debtor to the creditor: the Mahfuz bin Ahmeds of East Africa could hold onto their homes and *shambas*, even as the tides of the market turned against them. And as Murison transcribed the judgment into the first edition of the *Zanzibar Law Reports* years later, the headnote would confirm it: "The common form of Beikhiyar mortgage prevailing in Zanzibar is a mortgage by conditional sale within the meaning of Section 58 of the Transfer of Property Act, and not an absolute sale."[31] Through a simple act of transcription, his declaration became part of the legal corpus.

The *Khiyār* as "Muslim" Mortgage, 1914–1930: The *Hafiz* Case

As the years progressed, British judges remained steadfast in their commitment to creating a property rights regime across the empire that would balance the rights of debtors and creditors. Like before, they wanted to ensure that planters and other commercial actors facing the threat of failure or default would not have to risk dispossession, while also staying mindful of the rights of creditors and the risks they faced. The *khiyār* sale, then, continued to be regarded as a mortgage, blocking all attempts by creditors to dislodge their debtors from their homes while upholding their right to the money owed to them.

Some things had changed, though. On New Year's Day in 1917, officials replaced the TPA with the Transfer of Property Decree, which preserved the bulk of the TPA's text but restricted it from applying to

[31] 1 ZLR 189.

subjects of the Sultan – incidentally, the bulk of the region's debtors.[32] In practice, the Decree amounted to a repeal of the TPA, as Anglo-Indian contractual categories would no longer apply to most of the region's debt contracts. Untethered from Anglo-Indian statute, judges looked directly to works in Islamic jurisprudence to find the textual authority they needed to buttress their position on the *khiyār* – that the *khiyār* sale was a mortgage and nothing more. The effective repeal of the TPA did not change their position on how to read the contract; it just forced them to articulate it in new ways.

Interestingly, British judges resisted the impulse to do what one might have expected them to – that is, to refer to the dozens of digests on Anglo-Mohammedan law that had been produced in India during the eighteenth and nineteenth centuries. On more than one occasion, British courts refused to apply Anglo-Mohammedan law to disputes surrounding land, property, or *wakfs*. Anglo-Mohammedan law, they argued, might have been suitable for the Muslims of India, but was less so for those of East Africa, as the "local Mohammedan law of India was different from that of Zanzibar."[33] In Zanzibar and East Africa, judges relied on what they considered the key works in Islamic law – not coincidentally, these were texts that were available to them through a newly established government printer – though at times they would look to India for guidance on how to interpret them (see Chapter 8).

One dispute illustrated the new approach to Islamic law well. In 1894, Mohammed bin Hamad Al-Busa'idi, one of the former Sultan's ministers and relatives, found himself indebted to a *Bania* to the tune of MTD 31,766 – a heavy load, which he had likely accumulated over the course of a lifetime. As security for the debt, Mohammed hypothecated one of his houses and a large *shamba* to his creditor through a *khiyār* sales *waraqa*. Mohammed died soon after, but just before his death the Sultan agreed to settle the debt with the *Bania* for the compromised sum of MTD 23,500 – and as the new holder of the *waraqas*, the Sultan later took over the properties in satisfaction of the sum he paid on Mohammed's behalf.

Twenty years later, in 1914 – three years before the Transfer of Property Decree replaced the TPA – the former minister's son Hafiz lodged a petition in court, arguing that the Sultan had acquired the property in contravention of the *khiyār* rules; as the heir to the *khiyār* arrangement, he alone had the right to annul the sale. The court dismissed the claim on the grounds that it was too old and also without basis in the law. A *qāḍi*

[32] J.N.D. Anderson, *Islamic Law in Africa* (Oxford, UK: Routledge, 1955), 61–66; *Sheikh Burhan bin Abdulaziz El-Amawi* v. *Khalfan bin Salim El-Barwani and Another* (1929) 4 ZLR 92.

[33] *Gazette for Zanzibar and East Africa*, No. 1032 (November 6, 1911), 6–8.

sitting in on the session opined that the *khiyār* sale between the former minister and the *Bania* had expired before the Sultan paid off the debt; because nobody had expressed any interest in keeping the arrangement alive, the Sultan's payment to the creditor constituted a valid purchase of the debt and, by extension, the hypothecated properties. The judge presiding over the session agreed, but on slightly different grounds: "the procedure of allowing something in the nature of equitable relief in these *bei-kiyar* [sic] transactions which has become the practice of the British Court did not obtain in those days, and certainly not in the Sultan's Court," he wrote. The practice of extending the contract, he effectively argued, was a new one; he would not apply it retroactively.

Undeterred, Hafiz lodged an appeal at the Sultan's Court – a court of appeal for the Sultan's subjects that was headed by British judges bound to administer Islamic law. To argue his case, he hired the now-seasoned veteran of *khiyār*-related disputes Framji Rabadina. Drawing on cases from Calcutta and Madras, Rabadina argued that the law of limitations did not prevent his client from pressing his case, and that his claim to the property was a valid one.

His timing could not have been any better. Presiding over the Sultan's Court was Judge Murison, who had decided in the *Mahfuz* case nine years earlier that the TPA overruled Islamic law. This time, the judge's opinion had changed, in no small part because of the Transfer of Property Decree. The *qāḍi's* opinion on the document, he suggested, was "not quite an exhaustive pronouncement of the Mahommedan [sic] law." Looking to what he perceived to be the authoritative texts himself – at least one of which the *qāḍi* had pointed him to – he declared that "it is stated in the Sherhu-Nil [Mohammed ibn Yusuf Atfiyish's legal commentary, *Sharḥ Kitāb al-Nīl*] (p. 553 of Vol. 4) that if the time named in a *bei-kiyar waraka* [sic] expires and the parties neither cancel nor confirm the *bei-kiyar* transaction, the transaction stands good." To clear up any confusion, he elaborated on the point:

> "The expression 'stands good,' like a very great part of the Sheria of Islam, is liable to misinterpretation. It does not mean that the transaction is good as a sale. It means, at most, that it stands good as a mortgage. Thus it is stated in the book *Khazaini el Athar* (Ch. VII., Vol. VI.) that 'the Kathi bin Abadan said that if the conditional or complete sale is cancelled by the mortgagor the money due to the mortgagee will have to be recovered from the mortgaged property as against the unsecured creditors, and if the cancellation is made by the mortgagee there are different views; but bin Abadan says that the mortgagee's right comes first.' This latter view is in accordance with equity as understood in England and in my opinion is correct."

Murison's opinion identified the spirit of the *khiyār* sale as jurists from Al-Khalili onward had understood it, but it was his understanding of the principle of equity – or, more precisely, "justice, equity, and good conscience" – in England (and, by extension, India) that shaped his approach to the contract.[34] As in the past, Murison was inclined to stave off the threat of foreclosure – to keep the wheels of finance greased while avoiding cutting the ties that bound creditors to debtors in ongoing relationships of economic obligation. This inclination, couched in the language of equity, guided his reading of the texts in front of him, which included Aṭfiyyish's *Sharḥ Kitāb al-Nīl*, Ibn Hajar Al-Haytami's *Tuḥfat al-Muḥtāj fī Sharḥ al-Minhāj*, and two other works: Mohammed bin Ibrahim Al-Kindi's twelfth-century *Bayān al-Sharʿ lil-Aṣl wal-Farʿ*, and the *Khazaini al-Athar*.[35] As he moved through the texts, he drew on Anglo-Indian case law to make sense of certain questions. He cited a case from Calcutta another from Bombay in his commentary on how to infer the confirmation of a sale from conduct, asserting that the issue was one that was "quite familiar in the English law."[36] He dispensed of other aspects of the case in very much the same fashion: a blending together of Islamic and Anglo-Indian legal categories that was at times perhaps too seamless.[37]

In his approach to the *khiyār* transaction, Murison was not breaking new epistemological ground; he was re-articulating a position that he and other judges had been developing for a few decades – that as a mortgage rather than a sale, the *khiyār* stood over even after the redemption period had expired. With the repeal of the TPA, he now had to look for new bottles to hold his old wine; by looking directly to Muslim legal texts and reading through the lens of Anglo-Indian jurisprudence, he was able to boldly express himself in a new language – to look to *fiqh* texts himself, without the interpretive mediation of the *qāḍi*. And again, he wrote out his headnote, repeating what he had declared just before: "If

[34] Elke Stockreiter notes that judges approached Islamic law in a way that they felt was "in accordance with the common law principles of 'justice, equity, and good conscience', while at the same time preserving the local law with alterations"; idem, "'British Kadhis' and 'Muslim Judges': Modernisation, Inconsistencies and Accommodation in Zanzibar's Colonial Judiciary," *Journal of Eastern African Studies*, Vol. 4, No. 3 (2010), 565. In British India, the principle applied to the administration of Islamic law, although it did not affect "rules which the Courts have expressly been directed to apply to Mahomedans," such as marriage or inheritance. Sir Dinshah Fardunji Mulla, *Principles of Mahomedan Law*, 2nd ed. (Bombay: Thacker and Company, 1907), 2–3.

[35] I have been unable to identify the latter text.

[36] *The British Resident* v. *Hafiz bin Mohammed* (1916), 1 ZLR 526.

[37] On a related point in the case, the judge had to decide whether the Sultan's actions vis-à-vis the property rendered him a *ghasib* (usurper). After going through several *fiqh* texts, he concluded that "as a *ghasib* he [the Sultan] is liable to account for his use of the property on a basis which is... identical with the liability of an English trustee." *The British Resident* v. *Hafiz bin Mohammed* (1916), 1 ZLR 526.

the time named for redemption in a *bei-kiyar* expires and the parties neither confirm it nor cancel it the *bei-kiyar* stands good, that is, as a mortgage" – this time adding that "evidence of the conduct of the parties to such a deed is admissible to show an intention to confirm or cancel the *bei-kiyar*."[38] With that caveat – with the reinterpretation of Islamicate legal discourses on sales in the language of Anglo-Indian law – the narrative of the transformation of the *khiyār* sale into an Anglo-Indian Muslim mortgage was all but complete.

Conclusion

Right around the time he issued his opinion in the *Hafiz* case, Murison was hard at work on the compilation of the *Zanzibar Law Reports*, which he would finally publish in 1919. By the time he published them, he had already moved up the ranks – first to Advocate-General and then Chief Secretary. The *Zanzibar Law Reports*, which compiled, annotated, and indexed a selection of court decisions from between 1868 and 1918, was to be his lasting legacy to the legal history of East Africa – an admixture of Indian decisions, statute, and selections from Muslim *fiqh*, all marshaled in the service of imperial legal administration.

The narrative he crafted seemed to have stuck remarkably well. Scarcely a year after Murison published the first set of law reports, the British judge Gilchrist Alexander arrived at his appointment to the recently established High Court in the East African port city of Dar es Salaam. Reflecting on his work years later, the judge marveled at the type of law he administered. "Our law," he wrote, "was based on the law and procedure of India," adding that "it struck me as somewhat amusing that for so many years, I should have been administering justice according to English law to Indians in Fiji… and that now I should be called upon to administer justice to Africans according to Indian law." The introduction of Indian law to East Africa, he noted, had a traceable path. "The Indian form of law in Tanganyika, as in other parts of East Africa," he wrote, "is explained by Zanzibar's former connections with the High Court of Bombay. From Zanzibar legal influences spread to the adjoining mainland of Africa."[39]

Alexander's memoir recalled one of the main frontiers of an Anglo-Indian empire of law in the Indian Ocean. As Indian institutions and legislation traveled to the ports of the Indian Ocean, an Anglo-Indian

[38] 1 ZLR 526.
[39] Alexander, *Tanganyika Memories*, 24.

empire of law slowly emerged; commercial nodes like Muscat, Aden, Mombasa, Zanzibar, and Bahrain marked the first frontiers. Judges like Alexander and Murison formed one of the circuits through which law traveled across the ocean's basin: Alexander had just arrived in East Africa from Fiji; that year, Murison had left Zanzibar for the Straits Settlement, where he took up the post of Attorney General and, later, Chief Justice; he was knighted in 1924.[40] As judges circulated between different colonies and protectorates in the Indian Ocean, a coherent, self-referencing body of imperial law matured, one which often looked to India for "inspiration, precedents, and personnel for colonial administration."[41]

At the same time, however, Alexander's brief sketch of the travels of Anglo-Indian law to East Africa is perhaps too seamless. Taken at face value, it suggests that codes, acts, and case law traveled smoothly from one shore to another – that the process was certain, uncontested, and linear.[42] This was a history of imperial law that owed less to the realities of juridical life than it did a conscious effort on the part of judges like Murison to construct a narrative of legal administration – a carefully-crafted corpus of law that would ultimately find expression in the *Zanzibar Law Reports* and, later, the *East African Law Reports*, and which would assist judges in administering British India's growing legal empire in the region. It set in writing a new lexicon of law and contracting that drew on practice but blended it with a particular vision of property, political community, and imperial law. As later judges waded through the thickets of Anglo-Indian law, Islamic law, and local practice, they relied on texts like these – texts that referenced other similar texts in India and other imperial domains – to guide them.

But much of this depended on the cooperation of East Africa's *qāḍis*. For all of the derisive remarks made in the *Gazette* and elsewhere on the unrefined nature *qāḍi* justice, it was clear that the new era of legal administration in East Africa relied on *qāḍis* as much as it did on textbooks.[43] Murison emphasized as much in the introduction to his law reports, when he stated that "A good deal of what has been done [in following Islamic law in the court system] is due to the assistance of the present

[40] "The Chief Justice: Retirement of Sir William Murison," *The Straits Times* (February 10, 1933), 11.

[41] Metcalf, *Imperial Connections*, 45.

[42] Later commentators seem to have adopted his view; see Allott, "The Development of the East African Legal Systems," 350.

[43] Stockreiter, *Islamic Law, Gender, and Social Change*, 4–5. See also *Gazette for Zanzibar and East Africa*, No. 56 (February 2, 1893), 9; *Gazette for Zanzibar and East Africa*, No. 1897 (June 2, 1928), 141–142, quoted in Stockreiter, "British kadhis," 565.

Kathis of Zanzibar – Sheikh Ahmed bin Smit, Sheikh Burhan bin Abdul Aziz, Sheikh Tahir bin Abu Bakr, and Sheikh Ali bin Mahomed [sic]."[44] A closer look at cases from the *Zanzibar Law Reports* made it clear that when it came to matters of economic life, British courts in East Africa relied just as much on *qāḍis* and Islamic legal texts as they did on Indian precedent.

But in calling on the *qāḍis*, the court tapped into another phenomenon: the advent of a new era in Islamic legal thinking in the Western Indian Ocean. When British judges wrote to *qāḍis* to ask their opinion or looked to the writings of Aṭfiyyish, they were unwittingly drawing on a current of Islamic legal thinking that was undergoing a renaissance in the region.

[44] 1 ZLR x.

7 Capital Moves

On the morning of August 11, 1923, an Arab named Saif bin Hamoud walked into the High Court at Zanzibar to appeal a case against the heirs of one ʻAbdullah bin Salam, another Arab who had migrated to Zanzibar from Oman. Their dispute was only five years old, but had roots in a series of debts, *waraqas*, and movements that dated back more than two decades. It had all started when ʻAbdullah, who owned a clove *shamba*, found himself deeply embroiled in debt to an Indian moneylender. ʻAbdullah had been borrowing from him for some time: twice a year, with every clove harvest, he would service his debts by supplying him with cloves, which his creditor then forwarded to members of his firm in Western India.

It's not clear why ʻAbdullah felt the need to sever his relationship with the moneylender, but at some point in 1902, he allegedly approached another Arab, Saleh bin Sulaiman, asking him for a loan of Rs 6,000 so that he could settle his accounts with his creditor. Saleh later alleged that as security, ʻAbdullah had sold by *khiyār* a property in Oman, from which he was supposed to realize an annual rent of Rs 600 – presumably in the harvest and sale of dates. Saleh traveled to Oman that same year to take possession of the property, leaving an agent (*wakīl*) in Oman to collect the property's rents and forward them to him in Zanzibar. Yet the property only realized Rs 360 every year, and ʻAbdullah was unable to pay more. Rather than trying to foreclose on the property, Saleh, who claimed that he did not want to take ʻAbdullah to court because he was "a big man," simply waited, collecting rent from the property every year – every year, that is, until ʻAbdullah passed away.

In 1910, as ʻAbdullah's heirs were sorting through his estate, Saleh lodged a petition at a magistrates' court, alleging that he had a claim upon ʻAbdullah's heirs to the tune of Rs 6,000, the amount he had loaned their father. His lawyer, Framji Rabadina, came well prepared: he argued that the court's customary practice, as demonstrated in the *Mahfuz* case five years earlier, was to read the *khiyār* sale as a mortgage and thus give the creditor the right to ask for his money to be returned. However, when asked to produce the *khiyār* sales *waraqa*, Saleh offered the court a burned document that nobody could read. He had accidentally burned the *waraqa*, he claimed, when he knocked over an oil lamp, causing the oil to pour out over the documents and burn off the most important sections. The document was also never registered at the consulate. When asked why, Saleh replied that he never registered it because it involved property in Muscat. He further claimed that he had previously bought Muscat property while in Zanzibar without registering the *waraqas*, including one plot of land worth MTD 2,700.[1]

Without the *waraqa*, however, it was difficult to tell what sort of transaction the deceased 'Abdullah bin Salam had agreed to. Saleh had rewritten the parts that he claimed had burnt off, but there was some doubt. The Indian lawyer Hornius Lascari, who was representing 'Abdullah's heirs, suggested that the document was more likely never a *khiyār* sale at all, but a *wakala* – a power of attorney – authorizing Saleh to take possession of the Oman property on behalf of 'Abdullah. The judge agreed: after polling three *qāḍis* on how to read the *waraqa* and consulting one Islamic legal text directly – Aṭfiyyish's *Sharḥ Al-Nīl*, which had become a standard reference in court – he suggested that the document was unlikely to be a *khiyār* sale and was most likely a *wakala* deed. 'Abdullah had property in Zanzibar, and if he had borrowed money from Saleh at all – and the judge was not altogether convinced that he had – it was unlikely that Saleh would have preferred land in Muscat to land in Zanzibar.[2]

Saleh's laywer lodged an appeal in the Supreme Court of His Highness the Sultan, but failed to get the verdict overturned.[3] And with the Sultan's Court's decision, all would seem to have been settled – except that it hadn't. Seven years after the court handed down its judgment, 'Abdullah bin Salam's heirs sold the Omani land to another Arab, Saif bin Hamoud, with one condition – that he was to travel to Oman and take it from Saleh bin Sulaiman, whom they claimed had been in "wrongful possession" of the land for nearly a decade! Saleh, it seemed, had circumvented the court's decision by absconding to Muscat and appealing to legal authorities there. When Saif left for Muscat to take possession of the land he had bought, he "met with difficulties of a legal nature." He returned to Zanzibar to get fresh certificates from the court, and then traveled back to Muscat, where "local authorities" upheld his claim to the property, but insisted that he pay MTD 1,400 to Saleh bin Sulaiman,

1 Petition by Saleh bin Sulaiman, ZNA HC 5/14 A and B.
2 Magistrate Court Judgment, ZNA HC 5/14 A and B.
3 Judgment from H.H. Supreme Court for Zanzibar, ZNA HC 5/14 A and B.

"who was to remain in possession until the sum was paid."[4] Frustrated, Saif returned to Zanzibar where he entered a successful claim against 'Abdullah bin Salam's heirs for the amount he had paid them for the Oman property.

The series of transactions and disputes between 'Abdullah bin Salam's family, Saleh bin Sulaiman, and Saif bin Hamoud highlights the major juridical tensions that remained in the Western Indian Ocean well after the entrenchment of British courts. On the face of it, the confusion stemmed from the inability of actors in the courtroom to read a *waraqa* whose provenance could not entirely be ascertained. At the same time, however, the case highlights the competing legal authorities that continued to jostle with one another in their attempts to define the *waraqa*: the British judge, the two Indian lawyers, and *qāḍis* who weighed in on the disputes – and then the "local authorities" in Oman, who intervened in the matter at several critical junctures. In a sense, the disputes between the three different parties open up the multiple legal worlds that Indian Ocean commercial actors traversed over the course of their lifetimes, but point to the gaps between those legal worlds – gaps that allowed actors like Saleh bin Sulaiman to retain possession of properties in Oman even though a court in Zanzibar ruled against him, or for the litigants to alternatively claim that the *waraqa* was a *khiyār* sale, a mortgage, or a *wakala* for taking possession of 'Abdullah's properties in Muscat.

The fact that the world of *waraqas*, *iqrārs*, *qāḍis*, *kātibs*, and jurists was still alive and well at the turn of the century even as the British imperial legal banner unfurled across the Indian Ocean owed a lot to developments that had taken place in Zanzibar, at the epicenter of British India's empire in the region. The establishment of an Arabic-language printing press in Zanzibar in the late 1870s allowed for the production of a range of different Islamic legal texts, injecting new life into Islamic legal writing around the region, as *fiqh* manuals and commentaries produced on the island made their way around East Africa and South Arabia, and as commercial actors sought out new opportunities beyond the established commercial centers of East Africa. The movements of creditors, debtors, legal claims, and texts between East Africa and South Arabia, then, reanimated a pre-colonial Indian Ocean contractual culture during a time of high imperialism.

As British India's legal empire in the Indian Ocean reached its zenith, then – as Murison took his compilation of cases to the government printer to publish the first edition of the *Zanzibar Law Reports* – there existed a whole other world of contracting in the region. As judges and

[4] *Seif bin Hamoud* v. *Mohamed bin Abdullah and Others* (1923) 2 ZLR 22.

lawyers reflected on *waraqas*, *khiyār* sales, and mortgages in the British courtrooms of East Africa, a transregional legal culture was flourishing – one in which *qāḍis*, *kātibs*, and jurists could actively engage in discussions about economic life, both in and outside of British courtrooms. These were legal arenas that largely existed beyond the purview of the empire and beyond the horizons of the courtrooms, though they intersected with them in revealing moments. And actors who were savvy enough to navigate these different juridical realms could stand to profit a great deal.

The Ibadhi *Nahḍa* in Africa and Arabia

There was something palpably different about Islamic juridical life in the Western Indian Ocean at the end of the nineteenth century. Although there were many developments in Islamic legal thinking over the previous hundred years or so, the 1880s and 1890s heralded the beginning of a new era – a renaissance (*nahḍa*) in Islamic thought. The *nahḍa*, spearheaded by a couple of key figures, received a major boost with the advent of a printing press in Zanzibar that devoted itself to the production of treatises in Islamic law and theology. Emboldened by the access to texts that the new press brought with it, a new generation of Muslim scholars emerged in South Arabia and East Africa.

The late nineteenth century *nahḍa* revolved around two key figures: ʻAbdullah bin Humayd Al-Salimi, in Oman, and Mohammed bin Yusuf Aṭfiyyish, in the Mzab Valley of Algeria.[5] Both regularly corresponded with one another, and the two shared a common educational background. Aṭfiyyish's older brother had studied in Oman sometime in the mid-nineteenth century and taught him when he returned to Mzab.[6] The younger Aṭfiyyish soon distinguished himself as a regional scholar of consequence, publishing the masterful commentary *Sharḥ Kitāb Al-Nīl* and a range of other tracts; he also developed extensive contacts with Muslim reformers in Egypt and even received decorations from the Ottoman Sultan.[7]

By contrast, Al-Salimi was very much a product of the world of jurisprudence and politics that had shaped Oman and East Africa over the centuries. He was born in 1869, just as Al-Khalili and ʻAzzan bin Qais declared the establishment of the Imamate on Oman's coast. And while

[5] For an excellent account of this *nahḍa*, see Amal D. Ghazal, *Islamic Reform and Arab Nationalism: Expanding the Crescent from the Mediterranean to the Indian Ocean (1880s to 1930s)* (London: Routledge, 2010).
[6] Wilkinson, *The Imamate Tradition of Oman*, 243.
[7] Ghazal, *Islamic Reform and Arab Nationalism*, 41–45.

he would have been too young to have been directly influenced by that moment in Oman's history, he undoubtedly bore its legacy. Al-Salimi's teacher was the jurist Saleh bin 'Ali Al-Harthi, who himself had been a student of Al-Khalili's, and who had joined forces with Al-Khalili and 'Azzan to oust the Sultan Salim bin Thuwaini and establish the Imamate (see Interlude). By birth and by learning, Al-Salimi was a continuation of Al-Khalili's world.

Al-Salimi's writings on the 'Azzan/Al-Khalili Imamate attested to his admiration for what his predecessors had accomplished. In his two-volume history, *Tuḥfat Al-A'yān fī Sīrat Ahl 'Umān [The Gift of the Notables to the History of the People of Oman]* he placed the 'Azzan regime at the end of a long list of Imamates stretching back in time to the beginnings of Omani history – a history of imams and jurists that stretched from the first Arab migrations to Oman until the present, broken only by temporary moments of disruption from outsiders and pretenders to the throne. Al-Salimi's work celebrated 'Azzan and Al-Khalili's achievements: their pacification of unruly tribes in the region, the success at defending Oman from attacks by the Wahhabis of Najd, and the even-handedness with which they dealt with the property of the Busa'idi sultans.[8] Even when Al-Salimi admitted the financial difficulties that 'Azzan and Al-Khalili faced, he was quick to point out that these were the results of the campaigns they undertook against hostile tribes and supporters of the Wahhabis rather than any sort of financial mismanagement.[9] His history of 'Azzan's Imamate constituted a counter-narrative to what British officials, the British Indian press, and supporters of the Busa'idi sultans had written.

Al-Salimi endowed his mentors with nicknames that placed them all within the same camp of Muslim reformers. Al-Khalili was "*Al-Muḥaqqiq*," or the Investigator – a sobriquet that Al-Salimi had given him because of his attention to the provenance of a question (*ta'ṣīl*) and its investigation (*taḥqīq*).[10] His own teacher, Al-Harthi, was alternatively "*Al-Shaykh*," a sign of Al-Salimi's respect for him, or "*Al-Muḥtasib*," a marker of the work he did as a marketplace inspector during the short-lived 'Azzan bin Qais Imamate. And Mohammed bin Yusuf Aṭfiyyish, whose legal commentary *Sharḥ Kitāb Al-Nīl* had circulated into Oman after having been printed in Zanzibar, earned the sobriquet "*Al-Quṭb*" – the axis, or pole – a testament to the influence his writings had on the

8 'Abdullah bin Humayd Al-Salimi, *Tuḥfat Al-A'yān fī Sīrat Ahl 'Umān*, Vol. 2 (Sib, Oman: Maktabat Al-Imām Nūr Al-Dīn Al-Sālimī, 2000) 254–290. The history was published decades after Al-Salimi's death in 1914.

9 Al-Salimi, *Tuḥfat Al-A'yān*, Vol. 2, 281–288.

10 Al-Khalili, *Ajwibat Al-Muḥaqqiq Al-Khalīlī*, Vol. 1, 14.

Ibadhi community. Al-Salimi brought together these figures into an intimate cast of characters that shaped Oman's modern intellectual history – a trans-regional and trans-historical community of scholars of which he, too, was a part.

He also made no secret of the contempt he had for the British and for their allies, the Al-Busa'idis. In *Tuḥfat Al-A'yān* he devoted a lengthy discussion to Turki's defeat of 'Azzan, highlighting Turki's arrival in "Christian" (i.e. British) ships from India and his murder of Al-Khalili, who in Al-Salimi's view had been betrayed by the British consul.[11] In an aside, Al-Salimi described how Al-Khalili had assumed that the British would not allow any harm to those under their protection (*lā yarḍawna fī dhimmatihim*), when they were in fact "the masters of intrigue, both then and now, and the enablers (*mudabbirūn*) of the coup against 'Azzan," adding that "the colonizers (*al-isti'māriyūn*) had no religion beyond their own needs."[12]

And yet, for all of his disdain for the Busa'idi sultans of Oman and Zanzibar, Al-Salimi owed them a great deal. At least some of his popularity lay in the publication of his writings in the Zanzibar printing press, which had been brought to the island in 1879 at the behest of Sultan Barghash bin Sa'id, a ruler with a taste for things modern and a voracious appetite for Arabic newspapers from Cairo.[13] Al-Salimi's treatment of Barghash, who was also the only Busa'idi ruler of Zanzibar to receive any sustained attention in *Tuḥfat al-A'yān*, was more even-handed. He wrote that Barghash had left "good legacies" (*ma'āthir ḥusna*), and while he mixed good deeds with bad (*khalaṭa 'amalan ṣāliḥan wa ākhar sayyi'an*) he did engage in pious acts, including the establishment of a steamship to carry pilgrims from Oman and East Africa to Mecca free of charge, and the printing of Ibadhi texts.[14]

Al-Salimi was right to praise the press: it was a major catalyst for Islamic scholarship in the region. Indeed, the first major publication to come out of it was a fitting homage to the new era it heralded: a projected 90-volume compendium on Ibadhi jurisprudence, the *Qāmūs Al-Sharī'a* written by the Omani jurist Jumayyil bin Khamis Al-Sa'di. The *Qāmūs*, which had been written in the mid-nineteenth century, celebrated the long lineage of Omani and North Africa Ibadhi scholars, but also portended the beginnings of a new era in Ibadhi *fiqh*. Its publication in Zanzibar and circulation between East Africa, North Africa, and South Arabia suggested a renewed interest in older texts and scholars – in a

11 Al-Salimi, *Tuḥfat Al-A'yān*, Vol. 2, 290–297.
12 Al-Salimi, *Tuḥfat Al-A'yān*, Vol. 2, 296, n. 1.
13 Sadgrove, "The Press," 156–157.
14 Al-Salimi, *Tuḥfat Al-A'yān*, Vol. 2, 241.

multi-generational community of jurists, *qāḍis*, and theologians, both dead and alive, that new scholars could insert themselves into.[15]

Of the works printed in Zanzibar, none would become as popular as Aṭfiyyish's *Sharḥ Kitāb Al-Nīl*, a fourteen-volume legal commentary that quickly established itself as the most authoritative exposition of Ibadhi *fiqh*.[16] Like most other texts of the commentary genre, the *Sharḥ* took on the whole gamut of Islamic positive law, from ritual (*'ibādāt*) matters to more mundane transactions (*mu'āmalāt*). What separated Aṭfiyyish's *Sharḥ* from other texts at the time, however, was its availability: as a printed text, it was more accessible, legible, and affordable. Much like Al-Sa'di's *Qāmūs* and other texts that shaped the renaissance in Ibadhi thinking, their portability was key. As printed books, the texts were far cheaper to produce than their manuscript counterparts and could be sent across the ocean or desert in bulk, particularly in the age of the steamship and railroad.[17] Works of Ibadhi scholarship were now much more widely studied by scholars in the Ibadhi world, and North African texts were just as accessible in Oman and East Africa as Omani and Zanzibari texts were in the Mzab.[18] Other texts, like the eleventh-century Shafi'i manual *Minhāj Al-Tālibīn*, or the famous sixteenth-century commentary *Tuḥfat Al-Muḥtāj fī Sharḥ Al-Minhāj* also circulated alongside them.

Unsurprisingly, the period that witnessed the expanded circulation of printed Islamic legal texts in Zanzibar also saw the emergence of a system of Islamic legal education along the East African coast – one that produced a new generation of *qāḍis* and scholars whose work would profoundly shape the legal history of the region. In the mid-1890s, the scholar 'Abdullah Bā Kathir established a *madrasa* at his home in Zanzibar, and by 1909 it covered all levels of Islamic learning, from elementary teaching for beginners to advanced studies for learned students and scholars. In 1901, scholars in Lamu built the Al-Riyāḍ mosque, where aspiring *qāḍis* and jurists would go to learn *tafsir* (Qur'anic exegesis), *fiqh*, and other disciplines. Graduates from these institutions often

15 Sadgrove, "The Press," 154–155; Only 19 of the 90 volumes were ever published.

16 The *Sharḥ* would become a standard reference text in British courts and among Muslim *qāḍis*. As the title suggested, the text was a commentary (*sharḥ*) on one of the more authoritative manuals of Ibadhi jurisprudence, the *Kitāb Al-Nīl*, written by 'Abdul-'Aziz Al-Thamini, a teacher to Aṭfiyyish's older brother.

17 For more on this, see James L. Gelvin and Nile Green "Introduction: Global Muslims in the Age of Steam and Print" in James Gelvin and Nile Green, eds. *Global Muslims in the Age of Steam and Print* (Berkeley, CA: University of California Press, 2013), 1–25; Nile Green, *Bombay Islam: The Religious Economy of the Western Indian Ocean, 1840–1915* (New York: Cambridge University Press, 2011), 92–99.

18 Wilkinson, *The Imamate Tradition of Oman*, 243.

ended up taking careers in the government as *qāḍis* and religious experts within the field of education.[19]

What distinguished this new generation of jurists and *qāḍis* from those who came before them was their deep appreciation for texts – particularly Arabic ones. In contrast to previous generations of East African juridical actors, who preferred an oral mode of transmission and who possessed only a limited literacy in Arabic, this generation was decidedly more "bookish," and preferred to spend their lessons learning from different works of reference – particularly Arabic texts like Aṭfiyyish's *Sharḥ Kitāb Al-Nīl*.[20] Scholars in Oman and East Africa also corresponded with one another from time to time on a range of subjects – including the *khiyār* sale. One Somali jurist who traveled around East Africa, 'Abdulaziz bin 'Abdulghani Al-Amawi, maintained a regular correspondence with jurists in Oman over the course of the late nineteenth century, in which thinkers on both sides of the Indian Ocean grappled with questions on law, commerce, and property.[21] His son, Burhan bin 'Abdulaziz – who enjoyed a lengthy career in the Zanzibar courts – carried on the tradition, exchanging letters with *qāḍis* and jurists from around Arabia.[22] Alongside the commercial instruments that circulated between Oman and East Africa, then, were the letters of jurists and *qāḍis*.

Alternative Legal Imaginaries in East Africa

When Saleh bin Sulaiman took his claim against 'Abdullah bin Salam's heirs to the lower court in Zanzibar in 1910, he could have hardly known that he was tapping into a trans-regional Ibadhi intellectual renaissance, or that his dispute with 'Abdullah's heirs would cast into relief the trans-oceanic movement of texts and actors that characterized the moment. And yet it did: as Saleh's lawyers drew on Indian statute and case law to make claims about how to read the *waraqa*, the judge and the *qāḍis* in the lower court drew on the texts and ideas that came out of Zanzibar's printing press and the *nahḍa* it supported. The judge himself referred to the *Sharḥ Kitāb Al-Nīl*, which he would have had access to because of the Zanzibar printers. The two *qāḍis* present in court, the chief Ibadhi *qāḍi* 'Ali bin Mohammed Al-Mandhiri and the Shafi'i *qāḍi* Tahir bin Abibaker

[19] Bang, *Sufis and Scholars of the Sea*, 144–150.
[20] Bang, *Sufis and Scholars of the Sea*, 128, 148.
[21] *As'ila wa Ajwiba min al-Shaykh 'Abdul-'Aziz bin 'Abdulghani Al-Amawi, Qāḍī Zinjibār [Questions and Answers from the Shaikh 'Abdul-'Aziz bin 'Abdulghani Al-Amawi, the Qāḍī of Zanzibar]* dated 13 Dhu Al-Qu'da 1299 [September 26, 1882], Mohammed bin Ahmed Al-Busa'idi Library, Seeb, Oman, Series 6, Vol. 589.
[22] *Wathā'iq Tārīkhiyya min Zinjibār [Historical Documents from Zanzibar]*, Mohammed bin Ahmed Al-Busa'idi Library, Seeb, Oman.

Al-Amawi, were both products of that *nahḍa*, both through the institutions they had studied in and the texts they read. The claims they made pointed to their position at the intersection of two worlds of law – a world of British Indian legal administration that they had to accommodate, but also an altogether different regime of reading *waraqas* and the property claims that underpinned them.

Before making his ruling, the magistrate presiding over Saleh's case posed a set of questions to the court's *qāḍis* about Saleh's *waraqa* and about the dispute more broadly. The bulk of the questions involved technicalities about the *waraqa* and transaction: whether 'Abdullah bin Salam was liable to make up the difference in projected rent and the amount realized, whether they recognized the handwriting on the *waraqa*, and more. Two questions, however, stood out in the weight of the answers that they would prompt: first, whether the court was able to hear cases relating to wealth in Oman; and second, whether the *waraqa*, genuine or not, could be taken as proof of a transaction between Saleh and 'Abdullah.

The *qāḍis* both dispensed with the questions in ways that revealed their competing impulses. Al-Amawi argued that the *waraqa* could not bear proof, and that its condition posed an obstacle to finding the strong sort of proof that the law required – namely verification by the *kātib* who wrote it or those who witnessed the transaction.[23] A witness, he reiterated later on in his opinion, constituted a stronger form of proof in the law than the *waraqa* itself did, particularly when a *waraqa* was as badly damaged as the one in front of him. Al-Mandhiri, however, suggested that there existed a regime of deed authentication beyond the social – that one could establish a document's authority without witnesses. He could not determine whether the *waraqa* was genuine, he said, because the handwriting on it was different from that of the *kātib* to which it was attributed (*mansūb*). More importantly, he argued, the *waraqa* "had no comparates (*qarā'in*) to support the supposition of its genuineness – corroborating documents like a copy in the court book (*daftar al-maḥkama*) or the consular registry, which he referred to using the Arabic phonetic transliteration, "*al-rigistar*."[24] The record-keeping regime of Zanzibar's legal bureaucracy, it seemed, had permeated into the evidentiary standards held by Islamic law. An authenticated copy could bolster the evidentiary value of a deed, speaking to its genuineness just as much as a live witness could.[25]

[23] Opinion of Shaikh Tahir bin Abibaker Al-Amawi (November 7, 1911), ZNA HC 5/14 A and B.

[24] Opinion of Shaikh 'Ali bin Mohammed (not dated), ZNA HC 5/14 A and B.

[25] The practice of looking to registers to corroborate documents presented in court was common among *qāḍis* elsewhere in the Islamic world, particularly in the Ottoman

In addition to their willingness to pander to the evidentiary requirements of the British courts, the *qāḍis* seemed open to re-interpreting the *khiyār* sale itself in order to meet the expectations of the British judges sitting with them. In his reflections on the contract, Al-Amawi commented that "these days the court has ruled that for the benefit of the subjects (*al-ṣilāḥ lil-ra'iyya*) the buyer [i.e. the creditor] has no claim to the wealth [i.e. the land] after the expiration date if the seller does not allow it, and that the sale was to be considered as being without consideration (*bidūna thaman al-mabya'*)." This, he continued was not in violation of the *shari'a*, for "in the *shar'* the sale is to be cancelled if there appears to be fraud (*ghabn*) involved."[26] The *qāḍi*, it seemed, was willing to mobilize his intellectual resources to shape the rulings on *khiyār* sales so as to meet the court's standards of equity, and even went so far as to consult Aṭfiyyish's *Sharḥ Kitāb Al-Nīl* to find textual support for his opinion.[27]

Even as their role as lawmakers shrank, then, Zanzibar and East Africa's *qāḍis* engaged with the colonial legal bureaucracy in ways that stimulated their creative thinking about contracts and law. Their work in British courts did not keep them from reading, thinking, and writing about property and contract. In some ways, their experiences may have provided them with opportunities to think through new sets of problems and new imperatives. As *qāḍis* worked to navigate the requirements placed on them by the British legal bureaucracy, they were forced to grapple with new texts (like the *Zanzibar Law Reports*), new questions about documents and evidence, and competing interpretations of contracts, sales, and property. What might on the face of it appear to be a bureaucratic confinement of the *qāḍis'* juridical work, then, could be reinterpreted as a new, creative phase in Islamic juridical thinking.[28]

At the same time, the *qāḍis*, who were products of new text-based forms of Islamic learning in East Africa, were engaging with other realms of Islamic scholarship and practice. Their work in the courts formed only one dimension of a rich legal and religious imaginary that extended well beyond the confines of the courtroom, the island, or even the East

Empire. Ahmed Akgündüz, "Shari'ah Courts and Shari'ah Records:The Application of Islamic Law in the Ottoman State," *Islamic Law and Society*, No. 16 (2009), especially 212–216.

26 Opinion of Shaikh Tahir bin Abibaker Al-Amawi (not dated), ZNA HC 5/14 A and B.

27 Translated opinion of Shaikh Taher bin Abibaker Al-Amawi (n.d., 1911), ZNA HC 5/14 A. While Shaikh Taher cites the volume and page number for his reference, I was not able to locate the passage in Atfiyish's volume; he was most likely using a much earlier edition.

28 Anne Bang has suggested that *qāḍis* still exercised considerable influence on the legal process into the early-twentieth century, and that a closed network of *qāḍis* "almost monopolized the judicial process." Bang, *Sufis and Scholars of the Sea*, 163.

African coast. In addition to their work as *qāḍis*, they were members of trans-regional Sufi groups and avid readers of texts produced in Oman and Hadramawt. The orders that the *qāḍis* belonged to, and the texts that they engaged with, spread along the East African coast and into the interior alongside the expanding British legal bureaucracy in the region, and were growing in popularity even at the zenith of British India's legal empire in the Western Indian Ocean.[29]

And there was plenty to suggest that *qāḍis* saw themselves as engaging in something that transcended the British courtroom, even as they acquiesced to the requirements of the British legal bureaucracy. In his opinions on the dispute between Saleh bin Sulaiman and the heirs of 'Abdullah bin Salam, Al-Amawi hinted at the existence of an alternative juridical regime and legal imaginary. When asked about whether the court could hear cases relating to wealth in Oman, Al-Amawi responded that it could, and that it was not impeded (*lā yusammā*) whether the two litigants were present in its jurisdiction (*mawjūdīn fī wilāyatihā*) or not. He continued: "In the *sharī'a* the *qāḍi's* ruling is upheld in any case relating to property that is absent, whether it is in his jurisdiction or another part of the world. We thus hold that this court can hear claims on all things that claims can be heard on, whether they are present in its jurisdiction or absent from it."[30]

By suggesting a universal *qāḍi* jurisdiction over property-related disputes, Al-Amawi in 1911 hearkened back to Al-Khalili's mid-nineteenth century notions of a regime of *iṭmā'ināna* in Indian Ocean contracting: a confidence in the stability of forms, instruments, and juridical actors as one traversed valleys, seas, and jungles.[31] In this regime of *iṭmā'ināna*, claims based on *waraqas* that were upheld by one *qāḍi* would be upheld by every other *qāḍi*, whether he was in Zanzibar, Mombasa, Muscat, "or another part of the world" – a striking illustration of his broad legal imaginary even within the limits of a new jurisdictional order. This wasn't just wishful thinking on Al-Amawi's part. Despite the continued growth of a British Indian legal bureaucracy in East Africa, there still existed a trans-oceanic world of contracting regulated by *qāḍis*, *kātibs*, jurists, merchants, and planters in places that British Indian law, however powerful its claims to jurisdiction might have been, could not reach.

And one didn't have to travel very far to get there. Just up the coast from British Indian legal strongholds like Zanzibar and Mombasa was

[29] Bang, *Sufis and Scholars of the Sea*, 128–131; Wilkinson, *The Arabs and the Scramble for Africa*, 151–152.
[30] Opinion of Shaikh Tahir bin Abibaker Al-Amawi (not dated), ZNA HC 5/14 A and B.
[31] For Al-Khalili's writings on this, see Chapter 3.

the port city of Barawa, once nominally a part of the dominions of the Sultans of Zanzibar. The relationship between the Sultan and his subjects at Barawa had always been somewhat contentious; at times he could make strong claims to authority in the port city, and at other times he found himself kept in check by local headmen.[32] But if the Sultan was nowhere to be found, Indian capital was. A number of Zanzibari merchants, it seemed, saw in Barawa a chance to invest their capital without the interference of British courts. The Khoja merchant Tharia Topan, for example, appears as a creditor in no less than thirty-five *waraqas* over seven years, loaning out an average of nearly MTD 140, in amounts as low as MTD 19 and as high as MTD 863 – mostly through his local agent, who operated a commercial and moneylending operation of his own.[33] The merchant Kanji Rajpar also appears as a creditor in eleven *waraqas*, and as a landowner in several others.[34] His lending portfolio, though smaller in size than Topan's, involved much more money: on average, Rajpar (or rather, his agent) loaned out roughly MTD 650, with loans as small as MTD 80 and as large as MTD 2,000. Unencumbered by British regulations, Indian merchants found outlets in nearby port cities.

All of the *waraqas* generated in Barawa seem to suggest that the regime of *waraqas*, jurists, and *kātibs* was alive and well. *Sijills* (registers) from the *qāḍi* court at Barawa from 1893 to 1900 contain hundreds of *iqrārs* of debt to merchants from Zanzibar and elsewhere. Many of the *iqrārs* were coupled with pledges of property through the vehicle of the *rahn* or short-term sales, and although nobody explicitly invoked the *khiyār* sale, inhabitants of Barawa drew on many different types of property, from boats to camels to stone houses, to access credit.[35] And across the Gulf of Aden from Barawa, in the towns of Hadramawt, men and women of all walks of life utilized instruments almost identical to the *khiyār* sales. There, they called it the *'uhda* (custody) sale, and it was a common enough feature of Hadrami commercial society that it attracted the attention of a number of Shafi'i jurists from the region.[36] In places

[32] W.F. Prideaux to Secretary to Government of India (n.d., 1874) ZNA AA2/14.

[33] See Alessandra Vianello and Mohamed M. Kassim, eds. *Servants of the Sharia: The Civil Register of the Qadis' Court of Brava, 1893–1900*, 2 vols. (Leiden, NL: Brill, 2006), Deeds 17–22, 84–86, 100–102, 108–123, 130–132, 145–146, 180–181.

[34] Vianello and Kassim, *Servants of the Sharia*, Deeds 14, 23, 30–32, 42–43, 65, 80, 83, 110, 126–129, 139, 232–233.

[35] There are hundreds of these reprinted in Vianello and Kassim, eds. *Servants of the Sharia*.

[36] See Linda Boxberger, "Avoiding *Ribā*: Credit and Custodianship in Credit and Custodianship in Nineteenth and Early-Twentieth Century Hadramawt," *Islamic Law and Society*, Vol. 5, No. 2 (1998), 196–213.

beyond the reach of British courts, then, a vernacular culture of contracting continued to flourish.

But when Al-Amawi made his argument for a universal *qāḍi* jurisdiction over property-related disputes, he wasn't thinking of Barawa or Hadramawt. As he sat and wrote down his opinion on the case before him for the sake of the British magistrate, he was imagining a jurisdiction that extended not just up the coast, but across the ocean. Like other *qāḍis* in East Africa, he was most likely thinking about Oman.

Oman and the Global Date Trade

When Saleh bin Sulaiman loaned out money to 'Abdullah bin Salam against property in Muscat in 1902, and when he fought to foreclose on it in 1910, he must have known that change was afoot in that port city across the sea. And more than seven years later, when Saif bin Hamoud agreed to buy the land in Muscat from 'Abdullah's heirs, even under condition that he would have to wrest control of that land from Saleh, he would have agreed to do so knowing how much the land was worth. Indeed, the very fact that Saleh bin Sulaiman, who first complained that the land wasn't worth enough for him to foreclose upon right away, still held onto that same land seven years later suggested something had changed.

And much had changed indeed. At the time he loaned out money to 'Abdullah, his commercial prospects in East Africa were probably looking less attractive than they had in years past. Since the development of the Uganda Railway, East Africa had become oversaturated with international capital, opportunities for Arab merchants had shrunk, and returns on loans to planters and ivory traders had diminished. The region was also overrun with lawyers and judges, who intervened in commercial contracting at every step of the process, regulating loans and *khiyār* sales more and more with every year that passed.[37] For a moneylender like Saleh, then, it was a bad time to be doing business in East Africa, at least when it came to *shambas*.

The interior trade did not offer much more. While the advent of the Uganda Railway was a boon to Indian merchants who were able to profit from hiring out workers to the railway or supplying them with provisions, for someone like Saleh, whose moneylending activities had little to do with railroad expansion, it offered less promise. Opportunities to engage in the ivory trade were also diminishing: by the century's close the Belgians had all but secured their hold over the Congo, and the

[37] For more on this, see Chapters 5 and 6.

Germans over Tanganyika. As the former strongmen of the interior of East Africa gave up their territories to the nascent European colonial powers, they had to contend with increasing restrictions on their mobility and higher taxes on their diminishing ivory trade. For all of their effort to fight the Europeans, people like Tippu Tip could not prevail, and they ended their days on the coast: Tippu Tip managed to wrangle a temporary position as Belgian consul; others like him lived on in relative obscurity.[38]

Not all was lost, though; as one door closed, others opened. At the time 'Abdullah and Saleh first contracted with one another, a commercial boom was unfolding across the sea, in Oman – a boom that would make somebody like Saleh feel confident that he would be able to derive a rent of Rs 600 per year from a property there. Oman distinguished itself in its relative freedom from commercial regulation. As lawyers, judges, and courts began intervening more into economic life in East Africa, commercial actors sought out opportunities in places that were far less bound up in red tape and fees – places where they could ply their trade without having to concern themselves with the legal technicalities that had come to define commercial contracting in places like Zanzibar or Mombasa.

By the end of the nineteenth century, the Omani date trade had expanded in dramatic ways, reaching many more consumers in Europe and America.[39] The trade in dates had been expanding slowly over the course of the second half of the nineteenth century – in part because of increasing Omani migration to East Africa, but largely because of an increased American interest in Omani dates.[40] By 1875, American merchants were importing nearly 10 million lbs of Omani dates a year.[41] Between 1899 and 1906, the earliest years for which there are published export figures, Muscat's date exports nearly doubled, from over $250,000 to almost $450,000 peaking at over $500,000 in 1902–1903.[42] The amount of dates exported only grew in the years that followed: by 1913, Muscat exported nearly 30 million lbs of dates, nearly twice that a

38 Bennett, *Arab Versus European*, 245–253.

39 Matthew S. Hopper, "The Globalization of Dried Fruit: Transformations in the East Arabian Economy, 1860s-1920s" in Gelvin and Green, eds. *Global Muslims in the Age of Steam and Print*, 161.

40 Matthew S. Hopper, *Slaves of One Master: Globalization and Slavery in Arabia in the Age of Empire* (New Haven, CT: Yale University Press, 2015), 51–79.

41 Hopper, "The Globalization of Dried Fruit," 162–164.

42 For the sake of consistency, I have converted these figures from British Pounds to US Dollars; in Lorimer, these figures are £52,000, £92,500, and £103,000 respectively. Lorimer, *Gazetteer of the Persian Gulf, Oman and Central Arabia*, Vol. 1 (Historical) Part II (Appendices), 2307.

decade later, and almost three times that amount by 1925.[43] In the first few decades of the twentieth century, then, the Omani date trade had swelled to truly global proportions. With this commercial transformation in mind – or at least the sense that the value of dates and property in Oman was on the rise – the prospect of loaning out money in Zanzibar against property an ocean away could seem like a good idea.

But perhaps no one could speak more to the growing date market than the Kutchi Bhattia Ratansi Purshottam, who profited directly from the expansion of the Omani date trade. Ratansi first arrived in Muscat in 1857, at the age of fourteen, to work as a clerk at his uncle's shop. He established his own business ten years later, most likely on capital borrowed from his uncle. It was a rough start for the young merchant: the port city fell to ʻAzzan bin Qais and Al-Khalili later that year, and Ratansi's commercial prospects would have looked uncertain at best. He was able to survive, though, and in time developed a thriving business that dealt in grain, coffee, textiles, and a range of different goods – including dates, which he exported to his own business offices in Karachi and his brother's business in Bombay.[44]

The records Ratansi kept paint a detailed picture of his involvement in the date trade. The first mention of dates in the *waraqas* he kept was a *khiyār* sale in July 1887 of a date garden by Sayyid Hilal bin Saʻid, a member of the Sultan's family.[45] Other *waraqas* from the late 1890s also highlight similar *khiyār* transactions between Ratansi and planters in Oman, in which they would borrow money and sell him their plantations – or in some cases, a set number of date palms – for a limited period of time.[46] His date trading was bound up in his moneylending and general trading activities: he would loan money and goods to middlemen operating in date-growing regions and expect them to forward him dates; the *iqrārs* were for amounts owed in the accounts they kept between them. His papers include a number of letters from the middlemen he did business with, all of whom would forward him information about prices for dates and other fruit, and would inform him of their ongoing negotiations with planter and transporters. One of Ratansi's middlemen was Al-Khalili's son ʻAbdullah, who seemed to prefer a quieter and less

[43] Hopper, "The Globalization of Dried Fruit," 164–165.

[44] Calvin H. Allen, "The Indian Merchant Community of Masqaṭ," *Bulletin of the School of Oriental and African Studies, University of London*, Vol. 44, No. 1 (1981), 46–47.

[45] Sayyid Hilal to Ratansi Purshottam (20 Shawwal 1304), Ratansi Purshottam Library, Mattrah, Oman (RPL) Arabic Documents Vol. 1.

[46] See also debt acknowledgment deed by Mansoor bin Humayd Al-Nakhli (24 Ramadan 1313 / March 9, 1896), and debt acknowledgment deed by Hamoud bin ʻAli Al-Ma'shary (11 Safar 1319 / May 30, 1901) RPL Arabic Documents Vol. 2; debt acknowledgment deed from Saʻid bin Rashid (1 Muharram 1321 / March 30, 1903).

Figure 6 Ratansi Purshottam

conspicuous life as a date trader over the political intrigues that his father had engaged in.[47]

Ratansi's date trading took on new significance when he began doing business with the New York-based firm of William Hills in 1905. Hills had been engaged in the date business for several years before contacting Ratansi. He and his older brother John had formed the Hills Brothers Company in 1893, and initially did the bulk of their business out of Basra, from which they would ship dates directly to their warehouse in Brooklyn. It was only in 1905, after John Hills died and a family feud broke up the firm, that William Hills decided to start up his own business and began looking for alternative suppliers.[48] He approached Ratansi just eight months after establishing himself as an independent date trader; another Indian merchant, Gopalji Walji, with whom both Ratansi and Hills had previous business dealings, suggested Ratansi as a possible partner.[49] Having dealt in dates for some time, and having an extensive

[47] 'Abdullah bin Sa'id bin Khalfan Al-Khalili to Ratansi Purshottam (12 Rabi' al-Awwal 1313 / September 2, 1895 and 12 Rajab 1313 / December 29, 1895), RPL Arabic Documents Vol. 2. On 'Abdullah's involvement in politics, see Wilkinson, *The Imamate Tradition of Oman*, 258–259.

[48] Hopper, "Globalization of Dried Fruit," 167–168.

[49] William Hills, Jr. to Ratansi Purshottam (October 27, 1905) RPL William Hills Documents. Invoice by Gopalji Walji (September 22, 1903).

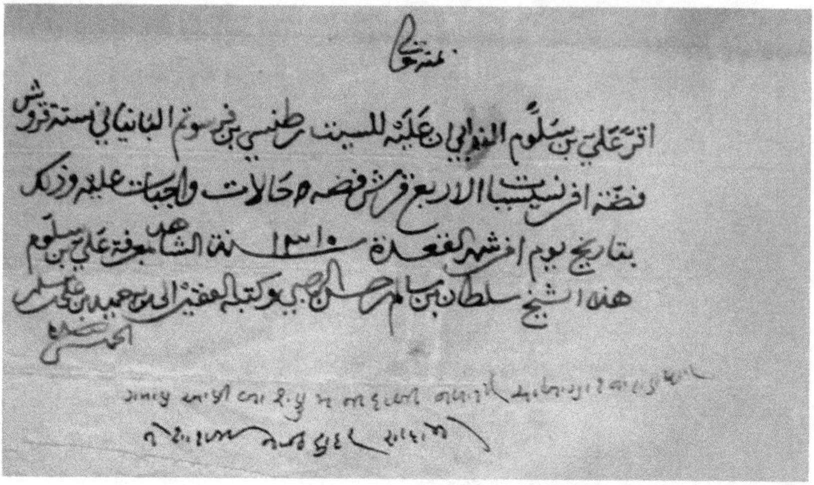

Figure 7 One of Ratansi's *waraqas*

network of middlemen and planters supplying him from the interior, Ratansi was well-placed to serve the needs of a prospective date trader like Hills. And Ratansi was able to mobilize his network towards his business with Hills, taking advantage of the opportunities that the New York-based firm offered him. Over the course of a few years, he shipped out tens of thousands of boxes of Omani dates.

To finance Hills's massive orders, Ratansi drew on the New York merchant's extensive credit network. In one letter, Hills enclosed letters of credit totaling GBP 6,000 to cover the costs of purchasing and packing the dates. Hills mentioned to Ratansi that Gopalji Walji normally took the letters to his bankers in Bombay and would draw drafts on them, which the Bombay bankers would cash and then credit to his account.[50] Through a network of bankers in London and Bombay, Hills and Ratansi directed global circuits of finance to Muscat and from there to middlemen operating on the coast and interior. In a way, Ratansi and other Indian merchants like him bridged date plantations in Oman to markets in Europe and the United States, mediating between global regimes of trade finance and local regimes of debt and property. These traders forged the international chains that linked Oman to Basra, Karachi, Bombay, and New York. What had once been a regional commodity had become transformed into a global one.

[50] William Hills, Jr., to Ratansi Purshottam (June 13, 1906), RPL William Hills Documents, 3–4.

Thus, when the Zanzibari Arabs Saleh bin Sulaiman and Saif bin Hamoud both jockeyed with one another for the right to 'Abdullah bin Salam's property in Oman, it was in this context – a time in which the growing date trade, made possible by merchants like William Hills and Ratansi Purshottam, had rendered land more valuable than it had been for decades. Saleh and Saif would have both known of the possibilities that land in Oman could offer, and would have been willing to risk a possible default by 'Abdullah bin Salam – or in Saif's case, the risk of a speculative purchase of land in the hands of a stranger across the sea – for the promise of rewards in the growing global date trade.

At the same time, in pursuing land in Oman, they banked on there being a legal system that would uphold their property rights – one that would not interfere with their relationships with their debtors nor impose limits on their ability to collect rent or, if necessary, foreclose on property. That Saleh was able to hold onto 'Abdullah bin Salam's properties in Oman for more than seven years after the courts in Zanzibar had ruled against him suggested that he knew something that the judges did not. And the fact that when Saif left Zanzibar for Muscat to take the land from Saleh but "was met with difficulties of a legal nature" indicates that Saleh had played the right cards. And he did: in 'Abdullah bin Salam's date garden, an ocean away, the Zanzibar court was nowhere to be seen, and commercial actors like Saleh could appeal to a completely different set of authorities to uphold his claims.

Al-Salimi, Finance, and the Date Trade

From his residence in Al-Qabil, an agricultural village in the northeast of Oman not far from the date plantations of the Batinah, the blind jurist 'Abdullah bin Humayd Al-Salimi might not have been able to see the globalization of Oman's date trade, but could feel the pressures it placed on local date farmers. Day after day, he responded to questions from merchants and planters, all of whom were in some way entangled in the webs of credit, finance, and *khiyār* sales that had by the late nineteenth century penetrated deep into the Omani interior. Through his pronouncements, Al-Salimi infused a trans-oceanic contractual culture with the renewed energy of the *nahḍa*.

As the property market in East Africa began to extend back into Oman at the time of the date trade, Al-Salimi was willing to furnish a legal framework that was supple enough to accommodate the range of transactions that merchants and financiers engaged in. At several points, Al-Salimi had to respond to legal questions arising from the increasing number of *khiyār* sales and *rahns* by East Africa-based Omanis of their home properties – properties like 'Abdullah bin Salam's. And the jurist was keen to guide his correspondents in whatever way he could.

As in the series of transactions between Saleh, Saif, and 'Abdullah, the mobility of people, capital, and property across the Indian Ocean rested in part on a system the rights and obligations between principals and the agents (*wakīls*) they appointed across the ocean. And people asked Al-Salimi many questions about their *wakīls*, whether they were based in East Africa (which they often referred to using "*Zanjibār*," or Zanzibar, as a synecdoche) or Oman.[51] His correspondents seemed especially concerned about *wakīls* tasked with selling property abroad (mostly in Oman, on behalf of principals in East Africa) who ended up taking the property for themselves, and the implications this might have for trans-oceanic property transactions.[52] In one instance, a Zanzibar-based Omani wanted to sell his property in Nizwa through a *wakīl*. After a series of missed opportunities with potential buyers, the *wakīl* decided to purchase the property himself, and paid his principal (i.e. the seller) most – but not all – of the asking price. Years later, presumably after the value of the land increased along with Oman's date boom, the principal decided that he wanted to annul the sale and take back the property. He approached a *qāḍi*, who then wrote to Al-Salimi outlining what had happened and asking for advice on what the seller's rights were. In his response, Al-Salimi upheld both parties' right to cancel the sale, affirming, moreover, that it passed to their heirs even after they died. Because the sale had not been completed – the buyer had not paid the full price – the seller retained the right to annul it. Until then, he argued, the buyer had a right to retain the property's harvest, since he occupied the land legally.[53] The jurist set out rights for both parties within the framework of a growing date trade: the original property owner had the right to reclaim his land, while the *wakīl*-cum-purchaser was able to retain whatever profits he had made in the interim.

Land constituted just one of the many forms of property that Omanis circulated around the Western Indian Ocean. Some Omanis executed *wakala* contracts for the production and purchase of clothing from Zanzibar; others used them for the sale and management of slaves.[54] In one question, a *qāḍi* looked to Al-Salimi for guidance on how to define the rights and liabilities in one particularly interesting trans-oceanic *wakala*. An Omani had appointed a *wakīl* to travel to East Africa and sell cloth there and use the profits to buy a female slave to bring back to Oman; anything left over was to be considered the *wakil's* payment. After selling

[51] Al-Salimi, *Jawābāt al-Imām al-Sālimī*, Vol. 4, 537–540, 543–544.
[52] Al-Salimi, *Jawābāt*, Vol. 4, 550–551.
[53] Al-Salimi, *Jawābāt*, Vol. 4, 310–311.
[54] Al-Salimi, *Jawābāt*, Vol. 4, 553–554.

off the cloth, the *wakīl* instead bought a group of slaves, both male and female, and transported them to the port of Sur, not far from Muscat. From there, he sent an elderly female slave to his principal, and kept the rest of the slaves to himself. This might have been fine had there not been one mishap: the elderly slave he sent died on her way there, prompting the principal to take his claim to the *qāḍi*, who then wrote to Al-Salimi. In his reply, Al-Salimi offered the *qāḍi* guidance on the extent of the *wakīl's* liability, and on how to best compensate the principal for his losses.[55] In another question, a woman in Zanzibar whose husband had traveled to Oman wrote to Al-Salimi asking about her right to oversee the marriage and divorce of slaves that he left her with.[56]

What Al-Salimi spent the most time dealing with, however, was death. When Omanis who moved between East Africa and South Arabia died, their heirs looked to Al-Salimi to help sort out the claims that heirs an ocean apart might have on the estates. For Al-Salimi, space was no deterrent to the rightful claims of an heir: in his response to a request for advice from the family of an Omani who had spent his years traveling between South Arabia and East Africa and died leaving families on both coasts, Al-Salimi contended that every heir had a right to the estate, and that he did not see "that distance or the sea was an obstacle to that" (*lā arā al-bu'd aw al-baḥar qāṭi'an li-dhālik*), a notion that resonates with Al-Amawi's ideas in Zanzibar about a universal *qāḍi* jurisdiction.[57]

But even if the ocean wasn't an obstacle to people's right to claim their inheritance, it could pose significant complications. As in the case between Saleh bin Sulaiman and 'Abdullah bin Salam's heirs, the time that it took to travel across the Western Indian Ocean and back left plenty of room for heirs to fashion their claims in ways that best suited their interests. In one case, the East African heirs to a property in Oman appointed a *wakīl* to dispose of the estate and return with the money. Upon his return, one of the heirs denied having ever authorized him to sell his inheritance, and had in the meantime sold off his share to an interested buyer.[58] Another case involved multiple *wakīls* and just as many instructions for the execution of a will of property in Oman from Zanzibar.[59] And in one particularly egregious case, an Omani husband to four wives spent his last days traveling around the East African coast, divorcing his Omani wives one by one as he married in East Africa. After his death, confusion lingered as to precisely which wives he divorced, and whether any one of them would have to withdraw her right to inherit from his estate.[60]

55 Al-Salimi, *Jawābāt*, Vol. 4, 539–540.
56 Al-Salimi, *Jawābāt*, Vol. 4, 542–543.
57 Al-Salimi, *Jawābāt*, Vol. 4, 58–60.
58 Al-Salimi, *Jawābāt*, Vol. 4, 49–50.
59 Al-Salimi, *Jawābāt*, Vol. 4, 127–128.
60 Al-Salimi, *Jawābāt*, Vol. 4, 192–193.

At times, death posed questions about what to do with property investments. One *qāḍi* relayed a story of an Omani who traveled to the Swahili Coast and took up residence there and, years later, invested in a plantation in Oman – one that he had never seen before. Because he lived abroad, the man appointed his daughter to look after the property and shared the harvest with her; after some time, he decided to gift it to her. However, when he passed away, other heirs came forward to claim their share of the plantation; the daughter then produced the deed through which her father had gifted her the property and brought witnesses to attest to her having managed it over the years. The *qāḍi* wanted to know whether her claim stood. Al-Salimi upheld the daughter's right: as long as the deed was good, he argued, the claim stood on its own, and none of the heirs had the right to demand the gift's annulment.[61]

As greater numbers of Omanis traveled between South Arabia and East Africa, taking with them people and property, they and their *qāḍis* looked to jurists like Al-Salimi to help them sort through the broad range of contracts, promises, rights, and obligations they generated.[62] In life or in death, Al-Salimi was their guide through the thickets of contracts, institutions, and law, and he was more than willing to draw on his legal knowledge in order to make their world more intelligible and navigable.

This was particularly true of the *khiyār* sale, which *qāḍis*, merchants, and planters frequently inquired about. They wrote to ask about the *khiyār* sale of land, of their harvest, and of irrigation rights, as well as the legal problems, concerns, and moral quandaries they faced in engaging in a form of contracting that had by then been in use for at least a half a century. Their questions showed a familiarity with the sale contract and an implicit acceptance of its use: unlike questions to Al-Khalili fifty years or so before, nobody writing to Al-Salimi suggested that the *khiyār* sale was a new practice. Indeed, the number of questions they brought up surrounding the sale – Al-Salimi's *fatwas* on sales record fifty-six questions directly related to the *khiyār* sale, compared to forty-six in Al-Khalili's *fatwas* – suggest that the contract had become an enduring fixture of a commercial society that was now facing its own commercial boom.

The questions were also all the more pressing now that international capital had made it into the date plantations by way of *Banias* like Ratansi Purshottam and others. Whereas Al-Khalili's *fatwas* from fifty years earlier barely mentioned *Banias*, Al-Salimi's correspondents made frequent

[61] Al-Salimi, *Jawābāt*, Vol. 4, 476–477.

[62] In one *fatwa*, Al-Salimi had to comment on whether a Zanzibari who had lured an Omani to East Africa under false promises of fortune was liable for any losses incurred by the Omani on the way there. Al-Salimi, *Jawābāt*, Vol. 4, 579–580.

mention of their Indian financiers – as moneylenders and merchants, but also as absentee property owners. One correspondent from 'Ibri, roughly 170 miles inland from Muscat, described how the rights to an irrigation canal (*falaj*) belonged to a "Dāmah bin Lālah," who nobody knew anything about. The correspondent, most likely a *qāḍi* or a neighboring planter, asked Al-Salimi how to deal with the rents that *falaj* generated, and whether it was necessary to search for Damah in Muscat and the areas surrounding it – and if Damah was not there, to travel all the way to India to find him. Al-Salimi replied that his correspondent's only responsibility was to guarantee the rents until Damah returned; nobody had a responsibility to seek the owner out, and neighbors could make use of the *falaj* or any other property until the absentee owner returned.[63]

The bulk of the questions surrounding *Banias*, however, involved their lending activities. Al-Salimi's correspondents wrote to him on at least a few different occasions to voice their concerns about their business relationships with their Indian financiers. One wrote to Al-Salimi explaining that in transactions with *Banias* "you take money in the form of a loan or debt (*bi-sabīl qarḍ aw daynan*) and you give him [your produce] to sell for you, and he takes a sales commission (*ijrat al-bay'*), and if you do not do that he does not give you money, and if you do the commission is lost to you, going to him and to others." The letter did not involve a question, but Al-Salimi took it as an expression of moral qualms. He reassured his correspondent: "it is to you to take the loan (*lak an taqriḍ*), and his ill intentions and bad practices will not affect you (*lā yaḍirrak sū' qaṣdih wa sū' fi'lih*)."[64] Omani planters were not morally responsible for having to engage in unequal commercial relationships. Rather, Al-Salimi reserved his ire for Muslim moneylenders – either a reference to Khoja moneylenders or, more likely, the Arab middlemen lending out the *Bania's* capital in the interior. Al-Salimi was unequivocal in his rejection of the practice: "he [i.e. the Muslim lender] is the *Bania's* brother in that [the loan] (*huwa akhū al-bānyān fī dhālik*), and *ribā* is forbidden (*ḥarām*) from everyone."[65]

For all of his contempt for *Banias* and other lenders, though, Al-Salimi upheld their rights as commercial actors. One *qāḍi* wrote to him asking about the permissibility of settling accounts between *Banias* when they most likely involved interest-bearing loans and other corrupt (*fāsid*) transactions. Al-Salimi had no objections to the *qāḍi* settling their accounts, particularly if he had no specific knowledge of any

[63] Al-Salimi, *Jawābāt*, Vol. 4, 529–530.
[64] Al-Salimi, *Jawābāt*, Vol. 4, 439.
[65] Al-Salimi, *Jawābāt*, Vol. 4, 395.

impermissible activity.[66] In another opinion, he maintained the rights of *Banias* and other South Asian merchants to call on their debtors' heirs to make good on outstanding accounts.[67]

Whatever he thought of the moneylenders themselves, Al-Salimi voiced few objections to the general practice of *khiyār* sales taking place around him. Like Al-Khalili, he openly declared that using the *khiyār* sale as a means of selling a plantation's yield (*ghilla*) for a specified period of time was valid. He channeled the jurist's creative energies in a response to a question on whether a tree's yield was included in a *khiyār* sale. In a lengthy opinion in which he drew on a range of different legal texts, Al-Salimi contended that the issue was one grounded in the nature of the sale object itself. If the tree in question was sold before its fruit ripened, he wrote, then the fruit formed an inseparable part of the tree; because the fruit was not yet ripe, it could not be considered independent and thus remained in its original state. Much like Al-Khalili and Al-Shaqṣi before him, Al-Salimi drew on the metaphor of the flowering tree to argue that only by ripening could the fruit be considered as an independent object of sale. For Al-Salimi, this was largely an issue of value: unripe fruit had no use-value in itself (*lā naf'un lahā min ḥaythu dhātihā*); its use-value derived from its attachment to its mother, the tree (*min ḥaythu al-tabī'a li-ummahātihā*). Like a camel still in its mother's womb, fruit could have no existence of its own until it ripened.[68] In a date plantation sold before the time of harvest, then, the yield comprised an inseparable part of the sale.

Nor did Al-Salimi object to the growing practice of passing down the *khiyār* arrangement from one generation to another. The right of redemption in a *khiyār* sale, he wrote, "is a right that is inherited, and thus does not end with the death of the sellers, and undoubtedly transfers to their heirs until its period elapses."[69] While he was unsure as to whether the *khiyār* buyer (i.e. the creditor) could pass down his rights, he effectively validated the practice by presenting two competing opinions and leaving the question open.[70] Here, Al-Salimi displayed one of his many signs of willingness to accommodate the needs of an expanding commercial society.

But Al-Salimi made it clear that he was only willing to support changing commercial practices to a certain extent. Any contractual experiments

66 Al-Salimi, *Jawābāt*, Vol. 4, 595–596.

67 Al-Salimi, *Jawābāt*, Vol. 4, 206–207.

68 Al-Salimi, *Jawābāt*, Vol. 4, 257–60. The pregnant camel is a favorite example among Muslim jurists discussing uncertainty in sales contracts.

69 Al-Salimi, *Jawābāt*, Vol. 4, 229.

70 Al-Salimi, *Jawābāt*, Vol. 4, 268.

had to maintain their grounding in established rights and liabilities. Halfway through dealing with a seemingly endless list of queries about the permissibility of various configurations of *khiyār* transactions, Al-Salimi wrote that he no longer knew how to respond for the want of respect that people had for the rules surrounding the *khiyār* sale.[71] The questions, of course, kept coming in, and in an unusually candid moment an exasperated Al-Salimi wrote that he had "broken [his] pen in issuing *fatwas* on the *khiyār* due to people's misuse of it (*li-sū' mu'āmalat al-nās fīh*)." He then swore to his questioner that were he not coming to earnestly seek knowledge he would not have addressed his concerns with so much as one letter of the alphabet.[72]

What bothered Al-Salimi was that people were using the *khiyār* sale with no understanding of the contractual rights that underpinned it – that the contract had been reduced to a mere vehicle for flippantly usurious transactions. While he was willing to accommodate the sale of a plantation with its yield within a clearly-defined timeframe for its redemption, and was even willing to support the extension of that timeframe over several generations, he could not countenance transactions that clearly aimed to use the yield to service a debt over an indefinite period of time – transactions which effectively abrogated the seller's contractual rights. Here, he wrote, "people used it [the *khiyār*] without regard for justice, and turned it into a path to usury (*wa ja'alūh dharī'a ilā al-ribā*)." Al-Salimi ended his opinion by beseeching *kātibs* to join him in breaking their pens in the face of requests to engage in this sort of chicanery, if they had any respect for the integrity of their religion at all.[73]

In addition to his moral concerns surrounding land transactions, the jurist also had political concerns – namely, the implications of dealing in land with non-Muslims. Responding to a questioner who asked him about the legality of leasing property to Christians (*naṣāra*), he wrote that if the Christian enjoyed an inordinate amount of power (*quwwa*) in the area, then it was not permissible. This response was not simply a legal one; it reflected his assessment of the changing political dynamics in the Indian Ocean following the death of Sultan Sa'id, the partition of the Omani Empire by the British, and British support for the Busa'idi coup against 'Azzan bin Qais's Imamate. "The lease [of land] was the first instance of the Christians' entry into Zanzibar," he wrote, "and it assisted them in their mastery (*tamakkunihim*) in that land." He

[71] Al-Salimi, *Jawābāt*, Vol. 4, 296.
[72] Al-Salimi, *Jawābāt*, Vol. 4, 326–327.
[73] Al-Salimi, *Jawābāt*, Vol. 4, 302–303.

then immediately asked, "This was all seen, but where were the overseers (*al-nāẓirūn*)?!"[74]

Al-Salimi's response might have taken his questioner by surprise. Leasing land, especially to non-Muslims, was a common practice. For Al-Salimi, however, with control of land, whatever the means, loomed the threat of political power – and he had the example of East Africa to prove it. His response reflected his concerns about the changing nature of commercial contracting, its connection to the terrestrial landscape, and the imperial expansion it brought with it. As an heir to Al-Khalili's world, he knew, perhaps better than anyone else, that while *khiyār* sales and the economic relationships that grew out of them enabled commercial activity, they could also open the door to imperial intervention. He knew of what happened to Al-Khalili, and had seen the British Empire ride into South Arabia on *waraqas* and the open pages of Gujarati ledger books.

He also understood that land and title were legal constructions, and that the regime rested on flexible interpretations of legal and financial instruments in the face of a commercial boom. Whether or not the title transfers that the *waraqas* signaled were real and legally binding depended solely upon how those charged with enforcing commercial obligations read them. So long as conflicts arising from Indian Ocean transactions came before people like him – people who grasped the nature of the legal maneuverings surrounding land transactions and understood both social and economic realities, those ambiguities remained contained. But the interpretive tensions residing within *waraqas* raised the possibility that those reading them might reach alternative legal conclusions should those documents become subject to a more pluralistic juridical terrain, as they did in East Africa. For all of his work to facilitate a trans-regional property regime, then, Al-Salimi stopped short of permitting transactions that might have deep political implications – implications nested in the text and the recent history of the *waraqa* itself.

Conclusion

When he wrote back to his questioners, Al-Salimi made sure to stay close to the tenets of Islamic law as he understood them. Taken alone, Al-Salimi's writings would suggest that very little had changed in Omani legal discourses surrounding the *khiyār* sale and other contractual practices since the time of Al-Khalili. His references in his *fatwas* to the same actors, practices, and agricultural ontologies that Al-Khalili's writings had covered decades before made it seem like he was engaging in a stale,

[74] Al-Salimi, *Jawābāt*, Vol. 4, 303.

abstract discourse that was denuded of any sense of place and time. Even his history, the *Tuḥfat Al-A'yan*, could easily fool a reader into thinking it was little more than an homage to generations of scholars before him, from the founder of the Ibadhi *madhhab* to Al-Salimi's own teachers. On their own, Al-Salimi's writings give the impression of intellectual stagnation, of being stuck in a tradition whose age was showing, and whose relevance to a new economic world was limited.

And yet nothing could be further from the truth. Al-Salimi was neither thinking nor writing alone: he was part of a movement of scholars and jurists around the Indian Ocean whose writings sought to reassert a place for their own understandings of Islamic law at a time of high imperialism. Whether their writings took the form of histories, *fatwas*, treatises on jurisprudence, or short opinions hurriedly scribbled down on loose sheets of paper in a British courtroom, Muslim juridical actors from around the region worked to reinscribe their place in a constantly changing world of contracting. Their writings amounted to a counter-narrative to the one posed in the *Zanzibar Law Reports* – a denial of the ascendancy of British Indian law in the region, and an active attempt to re-inscribe their own authority in economic and juridical life, particularly in parts of the region that imperial jurisdiction could not reach. Al-Salimi's writings – his *fatwas*, the manuals of jurisprudence he authored, and his history – were as much products of this movement as they were attempts to assert its supremacy.

Al-Salimi also worked to make his vision a political reality. In 1913, just a year before he died, he and a group of other scholars nominated the tribal shaikh Salim bin Rashid Al-Kharusi as the new Imam of the Omani interior.[75] He was joined by a number of dissidents from Zanzibar, many of whom had failed in their attempts to put up a resistance to British involvement in local affairs and instead returned to Oman to join in the anti-British and anti-Busa'idi movements there.[76] Al-Kharusi's followers were able to successfully take key cities like Nizwa and Izki, but were unable to advance into Muscat and Muttrah, both of which were strongholds of the Sultanate and came under the protection of the British government. While relations between the Sultanate and Imamate were tense, the two polities persisted side by side, with a number of tribal buffer zones in between, until the mid-twentieth century.[77] And in the

75 Wilkinson, *The Imamate Tradition of Oman*, 249.

76 Wilkinson, *The Imamate Tradition of Oman*, 263–265.

77 This history is amply covered in Wilkinson, *The Imamate Tradition of Oman*, 249–273. Al-Salimi's son Mohammed also devoted a monograph to the history of the new Imamate, which he titled *Nahḍat Al-A'yān fī Ḥurriyat 'Umān [The Notables' Renaissance in the Liberation of Oman]* (Beirut: Dār Al-Jīl, 1998).

territories held by the Imamate, the civil administration was run by *qāḍis* who discharged their duties according to their understandings of Islamic law – people like Al-Salimi's correspondents, who continued to write to the jurist until his death in 1914.[78]

Merchants and litigants were savvy to what was going on around them. Faced with an uneven regulatory landscape, merchants took their money where it would be least encumbered by bureaucratic requirements, lawyers' fees, and troublesome legislation. Others, who stood to lose a great deal to unregulated capital and property markets in places like Oman and Barawa chose to hedge their bets with British courts in East Africa, appealing to the British courts to save their property from foreclosure. The legal strategies deployed by people like Saleh bin Sulaiman, Saif bin Hamoud, the children of 'Abdullah bin Salam, and countless others like them exposed the limits of each legal system, but also set into motion the very legal and intellectual processes that brought them into being. Well into the establishment of British protectorates in East Africa and South Arabia, then, the Anglo-Indian juridical regime continued to coexist alongside a number of other commercio-legal registers.

But there was only so much that the legal systems and the litigants could do when faced with real crisis. Over the course of the 1920s and 1930s, the Western Indian Ocean was rocked by an unyielding depression, and debtors all over faced the very real threat of foreclosure on their properties. As the relative prosperity of East Africa and South Arabia gave way to the prospect of economic and political collapse, an altogether different group of authorities stepped in to take the reins.

[78] Wilkinson, *The Imamate Tradition of Oman*, 270–273. Al-Salimi died a less sensational death than Al-Khalili: he fell off his donkey on his way to visiting one of his former teachers.

8 Unraveling Obligation

When Al-Salimi helped establish the Imamate in the interior of Oman in 1913, it was the end of history as he knew it. There was much to celebrate: by the end of that year, the forces of the Imamate had taken over much of the Omani interior, including many of the date-growing regions, and had deprived the Sultan of any chance at asserting jurisdiction beyond the coastal cities of Muscat and Muttrah. The vocally anti-British jurist and his rogue group of exiles from East Africa had realized their goal of creating a political alternative to a world of European empires and vassals like the Sultan of Muscat.

But for all of their ability to conquer territory and win over interior Omanis, the leaders of the Imamate were less certain when it came to the more mundane aspects of governance. Their ideological disdain for the Sultan and his relations with the British overlooked the fact that in order to generate revenue they needed access to the coast, both physically and financially. The date trade, which most of the Imamate's revenues were based upon, was intimately bound up in coastal finance and marketing, as was the trade in other produce. Moreover, many of the Imamate's leaders owned property and had family in Muscat; political tensions between the coast and interior created a climate of distrust that was harmful to interests on both sides.

Across the sea, things weren't much better. In Zanzibar, a gradual collapse in the market for cloves left most of the island's planter community in a virtually irreversible state of debt. Racked with frustration and drowning in red ink, planters' relationships with their merchant-financiers turned bitter, generating tensions that spilled over into the political arena. What had once been a place of opportunity had by 1930 become a place marred with political and economic instability. The troubles faced by economic actors and state officials in South Arabia and East Africa during the 1920s – troubles that were only exacerbated by the arrival of the worldwide economic depression in the 1930s – threatened to push the commercial arena to the verge of collapse. As creditors foreclosed on their debtors' properties, and as the ruling regime contended with the erosion of the economic foundations of their authority, it became clear that this was a moment of crisis. In Zanzibar, as in Muscat, the threat of financial collapse threatened to destabilize the social and political order that had reigned for nearly a century and shake the very foundations of British hegemony in the region. All of this set in motion processes that ultimately spelled the end of the region's contractual culture, washing the *waraqa* away with it.

Economic Transformation and Political Crisis, 1918–1930

The troubles that the Sultan of Muscat, Teymour bin Faisal Al-Busa'idi, faced as he struggled to balance his budget in 1918 were far beyond the capacities of one man. The gradual takeover of Zanzibar and East Africa by Britain and other European powers had created a whole body of disaffected merchants, jurists, and strongmen, all of whom had returned to Arabia and helped establish an Imamate in the interior of Oman. The new political geography that had taken shape in Southeast Arabia over the course of the past five years had left him with only the ports of Muscat and Muttrah as sources for revenue.

To make matters worse, the new leaders of the Imamate were hardly on good terms with the Sultan. They fumed at him for having been cut off from their *shambas* in Zanzibar, many of which were confiscated by the British government after the leaders' involvement in anti-British coup attempts, and for the punitive measures the Sultan took against their families in Muscat.[1] One leader, 'Isa bin Saleh Al-Harthi, whose father had taught Al-Salimi and supported the 'Azzan bin Qais takeover fifty years earlier, was particularly hard-hit, having owned considerable property around East Africa.[2]

The tensions between the Sultan in Muscat and his rivals in the Imamate strained revenues on both sides. The bulk of Oman's dates – its primary export – came from the interior, which was now under the control of the Imamate. These regions were now effectively cut off from Muscat, disrupting the movement of commodities that constituted the port city's life blood. And with no jurisdiction beyond Muscat and Muttrah, the Sultan was unable to ameliorate those losses with customs

[1] Some had gone so far as to hire lawyers in Zanzibar to pursue claims regarding their family properties. See also "Petition by Esa bin Saleh bin Ahmed El-Maskeri for the Restoration to Him of Certain Properties Belonging to His Father, Confiscated by Sultan Seyyid Hamoud" and "Petition Raya Binti Humaid El-Barwaniyya" ZNA AB 10/88.

[2] "Situation in Muscat and Oman, November 1919" IOR R/15/1/416, 70–76; Wilkinson, *The Imamate Tradition of Oman*, 264–265.

receipts from other ports: ships frequently chose to unload their wares in Omani ports where they did not have to pay customs duties, robbing the Sultan of one of his last sources of revenue.[3] To British officials observing the situation in Muscat in the early 1920s, this was an ally on the verge of bankruptcy.

The standoff between political figures on the coast and interior reverberated into the arena of agricultural finance. Whereas Indian traders like Ratansi Purshottam had once been happy to finance date production in the interior through middlemen and to use loans to secure shipments of dates, that was no longer the case. One British official commenting on the state of the date trade in 1920 highlighted how the political tensions of the previous five years had caused Indian traders to stop running accounts with producers in the interior. With the new political situation, he noted, "the dates are not paid for until they arrive on the coast, and the method of payment is partly in cash, and partly in rice and piece goods." Moreover, to address the uncertainties in the interior date trade, Indian merchants either paid less for the dates their producers brought to the coast or charged them more for the goods they sold them, buffering their shrinking supply with wider margins in their account books.[4] To add to the pressures that the interior producers faced, the Sultan raised the customs duties on dates coming from the interior to 25 percent, up from the normal 5 percent rate, coordinating with officials in India to ensure that Omani dhows without a pass from the Muscat customs house could not unload their cargoes.[5]

The interior tribes quickly caved to the pressure. In July 1920, an interior tribesman murdered the Imam, and interior leaders scrambled to elect a new head. They settled on Mohammed bin 'Abdullah Al-Khalili, the grandson of the jurist who had guided Omanis through some of the most rapid economic changes in recent memory. The choice was perhaps a deliberate one: Mohammed's father had worked as a middleman for Ratansi Purshottam in the date trade, brokering between the Indian merchant and interior date producers. His election thus signaled a desire to smooth relations between the interior and coast. And just three months after his election, the two sides reached a formal agreement regarding

[3] By this point, the Sultan's most dependable source of revenue was his customs receipts from Gwadar, which had once formed only a small component of the Sultanate's economic base. Political Agent, Muscat, to Civil Commissioner, Baghdad (February 8, 1920) IOR R/15/1/416, 138.

[4] "Situation in Oman as Regards the Negotiations and Measures Proposed," R/15/1/416, 216–217.

[5] Wilkinson, *The Imamate Tradition of Oman*, 250–251; "Situation in Oman as Regards the Negotiations and Measures Proposed," R/15/1/416, 216–217.

the movement of commodities and people, the levying of duties, and the mutual enforcement of justice.[6]

But the rapprochement between the Sultan and the Imamate did little to buoy profits in what was becoming a very crowded date trade. By the 1920s Muscat's date merchants began facing stiff competition from larger-scale farms in Basra.[7] Ratansi's partner William Hills had by 1908 already begun supplementing his Omani date supply with dates from Basra, where he established a branch of his firm. There, he joined dozens of other European and American firms that had already begun doing business out of the date-rich port city.[8] And by the 1930s, the death knell had sounded for what had been a short-lived boom in dates. Between 1925 and 1934, the total value of Omani date exports dropped by one-third, from over 3 million dollars to just under 1.8 million.[9] The declining export figures were only partly due to the effects of the worldwide depression: Oman's date merchants had also been hit by the emergence of expansive date farms in one of its largest markets, the United States.[10] By the end of the 1920s, American date farms were supplying consumers and retailers around the country; the Omani-American date trade had run its course.

The situation of producers and merchants across the Western Indian Ocean wasn't any more optimistic. In Zanzibar, the move towards widespread clove and coconut cultivation brought new perils to an already-volatile market. As economies that were increasingly dependent on the export of these two crops – of which cloves were the more valuable – Zanzibar and the neighboring island of Pemba developed new vulnerabilities to a constantly-changing market. The islands also faced new competition from abroad – from Madagascar, where clove exports had been steadily growing from the mid-nineteenth century onward, and from the United States, where the invention of synthetic clove oil threatened to dampen demand for Zanzibar cloves.[11]

Declining exports were exacerbated by the emergence of a worldwide agricultural crisis in the 1920s. During World War I, prices for agricultural commodities experienced an unprecedented boom as European nations' demand for food crops grew. Around the world, the surge in

6 Wilkinson, *The Imamate Tradition of Oman*, 269–270.
7 Hopper, "The African Presence in Arabia," 137–160.
8 Hopper, "The Globalization of Dried Fruit," 166–169.
9 Landen, *Oman Since 1856*, 405. Adjusted for inflation, the drop is closer to 28 percent, as 3 million dollars in 1925 had the same buying power as 2.3 million in 1934.
10 Hopper, "The Globalization of Dried Fruit," 173–177.
11 Gwynn Campbell, *An Economic History of Imperial Madagascar, 1750–1895: The Rise and Fall of an Island Empire* (New York: Cambridge University Press, 2005), 100, 188–189.

demand prompted farmers to expand agricultural acreage. However, when the war ended, agricultural prices worldwide experienced a dramatic collapse as farmers collectively produced far more than demand could sustain.[12] Although the core problem of global overproduction involved grains, the crisis reverberated in the agrarian economies of East Africa and Oman. In Zanzibar, clove prices dropped from highs of Rs 30 to an average price of roughly Rs 15 during the second half of the 1920s.[13] Later, the onset of the worldwide depression of the 1930s pulled the rug out from underneath the region's economies altogether. As markets worldwide nosedived, demand for East African goods plummeted. In Zanzibar and Pemba, the Depression effectively killed what little demand there was for ivory, while bringing the price of cloves to the lowest they had been in decades.[14]

Low prices, however, were just the beginning of the planter's woes and East Africa's troubles. For as the market shrank, so too did the financiers' patience with their debtors. Saddled with commodities that were no longer worth what they had paid for them, and frustrated by their inability to collect on their loans, Indian merchants turned to the only option they had left: foreclosure.

Debt and Dispossession

In November 1922, members of Pemba's Arab planter community, led by the former governor of Chake Chake, marched over to the British High Commissioner and presented him with a petition. The planters complained that they had become "heavily indebted to Indians" – that they were frequently obliged to borrow money at high interest rates in the hopes of being able to pay it back after the clove harvest. Although the seasonal indebtedness they grumbled about was a normal state of affairs for the planters, this time things were different. The planters noted that recently, the crop they collected frequently fell short of the accumulated interest, "and thus by degrees, year after year, we find ourselves losing one portion after another of our *shambas* and reduced to poverty."[15]

In 1920s Zanzibar, the reality of foreclosure – and especially the scale at which it took place – were both relatively new. Creditors had

12 Giovanni Federico, "Not Guilty? Agriculture in the 1920s and the Great Depression," *Journal of Economic History*, Vol. 65, No. 4 (2005), 949–976.

13 Report by K.P. Menon (1934), 16, ZNA AB 3/48.

14 Report by K.P. Menon (1934), 17, ZNA AB 3/48.

15 Address from Shaikh Sulaiman bin Mubarak Al-Ma'wali and other Arabs of Chake Chake to the High Commissioner for Zanzibar (November 24, 1922). He sent in a similar petition six months later, in June 1923. ZNA AB 14/2.

rarely foreclosed on properties before, in part because of the mutually understood rights and obligations underpinning the *khiyār* sale, but also because courts had kept them from doing so, interpreting the *khiyār* sale in such a way that it gave the debtor a chance to hold onto his property and pay off his debts. But now, faced with goods that could no longer fetch reasonable prices and debtors who were unable to find the money to close out their accounts, creditors opted to foreclose, and courts had no choice but to allow them to. And as the effects of the 1930s depression began to wash up onto the shores of the Western Indian Ocean, it swept up the land along with it, rocking the delicate balance of debt, property, and mutualism that had characterized economic life. In port cities around the region, debtors found their obligations to be increasingly unwieldy; one after another, they began to hand over their properties to their creditors in lieu of debts that they could neither service nor repay.

In Oman, the arrival of the Depression did not result in a crisis of foreclosures, in part because of the shifts in date finance that the tensions between the coast and interior had caused.[16] Indian merchants had since the mid-1910s shifted to dealing on a cash basis; there were relatively few hypothecated properties in Muscat – relative, at least, to Zanzibar – and creditors could hardly count on authorities upholding their claims to property in the interior, especially when the cash-strapped Imamate depended so dearly on those properties to generate its revenues.

But Oman hardly escaped the tumultuous 1920s and 1930s unburdened by debt. The gradual collapse of the date trade with the United States, Oman's most important market, dealt a devastating blow to the Sultan's finances. Faced with shrinking revenues, the Sultanate teetered on the verge of insolvency; the Sultan resorted to borrowing from Muscat's merchant community to keep the state apparatus afloat, putting up both personal and state property as collateral. According to one estimate at the end of 1919, he owed roughly Rs 250,000 in personal debts and another Rs 550,000 on security of the customs house – more than he would be able to repay with almost a decade of good revenues.[17]

Muscat's impending financial collapse worried British officials in India, who had invested a lot of time and energy into propping up the Sultanate over the past century or so. The Sultanate was of strategic importance to British shipping, and the Sultan was one of the Government of India's

16 Marc Valeri, however, suggests that there was a trend of foreclosure in 1930s Oman. See idem, "High Visibility, Low Profile: the Shiʿa in Oman Under Sultan Qaboos," *International Journal of Middle East Studies*, Vol. 42, No. 2 (2010), 255.

17 Political Agent, Muscat, to Civil Commissioner, Baghdad (December 11, 1919), IOR R/15/1/416, 27–46.

key allies in the fight against the slave and arms trade.[18] Moreover, Muscat's financial health was important to India's merchant communities, many of whom had invested in the port city. Nearly half of the Sultan's personal debts were to Indians, and at least two-thirds of the money he had borrowed against customs revenues came from the port's Indian merchants.[19] For the sake of fiscal solvency and for political expediency, the ruler had to stay.

In Zanzibar and Pemba, the problem was more widespread, but also more complicated. The first systematic attempt at collecting figures on property foreclosures in 1934 brought to the fore the magnitude of the problem, but represented it as an explicitly racialized one – a credit market of deep ethnic cleavages (see Tables 1 and 2). In Zanzibar, the statistics suggested that Arabs transferred nearly 30 plots of land worth just over Rs 80,000 to their Indian creditors in 1925; three years later, the number increased almost sixfold, to nearly 130 plots worth just over Rs. 650,000. By 1933, the numbers had dropped a little, but not enough to assuage debtors; a worrying trend of dispossession had clearly wrought havoc on the Arab landlord class. And debtors with smaller plots of land generally fared worse. Swahili debtors, whose plots of land were often smaller than their Arab counterparts, handed over 103 parcels of land worth nearly Rs 49,000 in 1925; three years later, those figures doubled. And higher numbers of Swahilis lost their lands to their Indian creditors than Arabs did – to say nothing of the lands they lost to their Arab creditors.[20]

Circumstances in Pemba, which was almost entirely dependent on the clove and coconut trade, proved even more dire. There, Indians foreclosed on almost 300 Arab *shambas* in 1926 – nearly ten times the number of foreclosures in Zanzibar during the previous year. The number peaked at 374 in 1932 – four times what Zanzibar saw during the same year. Their foreclosures on Swahili property reflected the same trend: in 1926, they were nearly eight times those in Zanzibar; and in 1932, there were nearly six times as many. Although the Pemba plots were only worth about half those in Zanzibar, the trend of dispossession of Arab and Swahili debtors was just as worrying.[21]

18 See also Johan Mathew, *Margins of the Market: Trafficking and Capitalism Across the Arabian Sea* (Berkeley, CA: University of California Press, 2016).

19 Political Agent, Muscat, to Civil Commissioner, Baghdad (December 11, 1919), IOR R/15/1/416, 36–40.

20 The high representation of Swahilis among the dispossessed is likely due to the vulnerability of their smaller harvests to downturns in prices as compared to the larger Arab *shamba* owners. At the same time, however, one has to consider how large the group "Swahili" might be, as it could potentially incorporate a much broader swath of the Zanzibari population than the smaller category of "Arab."

21 "Statistics Relating to the Transfers of Property as between Races," ZNA AB 47/25.

Table 1 *Number of Land Transfers in Zanzibar, 1925–1933*

	1925	1927	1928	1930	1931	1932	1933
Arab to Arab	207	178	217	205	142	137	142
Arab to Swahili	209	90	91	153	60	83	52
Arab to Indian	29	78	126	117	40	87	92
Swahili to Swahili	726	494	432	645	290	337	261
Swahili to Arab	130	113	147	130	82	101	75
Swahili to Indian	103	132	189	134	84	100	99
Indian to Indian	29	45	53	48	39	53	82
Indian to Arab	23	22	26	56	24	38	40
Indian to Swahili	42	29	40	92	29	29	29

Table 2 *Number of Land Transfers in Pemba, 1926–1933*

	1926	1927	1928	1929	1930	1931	1932	1933
Arab to Arab	508	438	628	364	531	365	608	269
Arab to Swahili	169	128	229	139	201	184	216	75
Arab to Indian	289	211	290	236	249	219	374	186
Swahili to Swahili	712	630	690	480	755	598	593	343
Swahili to Arab	488	431	603	270	317	309	461	167
Swahili to Indian	759	577	711	529	145	410	587	294
Indian to Indian	60	65	72	65	74	106	113	75
Indian to Arab	40	39	43	53	101	44	63	87
Indian to Swahili	59	34	63	80	129	80	67	23

The statistics officials collected furnished overwhelming evidence that foreclosure was more than a specter: represented as a distinctly racial problem, it had quickly become a politically destabilizing reality, and one with enormous implications. "Zanzibar," wrote the Attorney-General, "is an Arab State. It is the duty of the protecting government to assist the protected people, [and] it is impossible for us to stand by and take the risk of expropriation of His Highness's people."[22] If property formed the material basis of political community, then the large-scale dispossession of Arab landowners in an "Arab state" at the hands of their Indian financiers risked the transformation of the very foundations of the polity. And the solutions they proposed rested on a similarly racialized – though more caricatured – image of East African economic life.

22 Extracts from article written by C.F. Andrews in *The Statesman*, a Calcutta daily (1934), ZNA AB 3/48, 60.

The Battle for the Credit Market, 1920–1936

For some British officials in Zanzibar, the problem of indebtedness was, at its core, one of Arab economic sensibilities: the leisure that had formed such an integral component of *shamba* life in the past had now grown to eclipse the plantation's more strictly economic functions. And the problem was not simply a product of the times, but lay in the essential characteristics of the Arab and the African: extravagance, thriftlessness, and above all, a lack of economic foresight. "These people when they first came to these Islands must have been hard-working to have been able to do what they have done," wrote one official, "but it seems the far too easy way that money has been able to be made from the valuable products of the clove tree has had this degenerating effect on a once-industrious people." Affluence in times of plenty had given rise to laziness and improvidence.[23]

Officials who saw the problem of indebtedness in such individualistic terms saw a simple solution: restrict access to credit. "If his [the debtor's] credit is restricted, he will suffer," argued one official, "... but if he can get over this period (there seems to be no reason why he should not) it is possible that he may be turned into a really useful citizen again." The creditor would have to change too: "if the law can be made strong enough to prevent credit," he contended, "he [i.e. the creditor] will not always be able to keep up the price of necessities of life, for competition must bring them down again." By at least limiting the rate of interest on loans, the government could squeeze out avaricious creditors and rehabilitate the region's debtors.[24]

In the 1920s Indian Ocean, however, not all British officials were ready to support legislation that would interfere in credit markets. In Zanzibar the staunchest opposition to the legislation came from judges and lawyers, who saw them as a threat to the delicate balance between creditors and debtors in the region. Critics contended that restricting credit or limiting interest rates could just as easily achieve the opposite effect, stifling industry and enterprise by making access to capital more difficult. Drawing on passages from John Stuart Mill's *Principles of Political Economy*, one lawyer argued that government intervention in the credit market would raise the price of credit and make it more difficult for planters to access loans; it would discourage, rather than facilitate, economic activity.[25] Others argued that the state had no business interfering

[23] Report by B.C. Johnstone (February 1923) ZNA AB 47/26.
[24] Report by B.C. Johnstone (February 1923) ZNA AB 47/26.
[25] A.A. Stephens to the Chief Judge (June 20,1924) ZNA AB 14/2.

in a contract executed for a lawful purpose and for good consideration, especially when the parties were of full mental capacity.[26] Still others were of the opinion that interfering in credit markets would do nothing to rehabilitate native borrowers. One magistrate wrote that a native borrower would learn no more from attempts to restrict his ability to borrow than would a school boy "whom a vigilant prefect restrains from mortgaging his umbrella in order that he might stuff himself with chocolates or pork pies."[27] Another official contended that the very idea that one could legislate economic morality was misinformed, as the Government "shall not educate the native by too much spoon-feeding to take his proper place in the community."[28]

Part of what motivated the Zanzibar judiciary's staunch opposition to any attempt to place legal limits on interest was their conviction that any such move would falter when faced by the realities of *waraqa* practices on the ground. Judges and lawyers who had experience dealing with Indian merchants in the courtroom knew too well that any restriction on their ability to charge interest would be "defeated by the conclusion of clandestine arrangements between the Indians and the natives."[29] In a memorandum to the Zanzibar Attorney-General, a group of lawyers argued that legislation restricting access to credit or limiting the rate of interest would be easily evaded by actors who wrote up fictitious *waraqas* intended to mislead the court – *waraqas*, for example, would state that the debtor had borrowed Rs 500 when in fact they had only borrowed Rs 400. That sort of ruse, the laywers suggested, was only "a known difficulty: heaven help us from exploring the unknown in moneylending transactions."[30] Any legislation that targeted the moneylender, then, was doomed to a lifeless existence in the books alone.

Two cases highlighted the judicial tensions over how to read the *waraqa* against the backdrop of the global commercial downturn – cases important enough to be included in the *Zanzibar Law Reports*. In the summer of 1929, after several years of debates surrounding interest on loans, the children of Salim bin 'Abdullah Al-Barwani, a recently deceased Arab planter, filed a suit against the *qāḍi* Shaikh Burhan bin 'Abdulaziz Al-Amawi for a Rs 13,000 debt due to their father's estate – Rs 3,000 of which, they claimed, was rent (or *kod*) for three years (at the rate of Rs 1,000 per year). Al-Amawi, the defendant, was familiar

26 Letter from [name illegible] to Wallis (June 12, 1924) ZNA AB 14/2.
27 ZNA AB 47/10, 104.
28 ZNA AB 47/11, 36.
29 ZNA AB 47/10, 104.
30 Memo from Members of the Bar to the Attorney-General (June 20, 1924) ZNA AB 14/2.

with *khiyār* sales: he had penned a number of *waraqas* himself, and was able to counter Al-Barwani's heirs' claim well. Standing before the judge, the *qāḍi* argued that because *kod* constituted interest on the loan, and because Islamic law, which governed the transaction, forbade interest, the claim was void. Having already paid Rs 5,000 in *kod*, he only owed what remained of the principal amount loaned – Rs 5,000.[31]

To the panel of British judges presiding over the case, the *qāḍi* had no leg to stand on in claiming that his *kod* payments went towards paying off the principal owed rather than the interest. "The Mohammedan subjects of His Highness," wrote one judge, "were in the habit of entering into these *Beikhiar* [sic] transactions knowing full well their nature and being prepared to pay *kod* for the use of another man's money." The whole system of the *khiyār* sale with a stipulation for *kod*, he contended "was a polite fiction to enable persons needing money to obtain credit without incurring the possible guilt of dealing in transactions by way of interest." As such, the plaintiffs' claims for *kod* had to be admitted – but as *interest* rather than rent, and thus subject to a 6 percent cap. One judge even went so far as to proclaim that the time had come for Muslim jurists to abandon altogether the prohibition against interest in commercial transactions. "Credit," he declared in a long opinion following his judgment, "is the life's breath of modern commerce, and there can be no credit without interest. If, therefore, the modern Moslem is to take part in the commercial life of the community, it is necessary that he should be freed from the alleged prohibition against the taking of interest."[32]

However, not everyone expressed the same enthusiasm about tampering with a commercial instrument that had by the late 1920s become deeply entrenched in East African commercial society. Faced with a similar dispute less than a year after Al-Amawi's case, one judge held that *kod* had to be interpreted as precisely what the parties represented it to be – rent for a property leased. After reflecting on the many decades of court decisions surrounding the *khiyār* sale and the *waraqa*, the judge wrote that "to call *kod* interest involves two fictions in the document: the fictitious giving of possession and a fictitious name for interest. One, I think, is enough." *Kod*, he asserted, was to be treated as rent and awarded as such, irrespective of the rate of interest it effectively amounted to.[33] Together, the rulings on the two cases reflected the court's different

31 *Sheikh Burhan bin Abdulaziz El-Amawi* v. *Khalfan bin Salim El-Barwani and Another* (1929) 4 ZLR 90.

32 *Sheikh Burhan bin Abdulaziz El-Amawi* v. *Khalfan bin Salim El-Barwani and Another* (1929) 4 ZLR 96.

33 *Mahomed bin Mahfuth El-Fided by his attorney Oman bin Abdulla Gurnah* v. *Abdulla bin Salim bin Mbarak Ba-Saleh of Chwake* (1930) 4 ZLR 9.

impulses on how one might interpret the place of interest in financial practice – whether to read the *waraqa* for what it said, or to read into it for what it might amount to.

Any judicial tensions surrounding financial reforms in Zanzibar were ultimately overwhelmed by the pressures of the Great Depression. The continuing drop in clove prices through the 1930s, coupled with increasing agricultural indebtedness, weakened opposition to limiting the rate of interest on loans; the rising number of foreclosures overwhelmed it. Even when taking into account Arab repurchases of previously foreclosed land, officials estimated that between 1926 and 1933, Indian creditors came into possession of almost 2.3 million clove and coconut trees in Zanzibar and Pemba.[34] Amid such dislocation, officials conceded that the time had come for stronger regulations. "The only way to prevent a native from executing a deed of sale in favor of an Indian," wrote one British official in 1931, "is to prohibit such a transaction by law."[35]

If the 1920s reform attempts were partly stymied by a commitment to non-interference in credit markets, that was no longer the case in the 1930s; British accommodation of the *Bania* moneylender had reached its limits. After several decades of investment and economic development, British officials no longer viewed Indian financiers as necessary to the colonial East African economy, and the emergence of Indian nationalism elsewhere in the British Empire called into question their reliability as partners in the imperial project. Suspicion surrounding the role of Indian capital was especially heightened when it came to agricultural finance, and in the Kenyan highlands increasing numbers of White settlers effectively formed a barrier to Indian agricultural settlement and activity.[36] The tacit alliance between British officials and Indian merchants that had characterized much of the nineteenth century was beginning to show its seams.

In Zanzibar and Pemba, where Indian involvement in agricultural finance had gradually led to the establishment of a class of Indian landholders, there emerged a pronounced discourse surrounding the unproductive nature of Indian activities. "However anxious former Sultans may have been to induce Indian agriculturalists… to settle in Zanzibar," wrote one official in 1934, when the problem had reached its apex, "the position today is that with very few exceptions there is not resident on, or employed as tiller of, the soil any Indian agriculturalist at all." Most Indians, he argued, were

[34] ZNA AB 47/25.
[35] Letter to Chief Secretary (March 24, 1931) ZNA AB 14/68.
[36] Metcalf, *Imperial Connections*, 185–187.

"traders and shopkeepers," leaving most of the actual agricultural work to their Arab and Swahili tenants. He continued:

To the Zanzibar Indian a plantation is primarily a milch-cow and a source of income. He is not by instinct or by habit an agriculturalist, and though I have traced one example of a prosperous Indian family which lives on a plantation and has no other visible means of support, the general Indian custom is to remain in the towns and to rent out the plantations to agriculturalist tenants. A society constructed in this way will not be a healthy society.... It is clear that neither the agriculturalist communities nor the Government can view with equanimity the prospect of an urban Indian oligarchy monopolizing the plantations and managing them through a dependent, indebted and spiritless tenantry of Arabs and Swahilis.[37]

In the stereotypes that British officials had constructed to describe Zanzibar's agricultural economy, the Indian businessman was primarily a rent-seeking parasite – a profit-motivated miser whose interest in the upkeep of a plantation only stretched as far as his balance sheets. The Indian shift from agricultural finance to landholding, they thought, would ultimately lead to the degradation of commercial society – and, by extension, the landed foundations of political community in East Africa.

The racially polarized official discourse on East African commercial society was neither wholly local nor original; it had its roots in the Indian countryside. In Western India, British wariness of the dependence of the rural peasant on the moneylender had been growing for decades, reaching a crescendo in the 1920s when falling crop prices and mounting peasant indebtedness resulted in a similar trend of foreclosures. Recent developments in Punjab in particular provided an especially strong analogy for British officials in East Africa concerned with agricultural indebtedness. In the Punjabi countryside, rising crop output led to an increase in indebtedness on the part of peasant farmers, who took advantage of easy credit to finance growing consumption costs. When the farmers were unable to repay their debts, their moneylenders took to British courts and foreclosed on mortgaged farmland.[38] Thus, when British legislators looked at Indian merchants in East Africa, what they saw was an image of the moneylender of the Punjabi countryside, whose perceived avarice had made him the target of violence by tenant farmers for decades, and eventually the focus of much colonial policy. And in Arabs and Africans, British officials caught glimpses of the chronically indebted

[37] Government comments on the Menon Report (December 12, 1934) ZNA AB 3/48.

[38] See also Ian Talbot, "Punjab Under Colonialism: Order and Transformation in British India," *Journal of Punjab Studies*, Vol. 14, No. 1 (Spring 2007), 5–7. The Punjab Act also formed the basis for similar legislation in Bombay; see Catanach, *Rural Credit in Western India*, 40–41, 92–93.

Punjabi peasant, their sympathy for whom was only offset by what they regarded as opulent spending on lavish weddings and other forms of conspicuous consumption.[39]

Punjab not only inspired the tropes surrounding economic sensibility that British officials in East Africa mobilized, it also furnished the regulatory template for tackling the problem. To combat the trend of dispossession in Zanzibar, officials issued the Land Alienation Decree (LAD) in 1934 – a piece of legislation explicitly stating that Arabs and Africans were not to permanently alienate their land or lease it for more than two years to Indians without the consent of the British Resident, limiting them to usufructuary mortgages that did not come with the security of land.[40] Perhaps unsurprisingly, given the role of the Indian experience in framing the problem of agricultural indebtedness, officials modeled the Zanzibar decree on similar legislation in the Punjab in 1900, even taking many of its provisions verbatim from the Punjab Act. East Africa's problems of agricultural indebtedness thus became a replica of India's.

Alongside the LAD, British officials oversaw the implementation of another reform initiative: the establishment of the Clove Growers' Association (CGA), a quasi-official board headed by Omani Arab planters and government officials, which sought closer control over the marketing of cloves by providing loans to planters and controlling the costs of production, especially through labor rates. In exchange for help with the plantations inputs, planters would hand over their crop to the CGA, which would sell it on their behalf. Although its first years were marked by a lack of activity, by the 1930s the CGA began to play an important role for Arab planters: it bought cloves for guaranteed prices, resolved labor disputes, and supplied them with loans for whatever plantation maintenance was required.[41]

Taken together, the LAD and CGA effectively pulled the Indian merchant out of agricultural finance, replacing him with government-controlled institutions. By restricting Indian merchants' ability to give out loans against the security of land, and by taking over the provision of credit and marketing services to Zanzibar's planters, the Government's

[39] David Hardiman, *Feeding the Baniya: Peasants and Usurers in Western India* (New Delhi: Oxford University Press, 1996); David Hall-Matthews, *Peasants, Famine and the State in Colonial Western India* (London: Palgrave-Macmillan, 2005), 92–100; Catanach, *Rural Credit in Western India*, 11–13.

[40] By contrast, the *khiyār* sale approximated a usufructuary mortgage, but had always included land as security.

[41] The Clove Growers' Association, however, has yet to receive any serious treatment; most scholarship has only mentioned it in passing, despite the existence of a large cache of files at the Zanzibar National Archives. See ZNA AP series, and the Michael Lofchie collection at the University of California, Los Angeles.

reform program left no room for the Indian merchant in the island's clove trade. An Indian merchant dealing in cloves could now only purchase his supply in cash from the CGA – and even that was a concession that Indian merchants had to fight for. The British government in East Africa rolled out similar marketing reforms in Kenya and Uganda, cutting Indian merchants out of markets there as well.[42]

East Africa's Indian merchants refused to accept the new regulations without a fight. Almost immediately after the LAD's announcement, they mobilized their contacts in India in a trans-oceanic fight against the new program. Newspapers in East Africa and India immediately began rolling out articles and op-ed columns teeming with scathing criticism of the racial tropes that informed the new measures. In one of the first articles, published just a few weeks after the LAD was made public, the East Africa-based lawyer Bernard Wiggins suggested that the British administration in the region was "for the last three years consciously or unconsciously definitely anti-Indian."[43] Another article published just a month later included an entire section titled "Are Indians Foreigners?" in which the writer called into question the notion that Indian claims to political community in Zanzibar were any different from those made by Arabs and Africans. Many, he argued, had settled there for generations and were invited by the Sultan to settle in Zanzibar. "These Indians," the author asserted, "are no more 'foreigners' than the Arabs are."[44]

Critics of the LAD further contended that the problems that East Africa faced were the result of global economic changes, not the avarice or improvidence of local actors. Although some did argue that the Arabs' lack of economic foresight contributed to the increasing debt loads, most pointed to the Depression as the primary culprit.[45] Wiggins's defense of Indian merchant highlighted how "owing to the worldwide economic depression millions of people have lost millions of pounds in commercial undertakings," and suggested that the only reason heavy indebtedness had become a hot topic was "the depreciation in land values and produce prices" that the Depression had occasioned.[46] Another article pointed to the world economic depression as "the real cause of the low prices in the clove markets," adding that "to try thus by purely artificial methods to raise the price of cloves was not

[42] J.S. Mangat, *A History of the Asians in East Africa* (Oxford, UK: Clarendon Press, 1969), 156–161.
[43] "Zanzibar Government's Anti-Indian Decree," *Times of India* (July 18, 1934), 10.
[44] "Indians in Zanzibar Hit Hard by the New Legislation," *Times of India* (August 28, 1934), 10.
[45] S.A. Waiz, "Indians in Zanzibar: Effects of the Land Alienation Decree," *Times of India* (July 17, 1935), 14.
[46] "Zanzibar Government's Anti-Indian Decree," *Times of India* (July 18, 1934), 10.

even business speculation, it was gambling. What was worse still, it was gambling with public money." A better course, the author argued, was to ride out the Depression – to "let the world commerce in cloves have both its rise and fall." "Things," the author continued, "would right themselves, if only they were allowed to do so."[47] Through the Indian press, critics of the LAD hoped to turn the debate on indebtedness from one on the agency of individual actors to one on the global structures that shaped economic life on the island.

East Africa's Indians did not limit themselves to the press; they took political action as well. The summer after the Government issued the LAD, the British Resident received a telegram from the Secretary of State for the Government of India notifying him that Sir Maharaj Singh, a collector in the United Provinces, and K.P.S. Menon, his deputy, would be visiting Zanzibar to report on the local effects of the LAD on Indian interests.[48] Over three weeks, Menon (Singh had fallen ill) met with Indian merchants, moneylenders, lawyers, and administrative officials, many of whom expressed their discontentment with the new commercial landscape. To balance out his itinerary, he also briefly met with an Arab delegation, who alleged that the low price of cloves had most likely resulted from collusion among Indian merchants and middlemen, describing to him in detail the process by which an Indian foreclosed on his debtor's *shamba*. The delegation's head ended his speech by declaring that "if the *shambas* of this island belonging to Arabs and natives are possessed by foreign tribes, the industry of cloves will undoubtedly be diminished."[49]

Menon disagreed. In his assessment of the situation in Zanzibar following his visit, he repeated many of the claims vocalized in the Indian press. He criticized the racialized nature of the LAD, which he argued imported "the racial virus into this island, from which it has been happily free." He further lent his support to Indian complaints that the LAD allowed an Arab coming from Muscat or elsewhere, "however recent may be his arrival in the Protectorate and however ignorant he may be of agriculture," to buy and sell land while depriving Indians "settled in the country for generations and thoroughly well conversant with the art of agriculture" the right to do so.[50] His argument challenged the notion that political community in an "Arab state" necessarily had to be Arab;

47 "Indians in Zanzibar Hit Hard by the New Legislation," *Times of India* (August 28, 1934), 10.

48 Telegram from Secretary of State, Government of India, to British Resident, Zanzibar (July 31, 1934) ZNA AB 3/48.

49 Shaikh Sa'id bin Ali bin Jum'a Al-Mughairi to Menon (August 29, 1934), ZNA AB 3/48. Al-Mughairi would go on to pen a history of East Africa that many consider to be foundational. See Al-Mughairi, *Juhaynat Al-Akhbār*.

50 K.P.S. Menon Report (September 10, 1934), ZNA AB 3/48, 2–6.

Indians formed as much a part of the Zanzibari world writ large as Arabs from Oman did, and certainly more so than recent arrivals.

Menon reserved his most scathing critique, however, for the CGA, which he argued had "armed itself with the most powerful weapons for the purpose of eliminating Indian traders from the clove business," including exemptions from duties and income from levies imposed on other clove exports, as well as other protections.[51] He contended that the legislation establishing the CGA would reduce Indian merchants "not from opulence to poverty, but from poverty to starvation," ultimately driving them into exile.[52] The CGA, he argued, "strikes Indian traders as a Leviathan, brushing them aside, casting them adrift and trampling upon that freedom of trade which they have enjoyed for generations." Indians "whose forefathers opened up markets for and practically built up the clove trade, and who as financiers and exporters are primarily responsible for the growth of the industry from the parochial into world dimensions," he claimed, now felt the bitter humiliation of having to depend on the government for handouts.[53]

Menon's report only further whipped up the Indian press into a frenzy. Merchants, lawyers, and heads of Indian associations around East Africa and India quoted his report at length, using his observations to fuel their campaigns against the LAD and the CGA. The opposition had become so vocal that members of the British Government regularly took to the press themselves in defense of the measures they had taken, pointing to similar legislation put in place to protect cultivators in India.[54] But even they could do nothing to stop the onslaught of interviews, columns, and campaigns against them; by 1936, heads of the Imperial India Citizenship Association urged "leaders of all shades of opinion, irrespective of caste and creed" to apply "constant and vigorous pressure till justice is done to Indians in Zanzibar."[55] The trans-oceanic battle for the right to lend showed no signs of receding.

From the British consulate at Muscat, the noise on Zanzibar and the clove trade that had spread across the ocean and into the British press likely seemed far away. Officials in Muscat might have received copies of the *Times of India* and might have followed the debate on debt and economic regulation in Zanzibar and East Africa, but they were mostly

51 K.P.S. Menon Report (September 10, 1934), ZNA AB 3/48, 8.
52 K.P.S. Menon Report (September 10, 1934), ZNA AB 3/48, 11.
53 K.P.S. Menon Report (September 10, 1934), ZNA AB 3/48, 12.
54 See also "Moratorium in Zanzibar," *Times of India* (July 5, 1934), 10; "Recent Legislation in Zanzibar," *Times of India* (July 16, 1934), 9; "Indians in Zanzibar," *Times of India* (July 21, 1934), 12; "The Zanzibar Trouble," *Times of India* (January 29, 1935), 8.
55 "Indians in Zanzibar," *Times of India* (January 24, 1936), 3.

concerned with another kind of debt – one that attracted no media attention and no public outcry, and yet was no less important to the stability of a key ally of the Government of India. In Muscat, the problem was only partly driven by a sense of Arab improvidence – or rather, the perceived tendency of the Sultan to spend beyond his means and turn to his Indian creditors to bail him out. But unlike Zanzibar, the problem of Muscat's debt wasn't a question of personal finances as much as it was one of state administration – though in a fiscal regime that was intimately bound up in the person of the Sultan. As one official put it, it was "impossible to discriminate between the creditors" on the basis of whether or not they lent to the Sultan himself or to the state, on security of the customs house; the two were one and the same.[56] If the challenge in Zanzibar was how to bring about the solvency of planters and consumers, in Muscat the target was the Sultan and, by extension, the Sultanate.

To achieve their vision of a solvent Sultanate, British officials in Muscat set their eyes on the customs house – the nexus of the port city's commercial, personal, and administrative debts. Through the customs house, officials could strike at one of the pillars of the Sultanate's economy of obligation, bringing it more firmly under their control. In 1920, the Government of India approved a plan to advance a loan to the Sultan against the security of the customs house, which they would take over entirely. The customs house stood at the center of the Indian government's plan: instead of being run as a personal fiefdom, the customs house would be administered as a revenue-generating organ of the state.[57] And to realize their vision, they placed it under the directorship of three customs officials brought to Muscat from Egypt, Britain's other great experiment in economic regulation.[58] Through technocratic management, the Government of India surmised, the Sultanate's finances would be brought on a sounder footing.

At the same time, the Government of India sought a more direct hand in policymaking in the Sultanate – the appointment of a financial adviser, who would ensure that the Sultan's policies were in line

[56] Political Agent, Muscat, to Civil Commissioner, Baghdad (December 11, 1919) IOR R/15/1/416, 29.

[57] Officials undertook a similar customs reform program in Bahrain, where the ruler had similarly been farming out the customs house to Indian firms for at least a century. Onley, *Arabian Frontier of the British Raj*, 201–202, 207. The Gwadar customs house, however, was left out of the plan, and the Sultan continued to draw loans against it. Political Agent, Muscat, to Civil Commissioner, Baghdad (February 8, 1920) IOR R/15/1/416, 138.

[58] Uzi Rabi, *The Emergence of States in a Tribal Society: Oman Under Sa'id bin Taymur, 1932–1970* (Portland, OR: Sussex Academic Press, 2007), 51–52; Political Agent, Muscat, to Civil Commissioner, Baghdad (January 3, 1920) IOR R/15/1/452, 124–125.

with the fiscal health of the state. Eventually, they settled on Bertram Thomas, a civil servant who had served in Iraq during World War I before taking on an administrative post in Jordan. In 1925, Thomas was brought in to act as the Sultan's financial adviser – the financial *wazir* (or minister), as officials in the Government of India took to calling it – a post that he held until the early 1930s.[59] As financial *wazir*, Thomas both oversaw the fiscal regime in the Sultanate, but also attended other ministerial duties: he entered into negotiations on behalf of the Sultan, sat in on judicial proceedings both civil and criminal, and engaged in a range of different mundane matters of administration.[60] Fiscal governance in the Sultanate, it became clear, was not a separate domain of administration, but was intimately bound up in questions of law and politics.

The Era of the Expert, 1932–1938

The measures officials in Muscat had taken during the 1920s, including the reformation of the customs regime and the appointment of a financial *wazir* were by no means the end of the story. By the end of 1930, as the effects of the worldwide depression were still making themselves known, the Government of India's attempt at direct involvement in Muscat affairs through the financial *wazir* had run its course. Six years in, it was becoming alarmingly clear that Bertram Thomas was unsuited for the position. He had made a strong start but gradually found himself drawn to other pursuits – namely travel. "His chief interest is in exploration with its kindred subjects," fumed the Political Agent at Muscat, "and where his own interests are involved they will always be placed first." The solution, he declared, was to replace Thomas altogether: "I would feel more confident with an officer who kept his nose to the grindstone and confined his energies and attention to finance."[61]

After searching for someone who would be willing to relocate to Muscat, the Government of India settled on S.E. Hedgecock, a British officer who had also served in Iraq.[62] Hedgecock's tenure, however, was

[59] Rabi, *The Emergence of States in a Tribal Society*, 46.

[60] "Functions of the Financial Adviser," Political Resident, Bushire, to the Foreign Secretary to the Government of India, New Delhi (November 27, 1930) IOR R/15/1/452, 107–112.

[61] Political Agent, Muscat, to Political Resident, Bushire (April 6, 1930) IOR R/15/1/452, 17–19.

[62] Like Thomas, Hedgecock also fancied himself something of an anthropologist: during his time in Iraq, he and his wife undertook a study of the country's marsh-dwelling Arabs, which they published under the pseudonym "Fulanain" – literally, "two people." Fulanain, *The Marsh Arab: Hajji Rikkan* (Philadelphia: J.P. Lippincott and Company, 1928).

hardly any better than Thomas's; in fact, it was a good deal worse. In 1931, less than a year after he arrived at the port city, the new financial *wazir* drew up his resignation. The principal scheme he had in mind to reduce the state's liabilities and bring it to a point of solvency – a scheme involving a reduction in pay to British Indian troops stationed at Muscat – went entirely ignored.[63] The Government of India, which was loath to reduce the troops' pay, would not even reply to his letters, let alone consider his proposal. When he handed in his resignation, officials took it in stride: Hedgecock's terms of duty, wrote the Political Agent, "might be regarded as the visit of a financial expert (such as is the fashion nowadays for most small countries to receive) who has made certain financial recommendations, which have to be weighed against other considerations... and which will gradually be put into force as circumstances permit."[64]

The notion that Hedgecock might be considered as a financial expert for hire – and indeed, the idea that it was "the fashion nowadays" to have a financial expert – signaled a shift in British policymaking away from "the man on the spot" and towards consultants who drew on their experiences elsewhere in offering guidance to local governments. This one-size-fits-all approach to economic regulation encompassed a range of different subjects, from customs reform to land tenure and beyond. And "small countries" – protectorates like Muscat, Bahrain, Malaya, and other states throughout Africa and Asia – but even larger colonies like Egypt found themselves on the receiving end of this endless stream of experts.[65] Imperial policymaking had undergone a qualitative shift.

The shift to the expert made itself clearly visible in Zanzibar where British officials, faced with a public outcry from India that had become almost deafening, reached out to one such individual: Sir Ernest Dowson, an eminent land expert who had a distinguished career in the British Empire. By the time Dowson arrived in Zanzibar in 1934, he had already served as Director-General of the Survey Department of Egypt, had been a major figure in debates surrounding land reforms during the British Mandate in Iraq, and had proposed a system of land reforms

63 S.E. Hedgecock to Political Agent, Muscat (April 10, 1931) IOR R/15/1/452, 184–185.

64 Political Agent, Muscat, to Political Resident, Bushire (April 14, 1931) IOR R/15/1/452, 180–183.

65 See also Timothy Mitchell, *The Rule of Experts: Egypt, Technopolitics, Modernity* (Berkeley, CA: University of California Press, 2002); Omnia El-Shakry, *The Great Social Laboratory: Subjects of Knowledge in Colonial and Postcolonial Egypt* (Stanford, CA: Stanford University Press, 2007); Joseph Morgan Hodge, *Triumph of the Expert: Agrarian Doctrines of Development and the Legacies of British Colonialism* (Athens, OH: Ohio University Press, 2007).

for Palestine in 1926.[66] Like the Zanzibar Government, Dowson firmly believed in an approach to land tenure in which the state, not any communal leader, served as the arbiter of land rights.[67] He and many other experts like him saw the world before them in terms of aggregates – of national markets and states, rather than transactions between individuals. Through a mix of economic and legal reforms, he would redirect the vectors of economic life through the government bureaucracy.

In his sixty-two-page report on the agricultural situation in Zanzibar, Dowson drew on his experiences around the Middle East, but prefaced his study with a long note on India. While putting together the report, he wrote, he often relied on Malcolm Lyall Darling's work, *The Punjab Peasant in Prosperity and Debt*, which he applauded as "the most instructive book that I know on the subject of indebtedness among small-holders in conditions such as those of which he treats." Darling's views and conclusions, he wrote, had been eminently useful in his studies of agricultural indebtedness in Egypt, Palestine, and Iraq.[68] And in Zanzibar, where the Punjabi experience underpinned legislation and the imperial imaginary, Darling's approach fit especially well.

Dowson's report integrated legislation attempts and the stereotypes that framed them into a single, coherent vision of a rationalized Zanzibari agricultural economy, and articulated concrete steps towards its realization. Past attempts to diagnose the problem, Dowson noted, were predicated on the idea of a "peculiar mentality" among landowners in the Protectorate, including "innate improvidence, lack of thrift and love of ostentatious hospitality… and the disinclination of money lenders to foreclose and dispossess debtors."[69] By contrast, his approach involved a longer-term perspective on the Zanzibari economy. Although such long-standing factors as "lack of business capacity in debtors" and the lack of a comprehensive land register were important, more recent developments such as abolition, the movement of people into towns, and overproduction also figured into his analysis. In Dowson's writing, the scale of analysis had decidedly shifted from the micro to the macro.

Dowson's program chiefly sought the gradual elimination of agricultural indebtedness and the creation of self-sufficient economic actors. Rather than focus on the exclusion of certain actors and not others, "insistence should be laid in Government policy upon the constructive

[66] Toby Dodge, *Inventing Iraq: The Failure of Nation-Building and a History Denied* (New York: Columbia University Press, 2003), 101–130.
[67] Dodge, *Inventing Iraq*, 109–110.
[68] Sir Ernest Dowson's Report (1936), ZNA AB 47/23, 2.
[69] Sir Ernest Dowson's Report (1936), ZNA AB 47/23, 2.

necessity of preserving the existing rural population on the land and of developing their economic self-dependence." The government, Dowson thought, also ought to make provisions to allow Indians who were genuinely interested in farming land to do so. The LAD was thus misdirected, since "it is surely a sign of stagnation and weakness to exclude new blood, new ideas, and new capital from agriculture as from other industries."[70] With the proper safeguards in place, he thought, one could preserve the place of the land-holders, promote the composition of existing debts, and, more generally, introduce healthier relations between urban creditors and rural debtors.

But not everyone deserved to maintain their position. "From the point of view of the public interest and the maintenance of a healthy agricultural industry," he wrote, "the continuous elimination of landholders who fail (whether through debt or otherwise) is generally regarded elsewhere as a salutary operation economically, which prevents the accumulation of unproductive debt and keeps the industry purged of its weaker and less capable elements." In Zanzibar, courts had put off the Darwinian purging process for too long, and the island now lacked a reserve of equipped successors to the landholders. "It is feared," Dowson wrote, "that many of the sick cannot be saved." The rest, he imagined, would respond well to assistance, eventually developing "in every way possible a riper and more alert sense of the economic and business aspects of agriculture among all members of the industry."[71]

Law was critical to the process of nursing Zanzibar back to health; the courtroom would serve as the handmaiden of the rehabilitation process. As the locus of debt settlement and the point at which the growing regulatory state and commercial society most vividly intersected, courts were ideally suited to carry out Dowson's vision. "No body other than a regular Court of Justice," he wrote, "can command the unquestioning confidence in its judicial integrity and competence that must constitute the foundation of any settlement of existing debts."[72] To Dowson, the court had to facilitate debt settlement on a case-by-case basis, restoring the earning capacity of the mass of agricultural holdings encumbered by debt by institutionalizing periodic payments to the creditor while always working to preserve the land's earning power.[73] The ultimate goal of the legal process was not to clearly decide in favor of one party or another, but to arrive at a sustainable arrangement wherein the creditor got his due as the debtor continued to participate in agriculture – or

70 Sir Ernest Dowson's Report (1936), ZNA AB 47/23, 28.
71 Sir Ernest Dowson's Report (1936), ZNA AB 47/23, 26.
72 Sir Ernest Dowson's Report (1936), ZNA AB 47/23, 37.
73 Sir Ernest Dowson's Report (1936), ZNA AB 47/23, 33.

alternatively, facilitating the transfer of *shambas* into the hands of owners who were invested in maintaining its productivity. His report reflected earlier notions of land as the material foundation for political community, but wed them to a vision of more disembedded and rational market economy at work.

Dowson's plan echoed in the courtroom, where officials had for a few years been grasping at different solutions to adjust the increasingly unequal relationship between creditors and debtors. In their execution of Dowson's vision for debt settlement, courts effectively coordinated between the different actors who had a stake in the matter: the debtors, the creditors, and the CGA. By imbricating themselves in the new institutional structure of the clove industry, courts effectively replaced the bonds of obligation that had once tied Indian Ocean actors together with institutions that the now-developed state bureaucracy could both monitor and regulate. As the 1930s wore on, planters who found themselves inundated with debt could come before the court to plead bankruptcy and ask for a degree of relief. They could count on the judge to oversee the processes of determining the actual amount and nature of the debt, assessing the earning capacity of a debtor's *shamba*, and fashioning a plan between the debtor, the creditor, and the CGA so that debtors could service their debts while maintaining enough of an income to live off of.[74] If debtors were uninterested in continuing their agricultural responsibilities, courts auctioned off their *shambas* in the hopes that they might generate enough cash to satisfy the creditors and that they might pass into the hands of a buyer who would take an interest in recouping his or her investment.[75] The Zanzibari Sultanate of Arab landowners could persist, but in a much leaner form.

The New *Waraqa*

The changing regulatory landscape of the Western Indian Ocean left a visible imprint on the *waraqa*. As officials rolled out economic reforms and court proceedings unfolded over the 1920s and 1930s, officials devoted at least some of their energies to the *waraqa* and its place in the newly regulated commercial economy. What had once circulated beyond the grasp of the Busa'idi Sultanate had by the 1930s become all but thoroughly ensconced in the new British-headed regulatory regime.

[74] See, for example, *Said bin Mohammed El-Kuweti, Insolvent* (1938) ZNA HC 2/1445 A and B. The CGA also ran its own court, the records of which I have not had the opportunity to explore. See ZNA AP 50 and ZNA AP 51 series.

[75] See, for example, *Mahomed bin Zahran bin Mahomed El-Kindi, Insolvent* (1938) ZNA HC 2/1455.

The *waraqa* was no longer an instrument that coordinated between commercial and legal actors alone; it had become an instrument through which the governmental bureaucracy could actively intervene in everyday transactions.

The state visually interceded in the form of the *waraqa* itself. In Muscat, *waraqa* registration procedures changed early on – even before the customs regime itself underwent a transformation. Whereas economic actors in those ports were once able to freely call a scribe to draw up an agreement between them, by 1913 the process had to pass through government supervision. The only valid legal instruments were those printed on government-issued paper, drawn up and notarized by a government official. The changes made themselves visible on the *waraqas*: emblazoned across the top of Muscat *waraqas* was a government logo, along with the stern declaration that "it is not acceptable that a legal contract be written [*lā yubāḥ an yuktab al-sanad al-sharʿī*] for a sale, a pledge, an agency [*tawkīl*], a guarantee, a verification, or any type of obligation [*ayy nawʿ min al-iqrārāt*] except on these *waraqas*."[76] Other port cities near Muscat also adopted similar forms.[77] The wording of the contracts on the documents themselves had not changed very much, but the government's oversight of the contracting process could not have been missed by anyone involved. Moreover, the new *waraqas* came with a fee: further up the Persian Gulf, in Bahrain, for example, a single sheet cost 2 Annas, equivalent to one half of a Rupee. The contracting process, which had once occurred completely outside of the framework of the state, had by the 1930s become one of the sources of government revenue.

The *waraqa's* transformation in Muscat, however, was not nearly as visible as it was in Zanzibar. In his report, Dowson called attention to the need to change the *waraqa* so as to strip it of the ambiguity which had vexed officials for so long. For Dowson, documents embodying loan transactions needed to be "written in a language, and if possible a script, comprehensible to both parties," both to facilitate the intelligibility of these transactions to inexperienced court officials, but also to help to eventually establish a land registry.[78] The land registry never materialized, but the *waraqa* form that had dominated the commercial landscape of the Indian Ocean for at least a century had almost completely disappeared. By the 1930s, it had been all but completely replaced by an English-language mortgage deed – one typed up by a court clerk in the presence of an advocate. In the new deed, the clerk clarified all of the

[76] Debt Acknowledgment from ʿAli bin Yusuf Al-Hijali to Saleh bin Salem Al-Dallal (1335 A.H.), RPL Arabic Deeds, Vol. 4.

[77] On Bahrain, see Bishara "A Sea of Debt," 452–463.

[78] Sir Ernest Dowson's Report (1936), ZNA AB 47/23, 25.

details of the transaction: the amount loaned, the rate of interest, the precise terms of repayment, and the rules surrounding default. When describing the properties being mortgaged, the clerk was careful to note the number of clove and coconut trees, their size ("large" or "small"), and, if possible, the registration number of the old *waraqa* drawn up at the time the borrower originally bought the property.[79] One could only catch glimpses of the old contractual culture in the new forms.

In addition, Zanzibar's courts enforced provisions that regulated the very act of lending money by requiring that moneylenders take out licenses for their practice. When a dispute landed in court, the judges would determine whether the creditor in question was a moneylender, and if so, whether he had registered himself as such. Those who did not register could not recover debts in court, and further faced possible fines.[80] As the 1930s drew to a close, the British administration in Zanzibar enacted additional legislation mandating that those who wanted to borrow money on the security of land could do so only with explicit consent – not from the Resident, as had been the case before, but from a Land Alienation Board. The latter would thoroughly scrutinize the details of the loan for any irregularities and ensure that the debtors applied the money they borrowed to approved (i.e. agricultural) purposes. The legislation further set established proportions of the value of the land to the loan, and required that debtors taking on loans have at least one piece of land left unencumbered.[81]

By the 1940s, then, a creditor and debtor who wanted to enter into a contract with one another could no longer simply call a scribe to lend a legal lexicon to an open-ended and flexible economic relationship, as they had in the past. Those who wanted to leave an official, enforceable record of their transaction had to hire an attorney, prepare a lot of paperwork, and clear through several stages of bureaucracy before they could legally lend or borrow. The *khiyār* sale and *waraqa* as people knew it had all but disappeared. As one scholar doing fieldwork in Zanzibar in 1950 observed, "such mortgages as are now created are almost invariably in the usual English form, and Islamic forms of mortgage may be said to no longer exist in Zanzibar."[82] And although reports from as late as 1952

79 For one example of many, see ZNA HC 3/3824, which includes a 1933 mortgage deed. *Waraqas* from the 1920s already exhibited some standardized markings, including pre-stamped paper that included fields for the names of the counterparties and the registration date. See, for example, ZNA AM 5/5.

80 Bose, *A Hundred Horizons: The Indian Ocean in the Age of Global Empires* (Cambridge, MA: Harvard University Press, 2006), 104.

81 Land was not to be worth less than 60 percent of the amount borrowed. "Legal Report on Land Alienation Decree," (June 16, 1939) ZNA AB 40/1.

82 Anderson, *Islamic Law in Africa*, 66.

بسم الله الرحمن الرحيم

Figure 8 A debt *iqrār* on a state-issued *waraqa* from Muscat

point to persistent maneuverings on the part of debtors and creditors to sidestep the cumbersome restrictions that had been placed on the credit market, those were exceptions to the broader trend.[83] Dowson's vision had triumphed, but at the cost of the central artifact of the region's century-long economic and legal transformation.

[83] Senior Commissioner of Agriculture to Chief Secretary (October 8, 1952) ZNA AB 40/1.

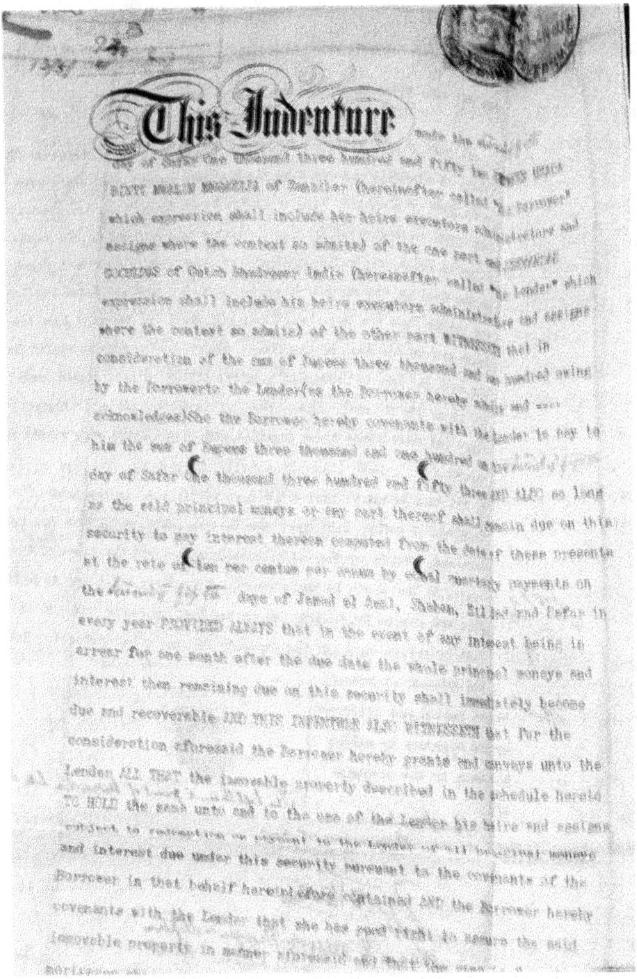

This Indenture made the [illegible] day of Safar One thousand three hundred and fifty two BETWEEN [illegible] BINTI MWALIM MGHEIRI of Zanzibar (hereinafter called "the Borrower" which expression shall include her heirs executors administrators and assigns where the context so admits) of the one part and [illegible] of Cutch Mandvee India (hereinafter called "the Lender" which expression shall include his heirs executors administrators and assigns where the context so admits) of the other part WITNESSETH that in consideration of the sum of Rupees three thousand and one hundred owing by the Borrower to the Lender (as the Borrower hereby admits and [illegible] acknowledges) the Borrower hereby covenants with the Lender to pay to him the sum of Rupees three thousand and one hundred on the [illegible] day of Safar One thousand three hundred and fifty three AND ALSO so long as the said principal moneys or any part thereof shall remain due on this security to pay interest thereon computed from the date of these presents at the rate of ten per centum per annum by equal quarterly payments on the [illegible] days of Jamad el Awal, Shaban, Zilkad and Safar in every year PROVIDED ALWAYS that in the event of any interest being in arrear for one month after the due date the whole principal moneys and interest then remaining due on this security shall immediately become due and recoverable AND THIS INDENTURE ALSO WITNESSETH that for the consideration aforesaid the Borrower hereby grants and conveys unto the Lender ALL THAT the immovable property described in the schedule hereto TO HOLD the same unto and to the use of the Lender his heirs and assigns subject to redemption on payment to the Lender of all principal moneys and interest due under this security pursuant to the covenants of the Borrower in that behalf hereinbefore contained AND the Borrower hereby covenants with the Lender that she has good right to assure the said immovable property in manner aforesaid and that [illegible]

Figure 9 The new Zanzibar registered debt deed

Conclusion

For British officials in East Africa and Oman, the Indian Ocean economy of obligation had by the 1930s run its course. External pressures on the chains of obligation that linked the region's different ports and actors together – the worldwide agricultural crisis and the worldwide economic depression – called for a rethinking of the legal and institutional bases of economic life. Officials focused not so much on obliterating the bonds of debt and obligation that had long characterized economic life in the region as on establishing a new legal framework that they thought would achieve a vision of solvency while maintaining a stable socio-political infrastructure. In a sense, they refashioned economic life so that it reflected the imperatives of a new construct – the national economy – rather than the impulses of individuals.

There were other changes afoot as well. In Oman, the ascension of a new Sultan, Sa'id bin Teymour in 1932 marked the beginning of an enormous change in the Sultanate's administration. Confident that he would be able to put the Sultanate back on a stronger financial footing, the new Sultan took over the administration of the customs house from the Government of India, completing the transformation of the customs house into an exclusive organ of the state. The young Sultan had a right to be optimistic about his country's future: he had recently learned of the potential that Oman, like many of its neighbors in the Arabian Peninsula, held substantial oil deposits. It would take some time before Oman would be able to export oil, but in the meantime he could count on income from concession agreements he had signed with oil exploration companies.[84]

Things were not so sanguine in East Africa. In 1937, after repeated calls in the Indian press to end the Land Alienation Decree and the CGA failed to result in any meaningful change, merchants and legislators in the Indian National Congress chose to boycott Zanzibar's cloves altogether.[85] The results were disastrous: in retaliation against the boycott, the island's Arab planters, under the aegis of the recently-formed Arab Association, mobilized against the Indians. They took to the press to warn the islanders of the dangers that Indian moneylenders posed to the island's Islamic fabric and urged them to support a counter-boycott of Indian shops; meanwhile, Arabs roamed the *shambas* looking to ensure support for their campaign and to intimidate Indian shopkeepers. The standoff between the two sides precipitated what would become a decades-long series of newspaper battles and political jockeying – one that would set the stage for a bloody revolution in 1964.[86] What had once been a relationship characterized by economic mutualism had degenerated into one marred by economic tensions and racial caricatures.

The troubles in Zanzibar made life in the interior of Oman very difficult. Because the Imamate was dependent on trade with East Africa and India for its income in a way that the Sultan was not anymore, the

[84] See also Wilkinson, *The Imamate Tradition of Oman*, 274–298.

[85] Mangat, *A History of the Asians in East Africa*, 166–167.

[86] Jonathon Glassman, *War of Words, War of Stones: Racial Thought and Violence in Colonial Zanzibar* (Bloomington, IN: Indiana University Press, 2011), 45–46.

worsening Arab fortunes on the coast reverberated across the Indian Ocean, as the Imamate's principal trading partner lost much of its economic stability. Indian independence and the temporary suspension of date and dried fish import permits that came with it further crippled the Imamate economy. The situation was only made worse by the decline in the Maria Theresa Dollar, the accepted currency in the interior, from an exchange rate of Rs 2.6 in 1946 to Rs 1.6 in 1948.[87] For the Sultan in Muscat, the Imamate's financial woes offered up an unexpected opportunity. Buoyed by oil receipts and money he had made speculating on currency, the Sultan was able to buy over many of the interior tribes and, after a series of splinters in the interior, launched a bloodless coup in which he took over Nizwa and other Imamate strongholds. By 1956, he was able to proclaim himself sovereign of the Omani coasts and interior, traveling through the country in a motorcade fueled with the new source of political authority in the country.[88]

No matter where one chooses to end the story, whether in 1940, 1956 or 1964, by the mid-twentieth century, the Indian Ocean economy had undergone a fundamental transformation. Instead of an economy in which long chains of obligation bound producers, merchants, consumers, and rulers together, what they would have seen in the mid-twentieth century was an economy heavily regulated by governments and their bureaucratic organs. Gone were the days in which *Banias*, brokers, shopkeepers, and planters shaped the flow of credit and goods in the region; these were the days of banks, cooperative societies, marketing boards, and state institutions.

And a key element of the region's commercial past was conspicuously absent from the Indian Ocean world of the mid-twentieth century: the *waraqa*. Once the region's commercial instrument *par excellence*, the *waraqa* as nineteenth-century actors knew it had all but disappeared from Indian Ocean commercial society by the 1940s. As the bonds of obligation that tied actors to one another in the face of a booming economy began to break under the pressures of the worldwide depression and modern techniques of regulation, the written manifestation of these bonds gave way to mortgage forms and registered loans. Ironically, then, the same set of economic forces that brought about the Indian Ocean contractual culture – the region's integration into world markets – also brought about that culture's quiet demise.

87 Wilkinson, *The Imamate Tradition of Oman*, 302.

88 I am glossing over a very detailed series of events at a crucial moment in Oman's political history, and 1956 was hardly the final victory for the Sultans, who had to deal with a series of uprisings until the 1970s. See also Wilkinson, *The Imamate Tradition of Oman*, 300–315; Rabi, *The Emergence of States in a Tribal Society*, 71–128. For an account of the motorcade, see James Morris, *Sultan in Oman* (London: Century, 1957).

Epilogue

In early December, 2014, I sat down to dinner with Vimal Purecha and his family in an Afghani restaurant in Falls Church, VA, just outside of Washington, D.C. The last time I had seen Vimal was five years earlier, when I flew to Muscat to see a small collection of *waraqas* in his family library – *waraqas* that belonged to his great, great grandfather, Ratansi Purshottam. When I went to Vimal's in 2009, I was just beginning my long research year, which would take me to the Persian Gulf, East Africa, India, and England; his collection of *waraqas* would be among the first to spark my interest in these documents and the social, political, and legal lives they had. At the time, I had no answers, only questions. This time was different, though. I had spent the past five years thinking about *waraqas* and the histories they inhabited. This time, it was Vimal who had questions.

As we sat down to enjoy the plates of cooked vegetables the servers brought us – *'ashā' al-banyān*, or "the *Bania* dinner," as he called it – Vimal asked what should have been a simple question: was it true that when debts were paid off the *waraqas* were supposed to be destroyed? He recalled a time in the early 1970s when people from the interior of Oman would come to the Purechas' waterfront office in Muttrah (the office sign still bears the name of Ratansi Purshottam) to pay off their decades-old debts. They would bring their copy of their 1920s *waraqas* with them, pay what they owed at the rate of one Omani riyal per two MTD – an exchange rate set by Sultan Qaboos shortly after his accession in 1970 – and ask for both *waraqas* to be destroyed. If that was the case, he asked, were the *waraqas* that remained in the collection outstanding debts? As a claim, was the *waraqa* still alive?

It was a loaded question, and one that I hesitated to give a simple answer to. At the core of what he was asking, at least to me, was the question of what the documents were – what sort of legal standing they had, and whether that persisted for the 150 years since they had first been written up. I couldn't answer him then; instead, I spent the two-hour drive from Falls Church to Richmond thinking about his question, and reflecting on the long history that brought the *waraqas* from the plantations in which they were drawn up to the archives and collections in which I first encountered them.

Vimal's question suggested one understanding of the relationship between *waraqas* and the law: first, that law was singular, coming down from rulers or the state, and that this singular law regulated instruments like the *waraqa*. In many ways he was right, and during the 1970s this was probably the most accurate way of thinking about the *waraqa* and what it was supposed to reflect. But to take that moment of regulation and to project it back onto the past risks flattening a long history of law and economic life in the Indian Ocean, subjugating it to the state-centered narratives that have done so much to cloud our imaginations and shift focus away from the universe of legal possibility.

As an artifact of Indian Ocean economic life, the *waraqa* was as dense and rich as it was slim and formulaic. Seen as a single object, it spun tales of debt and commerce, of fortunes made and lost, and of lives transformed as they crossed the sea and sank themselves into new soil. But seen as one of thousands – as a mass of paper that stretched between South Arabia and East Africa – it intertwined itself with a legal and bureaucratic background, burying itself in *fatwas*, registers, case files, and reports. It quickly became clear to me, then, that to understand what the *waraqa* meant for Indian Ocean history I had to not only look *through* it to see a world of commerce and obligation, but I had to look *at* it as an artifact, unpacking the different practices and discourses that conjured it into being and shaped its place in a changing economic, legal, and political landscape. And seen as a part of a whole – one component of a broader assemblage of actors, texts, ideas, and institutions – the document had a lot to tell us about itself.

The *Waraqa's* Other Shores

Vimal's question to me, and his interpretation of the *waraqa* as a debt contract between his great-grandfather and debtors past localized the history of a document that was anything but local in its contours. The history I've written here placed the *waraqa* within a world on the move – in a history of actors, goods, properties, ideas, concepts, and institutions that circulated between South Arabia, East Africa, and India. But even then – even in its presumed breadth – the narrative I've presented has maintained its focus on specific port cities, sets of actors and discourses, in part to preserve analytic depth. And I chose to take that path while knowing that it was only one of many crisscrossing stories of *waraqas* around the region – constellations of actors, instruments, and institutions that together formed a heterogeneous universe of contracting around the Indian Ocean.

Just up the Persian Gulf from Muscat, on the island of Bahrain, economic actors were experiencing many of the same transformations that we saw in Oman and East Africa, and making use of similar instruments to capture changing commercial opportunities or to ride out similar changing economic and legal ties. The details are of course different: the island's economic mainstay was not in agriculture (though there was plenty of that around) but was instead the pearl trade; dhow captains, pearl divers, and Arab and Indian pearl merchants took the place of Oman and East Africa's planters and ivory traders. But when one takes a step back and the details recede into the background, the outlines are remarkably similar: the usage of particular debt instruments to bind together divers, captains, local pearl traders, and regional merchants during a time of commercial boom; appeals by different actors to local legal institutions and British courts at different stages of boom and bust in the global pearl market; and a frenzied rush to stave off property dispossession after the global economic depression of the 1930s.[1]

And there are other places where the histories of these credit instruments connect more directly to the histories of the *waraqas* of Oman and East Africa. The *'uhda* sales contracts of the towns of Hadramawt in South Yemen extend the narrative of the *khiyār* sale into a different, but related, Muslim discursive sphere; were the records of the courts of Aden available to us, they would no doubt tell us a great deal about the colonial careers of those instruments.[2] Meanwhile, the *iqrārs* and *waraqas* of Barawa on the Benadir Coast of Somalia peer at us from the pages of the *qāḍi* records there, replete with Italian consular markings, patiently awaiting their historian.[3]

And then there was an entire menu of contracts and instruments in South Asian history – some that were utilized in metropolitan centers like Bombay and Calcutta, and others that were taken on the road by Indian merchants in their travels to Eurasia and Southeast Asia.[4] One

1 Bishara, "A Sea of Debt," 80–92, 103–111, 342–403, 452–463.

2 Boxberger, "Avoiding *Ribā*."

3 Vianello and Kassim, *Servants of the Sharia*.

4 Marina Bernadette Victoria Martin, "An Economic History of Hundi, 1858–1978" (Ph.D. Dissertation, London School of Economics, 2012); idem, "Hundi/Hawala: The Problem of Definition," *Modern Asian Studies*, Vol. 43, No. 4 (2009): 909–937; Birla, *Stages of Capital*; Rudner, *Caste and Capitalism in Colonial India*; Levi, *The Indian Diaspora in Central Asia and its Trade, 1550–1900*; Dale, *Indian Merchants and Eurasian Trade, 1600–1750;* Amrith, *Crossing the Bay of Bengal*, 81–83.

might imagine the histories of those instruments as running parallel to that of the *waraqa*, their trajectories being shaped by similar forces of boom and bust, and the possibilities that they offered either opened up or constrained by a changing legal landscape that consisted of a mix of native and colonial legal institutions. But there are points of intersection between the narratives as well: after all, one couldn't possibly understand what *waraqas* meant to the Indian merchants who mobilized them in South Arabia and East Africa without placing them within a broader universe of South Asian financial instruments.[5]

Construed more broadly, then, the history of law and economic life that I've written around the *khiyār* sale and *waraqa* echoes around the shores of the Western Indian Ocean. In a sense, there were many similar *waraqas* around the region, whether they dealt in dates and cloves in Oman and East Africa, real estate in Hadramawt, livestock in Barawa, pearls in Bahrain, or agrarian produce in India. Each of their histories was different in its particularities but familiar in their outlines, following narrative arcs that sometimes revealed remarkable intersections. The history of the *waraqa* that I have told here, then, forms but one dense thread in a broader regional history – or rather a tapestry comprising regional *histories* of debt, obligation, law, and economic life in the Indian Ocean, and the assemblages of ideas, discourses, practices, artifacts, and actors that gave them each their shape.

Inscribing Law into Economic Life

How might one think about the histories of the broader universe of Indian Ocean *waraqas*? Vimal's question on the debts that underpinned the *waraqas* and their enforceability offered one possibility – one that had its roots in a literature on law and the economic trajectories of different civilizations. In its most recent incarnation, that debate has taken the form of what we have come to call New Institutional Economics (NIE) – a sub-field of economic history that explores the legal underpinnings of economic development in different societies that has highlighted how different rules (labeled "institutions") shape the incentive structures that motivate economic performance. Institutions, they have declared, are the principal determinants of the economic success or failure of communities, countries, and sometimes even entire civilizations.[6] Within the

[5] Hollian Wint's dissertation goes some way towards connecting these histories. Idem, "Credible Relations."

[6] The literature is a long one. For illustrative examples, see also Douglass C. North, *Institutions, Institutional Change and Economic Performance* (New York: Cambridge University Press, 1990); idem, *Structure and Change in Economic History* (New York: W.W. Norton,

framework of this new economic history, scholars could revisit historical phenomena like trade networks, mercantile tribunals, and land tenure, injecting them with new insights and a renewed sense of purpose.[7]

Historians of the Muslim commerce have had good reason to find in the NIE turn a compelling framework for thinking about their subjects. Since its inception, the literature on the economic history of the Islamic world has grappled with the place of Islamic law in Muslim economic life – some explicitly, others more tangentially.[8] Interest in the subject waned for roughly twenty-five years before new work in NIE inspired a new generation of scholars, many of whom embraced the work of North, Avner Greif, and others to call attention to the eagerness of Muslim (and non-Muslim) actors to draw law into their commercial transactions. The economic implications of Islamic law varied from one context to another, but the majority of scholars seemed to embrace a view that suggested long-term consequences for short-term contractual choices.[9]

But that's only one dimension of the picture. The history of law and economic life is not simply one of actors drawing on different institutions to shape their commercial destinies; it's also about how they imagined law to work in economic life, how they made claims to law-making through their actions, and the writings they mobilized to achieve those goals. Undergirding their strategies were the very material artifacts through which actors made claims to the regulation of the economic sphere: the genres of the Indian Ocean credit economy that gave it its texture from the end of the eighteenth century (if not well before) to the middle of the twentieth.[10] A range of different texts – *waraqas*, *fatwas*,

1982); Daron Acemoğlu and James Robinson, *Why Nations Fail: The Origins of Power, Prosperity, and Poverty* (New York: Profile Books, 2012); Jean-Philippe Platteau, *Institutions, Social Norms, and Economic Development* (Amsterdam: Hardwood Academic Publishers, 2000).

7 The list of scholars who have taken to the NIE turn with gusto is a long one, ranging from historians of the ancient economy to those of the modern Atlantic. See, for example, Dennis P. Kehoe, *Law and the Rural Economy of the Roman Empire* (Ann Arbor, MI: University of Michigan Press, 2007); Aslanian, *From the Indian Ocean to the Mediterranean*; Jeremy Adelman, *Republic of Capital: Buenos Aires and the Legal Transformation of the Atlantic World* (Stanford, CA: Stanford University Press, 1999).

8 Early works include Udovitch, *Partnership and Profit*; Rodinson, *Islam and Capitalism*; Ronald C. Jennings, "Loans and Credit in Early 17th Century Ottoman Judicial Records: The Sharia Court of Anatolian Kayseri," *Journal of the Economic and Social History of the Orient*, Vol. 41, No. 2–3 (1973): 168–216.

9 See also Avner Greif, *Institutions and the Path to the Modern Economy: Lessons from Medieval Trade* (New York: Cambridge University Press, 2005); Kuran, *The Long Divergence*; Lydon, *On Trans-Saharan Trails*. For a useful counterpoint, see Maya Shatzmiller, "Economic Performance and Economic Growth in the Early Islamic World," *Journal of the Economic and Social History of the Orient*, Vol. 54 (2011), 132–184.

10 See also Mary Poovey, *Genres of the Credit Economy: Mediating Value in Eighteenth- and Nineteenth-Century Britain* (Chicago: University of Chicago Press, 2008).

legal treatises, consular registers, case files, and more – constituted the genres that actors mobilized to make claims to legality, and formed the backbone of the legal cultures of the Western Indian Ocean.

What, then, does it mean when we speak of a body of "Islamic law" giving shape to an entire economic history? What the relationship is between this body of law and the different commercial practices that animated economic life in the region, and how did it later articulate with an expanding regime of imperial law? If the history of the *waraqa* in the Indian Ocean tells us anything at all, it is that what made the nineteenth-century transformation of production, finance, and trade was not some monolithic "Islamic law," but a constellation of different discourses, concepts, instruments, and practices: changing markets, yes, but also expanding notions of legal personhood, changing agricultural ontologies, a new conceptual foundation for commercial contracting, a set of instruments that allowed for those possibilities, and a group of actors that were willing to mobilize them to capture new opportunities. To pick these apart in order to highlight either the material components of it all (i.e. changing markets, and a set of economic actors and institutions) or the intellectual, discursive, and ontological components that animated them flattens the texture of law and reduces economic life to basic mechanics.[11]

By the middle of the nineteenth century a clear conversation surrounding *waraqas* and a new form of contracting called the *khiyār* sale had emerged between merchants, planters, *kātibs*, *qāḍis*, and jurists. The conversation, which moved from the space of *waraqas* that economic actors and their *kātibs* produced to the loose folios of questions that merchants and *qāḍis* posed to jurists and the *fatwas* they responded with, reflected the changing contractual practices that actors around the Indian Ocean began to engage in as the commercial world around them offered new possibilities for wealth and mobility. The carefully scripted conversation between the contracting parties and the jurists pointed to a growing world of economic and legal possibilities that *waraqas* enabled – a vernacular legal and commercial culture that merchants, planters, *kātibs*, and jurists all participated in, and on which no one group could make more authoritative claims than another. This circulation of forms, categories, discourses, and artifacts like the *waraqa*, and the sets of actors who made it all possible – a juridical society of *qāḍis*, jurists, and scribes – formed the basis of what they would have known to be "the Indian Ocean arena."

[11] I am drawing here on the useful set of ideas articulated in Kenneth Lipartito's article, "Reassembling the Economic: New Departures in Historical Materialism," *American Historical Review*, Vol. 121, No. 1 (2016), 101–139.

This was Islamic law in economic life: not centuries-old rulings handed down by jurists on licit and illicit commercial contracting, but an ad-hoc exploration of commercio-legal possibility, both in the world of trade and in the realm of jurisprudence. Jurists did not conjure up contractual categories on their own; the partnerships, sales contracts, and rules surrounding loans, labor hiring, and a host of other everyday transactions all grew out of a minutely-choreographed dance between commercial and legal actors, mediated by the different texts, instruments, and discourses that they mobilized in their day-to-day exchanges. Even the *muḍāraba* – the *commenda*-style partnership institution that has attracted the attention of so many economic historians of the Islamic world – likely emerged in the same way.[12] Reading Islamic commercial law, then, requires the reconstruction of the contexts, actors, writings, and exchanges – both actual and discursive – that constituted it. These did not only exist in the ether of jurisprudence; rather, they might be more productively thought of as a collection of many local, context-specific relationships of people, texts, capital, and goods that were worked into connection with one another, gradually anchoring themselves in particular juristic discourses. The legal categories that historians have relied on to describe Muslim commerce, then, emerged out of these assemblages; the work of the historian is to reconstruct them in their local contexts, rather than to rely on them as trans-historical descriptors – or worse yet, explanations for Muslim economic success or failure.

The assemblages that gave meaning to the *khiyār* sale – or, by extension, the *muḍāraba*, the *ʿinan* partnership, or any of the other forms of "Muslim" contracting – didn't materialize out of thin air; they accumulated over time. None of these forms of contracting would have started off as being inherently "Islamic" or even legal; the *khiyār* sale's career suggests it is that only after a form of contracting becomes more common does it attract the regulatory impulses of jurists. A single question might touch off a discussion; a series of questions, however, can bring a whole discourse into being. And over time, sets of actors, ontologies, and concepts accumulate around the contracts, which are then anchored in particular texts – which then form part of the assemblage – and practices.

[12] On the *muḍāraba*, see also Abraham L. Udovitch, "At the Origins of the Western Commenda: Islam, Israel, Byzantium?," *Speculum*, Vol. 37, No. 2 (1962), 198–207; idem, *Partnership and Profit in Medieval Islam*, 170–248; Sebouh Aslanian, "The Circulation of Men and Credit: The Role of the Commenda and the Family Firm in Julfan Society," *Journal of the Economic and Social History of the Orient*, Vol. 50, No. 2 (2007), 124–170; Kuran, *The Long Divergence*, 50–52; Lydon, *On Trans-Saharan Trails*, 290–293. This, of course, is to say nothing of the countless books on Islamic finance that have been published over the past fifteen to twenty years.

Only then, perhaps, might a commercial practice become institutionalized as a "Muslim" contract, moving from the domain of "commerce" and into the domain of "law."

And these assemblages were not necessarily limited to "Muslim" actors or texts. From its outset, the Islamic legal system was shaped by competing imperatives and contended with intersecting legal regimes.[13] In the nineteenth-century Western Indian Ocean, the list included a growing body of British courts in India, Arabia, and East Africa that began looking to the *waraqa* and the world it inhabited as an object of regulation. The *waraqa* stood at the center of these waves of regulation, from the first contact in British consular registers during the 1860s and 1870s to the onslaught of regulations in the 1930s, as British officials drew on their experiences in India, Iraq, and elsewhere to guide their actions in South Arabia and East Africa.

Muslim juridical actors did not close themselves off to this vector of history; they actively engaged with it. They staffed British legal bureaucracies across the Western Indian Ocean, guided British judges through Muslim legal treatises, took up work as *qāḍis* and interpreters, and tailored their own lexicons to meet the expectations that their new roles placed on them. As the British imperial legal banner unfurled across the Indian Ocean, then, Muslim juridical actors enrobed themselves within it. The actions they took, the texts they produced, and the discussions they engaged in precipitated a decades-long conversation with British officials about the place of Islamic law within this changing capitalist world – one that highlighted the primacy of the printed legal text over the more open-ended assemblage.[14] But the narratives aren't what we might expect: despite the fact that British judges ultimately made the final decision, *qāḍis* and other legal actors did engage with them.

[13] See also Abaraham L. Udovitch, "Islamic Law and the Social Context of Exchange in the Medieval Middle East," *History and Anthropology*, Vol. 1 (1985), 445–465; S.D. Goitien, *A Mediterranean Society: The Jewish Communities of the World as Portrayed in the Documents of the Cairo Geniza, Vol. 2: The Community* (Berkeley, CA: University of California Press, 1967), 311–410; Kuran, *The Long Divergence*, 169–188. As Marshall Hodgson pointed out, even when the discursive force of what we consider to be "the Islamic" was the most forceful, it was hardly ever the only one in existence; non-Muslim groups constituted integral elements in the complex of social relations that came to define the Islamic world. Marshall Hodgson, *The Venture of Islam: Conscience and History in a World Civilization, Vol. 1: The Classical Age of Islam* (Chicago: University of Chicago Press, 1974), 58–60. This was no less true for the Islamic laws surrounding transactions, in which practices that lay outside of the realm of jurisprudence were fundamentally constitutive of jurists' discourses on what "the law" might be.

[14] This might be thought of as a process of punctualization or simplification – or, alternatively, as a precarious process of translation wherein the text was able to stand in for the assemblage. John Law, "Notes on the Theory of the Actor-Network: Ordering, Strategy and Heterogeneity," *Systems Practice*, No. 5 (1992), 379–393.

Courtroom actors, it seemed, all understood that this was a shared arena of lawmaking – that people could make claims about the place of Islamic law in economic life by speaking in multiple languages and registers. The advent of a British colonial legal bureaucracy in East Africa, then, might have reanimated discussions on Islamic law in ways that scholars have yet to completely come to terms with.[15]

By the 1940s, the multiple discourses and practices that delineated the boundary between Islamic law and economic life were waning. The vision of a marketplace that jurists, merchants, and *kātibs* had contributed to was slowly replaced by another vision – that of the national economy, complete with the organs of the state bureaucracy and the paper technologies that governed it. But as some possibilities closed off, others opened up. Across the Arabian Sea, in the newly independent states of India and Pakistan, Muslim scholars began to envision a new domain for Islamic law in economic life, one that combined Islamic legal precepts with the emergent discipline of economics – a field that scholars later named "Islamic economics."[16]

These discourses and the assemblages they pulsed through were always contingent. Getting at the shape they might take requires a move away from the trans-regional, trans-historical studies on the history of Islamic law and Muslim commercial society that we have seen far too much of, grounding them instead in a particular geographical and temporal context. Of course, the texts that are mobilized within that context might immediately point to worlds beyond – the usage of a sixteenth-century Hejazi *fiqh* manual in a nineteenth-century British court in Zanzibar, for example – but once we reimagine these as belonging to particular assemblages that form at particular moments in time, whether a particular text "belongs" to that context becomes less relevant. Of greater significance are the events that trigger the availability of different texts and instruments and shape the possibilities for assemblages in a particular place (however broadly defined) and time.

The history of the *waraqa* thus asks us to situate law more firmly within a world of changing practices and institutions, and to place it amidst the

[15] For a notable exception to this trend, see Seema Alavi, *Muslim Cosmopolitanism in the Age of Empire* (Cambridge, MA: Harvard University Press, 2015).

[16] Timur Kuran, "The Genesis of Islamic Economics: A Chapter in the Politics of Muslim Identity," *Social Research*, Vol. 64, No. 2 (Summer 1997), 301–338; Julia Stephens, "Governing Islam: Law and Religion in Colonial India" (Ph.D. Dissertation, Harvard University, 2013); Muhammad Hamidullah, "Haidarabad's Contribution to Islamic Economic Thought and Practice," *Die Welt Des Islams*, Vol. 4, No. 2/3, New Series (1955), 73–78; idem, "Islam's Solution of the Basic Economic Problems," *Islamic Culture*, Vol. 10, No. 2 (April 1936), 213–233. I am grateful to Julia Stephens for many of these references.

wide range of actors who could make claims to it. It pushes us to disentangle the web of discourses, practices, artifacts, institutions, and histories that constituted "Islamic law" in economic life and to reassemble them in their local (or trans-local), contingent contexts. This is not to discount the importance of big arguments that stretch out across space and time; rather, it is to say that without attention to the local context, historians end up relying more on trans-historical abstractions than they do grounded, lived categories. Islamic law didn't only reside in the textbooks of medieval jurisprudence, nor did it move in the abstract. It lived in the *waraqas*, *fatwas*, court cases, petitions, registries, actors, and practices that made claims to it on a daily basis.[17] When I imagine Islamic law doing its work in finance, production, or commerce, I see a malleable grammar of contracting that can take many different shapes in many different contexts, but which fundamentally does the work of connecting objects to concepts, and materials to the human constructs that give them meaning. It is the language for ordering the material world ontologically, for framing the possibilities of assemblages that might form around those ontologies, and it lends actors a vocabulary with which to coordinate those assemblages.

The *Waraqa*, the Law, and the History of the Indian Ocean

Of course, the question Vimal Purecha posed to me at dinner still stands. Put differently, his question asked how we ended up with the *waraqas* before us, and what it meant that these commercio-legal instruments remained intact. As my extended detour above on *waraqas*, law, and economic life in the Indian Ocean suggests, there isn't one clear answer. A *waraqa* could have many different meanings, purposes, and lives. Vimal's understanding of the *waraqas* his family held onto – that they were documents on which they could make positive legal claims – was in part true. In a sense, claim-making in specific contexts was the whole point of the *waraqa*. But within those *waraqas* – in their journeys from the hands of merchants and planters and into the pages of *fatwa* collections and consular registries, into courtrooms and through the networks of *qāḍis*, judges, and litigants that underpinned them – existed the

17 Messick, *The Calligraphic State*, 133–200; "Just Writing: Paradox and Political Economy in Yemeni Legal Documents," *Cultural Anthropology*, Vol. 4, No. 1 (1989), 26–50; "Textual Properties: Writing and Wealth in a Shari'a Case," *Anthropological Quarterly*, Vol. 68, No. 3 (1995), 157–170; "Transactions in 'Ibb: Economy and Society in a Yemeni Highland Town" (PhD Dissertation, Princeton University, 1978), 404–438.

possibility of many different narratives of law and economic life, both in the Indian Ocean and in the Islamic world more generally.

In framing the relationship between law and economic life as one of assemblages, I am purposefully moving away from an understanding of law as a positive body of rulings that is brought to bear on a world of transactions. That conception of law has not gotten us very far, especially when it has come to the economic history of the Islamic world. Even the very beginnings of the literature on Islam and capitalism were wrought with fundamental disagreements on whether Islamic law had any bearing on economic life, not least of all because of the vexing question of whether the prohibition on interest mattered, whether anyone followed it, and other related distractions.[18] And if the literature on Islamic finance and the moral anxieties surrounding it (but is it *really* Islamic?) tell us anything, it's that we haven't moved too far along at all.[19] In some ways, Vimal's question, as innocent as it was of the attacks I'm leveling at the literature here, bore the weight of decades of understanding law as an unfolding text of decisions, rulings, and legislation.

Thinking about the sorts of *waraqas* Vimal had in his family library allowed me to see the possibility of conceiving of Islamic law in a way that opens doors to understanding a range of different practices in finance, production, and commerce as potentially "Islamic" – yes, even Islamic finance, that *bête noire* of Islamic legal scholars. But it also (and perhaps more importantly) further pries open the field to a whole new set of questions on the histories of law, finance, and commerce, and the genres of writing that conjured up, captured, and constrained the universe of possibility.

I began this book by calling it a legal history of economic life in the Western Indian Ocean. Perhaps all I've been able to do is describe how a particular contractual culture – one that stretched from South Arabia to East Africa – came to assume the form it did over the course of the nineteenth and early twentieth centuries, and how it all coalesced around a small set of instruments and forms of exchange. But if we return to what the *qāḍi* in the case of Muṣabbah's *waraqa* (see Chapter 4) said – that

[18] Braudel acknowledged the existence of interest-bearing loans in the Muslim world but notes that on the whole "credit was poorly developed"; see Fernand Braudel, *Civilization and Capitalism*, Vol. 3 (New York: Harper and Row, 1984): 472–474. See also Rodinson, *Islam and Capitalism*; Jennings, "Loans and Credit in Early 17th Century Ottoman Judicial Records"; and more recently, Timur Kuran, *The Long Divergence*, 143–166.

[19] For academic treatments of the subject, see also Timur Kuran, *Islam and Mammon: The Economic Predicaments of Islamism* (Princeton University Press, 2004); Mahmoud El-Gamal, *Islamic Finance: Law, Economics, Practice* (New York: Cambridge University Press, 2006); Mohammed Hashim Kamali, *Islamic Commercial Law: An Analysis of Futures and Options* (Cambridge: The Islamic Texts Society, 2000).

there were many thousands of *waraqas* like Musabbah's – then the legal vistas of economic life around the Indian Ocean open up to the historian. Construed more broadly, each *waraqa*, whether in Zanzibar, Bahrain, Aden, or Bombay, had its own history, and was produced by assemblages of actors, ideas, institutions, and texts both mandarin and mundane. What's left, then, is to unpack them – starting not with abstract categories, but with local contexts and practices.

Bibliography

Primary Sources

Archives

Bushihri Archive, Manama, Bahrain

Miscellaneous Arabic Deeds

India Office Records, British Library, London (IOR)

R/15/1: Political Resident, Bushire
R/15/2: Political Agency, Bahrain
R/15/3: Political Agency, Bahrain: Court Records
R/15/5: Political Agency, Kuwait
R/15/6: Political Agency, Muscat

Maharashtra State Archives, Mumbai, India (MSA)

Judicial Department
Political Department

Ratansi Purshottam Library, Muscat, Bahrain (RPL)

Miscellaneous Arabic Deeds
Date Trade Files

Zanzibar National Archives, Zanzibar, Tanzania (ZNA)

Consular Records
AA 2: General Correspondence, 1837–1890
AA 3: Bombay Correspondence, 1840–1884
AA 4: Government of India Correspondence, 1874–1887
AA 7: Court Records, 1855–1891
AA 12: Miscellaneous, 1837–1914

Secretariat Files

AB 3: Executive and Legislative Council, 1908–1964
AB 14: Banks and Currency, 1909–1960

AB 27: World Wars and Treaties, 1886–1956
AB 40: Land and Survey Records, 1910–1959
AB 47: Mortgage and Debt Settlement, 1920–1957
AB 62: Judicial and Legal Departments, 1900–1964

Deeds of Sale and Mortgages

AM 1: General Deed Register, 1865–1920
AM 3: General Deeds, 1877–1881

Court Files

HC 2: High Court: Insolvency, 1887–1962
HC 3: High Court: Civil Cases, 1908–1948
HC 5: High Court: Civil Appeals, 1898–1949
HC 6: High Court: Criminal Appeals, 1897–1940
HC 7: H.B.M. and Consular Court: Civil Cases, 1875–1939
HC 8: H.H. the Sultan's Court: Civil Cases, 1898–1924

Published Primary Sources

Arabic

Aṭfiyyish, Mohammed bin Yusuf. *Sharḥ Kitāb al-Nīl wal-Shifā' al-'Alīl*, 17 vols. 3rd ed. Jeddah: Al-Irshad Press, 1985.

Ibn Hajar, *Tuḥfat al-Muḥtāj bi-Sharḥ al-Minhāj*, 4 vols. Beirut: Dār al-Kutub al-'Ilmiyya, 1971.

Al-Khalili, Sa'id bin Khalfan, *Ajwibat Al-Muḥaqqiq Al-Khalili*, 6 vols. Muscat: Maktabat Al-Jīl Al-Wā'id, 2013.

Al-Mughairi, Sa'id bin 'Ali. *Juhaynat al-Akhbār fī Tārīkh Zanjibār*, 4th ed. Muscat: Ministry of Heritage and Culture, 2001.

Ibn Rushd, *Al-Bayān wal-Taḥṣīl wal-Sharḥ wal-Tawjīh wal-Ta'līl fī Masā'il al-Mustakhraja*. 20 vols. Beirut: Dār al-Gharb al-Islāmī, 1988.

Al-Rustaqi, Khamis bin Sa'id Al-Shaqṣi. *Manhaj Al-Talibin wa Balāgh Al-Rāghibin*, 10 vols. Muscat, Oman: Maktabat Masqaṭ 2006.

Al-Salimi, 'Abdullah bin Ḥumayd. *Tuḥfat Al-A'yān fī Sīrat Ahl 'Umān*, 2 vols. Sib, Oman: Maktabat Al-Imām Nūr Al-Dīn Al-Sālimī, 2000.

Jawābāt Al-Imām Al-Sālimi, 7 vols. 2nd ed. Muscat, Oman: Ministry of Awqaf and Religious Affairs, 1999.

Al-Salimi, Muhammad bin 'Abdullah b. Ḥumayd. *Nahḍat Al-A'yān bi Ḥurriyat 'Umān [The Notables' Renaissance in the Liberation of Oman]*. Beirut: Dār Al-Jīl, 1998.

Other

Accounts and Papers of the House of Commons. London: Harrison and Sons, 1876.

Aitchison, C.U., ed. *A Collection of Treaties, Engagements, and Sunnuds Relating to India and Neighboring Countries*, 7 vols. Calcutta: Foreign Office Press, 1876.

Alexander, Gilchrist C. *Tanganyika Memories: A Judge in the Red Kanzu*. London: Blackie and Sons, 1936.

Australian Dictionary of Biography, Vol. 3. Carlton, Vic.: Melbourne University Press, 1969.

Bakari, Mtoro bin Mwinyi. *The Customs of the Swahili People: The Desturi Za Waswahili of Mtoro Bin Mwinyi Bakari and Other Swahili Persons*, trans. J.W.T. Allen. Berkeley, CA: University of California Press, 1981.

Beach, Wooster. *The American Practice of Medicine*, 3 vols. New York: Charles Scribner, 1852.

Bennett, Norman Robert and George E. Brooks. *New England Merchants in Africa: A History through Documents, 1802–1856*. Boston: Boston University Press, 1965.

Brode, Heinrich. *Tippoo Tib, the Story of his Career in Central Africa*. London: The India Office, 1907.

Brooke, Douglas and Wheelton Sladen, eds. *Who's Who, 1907: An Annual Autobiographical Dictionary*. London: Adam and Charles Black, 1907.

Who's Who 1903: An Annual Biographical Dictionary. London: Adam and Charles Black, 1903.

Broyon-Mirambo, Philippe. "Description of the Unyamwesi, the Territory of King Mirambo, and the Best Route Thither from the East Coast," *Proceedings of the Royal Geographic Society of London*, Vol. 22, No. 1, 1877–1878: 28–38.

Burton, Richard F. *Zanzibar: City, Island, and Coast*, 2 vols. London: Tinsley Brothers, 1872.

Lake Regions of Central Africa, 2 vols. London: Longman, Green, Longman and Roberts, 1860.

Commons, John R. *Institutional Economics: Its Place in Political Economy*. New York: Macmillan, 1934.

Cruttendren, C.J. "Notes on the Mijjertheyn Somalees," *Journal of the Asiatic Society of Bengal*, Volume 13, Part 1, No. 149 (1844): 319–335.

Dictionary of National Biography, 1885–1900, 63 vols. London: Smith, Elder & Co, 1885–1900.

Fitzgerald, William Walter Augustine. *Travels in the Coastlands of British East Africa and the Islands of Zanzibar and Pemba*. London: Chapman and Hall, 1898.

Foster, Joseph. *Men-At-The-Bar: A Biographical Hand-list of the Members of the Various Inns of Court, Including Her Majesty's Judges, Etc.*, 2nd ed. London: Hazell, Watson, and Viney, 1885.

Fulanain. *The Marsh Arab: Hajji Rikkan*. Philadelphia: J.P. Lippincott and Company, 1928.

The Gazette for Zanzibar and East Africa. Zanzibar: Government Printers, 1892–1963.

Gorgas, Ferdinand J.S. *Dental Medicine: A Manual of Dental Materia Medica and Therapeutics for Practitioners and Students*. Philadelphia: P. Blakiston, Son, & Co: 1884.

Gullain, M. *Documents Sur L'Histoire, La Geographie, et Le Commerce L'Afrique Orientale*. Paris: Arthur Bertrand, 1856.

Hamdun, Said and Noël King, eds. *Ibn Battuta in Black Africa*. Princeton, NJ: Markus Weiner Publishers, 1995.

Hoffer, Leopold, ed. *The Chess-Monthly*, Vol. 2 (September, 1880–August, 1881): 265.

Hughes, Thomas Patrick. *A Dictionary of Islam*. London: W.H. Allen & Co, 1895.

Hutchinson, Edward. *The Slave Trade of East Africa*. London: Sampson Low, 1874.

Ibn Rushd, *The Distinguished Jurist's Primer*, 2 vols. Reading, UK: Garnet Publishing, 1995.

Ibn Sallam, Abu 'Ubayd ibn Al-Qasim. *The Book of Revenue: Kitāb Al-Amwāl*. Garnet, NY: Ithaca Press, 2006.

The Indian Law Reports.

Keynes, John Maynard. *Indian Currency and Finance*. London: Royal Economic Society, 1913.

The Law Journal: Comprising Cases from the Bench of Chancery, King's Bench, and Common Pleas. Vol. 40. London: The Law Journal, 1905.

Captain Loarer, "L'Ile de Zanzibar," *Revue de l'Orient*, Vol. 9, 1851: 240–299.

Lorimer, J.G. *The Gazetteer of the Persian Gulf, Oman and Central Arabia*. Slough, UK: Archive Editions, 1905/1987.

Lyne, Robert Nunez. *Zanzibar in Contemporary Times: A Short History of the Southern East in the Nineteenth Century*. London: Hurst and Blackett, Ltd, 1905.

Al-Marjebi, Hamad bin Mohammed. *Maisha ya Hamed bin Muhamed El Murjebi, Yaani Tippu Tip, Kwa Maneno Yake Mwenyewe*, edited by W.H. Whitely. Nairobi: East African Literature Bureau, 1971.

Maurizi, Vicenzo. *History of Seyd Said, Sultan of Muscat*. London: John Booth, 1819.

Montgomery-Massingberd, Hugh. *Burke's Irish Family Records*. London, UK: Burkes Peerage Ltd, 1976.

Morris, James. *Sultan in Oman*. London: Century, 1957.

Mukhopadhyay, Pandit Upendranath and Priya Sankar Majumdar. *Privy Council Judgments on Appeal from India*, 9 vols. [electronic reproduction]. Hathitrust Digital Library, 2011.

Mulla, Dinshah Fardunji. *Principles of Mahomedan Law*, 2nd ed. Bombay: Thacker and Company, 1907.

Niebuhr, Carsten. *Travels through Arabia and Other Countries in the East*, 2 vols. London: T. Vernor, 1792.

Osgood, William. *Notes of Travel or Recollections of Majunga, Zanzibar, Muscat, Aden, Mocha, and Other Eastern Ports*. Salem: George Creamer, 1854.

Pelly, Lewis. "Remarks on the Tribes, Trade, and Resources Around the Shore Line of the Gulf," *Transactions of the Bombay Royal Geographic Society*, Vol. 17, 1865: 32–103.

Piggott, Francis T. *Exterritoriality: The Law Relating to Consular Jurisdiction and to Residence in Oriental Countries*. London: William Clowes and Sons, 1892.

Report from the Select Committee on the Sale of Corn: With the Minutes of Evidence, Appendix, and Index. London: House of Commons, July 25, 1834.

Reute, Emily. *Memoirs of an Arabian Princess*. New York: D. Appleton & Co, 1888.

Robinson, Heaton Bowstead, ed. *Narrative of Voyages to Explore the Shores of Africa, Arabia, and Madagascar; Performed in H.M. Ships "Leven" and "Barracouta," Under the Direction of Capt. W.F.W. Owen, R.N.*, 2 vols. London: Richard Bentley, 1833.

Ruschenbeger, William. *Narrative of a Voyage Round the World During the Years 1835, 1836 and 1837, Including an Embassy to the Sultan of Muscat and the King of Siam*, 2 vols. London: Richard Bentley, 1838.

Salvadori, Cynthia, ed. *We Came in Dhows*, 3 vols. Nairobi: Paperchase Kenya Ltd, 1996.

Smith, Adam. *An Inquiry into the Nature and Causes of the Wealth of Nations*, 2 vols. Paris: Levrault Freres, 1801.

Stigant, C.H. *The Land of Zinj: Being an Account of British East Africa, its Ancient History and Present Inhabitants*. London: Constable and Company Ltd, 1913.

The Straits Times.

Sturgess, H.A.C. ed. *Register of Admissions to the Honourable Society of the Middle Temple. From the Fifteenth Century to the Year 1944*. London: Butterworth & Co., 1949.

The Times of India.

University of Bombay: The Calendar for the Year 1906–1907. Bombay: Government Press, 1906.

Vaughn, John Henry. *The Dual Jurisdiction in Zanzibar*. Zanzibar: Zanzibar Government Printers, 1935.

Vianello, Alessandra and Mohamed M. Kassim, eds. *Servants of the Sharia: The Civil Register of the Qadis' Court of Brava, 1893–1900*, 2 vols. Leiden, NL: Brill, 2006.

Weber, Max. *The History of Commercial Partnerships in the Middle Ages*. Lanham, MD: Rowman and Littlefield, 2003.

Wellsted, J.R. *Travels in Arabia*, 2 vols. London: John Murray, 1838.

Zanzibar High Court. *Law Reports Containing Cases Determined by the High Court for Zanzibar and on Appeal Therefrom by the Court of Appeal for Eastern Africa and by the Privy Council.* 8 vols. Zanzibar: Zanzibar Government Printer, 1919–1956.

Secondary Sources

Unpublished Works

Allen, Calvin. "Sayyids, Shets and Sultans: Politics and Trade in Muscat Under the Al Bu Said, 1785–1914." Ph.D. Dissertation, University of Washington, 1978.

Bathurst, R.D. *The Ya'rubi Dynasty of Oman*. Ph.D. Dissertation, Oxford University, 1967.

Bishara, Fahad Ahmad. "A Sea of Debt: Histories of Commerce and Obligation in the Western Indian Ocean, c. 1850–1950." Ph.D. Dissertation, Duke University, 2012.

Fraas, Arthur Mitchell. "'They Have Travailled into a Wrong Latitude': The Laws of England, Indian Settlements, and the British Imperial Constitution, 1726–1773." Ph.D. Dissertation, Duke University, 2011.

Hopper, Matthew S. "The African Presence in Arabia: Slavery, the World Economy, and the African Diaspora in Eastern Arabia, 1840–1940." Ph.D. Dissertation, University of California, Los Angeles, 2006.

Johansen, Baber. "The Legal Personality (*Dhimma*) in Islamic Law: How to Separate Personal Obligations from Goods and Secure Credit for the Insolvent." Paper presented at the workshop "Before and Beyond Europe: Economic Change in Historical Perspective," hosted by the Economic Growth Center, Yale University, February 25–26, 2011.

Kranzer, Jonas. "Warengeschichte des Elfenbeins im 19. und 20. Jh." Unpublished Ph.D. Dissertation, University of Konstanz, Germany, 2010.

McDow, Thomas F. "Arabs and Africans: Commerce and Kinship from Oman to the East African Interior." Ph.D. Dissertation, Yale University, 2008.

Messick, Brinkley. "Transactions in 'Ibb: Economy and Society in a Yemeni Highland Town." PhD Dissertation, Princeton University, 1978.

Samuels, Peter Satyanand. "Dysmorphic Sovereignty: Colonial Railroads, Eminent Domain, and the Rule of Law in British India, 1824–1857." Ph.D. Dissertation, Stanford University, 2014.

Stockreiter, Elke. "Tying and Untying the Knot: *Kadhi's* Courts and the Negotiation of Social Status in Zanzibar Town, 1900–1963." Ph.D. dissertation, School of Oriental and African Studies, 2008.

Published Works

Arabic

Al-Mahmoud, Abdulaziz. *Al-Qurṣān*. Doha, Qatar: Bloomsbury Press, 2011.

Al-Qasimi, Noor Mohammed. *Al-Wujūd Al-Hindī fī Al-Khalīj Al-'Arabī, 1820–1947 [The Indian Presence in the Gulf, 1820–1947]*. Sharjah, United Arab Emirates: Government Printers, 1996.

Al-Riyami, Nasser bin 'Abdullah. *Zanjibār: Shakhṣiyyāt wa Aḥdāth, 1868–1972 [Zanzibar: Personalities and Events, 1868–1972]*. Muscat: Maktabat Bayrūt, 2009.

English

Abu-Hakima, Ahmad Musatafa. *History of Eastern Arabia, 1750–1800: The Rise and Development of Bahrain, Kuwait, and Wahhabi Saudi Arabia*. Beirut: Khayats, 1965.

Acemoğlu, Daron and James Robinson. *Why Nations Fail: The Origins of Power, Prosperity, and Poverty*. New York: Profile Books, 2012.

Adelman, Jeremy. *Republic of Capital: Buenos Aires and the Legal Transformation of the Atlantic World*. Stanford, CA: Stanford University Press, 1999.

Akgündüz, Ahmed. "Shari'ah Courts and Shari'ah Records: The Application of Islamic Law in the Ottoman State," *Islamic Law and Society*, No. 16, 2009: 202–230.

Akinola, Olefumi A. "Reorganising the Farmers, c. 1930–1992: Structural Adjustment and Agricultural Politics in Ondo State, Southwestern Nigeria," *The Journal of Modern African Studies*, Vol. 36, No. 2, 1998: 239–240.

Alence, Rod. "Colonial Government, Social Conflict and State Involvement in Africa's Open Economies: The Origins of the Ghana Cocoa Marketing Board, 1939–46," *The Journal of African History*, Vol. 42, No. 3, 2001: 397–416.

Allen, Calvin H. "The Indian Merchant Community of Masqaṭ" *Bulletin of the School of Oriental and African Studies, University of London*, Vol. 44, No. 1, 1981: 39–53.

Alston, Lee. "Farm Foreclosures in the United States During the Interwar Period," *Journal of Economic History*, Vol. 43, No. 4, 1983: 885–903.

Alpers, Edward A, *The Indian Ocean in World History*. New York: Oxford University Press, 2014.

Altorki, Soraya and Donald P. Cole. *Arabian Oasis City: The Transformation of 'Unayzah*. Austin, TX: University of Texas Press, 1989.

Amrith, Sunil. *Crossing the Bay of Bengal: The Furies of Nature and the Fortunes of Migrants*. Cambridge, MA: Harvard University Press, 2014.

Anderson, J.N.D. *Islamic Law in Africa*. London: Frank Cass, 1970.

Armitage, David C. "The Elephant and the Whale: Empires of Land and Sea," *Journal for Maritime Research*, Vol. 9, No. 1, 2007: 23–36.

Arrighi, Giovanni. *The Long Twentieth Century: Money, Power and the Origin of Our Times*, 2nd ed. London: Verso, 2010.

Aslanian, Sebouh David. *From the Indian Ocean to the Mediterranean: The Global Trade Networks of Armenian Merchants from New Julfa*. Berkeley, CA: University of California Press, 2011.

"The Circulation of Men and Credit: The Role of the Commenda and the Family Firm in Julfan Society," *Journal of the Economic and Social History of the Orient*, Vol. 50, No. 2, 2007: 124–170.

Bang, Anne. *Sufis and Scholars of the Sea: Family Networks in East Africa, 1860–1920*. London: RoutledgeCurzon, 2003.

Beckert, Svenn. *Empire of Cotton: A Global History*. New York: Knopf, 2014.

"Emancipation and Empire: Reconstructing the Worldwide Web of Cotton Production in the Age of the American Civil War." *The American Historical Review*, Vol. 109, No. 5, 2004: 1405–1438.

Bennett, Norman R., *Arab Versus European: Diplomacy and War in Nineteenth-Century East Central Africa*. New York: Africana Publishing Company, 1986.

and George R. Brooks, Jr., eds. *New England Merchants in Africa: A History Through Documents, 1802–1865*. Boston: Boston University Press, 1965.

Benton, Lauren. *A Search for Sovereignty: Law and Geography in European Empires, 1400–1900*. New York: Cambridge University Press, 2009.

Law and Colonial Cultures: Legal Regimes in World History, 1400–1900. New York: Cambridge University Press, 2002.

Bhacker, M. Reda. *Trade and Empire in Muscat and Zanzibar: Roots of British Domination*. London: Routledge, 1994.

Bilder, Mary Sarah. *The Transatlantic Constitution: Colonial Legal Culture and the Empire*. Cambridge, MA: Harvard University Press, 2004.

Birla, Ritu. *Stages of Capital: Law, Culture and Market Governance in Late Colonial India*. Durham, NC: Duke University Press, 2009.

Bissell, William. *Urban Design, Chaos, and Colonial Power in Zanzibar*. Bloomington, IN: Indiana University Press, 2011.

Blythe, Robert. *The Empire of the Raj: India, Eastern Africa, and the Middle East, 1858–1947*. London: Palgrave, 2003.

Booth, Alan. "A Survey of Progressive Economic Thought in Interwar Britain: Strengths and Gaps," *The History of Economic Thought*, Vol. 50, No. 2, 2009: 74–88.

Bose, Sugata. *A Hundred Horizons: The Indian Ocean in the Age of Global Empire*. Cambridge, MA: Harvard University Press, 2011.

Peasant Labour and Colonial Capital: Rural Bengal since 1770. Cambridge, UK: Cambridge University Press, 1993.

Braudel, Fernand. *Civilization and Capitalism, Vol. 2: The Wheels of Commerce*. Berkeley, CA: University of California Press, 1992.

Civilization and Capitalism, Vol. 3: The Perspective of the World. London: William Collins Sons & Co, 1984.

Bulliet, Richard. *Conversion to Islam in the Early Period: An Essay in Quantitative History*. Cambridge, MA: Harvard University Press, 1979.

Burns, Kathryn. *Into the Archive: Writing and Power in Colonial Peru*. Durham, NC: Duke University Press, 2010.

Cain, P.J. and A.J. Hopkins. "Gentlemanly Capitalism and British Expansion Overseas II: New Imperialism, 1850–1945," *The Economic History Review*, Vol. 40, No. 1, 1987: 1–26.

"Gentlemanly Capitalism and British Expansion Overseas I: The Old Colonial System," *The Economic History Review*, Vol. 39, No. 4, 1986: 501–525.

Campbell, Gwyn, ed. *An Economic History of Imperial Madagascar, 1750–1895: The Rise and Fall of an Island Empire*. New York: Cambridge University Press, 2005.

"Introduction: Slavery and Other Forms of Unfree Labour in the Indian Ocean World," *Slavery and Abolition: A Journal of Slave and Post-Slave Societies*, Vol. 24, No. 2, 2003: ix–xxxii.

Catanach, I.J. *Rural Credit in Western India: Rural Credit and the Cooperative Movement in the Bombay Presidency, 1875–1930*. Berkeley, CA: University of California Press, 1970.

Chaudhuri, K.N. *Trade and Civilization in the Indian Ocean: An Economic History from the Rise of Islam to 1750*. Cambridge, UK: Cambridge University Press, 1985.

Cohen, Abner. "Cultural Strategies in the Organization of Trading Diasporas," in Claude Messiloux, ed., *The Development of Indigenous Trade and Markets in West Africa*. Oxford: Oxford University Press, 1971: 266–281.

Cohn, Bernard S. "Some Notes on Law and Change in North India," *Economic Development and Cultural Change*, Vol. 8, No. 1, 1959: 79–93.

Cooper, Frederick. *From Slaves to Squatters: Plantation Labor and Agriculture in Zanzibar and Coastal Kenya, 1890–1925*. Portsmouth. NH: Heinemann, 1997.

Plantation Slavery on the East Coast of Africa. New Haven, CT: Yale University Press, 1977.

Cohn, Bernard S. *Colonialism and Its Forms of Knowledge: The British in India*. Princeton, NJ: Princeton University Press, 1996.

Coulson, N.J. *Succession in the Muslim Family*. New York: Cambridge University Press, 1971.

Curtin, Philip D. *Cross-Cultural Trade in World History*. New York: Cambridge University Press, 1984.

Das Gupta, Uma, ed. *The World of the Indian Ocean Merchant, 1500–1800: Collected Essays of Ashin Das Gupta*. New Delhi: Oxford University Press, 2001.

Dale, Stephen Frederic. *Indian Merchants and Eurasian Trade, 1600–1750*. New York: Cambridge University Press, 1994.

Davies, Charles E. *The Blood Red Arab Flag: An Investigation into Qasimi Piracy, 1797–1820*. Exeter, UK: University of Exeter Press, 1997.

De, Rohit. "The Two Husbands of Vera Tiscenko: Apostasy, Conversion, and Divorce in Late Colonial India," *Law and History Review*, Vol. 28, No. 4, 2011: 1011–1041.

Desai, Gaurav. *Commerce with the Universe: Africa, India, and the Afrasian Imagination*. New York: Columbia University Press, 2013.

Desan, Christine S. "Coin Reconsidered: The Political Alchemy of Commodity Money," *Theoretical Inquiries in Law*, Vol. 11, No. 1, 2010: 361–409.

Dodge, Toby. *Inventing Iraq: The Failure of Nation-Building and a History Denied*. New York: Columbia University Press, 2003.

Edwards, Laura F. *The People and Their Peace: Legal Culture and the Transformation of Inequality in the Post-Revolutionary South*. Chapel Hill, NC: University of North Carolina Press, 2009.

El-Shakry, Omnia. *The Great Social Laboratory: Subjects of Knowledge in Colonial and Postcolonial Egypt*. Stanford, CA: Stanford University Press, 2007.

Ellickson, Robert C. *Order Without Law: How Neighbors Settle Disputes*. Cambridge, MA: Harvard University Press, 1996.

Farrant, Leda. *Tippu Tip and the East African Slave Trade*. London: Hamish Hamilton, 1975.

Fattah, Hala. *The Politics of Regional Trade in Iraq, Arabia and the Gulf, 1745–1900*. Albany, NY: SUNY Press, 1997.

Fenster, Thelma and Daniel Lord Smail, eds. *Fama: The Politics of Talk and Reputation in Medieval Europe*. Ithaca, NY: Cornell University Press, 2003.

Fields, Michael. *The Merchants: The Big Business Families of Saudi Arabia and the Gulf States*. Woodstock, NY: Overlook Press, 1985.

Fitzmaurice, Andrew. *Sovereignty, Property, and Empire, 1500–1900*. Cambridge, UK: Cambridge University Press, 2014.

Fontana, Biancamaria. *Rethinking the Politics of Commercial Society: The Edinburgh Review, 1802–1832*. New York: Cambridge University Press, 1985.

Ford, Lisa. *Settler Sovereignty: Jurisdiction and Indigenous People in America and Australia, 1788–1836*. Cambridge, MA: Harvard University Press, 2010.

Freyer, Tony. "Negotiable Instruments and the Federal Courts in Antebellum American Business," *Business History Review*, Vol. 50, No. 4, 1976: 435–455.

Fuccaro, Nelida. *Histories of City and State in the Persian Gulf: Manama since 1800*. New York: Cambridge University Press, 2009.

Fuller, Lon. *Legal Fictions*. Stanford, CA: Stanford University Press, 1967.

Furber, Holden. *Rival Empires of Trade in the Orient 1600–1800*. Minneapolis, MN: University of Minnesota Press, 1978.

Gelvin, James and Nile Green, eds. *Global Muslims in the Age of Steam and Print*. Berkeley, CA: University of California Press, 2013.

Ghazal, Amal D. *Islamic Reform and Arab Nationalism: Expanding the Crescent from the Mediterranean to the Indian Ocean (1880s–1930s)*. New York: Routledge, 2010.
Ginsburg, Carlo. *The Cheese and the Worms: The Cosmos of a Sixteenth-Century Miller*. Baltimore, MD: Johns Hopkins University Press, 1980.
Gissibel, Bernhard. "German Colonialism and the Beginnings of International Wildlife Preservation in East Africa," *German Historical Institute Bulletin*, Supplement 3, 2006: 121–142.
Glasner, David and Thomas F. Cooley, eds. *Business Cycles and Depressions: An Encyclopedia*. New York: Garland Publishing, 1997.
Glassman, Jonathon. *War of Words, War of Stones: Racial Thought and Violence in Colonial Zanzibar*. Bloomington, IN: Indiana University Press, 2011.
Feasts and Riot: Revelry, Rebellion and Popular Consciousness on the Swahili Coast, 1856–1888. London: James Currey, 1995.
"The Bondsman's New Clothes: The Contradictory Consciousness of Slave Rebellions on the Swahili Coast," *Journal of African History*, Vol. 32, 1991: 277–312.
Goitein, S.D. *A Mediterranean Society: The Jewish Communities of the World as Portrayed in the Documents of the Cairo Geniza*, 6 vols. Berkeley, CA: University of California Press, 1967.
Goldberg, Jessica. *Trade and Institutions in the Medieval Mediterranean: The Geniza Merchants and their Business World*. New York: Cambridge University Press, 2012.
Goswami, Chhaya. *The Call of the Sea: Kachchhi Traders in Muscat and Zanzibar, c. 1800–1880*. New Delhi: Orient Blackswan, 2011.
Gran, Peter. *Islamic Roots of Capitalism: Egypt, 1760–1840*. Austin, Texas: University of Texas Press, 1979.
Granovetter, Mark. "Economic Action and Social Structure: The Problem of Embeddedness," *American Journal of Sociology*, Vol. 91, 1985: 481–510.
Gray, Sir John. *The British in Mombasa, 1824–1826: Being a History of Captain Owen's Protectorate*. London: Macmillan, 1957.
Green, Nile. *Bombay Islam: The Religious Economy of the Western Indian Ocean, 1840–1915*. New York: Cambridge University Press: 2011.
Gregory, Robert C. *South Asians in East Africa: An Economic and Social History, 1890–1980*. Boulder, CO: Westview Press, 1993.
Greif, Avner. *Institutions and the Path to the Modern Economy: Lessons from Medieval Trade*. New York: Cambridge University Press, 2005.
Hall, Richard. *Empires of the Monsoon: A History of the Indian Ocean and its Invaders*. London: HarperCollins, 1998.
Hall-Matthews, David. *Peasants, Famine and the State in Colonial Western India*. London: Palgrave-Macmillan, 2005.
Hanaway, Joseph and Richard Cruess. *McGill Medicine: The First Half-Century, 1829–1885*, 2 vols. Quebec: McGill-Queen's University Press, 1996.
Hardiman, David. *Feeding the Baniya: Peasants and Usurers in Western India*. New Delhi: Oxford University Press, 1996.
Harms Robert D. and Bernard K. Freamon and Michael Morony, eds. *Indian Ocean Slavery in the Age of Abolition*. New Haven, CT: Yale University Press, 2014.

Hartog, Hendrik. "Pigs and Positivism," *Wisconsin Law Review*, 1985: 899–935.
Heard-Bey, Frauke. *From Trucial States to United Arab Emirates*. London: Longman, 1996.
Al-Hijji, Yacoub H. *Kuwait and the Sea: A Brief Economic and Social History*. London: Arabian Publishing, 2010.
Hill, M.F. *The Permanent Way: The Story of the Kenya and Uganda Railway*, 2 vols. East Africa Literature Bureau, 1976.
Ho, Engseng. "Afterword: Mobile Law and Thick Transregionalism," *Law and History Review*, Vol. 32, No. 4, 2014: 883–889.
The Graves of Tarim: Genealogy and Mobility Across the Indian Ocean. Berkeley, CA: University of California Press, 2006.
"Empire Through Diasporic Eyes: A View from the Other Boat," *Comparative Studies in Society and History*, Vol. 46, No. 2, 2004: 210–246.
Hodge, Joseph Morgan. *Triumph of the Expert: Agrarian Doctrines of Development and the Legacies of British Colonialism*. Athens, OH: Ohio University Press, 2007.
Hodgson, Marshall. *The Venture of Islam: Conscience and History in a World Civilization*, 3 vols. Chicago: University of Chicago Press, 1974.
Hoffer, Peter. "Very Flawed Founders," *Review of Law's Imagined Republic: Popular Politics and Criminal Justice in Revolutionary America*, by Wilf. Steven Robert. *H-Law, H-Net Reviews*, June, 2010. <www.h-net.org/reviews/showrev.php?id=30481> Accessed February 21, 2015.
Hopper, Matthew S. *Slaves of One Master: Globalization and Slavery in Arabia in the Age of Empire*. New Haven, CT: Yale University Press, 2015.
"The Globalization of Dried Fruit: Transformations in the Eastern Arabian Economy, 1860s–1920s," in James Gelvin and Nile Green, eds. *Global Muslims in the Age of Steam and Print*. Berkeley, CA: University of California Press, 2013.
Hull, Matthew. *Government of Paper: The Materiality of Bureaucracy in Urban Pakistan*. Berkeley, CA: University of California Press, 2012.
"The File: Agency, Authority, and Autography in a Pakistan Bureaucracy," *Language and Communication*, Vol. 23, No. 3–4, 2003: 287–314.
Hulsebosch, Daniel. *Constituting Empire: New York and the Transformation of Constitutionalism in the Atlantic World, 1664–1830*. University of North Carolina Press, 2005.
Hunwick, John and Eve Trout-Powell. *The African Diaspora in the Mediterranean Lands of Islam*. Princeton, NJ: Marcus Wiener, 2002.
Hurst, James Willard. *Law and Economic Growth: A Legal History of the Lumber Industry in Wisconsin, 1836–1915*. Cambridge, MA: Harvard University Press, 1964.
Law and the Conditions of Freedom in the Nineteenth-Century United States. Madison, WI: University of Wisconsin Press, 1956.
Hussin, Iza. "Circulations of Law: Cosmopolitan Elites, Global Repertoires, Local Vernaculars," *Law and History Review*, Vol. 32, No. 4, 2014: 773–795.
Iliffe, John. *A Modern History of Tanganyika*. Cambridge, UK: Cambridge University Press, 1979.
Israel, Jonathan. "Diasporas Jewish and non-Jewish and the World Maritime Empires," in Ina Baghdiantz-McCabe, Gelina Harlaftis, and Ioanna

Pepelasis Minoglu, eds. *Diaspora Entrepreneurial Networks: Four Centuries of History*. New York: Berg, 2005: 3–26.

Johansen, Baber. *Contingency in a Sacred Law: Legal and Ethical Norms in the Muslim Fiqh*. Leiden: E.J. Brill, 1999.

Johnson, Walter. *River of Dark Dreams: Slavery and Empire in the Cotton Kingdom*. Cambridge, MA: Harvard University Press, 2013.

Kayaoglu, Turan. *Legal Imperialism: Sovereignty and Extraterritoriality in Japan, the Ottoman Empire and China*. New York: Cambridge University Press, 2010.

Kehoe, Dennis P. *Law and the Rural Economy of the Roman Empire*. Ann Arbor, MI: University of Michigan Press, 2007.

Kelly, J.B. *Britain and the Persian Gulf, 1795–1880*. Oxford, UK: Clarendon Press, 1968.

Kerr, Ian. *Building the Railways of the Raj, 1850–1900*. Oxford, UK: Oxford University Press, 1995.

Kessler, Amalia D. *A Revolution in Commerce: The Parisian Merchant Court and the Rise of Commercial Society in Eighteenth-Century France*. New Haven, CT: Yale University Press, 2011.

Kolsky, Elizabeth. *Colonial Justice in British India: White Violence and the Rule of Law*. New York: Cambridge University Press, 2010.

Kostal, R.W. *Law and English Railway Capitalism, 1825–1875*. New York: Oxford University Press, 1998.

Kozlowski, Gregory C. *Muslim Endowments and Society in Colonial India*. New York: Cambridge University Press, 1985.

Kugle, Scott Alan. "Framed, Blamed and Renamed: The Recasting of Islamic Jurisprudence in Colonial South Asia," *Modern Asian Studies*, Vol. 35, No. 2, 2001: 257–313.

Kuran, Timur. *The Long Divergence: How Islamic Law Held Back the Middle East*. Princeton, NJ: Princeton University Press, 2011.

Islam and Mammon: The Economic Predicaments of Islamism. Princeton, NJ: Princeton University Press, 2004.

"The Absence of the Corporation in Islamic Law: Origins and Persistence," *American Journal of Comparative Law*, Vol. 53, 2005: 785–834.

Landen, Robert G. *Oman Since 1856: Disruptive Modernization in a Traditional Arab Society*. Princeton, NJ: Princeton University Press, 1967.

Latour, Bruno. *Reassembling the Social: An Introduction to Actor-Network-Theory*. Oxford, UK: Oxford University Press, 2005.

Levi, Scott. *The Indian Diaspora in Central Asia and its Trade, 1550–1900*. Leiden: E.J. Brill, 2002.

Low, D.A. and A. Smith, eds. *History of East Africa*, 3 vols. Oxford: Clarendon Press, 1976.

Low, Michal Christopher. "Introduction: The Indian Ocean and Other Middle Easts," *Comparative Studies of South Asia, Africa, and the Middle East*, Vol. 34, No. 3, 2014: 549–555.

Lydon, Ghislaine. "A Paper Economy of Faith Without Faith in Paper: A Reflection on Islamic Institutional History," *Journal of Economic Behavior and Organization*, Vol. 71, 2009: 647–659.

On Trans-Saharan Trails: Islamic Law, Trade Networks and Cross-Cultural Exchange in Nineteenth-Century Western Africa. New York: Cambridge University Press, 2009.

Machado, Pedro. *Ocean of Trade: South Asian Merchants, Africa, and the Indian Ocean, c. 1750–1850*. New York: Cambridge University Press, 2014.

Mangat, J.S. *A History of the Asians in East Africa*. Oxford, UK: Clarendon Press, 1969.

Margariti, Roxani. "Mercantile Networks, Port Cities, and "Pirate" States: Conflict and Competition in the Indian Ocean World of Trade before the Sixteenth Century," *Journal of the Economic and Social History of the Orient*, Vol. 58, 2008: 543–577.

Markovits, Claude. *The Global World of Indian Merchants, 1750–1947: Traders of Sind from Bukhara to Panama*. New York: Cambridge University Press, 2000.

Massud, Muhammad Khalid, Brinkley Messick and David S. Powers, eds. *Islamic Legal Interpretation: Jurists and their Fatwas*. Cambridge, MA: Harvard University Press, 1996.

Mathew, Johan. *Margins of the Market: Trafficking and Capitalism Across the Arabian Sea*. Berkeley, CA: University of California Press, 2016.

Mawani, Renisa and Iza Hussin, "The Travels of Law: Indian Ocean Itineraries," *Law and History Review*, Vol. 32, No. 4, 2014: 733–747.

Mauss, Marcel. *The Gift: The Form and Reason for Exchange in Archaic Societies*. New York: W.W. Norton, 1990.

McDow, Thomas F. "Deeds of Freed Slaves: Manumission and Economic and Social Mobility in Pre-Abolition Zanzibar," in Robert Harms, Bernard K. Freamon, and David W. Blight, *Indian Ocean Slavery in the Age of Abolition*. New Haven, CT: Yale University Press, 2014: 60–79.

McMahon, Elizabeth. *Slavery and Emancipation in Islamic East Africa: From Honor to Respectability*. New York: Cambridge University Press, 2013.

Meredith, David. "State Controlled Marketing and Economic "Development": The Case of West African Produce during the Second World War," *The Economic History Review*, New Series, Vol. 39, No. 1, 1986: 77–91.

Merry, Sally Engle. *Getting Justice and Getting Even: Legal Consciousness Among Working-Class Americans*. Chicago: University of Chicago Press, 1990.

Messick, Brinkley. "Property and the Private in a Sharia System," *Social Research*, Vol. 70, No. 3, 2003: 711–734.

"Textual Properties: Writing and Wealth in a Yemeni Sharia Case," *Anthropology Quarterly*, Vol. 68, No. 3, 1995: 157–170.

The Calligraphic State: Textual Domination in a Muslim Society. Berkeley, CA: University of California Press, 1993.

"Just Writing: Paradox and Political Economy in Yemeni Legal Documents," *Cultural Anthropology*, Vol. 4, No. 1, 1989: 26–50.

Metcalf, Thomas. *Imperial Connections: India in the Indian Ocean Arena, 1860–1920*. Berkeley, CA: University of California Press, 2008.

Mitchell, Timothy. *The Rule of Experts: Egypt, Technopolitics, Modernity*. Berkeley, CA: University of California Press, 2002.

Nadri, Ghulam Ahmed. *Eighteenth-Century Gujarat: The Dynamics of Its Political Economy*. Leiden: Brill, 2009.

Ng'ong'ola, Clement. "Malawi's Agricultural Economy and the Evolution of Legislation on the Production and Marketing of Peasant Economic Crops," *Journal of Southern African Studies*, Vol. 12, No. 2, 1986: 240–262.

North, Douglass C. *Institutions, Institutional Change and Economic Performance*. New York: Cambridge University Press, 1990.

Structure and Change in Economic History. New York: W.W. Norton, 1982.

Nugent, Jeffrey and Theodore H. Thomas, eds. *Bahrain and the Gulf: Past Perspectives and Alternative Futures*. London: Croom Helm, 1985.

Nussdorfer, Laurie. *Brokers of Public Trust: Notaries in Early Modern Rome*. Baltimore, MD: Johns Hopkins University Press, 2009.

Ogborn, Miles. "Writing Travels: Power, Knowledge and Ritual on the English East India Company's Early Voyages," *Transactions of the Institute of British Geographers*, Vol. 27, No. 2, 2002: 155–171.

Onley, James. "Britain and the Gulf Shaikhdoms, 1820–1971: The Politics of Protection," *Georgetown Center for International and Regional Studies, Occasional Paper No. 4* (2009).

The Arabian Frontier of the British Raj: Merchants, Rulers and the British in the Nineteenth-Century Gulf. Oxford, UK: Oxford University Press, 2007.

"The Politics of Protection in the Gulf: The Arab Rulers and the British Resident in the Nineteenth Century," *New Arabian Studies*, Vol. 6, 2004: 30–92.

Panandikar, S.G. "Banking," in V.B. Singh, ed. *Economic History of India, 1857–1956*. Mumbai: Allied Publishers, 1975.

Pearson, M.N. *The Indian Ocean*. London: Routledge, 2003.

Port Cities and Intruders: The Swahili Coast, India and Portugal in the Early Modern Era. Baltimore, MD: Johns Hopkins University Press, 1998.

Peirce, Leslie. *Morality Tales: Law and Gender in the Ottoman Court of Aintab*. Berkeley, CA: University of California Press, 2003.

Polanyi, Karl. *The Great Transformation*. New York: Reinhardt Press, 1944.

Poovey, Mary. *Genres of the Credit Economy: Mediating Value in Eighteenth and Nineteenth-Century England*. Chicago: University of Chicago Press, 2008.

Pouwels, Randall L. *Horn and Crescent: Cultural Change and Traditional Islam on the East African Coast, 800–1900*. New York: Cambridge University Press, 2002.

Powers, David S. *Law, Society, and Culture in the Maghrib, 1300–1500*. New York: Cambridge University Press, 2002.

Prange, Sebastian. "A Trade of No Dishonor: Piracy, Commerce, and Community in the Western Indian Ocean, Twelfth to Sixteenth Century," *The American Historical Review*, Vol. 116, No. 5, 2011: 1269–1293.

Prasad, Ritika. *Tracks of Change: Railways and Everyday Life in Colonial India*. New York: Cambridge University Press, 2015.

Prestholdt, Jeremy. *Domesticating the World: East African Consumerism and the Genealogies of Globalization*. Berkeley, CA: University of California Press, 2008.

"On the Global Repercussions of East African Consumerism," *The American Historical Review*, Vol. 109, No. 3, 2004: 755–781.

Al-Qasimi, Sultan bin Mohammed. *The Myth of Arab Piracy in the Gulf*. London: Routledge, 1986.

Rabi, Uzi. *The Emergence of States in a Tribal Society: Oman Under Sa'id bin Taymur, 1932–1970*. Portland, OR: Sussex Academic Press, 2007.

Raman, Bhavani. *Document Raj: Writing and Scribes in Early Colonial South India*. Chicago: University of Chicago Press, 2012.

Rasmussen, Dennis C. *The Problems and Promise of Commercial Society: Adam Smith's Response to Rousseau*. University Park, PA: Pennsylvania State University Press, 2008.

Ray, Rajat Kanta. "Asian Capital in the Age of European Domination: The Rise of the Bazaar, 1800–1914," *Modern Asian Studies*, Vol. 29, No. 3, 1995: 449–554.

Reeves, Peter, ed. *The Encyclopedia of the Sri Lankan Diaspora*. Singapore: Editors Didier Millet, 2013.

Reid, John Philip. *Law for the Elephant: Property and Social Behavior on the Overland Trail*. San Marino, CA: The Huntington Library, 1980.

Risso, Patricia. *Merchants and Faith: Muslim Commerce and Culture in the Indian Ocean*. Boulder, CO: Westview Press, 1995.

Rockel, Stephen J. "Slavery and Freedom in Nineteenth Century East Africa: The Case of Waungwana Caravan Porters," *African Studies*, Vol. 68, No. 1, 2009: 87–109.

Carriers of Culture: Labor on the Road in Nineteenth-Century East Africa. London: James Currey, 2006.

Rodinson, Maxime. *Islam and Capitalism*. London: Al-Saqi, 2007.

Rudner, David West. *Caste and Capitalism in Colonial India: The Nattukottai Chettiars*. Berkeley, CA: University of California Press, 1994.

Sadgrove, Philipo, ed. *Printing and Publishing in the Middle East*. Oxford: Oxford University Press, 2008.

Schacht, Joseph. *An Introduction to Islamic Law*. Oxford: Clarendon Press, 1964.

Schaefer, Charles. "'Selling at a Wash:' Competition and the Indian Merchant Community in Aden Crown Colony," *Comparative Studies of South Asia, Africa and the Middle East*, Vol. 19, No. 2, 1999: 16–23.

Schmitthener, Samuel. "A Sketch of the Development of the Legal Profession in India," *Law & Society Review*, Vol. 3, No. 2/3, 1968–1969: 337–382.

Seed, Patricia. *American Pentimento: The Invention of Indians and the Pursuit of Riches*. Minneapolis, MN: University of Minnesota Press, 2003.

Sewell, William H., Jr. "A Strange Career: The Historical Study of Economic Life," *History and Theory*, Theme Issue 49, 2010: 146–166.

Sharafi, Mitra. *Law and Identity in Colonial India: Parsi Legal Culture, 1772–1947*. New York: Cambridge University Press, 2014.

Sheriff, Abdul. "Social Mobility in Indian Ocean Slavery: The Strange Career of Sultan b. Aman," in Robert Harms, Bernard K. Freamon, and David W. Blight, *Indian Ocean Slavery in the Age of Abolition*. New Haven, CT: Yale University Press, 2014: 143–159.

Dhow Cultures of the Indian Ocean: Cosmopolitanism, Commerce, Islam. New York: Columbia University Press, 2010.

Slaves, Spices and Ivory in Zanzibar. Oxford: James Currey, 1987.

Smail, Daniel Lord. *The Consumption of Justice: Emotions, Publicity, and Legal Culture in Marseille, 1264–1423*. Ithaca, NY: Cornell University Press, 2003.

Smith, Barbara J. *The Roots of Separatism in Palestine: British Economic Policy, 1920–1929*. Syracuse, NY: Syracuse University Press, 1983.

Solberg, Carl E. *The Prairies and the Pampas: Agrarian Policy in Canada and Argentina, 1880–1930*. Stanford, CA: Stanford University Press, 1987.

Sood, Gagan. "Sovereign Justice in Precolonial Maritime Asia: The Case of the Mayor's Court of Bombay, 1726–1798," *Itinerario*, Vol. 37, No. 2, 2013: 46–72.

"'Correspondence is Equal to Half a Meeting': The Composition and Comprehension of Letters in Eighteenth-Century Islamic Eurasia," *Journal of the Economic and Social History of the Orient*, Vol. 50, No. 2–3, 2007: 172–214.

Spiegel, Henry W. *The Growth of Economic Thought*, 3rd ed. Durham, NC: Duke University Press, 1991.

Steensgaard, Niels. *Carracks, Caravans and Companies: The Structural Crisis in the European-Asian Trade in the Early Seventeenth Century*. Lund: Studentlitteratur, 1973.

Stephens, Julie. "The Phantom Wahhabi: Liberalism and the Muslim Fanatic in Mid-Victorian India," *Modern Asian Studies*, Vol. 47, No. 1, 2013: 22–52.

Stiles, Erin. *An Islamic Court in Context: An Ethnographic Study of Judicial Reasoning*. New York: Palgrave Macmillan, 2009.

Stockreiter, Elke. "'British kadhis' and 'Muslim Judges': Modernisation, Inconsistencies and Accommodation in Zanzibar's Colonial Judiciary," *Journal of Eastern African Studies*, Vol. 4, No. 3, 2010: 560–576.

Subramanian, Lakshmi. *Indigenous Capital and Imperial Expansion: Bombay, Surat and the West Coast*. New York: Oxford University Press, 1998.

Subrahmanyam, Sanjay. "Introduction: The Indian Ocean Between Empire and Nation," in *Maritime India*. New Delhi: Oxford University Press, 2004.

The Career and Legend of Vasco da Gama. New York: Cambridge University Press, 1997.

"Of Imarat and Tijarat: Asian Merchants and State Power in the Western Indian Ocean, 1400 to 1750," *Comparative Studies in Society and History*, Vol. 37, No. 4, 1995: 750–780.

Szombathy, Zoltán. "Genealogy in Medieval Muslim Societies," *Studia Islamica*, No. 95, 2002: 5–35.

Talbot, Ian. "Punjab Under Colonialism: Order and Transformation in British India," *Journal of Punjab Studies*, Vol. 14, No. 1, 2007: 3–10.

Tomlinson, B.R. *The Economy of Modern India: From 1860 to the Twenty-First Century*. New York: Cambridge University Press, 2013.

Trivellato, Francesca. *The Familiarity of Strangers: The Sephardic Diaspora, Livorno, and Cross-Cultural Trade in the Early Modern Period*. New Haven: Yale University Press, 2009.

Udovitch, Abraham. "Islamic Law and the Social Context of Exchange in the Medieval Middle East," *History and Anthropology*, Vol. 1, No. 2, 1985, pp. 445–465.

Partnership and Profit in Medieval Islam. Princeton, NJ: Princeton University Press, 1970.

"At the Origins of the Western Commenda: Islam, Israel, Byzantium?" *Speculum*, Vol. 37, No. 2, 1962: 198–207.

Valeri, Marc. "High Visibility, Low Profile: The Shi'a in Oman Under Sultan Qaboos," *International Journal of Middle East Studies*, Vol. 42, No. 2, 2010, pp. 251–268.

Vardi, Liana. *The Physiocrats and the World of the Enlightenment*. New York: Cambridge University Press, 2012.

Vickery, Kenneth P. "Saving Settlers: Maize Control in Northern Rhodesia," *Journal of Southern African Studies*, Vol. 11, No. 2, 1985: 212–234.

Yahaya, Nurfadzilah. "Legal Pluralism and the English East India Company in the Straits of Malacca during the Early Nineteenth Century," *Law and History Review*, Vol. 33, No. 4, 2015: 945–964.

Wakin, Jeannette, ed. *The Function of Documents in Islamic Law: The Chapter of Sales in Al-Tahawi's Kitab al-Shurūt al-Kabīr*. Albany, NY: SUNY Albany, 1972.

Ward, Kerry. *Networks of Empire: Forced Migration in the Dutch East India Company*. New York: Cambridge University Press, 2009.

Washbrook, David C. "Law, State and Agrarian Society in Colonial India," *Modern Asian Studies*, Vol. 15, No. 3, 1981: 649–721.

Watson, Alan. *Slave Law in the Americas*. University of Georgia Press, 1989.

Weiss, Bernard G. *The Spirit of Islamic Law*. Athens, GA: University of Georgia Press, 1998.

Westlake, J. "The Muscat Dhows," *The Law Review Quarterly*, Vol. 23, 1907: 83–87.

Wilf, Steven. *Law's Imagined Republic: Popular Politics and Criminal Justice in Revolutionary America*. New York: Cambridge University Press, 2010.

Wilkinson, John C. *The Arabs and the Scramble for Africa*. Sheffield, UL: Equinox Publishing, 2015.

The Imamate Tradition of Oman. New York: Cambridge University Press, 1987.

Index